Chaos Engineering

Chaos Engineering

SITE RELIABILITY THROUGH CONTROLLED DISRUPTION

MIKOLAJ PAWLIKOWSKI

FOREWORDS BY CASEY ROSENTHAL AND DAVE RENSIN

MANNING

SHELTER ISLAND

For online information and ordering of this and other Manning books, please visit
www.manning.com. The publisher offers discounts on this book when ordered in quantity.
For more information, please contact

Special Sales Department
Manning Publications Co.
20 Baldwin Road
PO Box 761
Shelter Island, NY 11964
Email: orders@manning.com

Manning Publications Co.
20 Baldwin Road
PO Box 761
Shelter Island, NY 11964

Development editor:	Toni Arritola
Technical development editor:	Nick Watts
Review editor:	Mihaela Batinic
Production editor:	Deirdre S. Hiam
Copy editor:	Sharon Wilkey
Proofreader:	Melody Dolab
Technical proofreader:	Karsten Strøbæk
Typesetter:	Dennis Dalinnik
Cover designer:	Marija Tudor

ISBN: 9781617297755
Printed in the United States of America

To my father, Maciej, who always had this inexplicable faith in my abilities.
I miss you, man.

brief contents

contents

foreword

As is often the case with new and technical areas, *Chaos Engineering* is a simple title for a rich and complex topic. Many of its principles and practices are counterintuitive—starting with its name—which makes it doubly challenging to explain. The early days of a new topic, however, are precisely the time when we need to find and distribute the easy-to-understand explanations.

I'm very pleased to say this book does exactly that.

An oft repeated scientific dictum is that "if you can't explain it simply, then you don't really understand it." I can safely say to you that Mikolaj clearly understands chaos engineering because in these pages he explains its principles and practices with a simplicity and practical use that is uncommon for technical books.

This, however, brings us to the main question. Why on earth would any reasonable person want to introduce *chaos* into their systems? Things are complicated enough already in our lives, so why go looking for trouble?

The short answer is that if you don't look for trouble, you won't be prepared when it comes looking for you. And eventually, trouble comes looking for all of us.

Testing—at least as we have all understood the term—will not be of much help. A *test* is an activity you run to make sure that your system behaves in a way that you expect under a specific set of conditions.

The biggest source of trouble, however, is not from the conditions we were expecting, but from the conditions that never occurred to us. No amount of testing will save us from emergent properties and behaviors. For that, we need something new.

We need chaos engineering.

If this is your first book on chaos engineering, you have chosen wisely. If not, then take solace in the fact that you are about to begin a journey that will fill in the gaps of your understanding and help you glue it all together in your mind.

When you are finished, you will feel more comfortable (and excited) about applying chaos engineering to your systems, and probably more than a little anxious about what you will find.

I am very pleased to have been invited to write these words and grateful to have a book like this available the next time someone asks me, "What is chaos engineering?"

—DAVID K. RENSIN, Google

foreword

If Miko didn't write this book, someone else would have to. That said, it would be difficult to find someone with Miko's history and experience with chaos engineering to put such a practical approach into writing. His background with distributed systems and particularly the critical and complex systems at Bloomberg, combined with his years of work on PowerfulSeal, give him a unique perspective. Not many people have the time and skill of working in the trenches on chaos engineering at an enterprise level.

This perspective is apparent in Miko's pragmatic approach. Throughout the chapters, we see a recurring theme that ties back to the value proposition of doing chaos engineering in the first place: risk and contract verification, holistic assessment of an entire system, and discovery of emergent properties.

One of the most common questions we hear with respect to chaos engineering is "Is it safe?" The second question is usually "How do I get started with chaos engineering?" Miko brilliantly answers both by including a virtual machine (VM) with all the examples and code used in the book. Anyone with basic knowledge of running an application can ease into common and then more advanced chaos engineering scenarios. Mess something up? No worries! Just turn off the VM and reload a new copy. You can now get started with chaos engineering, and do so safely, as Miko facilitates your learning journey from basic service outages (killing processes) to cache and database issues through OS- and application-level experiments, being mindful of the blast radius all the while.

Along the way, you'll get introduced to more advanced topics in system analysis, like the sections on Berkeley Packet Filter (BPF), `sar`, `strace`, and `tcptop`—even virtual machines and containers. Beyond just chaos engineering, this book is a broad education in SRE and DevOps practices.

The book provides examples of chaos engineering experiments across the application layer, at the operating system level, into containers, on hardware resources, on the network, and even in a web browser. Each of these areas alone is worthy of an entire chapter, if not book; you get the benefit of exploring the full breadth of possible experiments with an experienced facilitator to guide you through. Miko hits different ways each area can be affected in just the right level of detail to give you confidence to try it yourself in your own stack.

It's all very practical, without glossing over the nuances of understanding technical trade-offs; for example, in chapter 8 Miko weighs the pros and cons of modifying application code directly to enable an experiment (easier, more versatile) versus using another layer of abstraction such as a third-party tool (safer, scales better across contexts). These are the appropriate considerations for a pragmatic and tactical approach to implementing chaos engineering. I can say with confidence that this balance has not been struck in the literature on this subject prior to this book, making it an instant addition to the canon.

If you are chaos-curious, or even if you are well-versed in the history and benefits of chaos engineering, this book will take you step-by-step, safely, into the practice. Following along with the exercises will give you practical experience under your belt, and examples and pop quizzes included in the VM reinforce the takeaway learning. You will emerge with a better understanding of complex systems, how they work, and how they fail. This will, of course, allow you to build, operate, and maintain systems that are less likely to fail. The safest systems are, after all, the most complex ones.

—CASEY ROSENTHAL
Former manager of the Chaos Engineering Team at Netflix
CEO and cofounder of Verica.io

preface

People often ask how I ended up doing chaos engineering. I tend to tell them that I needed a sleeping aid. And chaos engineering is vegan-friendly and surprisingly effective for that purpose. Let me explain.

Back in 2016, through a lucky coincidence, I started working on a cutting-edge project based on Kubernetes. Nobody gets fired for choosing Kubernetes in 2020, but back then it was rather risky. Kubernetes v1.2 came as a bunch of moving parts, and bug fixes were rolling out quicker than we could install them.

To make it work, my team needed to build real operational experience, and do it fast. We needed to know how things worked and broke, how to fix them, and how to get alerted when that happened. And the best way to do that, we reasoned, was to break them preemptively.

This practice, which I later learned to call *chaos engineering* for the extra cool factor, turned out to be very effective at reducing the number of outages. And that, in turn, was better for my sleep quality than the expensive, bamboo-coated, memory foam pillow I have. Fast-forward a few years, and chaos engineering is one my primary interests. And I'm not alone—it is quickly becoming an invaluable tool to engineers around the world.

Today chaos engineering suffers from a few serious problems. In particular, the urban myths (that it's about randomly breaking things in production), a lack of quality content that teaches people how to do it well, and the initially counterintuitive mindset that needs to be adopted (failure will happen, so we need to be ready).

I wrote this book to fix these problems. I want to move chaos engineering from the funky zone to a legitimate, science-based methodology that's applicable to any system, software or otherwise. I want to show that you don't need to have massive scale to benefit from it, and that it can give you a lot of value for a little investment.

This book is designed for all curious software engineers and developers who want to build more reliable systems, however tiny or humongous they might be. And it gives them the right tools, from the Linux kernel all the way up to the application or browser level.

I've put a lot of work into making this book what it is now, and I'm hoping that you get value—and a few laughs—out of it. And finally, let's stay in touch. If you'd like to hear more from me, subscribe to my newsletter at https://chaosengineering.news. And if you like (or hate) the book, reach out and tell me all about it!

acknowledgments

I'll be honest: if I knew just how much time it would take to write this book, I'm not sure I'd have signed up in the first place. But now that I can almost smell the freshly printed copies, I'm really glad that I did!

A long list of people really helped make it happen, and they all deserve a massive thank you.

Tinaye, thank you for the endless streams of freshly brewed tea and for taking up a brand-new hobby to reduce my feeling of guilt about always being busy. You really helped me get through that; thank you!

Thank you to my good friends Sachin Kamboj and Chris Green, who somehow managed to read through the first, unpolished drafts of these chapters. That required true grit, and I'm very thankful.

A massive thank you to my editor, Toni Arritola, who not only fiercely guarded the quality of this book and always detected any slip-ups I was trying to sweep under the carpet, but also did all of that while putting up with my sense of humor. And she never tried explaining that it's not spelled "humour" across the pond.

Thank you to the rest of the staff at Manning: Deirdre Hiam, my project editor; Sharon Wilkey, my copyeditor; Melody Dolab, my proofreader; and Karsten Strøbæk, my technical proofreader.

Thank you to all the reviewers: Alessandro Campeis, Alex Lucas, Bonnie Malec, Burk Hufnagel, Clifford Thurber, Ezra Simeloff, George Haines, Harinath Mallepally, Hugo Cruz, Jared Duncan, Jim Amrhein, John Guthrie, Justin Coulston, Kamesh Ganesan, Kelum Prabath Senanayake, Kent R. Spillner, Krzysztof Kamyczek, Lev

Andelman, Lokesh Kumar, Maciej Drożdżowski, Michael Jensen, Michael Wright, Neil Croll, Ryan Burrows, Satadru Roy, Simeon Leyzerzon, Teresa Fontanella De Santis, Tobias Kaatz, Vilas Veeraraghavan, and Yuri Kushch, as well as Nick Watts and Karsten Strøbæk, who relentlessly called me out on any vagueness and broken code samples.

Thank you to my mentor, James Hook, who allowed chaos engineering to happen in my project in the first place. That decision years later resulted in the words you're reading right now.

Finally, I'd like to thank the GitHub community for being awesome. Thank you to everyone who contributed to PowerfulSeal, Goldpinger, or other projects we worked on together. It's an amazing phenomenon, and I hope it never stops.

about this book

The goal of this book is to help turn chaos engineering into a mature, mainstream, science-based practice, accessible to anyone. I strongly believe that it might offer some of the best return on investment you can get, and I want everyone to be able to benefit from that.

One of the challenges of writing a book like this is that chaos engineering doesn't focus on any single technology or programming language. In fact, it can be used on all kinds of stacks, which is one of its advantages. You can see that reflected in this book—each chapter is focused on a popular situation a software engineer might find themselves in, dealing with different languages, layers of the stack, and levels of control over the source code. The book uses Linux as the primary operating system, but the principles it teaches are universal.

Who should read this book

This book is for anyone who wants to make their systems more reliable. Are you an SRE? A full-stack developer? Frontend developer? Do you work with JVM, containers, or Kubernetes? If you said yes to any of these, you will find chapters of this book written for you. The book assumes a minimal familiarity with running day-to-day commands on Linux (Ubuntu). This is not an introduction to all of these things, and I assume a basic understanding of them so that we can dive deep (notable exceptions are Docker and Kubernetes, which are relatively new technologies, and we do cover how they work first).

How this book is organized: a roadmap

The book ships 13 chapters, split across three parts.

After chapter 1 introduces chaos engineering and the reasons for implementing it, part 1 lays the groundwork for further understanding what chaos engineering is about:

- Chapter 2 shows a real-world example of how a seemingly simple application might break in unexpected ways.
- Chapter 3 covers observability and all the tools that you're going to need to look under the hood of your system.
- Chapter 4 takes a popular application (WordPress) and shows you how to design, execute, and analyze a chaos experiment on the networking layer.

Part 2 covers various technologies and stacks where chaos engineering shines:

- Chapter 5 takes you from a vague idea of what Docker is, to understanding how it works under the hood and testing its limitations using chaos engineering.
- Chapter 6 demystifies system calls—what they are, how to see applications make them, and how to block them to see how resistant to failure these applications are.
- Chapter 7 shows how to inject failure on the fly into the JVM, so that you can test how a complex application handles the types of failure you're interested in.
- Chapter 8 discusses baking failure directly into your application.
- Chapter 9 covers chaos engineering . . . in the browser (using JavaScript).

Part 3 is dedicated to Kubernetes:

- Chapter 10 introduces Kubernetes, where it came from, and what it can do for you.
- Chapter 11 covers some higher-level tools that let you implement sophisticated chaos engineering experiments quickly.
- Chapter 12 takes you deep down the rabbit hole of how Kubernetes works under the hood. To understand its weak points, you need to know how it works. This chapter covers all the components that together make Kubernetes tick, along with ideas on how to identify resiliency problems using chaos engineering.

Finally, the last chapter talks about chaos engineering beyond the machines:

- Chapter 13 shows that the same principles also apply to the other complex distributed systems that you deal with on a daily basis—human teams. It covers the chaos engineering mindset, gives you ideas for games you can use to make your teams more reliable, and discusses how to get buy-in from stakeholders.

About the code

The book contains various snippets of code along with the expected output to teach you how to use different tools. The best way to run them is to use the Ubuntu VM that ships with this book. You can download it, as well as all the source code, from https://github.com/seeker89/chaos-engineering-book.

liveBook discussion forum

Purchase of Chaos Engineering includes free access to a private web forum run by Manning Publications, where you can make comments about the book, ask technical questions, and receive help from the author and from other users. To access the forum, go to http://mng.bz/5jEO. You can also learn more about Manning's forums and the rules of conduct at https://livebook.manning.com/#!/discussion.

Manning's commitment to our readers is to provide a venue where a meaningful dialogue between individual readers and between readers and the author can take place. It is not a commitment to any specific amount of participation on the part of the author, whose contribution to the forum remains voluntary (and unpaid). We suggest you try asking the author some challenging questions lest his interest stray! The forum and the archives of previous discussions will be accessible from the publisher's website as long as the book is in print.

about the author

Mikolaj Pawlikowski is a software engineer in love with reliability. Yup, "Miko" is fine!

If you'd like to hear more, join his newsletter at https://chaosengineering.news. To reach out directly, use LinkedIn or @mikopawlikowski on Twitter.

If you'd like to get involved in an open source chaos engineering project and hang out virtually, check out PowerfulSeal at https://github.com/powerfulseal/powerfulseal/. See chapter 11 for more details.

And finally, Miko helps organize a yearly chaos engineering conference. Sign up at https://www.conf42.com.

about the cover illustration

The figure on the cover of *Chaos Engineering* is captioned "Homme de Buccari en Croatie," or man from Bakar (Buccari) in Croatia. The illustration is taken from a collection of dress costumes from various countries by Jacques Grasset de Saint-Sauveur (1757–1810), titled *Costumes de Différents Pays*, published in France in 1797. Each illustration is finely drawn and colored by hand. The rich variety of Grasset de Saint-Sauveur's collection reminds us vividly of how culturally apart the world's towns and regions were just 200 years ago. Isolated from each other, people spoke different dialects and languages. In the streets or in the countryside, it was easy to identify where they lived and what their trade or station in life was just by their dress.

The way we dress has changed since then and the diversity by region, so rich at the time, has faded away. It is now hard to tell apart the inhabitants of different continents, let alone different towns, regions, or countries. Perhaps we have traded cultural diversity for a more varied personal life—certainly for a more varied and fast-paced technological life.

At a time when it is hard to tell one computer book from another, Manning celebrates the inventiveness and initiative of the computer business with book covers based on the rich diversity of regional life of two centuries ago, brought back to life by Grasset de Saint-Sauveur's pictures.

Into the world of
chaos engineering

This chapter covers

- What chaos engineering is and is not
- Motivations for doing chaos engineering
- Anatomy of a chaos experiment
- A simple example of chaos engineering in practice

What would you do to make absolutely sure the car you're designing is safe? A typical vehicle today is a real wonder of engineering. A plethora of subsystems, operating everything from rain-detecting wipers to life-saving airbags, all come together to not only go from A to B, but to protect passengers during an accident. Isn't it moving when your loyal car gives up the ghost to save yours through the strategic use of crumple zones, from which it will never recover?

Because passenger safety is the highest priority, all these parts go through rigorous testing. But even assuming they all work as designed, does that guarantee you'll survive in a real-world accident? If your business card reads, "New Car Assessment Program," you demonstrably don't think so. Presumably, that's why every new car making it to the market goes through crash tests.

Picture this: a production car, heading at a controlled speed, closely observed with high-speed cameras, in a lifelike scenario: crashing into an obstacle to test the system as a whole. In many ways, *chaos engineering is to software systems what crash tests are to the car industry*: a deliberate practice of experimentation designed to uncover systemic problems. In this book, you'll look at the why, when, and how of applying chaos engineering to improve your computer systems. And perhaps, who knows, save some lives in the process. What's a better place to start than a nuclear power plant?

1.1   *What is chaos engineering?*

Imagine you're responsible for designing the software operating a nuclear power plant. Your job description, among other things, is to prevent radioactive fallout. The stakes are high: a failure of your code can produce a disaster leaving people dead and rendering vast lands uninhabitable. You need to be ready for anything, from earthquakes, power cuts, floods, or hardware failures, to terrorist attacks. What do you do?

You hire the best programmers, set in place a rigorous review process, test coverage targets, and walk around the hall reminding everyone that we're doing serious business here. But "Yes, we have 100% test coverage, Mr. President!" will not fly at the next meeting. You need contingency plans; you need to be able to demonstrate that when bad things happen, the system as a whole can withstand them, and the name of your power plant stays out of the news headlines. You need to go looking for problems before they find you. That's what this book is about.

Chaos engineering is defined as "the discipline of experimenting on a system in order to build confidence in the system's capability to withstand turbulent conditions in production" (Principles of Chaos Engineering, http://principlesofchaos.org/). In other words, it's a software testing method focusing on finding evidence of problems before they are experienced by users.

You want your systems to be reliable (we'll look into that), and that's why you work hard to produce good-quality code and good test coverage. Yet, even if your code works as intended, in the real world plenty of things can (and will) go wrong. The list of things that can break is longer than a list of the possible side effects of painkillers: starting with sinister-sounding events like floods and earthquakes, which can take down entire datacenters, through power supply cuts, hardware failures, networking problems, resource starvation, race conditions, unexpected peaks of traffic, complex and unaccounted-for interactions between elements in your system, all the way to the evergreen operator (human) error. And the more sophisticated and complex your system, the more opportunities for problems to appear.

It's tempting to discard these as rare events, but they just keep happening. In 2019, for example, two crash landings occurred on the surface of the Moon: the Indian Chandrayaan-2 mission (http://mng.bz/Xd7v) and the Israeli Beresheet (http://mng.bz/yYgB), both lost on lunar descent. And remember that even if you do everything right, more often than not, you still depend on other systems, and these systems can fail. For example, Google Cloud,[1] Cloudflare, Facebook (WhatsApp), and Apple all had major outages within about a month in the summer of 2019 (http://mng.bz/ d42X). If your software ran on Google Cloud or relied on Cloudflare for routing, you were potentially affected. That's just reality.

It's a common misconception that chaos engineering is only about randomly breaking things in production. It's not. Although running experiments in production is a unique part of chaos engineering (more on that later), it's about much more than that—anything that helps us be confident the system can withstand turbulence. It interfaces with site reliability engineering (SRE), application and systems performance analysis, and other forms of testing. Practicing chaos engineering can help you prepare for failure, and by doing that, learn to build better systems, improve existing ones, and make the world a safer place.

1.2 Motivations for chaos engineering

At the risk of sounding like an infomercial, there are at least three good reasons to implement chaos engineering:

- Determining risk and cost and setting service-level indicators, objectives, and agreements
- Testing a system (often complex and distributed) as a whole
- Finding emergent properties you were unaware of

Let's take a closer look at these motivations.

1.2.1 Estimating risk and cost, and setting SLIs, SLOs, and SLAs

You want your computer systems to run well, and the subjective definition of what *well* means depends on the nature of the system and your goals regarding it. Most of the time, the primary motivation for companies is to create profit for the owners and shareholders. The definition of *running well* will therefore be a derivative of the business model objectives.

Let's say you're working on a planet-scale website, called Bookface, for sharing photos of cats and toddlers and checking on your high-school ex. Your business model might be to serve your users targeted ads, in which case you will want to balance the total cost of running the system with the amount of money you can earn from selling these ads. From an engineering perspective, one of the main risks is that the entire site could go down, and you wouldn't be able to present ads and bring home the revenue. Conversely, not being able to display a particular cat picture in the rare event of a problem with the cat picture server is probably not a deal breaker, and will affect your bottom line in only a small way.

For both of these risks (users can't use the website, and users can't access a cat photo momentarily), you can estimate the associated cost, expressed in dollars per

---

[1] You can see the official, detailed Google Cloud report at http://mng.bz/BRMg.

unit of time. That cost includes the direct loss of business as well as various other, less tangible things like public image damage, that might be equally important. As a real-life example, Forbes estimated that Amazon lost $66,240 per minute of its website being down in 2013.[2]

Now, to quantify these risks, the industry uses *service-level indicators* (*SLIs*). In our example, the percentage of time that your users can access the website could be an SLI. And so could the ratio of requests that are successfully served by the cat photos service within a certain time window. The SLIs are there to put a number to an event, and picking the right SLI is important.

Two parties agreeing on a certain range of an SLI can form a *service-level objective* (*SLO*), a tangible target that the engineering team can work toward. SLOs, in turn, can be legally enforced as a *service-level agreement* (*SLA*), in which one party agrees to guarantee a certain SLO or otherwise pay some form of penalty if they fail to do so.

Going back to our cat- and toddler-photo-sharing website, one possible way to work out the risk, SLI, and SLO could look like this:

- The main risk is "People can't access the website," or simply the *downtime*
- A corresponding SLI could be "the ratio of success responses to errors from our servers"
- An SLO for the engineering team to work toward: "the ratio of success responses to errors from our servers > 99.95% on average monthly"

To give you a different example, imagine a financial trading platform, where people query an API when their algorithms want to buy or sell commodities on the global markets. Speed is critical. We could imagine a different set of constraints, set on the trading API:

- SLI: 99th percentile response time
- SLO: 99th percentile response time < 25 ms, 99.999% of the time

From the perspective of the engineering team, that sounds like mission impossible: we allow ourselves about only 5 minutes a year when the top 1% of the slowest requests average over 25 milliseconds (ms) response time. Building a system like that might be difficult and expensive.

Number of nines

In the context of SLOs, we often talk about the *number of nines* to mean specific percentages. For example, 99% is *two nines*, 99.9% is *three nines*, 99.999% is *five nines*, and so on. Sometimes, we also use phrases like *three nines five* or *three and a half nines* to mean 99.95%, although the latter is not technically correct (going from

---

[2] See "Amazon.com Goes Down, Loses $66,240 per Minute," by Kelly Clay, Forbes, August 2013, http://mng .bz/ryJZ.

99.9% to 99.95% is a factor of 2, but going from 99.9% to 99.99% is a factor of 5). The following are a few of the most common values and their corresponding downtimes per year and per day:

- 90% (*one nine*)—36.53 days per year, or 2.4 hours per day
- 99% (*two nines*)—3.65 days per year, or 14.40 minutes per day
- 99.95% (*three and a half nines*)—4.38 hours per year, or 43.20 seconds per day
- 99.999% (*five nines*)—5.26 minutes per year, or 840 milliseconds per day

How does chaos engineering help with these? To satisfy the SLOs, you'll engineer the system in a certain way. You will need to take into account the various sinister scenarios, and the best way to see whether the system works fine in these conditions is to go and create them—which is exactly what chaos engineering is about! You're effectively working backward from the business goals, to an engineering-friendly defined SLO, that you can, in turn, continuously test against by using chaos engineering. Notice that in all of the preceding examples, I am talking in terms of entire systems.

1.2.2 *Testing a system as a whole*

Various testing techniques approach software at different levels. *Unit tests* typically cover single functions or smaller modules in isolation. *End-to-end* (*e2e*) *tests* and *integration tests* work on a higher level; whole components are put together to mimic a real system, and verification is done to ensure that the system does what it should. *Benchmarking* is yet another form of testing, focused on the performance of a piece of code, which can be lower level (for example, micro-benchmarking a single function) or a whole system (for example, simulating client calls).

I like to think of chaos engineering as the next logical step—a little bit like e2e testing, but during which we rig the conditions to introduce the type of failure we expect to see, and measure that we still get the correct answer within the expected time frame. It's also worth noting, as you'll see in part 2, that even a single-process system can be tested using chaos engineering techniques, and sometimes that comes in really handy.

1.2.3 *Finding emergent properties*

Our complex systems often exhibit *emergent properties* that we didn't initially intend. A real-world example of an emergent property is a human heart: its single cells don't have the property of pumping blood, but the right configuration of cells produces a heart that keeps us alive. In the same way, our neurons don't think, but their interconnected collection that we call a *brain* does, as you're illustrating by reading these lines.

In computer systems, properties often emerge from the interactions among the moving parts that the system comprises. Let's consider an example. Imagine that you run a system with many services, all using a Domain Name System (DNS) server to find one another. Each service is designed to handle DNS errors by retrying up to 10 times. Similarly, the external users of the systems are told to retry if their requests ever fail. Now, imagine that, for whatever reason, the DNS server fails and restarts. When it comes back up, it sees an amount of traffic amplified by the layers of retries, an amount that it wasn't set up to handle. So it might fail again, and get stuck in an infinite loop restarting, while the system as a whole is down. No component of the system has the property of creating infinite downtime, but with the components together and the right timing of events, the system as a whole might go into that state.

Although certainly less exciting than the example of consciousness I mentioned before, this property emerging from the interactions among the parts of the system is a real problem to deal with. This kind of unexpected behavior can have serious consequences on any system, especially a large one. The good news is that chaos engineering excels at finding issues like this. By experimenting on real systems, often you can discover how simple, predictable failures can cascade into large problems. And once you know about them, you can fix them.

> **Chaos engineering and randomness**
>
> When doing chaos engineering, you can often use the element of randomness and borrow from the practice of *fuzzing*—feeding pseudorandom payloads to a piece of software in order to try to come up with an error that your purposely written tests might be missing. The randomness definitely can be helpful, but once again, I would like to stress that controlling the experiments is necessary to be able to understand the results; chaos engineering is not just about randomly breaking things.

Hopefully, I've had your curiosity and now I've got your attention. Let's see how to do chaos engineering!

1.3 Four steps to chaos engineering

Chaos engineering experiments (*chaos experiments*, for short) are the basic units of chaos engineering. You do chaos engineering through a series of chaos experiments. Given a computer system and a certain number of characteristics you are interested in, you design experiments to see how the system fares when bad things happen. In each experiment, you focus on proving or refuting your assumptions about how the system will be affected by a certain condition.

For example, imagine you are running a popular website and you own an entire datacenter. You need your website to survive power cuts, so you make sure two independent power sources are installed in the datacenter. In theory, you are covered—but in practice, a lot can still go wrong. Perhaps the automatic switching between power sources doesn't work. Or maybe your website has grown since the launch of the datacenter, and a single power source no longer provides enough electricity for all the servers. Did you remember to pay an electrician for a regular checkup of the machines every three months?

If you feel worried, you should. Fortunately, chaos engineering can help you sleep better. You can design a simple chaos experiment that will scientifically tell you what happens when one of the power supplies goes down (for more dramatic effect, always pick the newest intern to run these steps).

Repeat for all power sources, one at a time:

1 Check that The Website is up.
2 Open the electrical panel and turn the power source off.
3 Check that The Website is still up.
4 Turn the power source back on.

This process is crude, and sounds obvious, but let's review these steps. Given a computer system (a datacenter) and a characteristic (survives a single power source failure), you designed an experiment (switch a power source off and eyeball whether The Website is still up) that increases your confidence in the system withstanding a power problem. You used science for the good, and it took only a minute to set up. *That's one small step for man, one giant leap for mankind.*

Before you pat yourself on the back, though, it's worth asking what would happen if the experiment failed and the datacenter went down. In this overly-crude-for-demonstration-purposes case, you would create an outage of your own. A big part of your job will be about minimizing the risks coming from your experiments and choosing the right environment to execute them. More on that later.

Take a look at figure 1.1, which summarizes the process you just went through. When you're back, let me anticipate your first question: What if you are dealing with more-complex problems?

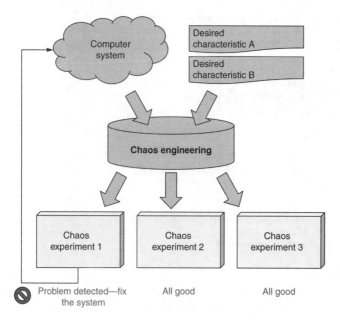

Figure 1.1 **The process of doing chaos engineering through a series of chaos experiments**

As with any experiment, you start by forming a hypothesis that you want to prove or disprove, and then you design the entire experience around that idea. When Gregor Mendel had an intuition about the laws of heredity, he designed a series of experiments on yellow and green peas, proving the existence of dominant and recessive traits. His results didn't follow the expectations, and that's perfectly fine; in fact, that's how his breakthrough in genetics was made.[3] We will be drawing inspiration from his experiments throughout the book, but before we get into the details of good craftsmanship in designing our experiments, let's plant a seed of an idea about what we're looking for.

Let's zoom in on one of these chaos experiment boxes from figure 1.1, and see what it's made of. Let me guide you through figure 1.2, which describes the simple, four-step process to design an experiment like that:

1 You need to be able to observe your results. Whether it's the color of the resulting peas, the crash test dummy having all limbs in place, your website being up, the CPU load, the number of requests per second, or the latency of successful requests, the first step is to ensure that you can accurately read the value for these

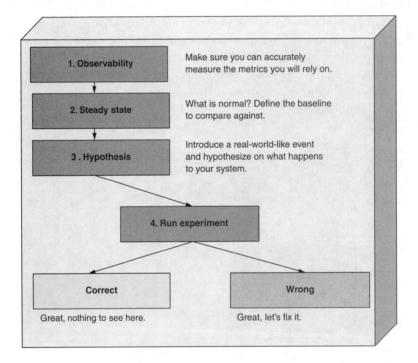

Figure 1.2   The four steps of a chaos experiment

---

[3] He did have to wait a couple of decades for anyone to reproduce his findings and for mainstream science to appreciate it and mark it "a breakthrough." But let's ignore that for now.

variables. We're lucky to be dealing with computers in the sense that we can often produce very accurate and very detailed data easily. We will call this *observability*.

2 Using the data you observe, you need to define what's *normal*. This is so that you can understand when things are out of the expected range. For instance, you might expect the CPU load on a 15-minute average to be below 20% for your application servers during the working week. Or you might expect 500 to 700 requests per second per instance of your application server running with four cores on your reference hardware specification. This normal range is often referred to as the *steady state*.

3 You shape your intuition into a hypothesis that can be proved or refuted, using the data you can reliably gather (observability). A simple example could be "Killing one of the machines doesn't affect the average service latency."

4 You execute the experiment, making your measurements to conclude whether you were right. And funnily enough, you like being wrong, because that's what you learn more from. Rinse and repeat.

The simpler your experiment, usually the better. You earn no bonus points for elaborate designs, unless that's the best way of proving the hypothesis. Look at figure 1.2 again, and let's dive just a little bit deeper, starting with *observability*.

1.3.1 *Ensure observability*

I quite like the word *observability* because it's straight to the point. It means being able to reliably see whatever metric you are interested in. The keyword here is *reliably*. Working with computers, we are often spoiled—the hardware producer or the operating system (OS) already provides mechanisms for reading various metrics, from the temperature of CPUs, to the fan's RPMs, to memory usage and hooks to use for various kernel events. But at the same time, it's often easy to forget that these metrics are subject to bugs and caveats that the end user needs to take into account. If the process you're using to measure CPU load ends up using more CPU than your application, that's probably a problem.

If you've ever seen a crash test on television, you will know it's both frightening and mesmerizing at the same time. Watching a 3000-pound machine accelerate to a carefully controlled speed and then fold like an origami swan on impact with a massive block of concrete is . . . humbling.

But the high-definition, slow-motion footage of shattered glass flying around, and seemingly unharmed (and unfazed) dummies sitting in what used to be a car just seconds before is not just for entertainment. Like any scientist who earned their white coat (and hair), both crash-test specialists and chaos engineering practitioners alike need reliable data to conclude whether an experiment worked. That's why observability, or reliably harvesting data about a live system, is paramount.

In this book, we're going to focus on Linux and the system metrics that it offers to us (CPU load, RAM usage, I/O speeds) as well as go through examples of higher-level metrics from the applications we'll be experimenting on.

Observability in the quantum realm

If your youth was as filled with wild parties as mine, you might be familiar with the double-slit experiment (http://mng.bz/MX4W). It's one of my favorite experiments in physics, and one that displays the probabilistic nature of quantum mechanics. It's also one that has been perfected over the last 200 years by generations of physicists.

The experiment in its modern form consists of shooting photons (or matter particles such as electrons) at a barrier that has two parallel slits, and then observing what landed on the screen on the other side. The fun part is that if you don't observe which slit the particles go through, they behave like a wave and interfere with each other, forming a pattern on the screen. But if you try to detect (observe) which slit each particle went through, the particles will not behave like a wave. So much for reliable observability in quantum mechanics!

1.3.2   *Define a steady state*

Armed with reliable data from the previous step (observability), you need to define what's normal so that you can measure abnormalities. A fancier way of saying that is to *define a steady state*, which works much better at dinner parties.

What you measure will depend on the system and your goals about it. It could be "undamaged car going straight at 60 mph" or perhaps "99% of our users can access our API in under 200ms." Often, this will be driven directly by the business strategy.

It's important to mention that on a modern Linux server, a lot of things will be going on, and you're going to try your best to isolate as many variables as possible. Let's take the example of CPU usage of your process. It sounds simple, but in practice, a lot of things can affect your reading. Is your process getting enough CPU, or is it being stolen by other processes (perhaps it's a shared machine, or maybe a cron job updating the system kicked in during your experiment)? Did the kernel schedule allocate cycles to another process with higher priority? Are you in a virtual machine, and perhaps the hypervisor decided something else needed the CPU more?

You can go deep down the rabbit hole. The good news is that often you are going to repeat your experiments many times, and some of the other variables will be brought to light, but remembering that all these other factors can affect your experiments is something you should keep in the back of your mind.

1.3.3   *Form a hypothesis*

Now, for the really fun part. In step 3, you shape your intuitions into a testable hypothesis—an educated guess of what will happen to your system in the presence of a well-defined problem. Will it carry on working? Will it slow down? By how much?

In real life, these questions will often be prompted by incidents (unprompted problems you discover when things stop working), but the better you are at this game, the more you can (and should) preempt. Earlier in the chapter, I listed a few examples of what tends to go wrong. These events can be broadly categorized as follows:

- External events (earthquakes, floods, fires, power cuts, and so on)
- Hardware failures (disks, CPUs, switches, cables, power supplies, and so on)
- Resource starvation (CPU, RAM, swap, disk, network)
- Software bugs (infinite loops, crashes, hacks)
- Unsupervised bottlenecks
- Unpredicted emergent properties of the system
- Virtual machine (Java Virtual Machine, V8, others)
- Hardware bugs
- Human error (pushing the wrong button, sending the wrong config, pulling the wrong cable, and so forth)

We will look into how to simulate these problems as we go through the concrete examples in part 2 of the book. Some of them are easy (switch off a machine to simulate machine failure or take out the Ethernet cable to simulate network issues), while others will be much more advanced (add latency to a system call). The choice of failures to take into account requires a good understanding of the system you are working on.

Here are a few examples of what a hypothesis could look like:

- On frontal collision at 60 mph, no dummies will be squashed.
- If both parent peas are yellow, all the offspring will be yellow.
- If we take 30% of our servers down, the API continues to serve the 99th percentile of requests in under 200 ms.
- If one of our database servers goes down, we continue meeting our SLO.

Now, it's time to run the experiment.

1.3.4 *Run the experiment and prove (or refute) your hypothesis*

Finally, you run the experiment, measure the results, and conclude whether you were right. Remember, being wrong is fine—and much more exciting at this stage!

Everybody gets a medal in the following conditions:

- If you were right, congratulations! You just gained more confidence in your system withstanding a stormy day.
- If you were wrong, congratulations! You just found a problem in your system before your clients did, and you can still fix it before anyone gets hurt!

We'll spend some time on the good craftsmanship rules in the following chapters, including automation, managing the blast radius, and testing in production. For now, just remember that as long as this is good science, you learn something from each experiment.

1.4 *What chaos engineering is not*

If you're just skimming this book in a store, hopefully you've already gotten some value out of it. More information is coming, so don't put it away! As is often the case, the devil is in the details, and in the coming chapters you'll see in greater depth how to execute the preceding four steps. I hope that by now you can clearly see the benefits of what chaos engineering has to offer, and roughly what's involved in getting to it.

But before we proceed, I'd like to make sure that you also understand what *not* to expect from these pages. Chaos engineering is not a silver bullet, and doesn't automatically fix your system, cure cancer, or guarantee weight loss. In fact, it might not even be applicable to your use case or project.

A common misconception is that chaos engineering is about randomly destroying stuff. I guess the name kind of hints at it, and Chaos Monkey (https://netflix.github .io/chaosmonkey/), the first tool to gain internet fame in the domain, relies on randomness quite a lot. But although randomness can be a powerful tool, and sometimes overlaps with fuzzing, you want to control the variables you are interacting with as closely as possible. More often than not, adding failure is the easy part; the hard part is to know where to inject it and why.

Chaos engineering is not just Chaos Monkey, Chaos Toolkit (https://chaostoolkit .org/), PowerfulSeal (https://github.com/bloomberg/powerfulseal) or any of the numerous projects available on GitHub. These are tools making it easier to implement certain types of experiments, but the real difficulty is in learning how to look critically at systems and predict where the fragile points might be.

It's important to understand that chaos engineering doesn't replace other testing methods, such as unit or integration tests. Instead, it complements them: just as airbags are tested in isolation, and then again with the rest of the car during a crash test, chaos experiments operate on a different level and test the system as a whole.

This book will not give you ready-made answers on how to fix your systems. Instead, it will teach you how to find problems by yourself and where to look for them. Every system is different, and although we'll look at common scenarios and gotchas together, you'll need a deep understanding of your system's weak spots to come up with useful chaos experiments. In other words, the value you get out of the chaos experiments is going to depend on your system, how well you understand it, how deep you want to go testing it, and how well you set up your observability shop.

Although chaos engineering is unique in that it can be applied to production systems, that's not the only scenario that it caters to. A lot of content on the internet appears to be centered around "breaking things in production," quite possibly because it's the most radical thing you can do, but, again, that's not all chaos engineering is about—or even its main focus. A lot of value can be derived from applying chaos engineering principles and running experiments in other environments too.

Finally, although some overlap exists, chaos engineering doesn't stem from chaos theory in mathematics and physics. I know: bummer. Might be an awkward question to answer at a family reunion, so better be prepared.

With these caveats out of the way, let's get a taste of what chaos engineering is like with a small case study.

1.5 A taste of chaos engineering

Before things get technical, let's close our eyes and take a quick detour to Glanden, a fictional island country in northern Europe. Life is enjoyable for Glandeners. The geographical position provides a mild climate and a prosperous economy for its hardworking people. At the heart of Glanden is Donlon, the capital with a large population of about 8 million people, all with a rich heritage from all over the world—a true cultural melting pot. It's in Donlon that our fictitious startup FizzBuzzAAS tries really hard to *make the world a better place.*

1.5.1 FizzBuzz as a service

FizzBuzzAAS Ltd. is a rising star in Donlon's booming tech scene. Started just a year ago, it has already established itself as a clear leader in the market of FizzBuzz as a Service. Recently supported by serious venture capital (VC) dollars, the company is looking to expand its market reach and scale its operations. The competition, exemplified by FizzBuzzEnterpriseEdition (https://github.com/EnterpriseQualityCoding/FizzBuzz-EnterpriseEdition) is fierce and unforgiving. The FizzBuzzAAS business model is straightforward: clients pay a flat monthly subscription fee to access the cutting-edge APIs.

Betty, head of sales at FizzBuzzAAS, is a natural. She's about to land a big contract that could make or break the ambitious startup. Everyone has been talking about that contract at the water cooler for weeks. The tension is sky-high.

Suddenly, the phone rings, and everyone goes silent. It's the Big Company calling. Betty picks up. "Mhm . . . Yes. I understand." It's so quiet you can hear the birds chirping outside. "Yes ma'am. Yes, I'll call you back. Thank you."

Betty stands up, realizing everyone is holding their breath. "Our biggest client can't access the API."

1.5.2 A long, dark night

It was the first time in the history of the company that the entire engineering team (Alice and Bob) pulled an all-nighter. Initially, nothing made sense. They could successfully connect to each of the servers, the servers were reporting as healthy, and the expected processes were running and responding—so where did the errors come from?

Moreover, their architecture really wasn't that sophisticated. An external request would hit a load balancer, which would route to one of the two instances of the API server, which would consult a cache to either serve a precomputed response, if it was fresh enough, or compute a new one and store it in cache. You can see this simple architecture in figure 1.3.

Finally, a couple of gallons of coffee into the night, Alice found the first piece of the puzzle. "It's kinda weird," she said as she was browsing through the logs of one of the API server instances, "I don't see any errors, but all of these requests seem to stop at the cache lookup." Eureka! It wasn't long after that moment that she found the problem: their code gracefully handled the cache being down (connection refused, no host, and so on), but didn't have any time-outs in case of no response. It was downhill

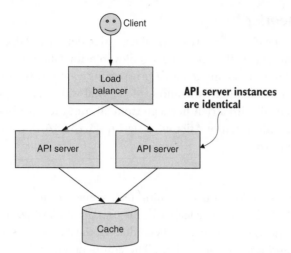

Figure 1.3   FizzBuzz as a Service technical architecture

from there—a quick session of pair programming, a rapid build and deploy, and it was time for a nap.

The order of the world was restored; people could continue requesting FizzBuzz as a Service, and the VC dollars were being well spent. The Big Company acknowledged the fix and didn't even mention cancelling its contract. The sun shone again. Later, it turned out that the API server's inability to connect to the cache was a result of a badly rolled-out firewall policy, in which someone forgot to whitelist the cache. Human error.

1.5.3   *Postmortem*

"How can we make sure that we're immune to this kind of issue the next time?" Alice asked, in what was destined to be a crucial meeting for the company's future.

Silence.

"Well, I guess we could preemptively set some of our servers on fire once in a while" answered Bob to lift up the mood just a little bit.

Everyone started laughing. Everyone, apart from Alice, that is.

"Bob, you're a genius!" Alice acclaimed and then took a moment to appreciate the size of everyone's eyeballs. "Let's do exactly that! If we could *simulate* a broken firewall rule like this, then we could add this to our integration tests."

"You're right!" Bob jumped out of his chair. "It's easy! I do it all the time to block my teenager's Counter Strike servers on the router at home! All you need to do is this," he said and proceeded to write on the whiteboard:

```
iptables -A ${CACHE_SERVER_IP} -j DROP
```

"And then after the test, we can undo that with this," he carried on, sensing the growing respect his colleagues were about to kindle in themselves:

```
iptables -D ${CACHE_SERVER_IP} -j DROP
```

Alice and Bob implemented these fixes as part of the setup and teardown of their integration tests, and then confirmed that the older version wasn't working, but the newer one including the fix worked like a charm. Both Alice and Bob changed their job titles to site reliability engineer (SRE) on LinkedIn the same night, and made a pact to never tell anyone they hot-fixed the issue in production.

1.5.4 *Chaos engineering in a nutshell*

If you've ever worked for a startup, long, coffee-fueled nights like this are probably no stranger to you. Raise your hand if you can relate! Although simplistic, this scenario shows all four of the previously covered steps in action:

- The *observability* metric is whether or not we can successfully call the API.
- The *steady state* is that the API responds successfully.
- The *hypothesis* is that if we drop connectivity to the cache, we continue getting a successful response.
- After *running the experiment*, we can confirm that the old version breaks and the new one works.

Well done, team: you've just increased confidence in the system surviving difficult conditions! In this scenario, the team was reactive; Alice and Bob came up with this new test only to account for an error their users already noticed. That made for a more dramatic effect on the plot. In real life, and in this book, we're going to do our best to predict and proactively detect this kind of issue without the external stimulus of becoming jobless overnight! And I promise that we'll have some serious fun in the process (see appendix D for a taste).

Summary

- Chaos engineering is a discipline of experimenting on a computer system in order to uncover problems, often undetected by other testing techniques.
- Much as the crash tests done in the automotive industry try to ensure that the car as a whole behaves in a certain way during a well-defined, real-life-like event, chaos engineering experiments aim to confirm or refute your hypotheses about the behavior of the system during a real-life-like problem.
- Chaos engineering doesn't automatically solve your issues, and coming up with meaningful hypotheses requires a certain level of expertise in the way your system works.
- Chaos engineering isn't about randomly breaking things (although that has its place, too), but about adding a controlled amount of failure you understand.
- Chaos engineering doesn't need to be complicated. The four steps we just covered, along with some good craftsmanship, should take you far before things get any more complex. As you will see, computer systems of any size and shape can benefit from chaos engineering.

Part 1

Chaos engineering fundamentals

Building a house tends to be much easier if you start with the foundation. This part lays the foundation for the chaos engineering headquarters skyscraper that we're going to build in this book. Even if you read only these three chapters, you will see how a little bit of chaos engineering on a real-life system can detect potentially catastrophic problems.

Chapter 2 jumps straight into the action, by showing you how a seemingly stable application can break easily. It also helps you set up the virtual machine to try everything in this book without worrying about breaking your laptop, and covers essentials like the blast radius.

Chapter 3 covers observability and all the tools that you're going to need to look under the hood of your system. Observability is the cornerstone of chaos engineering—it makes the difference between doing science and guessing. You will also see the USE methodology.

Chapter 4 takes a popular application (WordPress) and shows you how to design, execute, and analyze a chaos experiment on the networking layer. You will see how fragile the application can be to network slowness, so that you can design yours to be more resilient.

First cup of chaos and blast radius

This chapter covers

- Setting up a virtual machine to run through accompanying code
- Using basic Linux forensics—why did your process die?
- Performing your first chaos experiment with a simple bash script
- Understanding the blast radius

The previous chapter covered what chaos engineering is and what a chaos experiment template looks like. It is now time to get your hands dirty and implement an experiment from scratch! I'm going to take you step by step through building your first chaos experiment, using nothing more than a few lines of bash. I'll also use the occasion to introduce and illustrate new concepts like *blast radius*.

Just one last pit stop before we're off to our journey: let's set up the workspace.

DEFINITION I'll bet you're wondering what a *blast radius* is. Let me explain. Much like an explosive, a software component can go wrong and break other things it connects to. We often speak of a blast radius to describe the maximum number of things that can be affected by something going wrong. I'll teach you more about it as you read this chapter.

19

2.1   Setup: Working with the code in this book

I care about your learning process. To make sure that all the relevant resources and tools are available to you immediately, I'm providing a virtual machine (VM) image that you can download, import, and run on any host capable of running VirtualBox. Throughout this book, I'm going to assume you are executing the code provided in the VM. This way, you won't have to worry about installing the various tools on your PC. It will also allow us to be more playful inside the VM than if it was your host OS.

Before you get started, you need to import the virtual machine image into VirtualBox. To do that, complete the following steps:

1   Download the VM image:
   - Go to https://github.com/seeker89/chaos-engineering-book.
   - Click the Releases link at the right of the page.
   - Find the latest release.
   - Follow the release notes to download, verify, and decompress the VM archive (there will be multiple files to download).

2   Install VirtualBox by following instructions at www.virtualbox.org/wiki/Downloads.

3   Import the VM image into VirtualBox:
   - In VirtualBox, click File > Import Appliance.
   - Pick the VM image file you downloaded and unarchived.
   - Follow the wizard until completion.

4   Configure the VM to your taste (and resources):
   - In VirtualBox, right-click your new VM and choose Settings.
   - Choose General > Advanced > Shared Clipboard and then select Bidirectional.
   - Choose System > Motherboard and then select 4096 MB of Base Memory.
   - Choose Display > Video Memory and then select at least 64 MB.
   - Choose Display > Remote Display and then uncheck Enable Server.
   - Choose Display > Graphics Controller and then select what VirtualBox recommends.

5   Start the VM and log in.
   - The username and password are both `chaos`.

NOTE   When using VirtualBox, the Bidirectional check box under General > Advanced > Shared Clipboard activates copying and pasting in both directions. With this setting, you can copy things from your host machine by pressing Ctrl-C (Cmd-C on a Mac) and paste them into the VM with Ctrl-V (Cmd-V). A common gotcha is that when pasting into the terminal in Ubuntu, you need to press Ctrl-Shift-C and Ctrl-Shift-V.

That's it! The VM comes with all the source code needed and all the tools preinstalled. The versions of the tools will also match the ones I use in the text of this book.

All the source code, including the code used to prebuild the VM, can be found at https://github.com/seeker89/chaos-engineering-book. Once you've completed these steps, you should be able to follow everything in this book. If you find any issues, feel free to create an issue on that GitHub repo. Let's get to the meat of it by introducing an ironically realistic scenario!

> **TIP** I chose VirtualBox because it's free and accessible to all. If you and VirtualBox don't get along, feel free to use the image with whatever does float your boat. VMware is a popular choice, and you can easily google how to set it up.

2.2 Scenario

Remember our friends from Glanden from the previous chapter? They have just reached out for help. They are having trouble with their latest product: the early clients are complaining it sometimes doesn't work, but when the engineers are testing, it all seems fine. As a growing authority in the chaos engineering community, you agree to help them track and fix the issue they are facing. Challenge accepted.

This is a more common scenario than any chaos engineer would like to admit. Something's not working, the existing testing methods don't find anything, and the clock is ticking. In an ideal world, you would proactively think about and prevent situations like this, but in the real world, you'll often face problems that are already there. To give you the right tools to cope, I want to start you off with a scenario of the latter category.

In this kind of situation, you'll typically have at least two pieces of information to work with: the overall architecture and the application logs. Let's start by taking a look at the architecture of the FizzBuzz service, shown in figure 2.1.

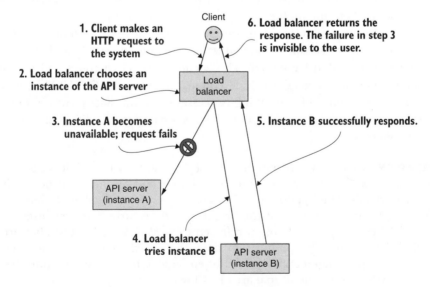

Figure 2.1 FizzBuzz as a Service technical architecture

As figure 2.1 illustrates, the architecture consists of a load balancer (NGINX) and two identical copies of an API server (implemented in Python). When a client makes a request through their internet browser (1), the request is received by the load balancer. The load balancer is configured to route incoming traffic to any instance that's up and running (2). If the instance the load balancer chooses becomes unavailable (3), the load balancer is configured to retransmit the request to the other instance (4). Finally, the load balancer returns the response provided by the instance of the API server to the client (5), and the internal failure is transparent to the user.

The other element you have at your disposal is the logs. A relevant sample of the logs looks like this (similar lines appear multiple times):

```
[14658.582809] ERROR: FizzBuzz API instance exiting, exit code 143
[14658.582809] Restarting
[14658.582813] FizzBuzz API version 0.0.7 is up and running.
```

While a little bit light on the details, it does provide valuable clues about what is going on: you can see that their API server instances are restarted and you can also see something called an exit code. These restarts are a good starting point for designing a chaos experiment. But before we do that, it's important that you know how to read exit codes like these and use them to understand what happened to a process before it died. With the *Criminal Minds* theme in the background, let's take a look at the basics of Linux forensics.

2.3   *Linux forensics 101*

When doing chaos engineering, you will often find yourself trying to understand why a program died. It often feels like playing detective, solving mysteries in a popular crime TV series. Let's put on the detective hat and solve a case!

In the preceding scenario, what you have at your disposal amounts to a *black-box* program that you can see died, and you want to figure out *why*. What do you do, and how do you check what happened? This section covers exit codes and killing processes, both manually through the kill command and by the Out-Of-Memory Killer, a part of Linux responsible for killing processes when the system runs low on memory. This will prepare you to deal with processes dying in real life. Let's begin with the exit codes.

> **DEFINITION**   In software engineering, we often refer to systems that are *opaque* to us as *black boxes*; we can see only their inputs and outputs, and not their inner workings. The opposite of a black box is sometimes called a *white box*. (You might have heard about the bright orange recording devices installed on airplanes. They are also often referred to as *black boxes*, because they are designed to prevent tampering with them, despite their real color.) When practicing chaos engineering, we will often be able to operate on entire systems or system components that are black boxes.

2.3.1 *Exit codes*

When dealing with a black-box piece of code, the first thing you might want to think about is running the program and seeing what happens. Unless it's supposed to rotate nuclear plant access codes, running it might be a good idea. To show you what that could look like, I wrote a program that dies. Let's warm up by running it and investigating what happens. From the provided VM, open a new bash session and start a mysterious program by running this command:

```
~/src/examples/killer-whiles/mystery000
```

You will notice that it exits immediately and prints an error message like this:

```
Floating point exception (core dumped)
```

The program was kind enough to tell us why it died: something to do with a floating-point arithmetic error. That's great for a human eye, but Linux provides a better mechanism for understanding what happened to the program. When a process terminates, it returns a number to inform the user of whether it succeeded. That number is called an *exit code*. You can check the exit code returned by the preceding command by running the following command at the prompt:

```
echo $?
```

In this case, you will see the following output:

```
136
```

This means that the last program that executed exited with code 136. Many (not all) UNIX commands return 0 when the command is successful, and 1 when it fails. Some use different return codes to differentiate various errors. Bash has a fairly compact convention on exit codes that I encourage you to take a look at (www.tldp.org/LDP/abs/html/exitcodes.html).

The codes in range 128–192 are decoded by using $128 + n$, where n is the number of the kill signal. In this example, the exit code is 136, which corresponds to $128 + 8$, meaning that the program received a kill signal number 8, which is SIGFPE. This signal is sent to a program when it tries to execute an erroneous arithmetic operation. Don't worry—you don't have to remember all the kill signal numbers by heart. You can see them with their corresponding numbers by running kill -L at the command prompt. Note that some of the exit codes differ between bash and other shells.

Remember that a program can return any exit code, sometimes by mistake. But assuming that it gives you a meaningful exit code, you know where to start debugging, and life tends to be good. The program did something wrong, it died, the cold kernel justice was served. But what happens if you suspect a murder?

Available signals

If you're curious about the various signals you can send (for example, via the `kill` command), you can list them easily by running the following command in your terminal:

```
kill -L
```

You will see output similar to the following:

```
 1) SIGHUP       2) SIGINT       3) SIGQUIT      4) SIGILL       5) SIGTRAP
 6) SIGABRT      7) SIGBUS       8) SIGFPE       9) SIGKILL     10) SIGUSR1
11) SIGSEGV     12) SIGUSR2     13) SIGPIPE     14) SIGALRM     15) SIGTERM
16) SIGSTKFLT   17) SIGCHLD     18) SIGCONT     19) SIGSTOP     20) SIGTSTP
21) SIGTTIN     22) SIGTTOU     23) SIGURG      24) SIGXCPU     25) SIGXFSZ
26) SIGVTALRM   27) SIGPROF     28) SIGWINCH    29) SIGIO       30) SIGPWR
31) SIGSYS      34) SIGRTMIN    35) SIGRTMIN+1  36) SIGRTMIN+2  37) SIGRTMIN+3
38) SIGRTMIN+4  39) SIGRTMIN+5  40) SIGRTMIN+6  41) SIGRTMIN+7  42) SIGRTMIN+8
43) SIGRTMIN+9  44) SIGRTMIN+10 45) SIGRTMIN+11 46) SIGRTMIN+12 47) SIGRTMIN+13
48) SIGRTMIN+14 49) SIGRTMIN+15 50) SIGRTMAX-14 51) SIGRTMAX-13 52) SIGRTMAX-12
53) SIGRTMAX-11 54) SIGRTMAX-10 55) SIGRTMAX-9  56) SIGRTMAX-8  57 SIGRTMAX-7
58) SIGRTMAX-6  59) SIGRTMAX-5  60) SIGRTMAX-4  61) SIGRTMAX-3  62) SIGRTMAX-2
63) SIGRTMAX-1  64) SIGRTMAX
```

2.3.2   *Killing processes*

To show you how to explicitly kill processes, let's play both the good cop and the bad cop. Open two bash sessions in two terminal windows. In the first one, run the following command to start a long-running process:

```
sleep 3600
```

Just as its name indicates, the `sleep` command blocks for the specified number of seconds. This is just to simulate a long-running process. Your prompt will be blocked, waiting for the command to finish. To confirm that the process is there, in the second terminal, run the following command to list the running processes (the f flag shows visually the parent-child relationships between processes):

```
ps f
```

In the following output, you can see `sleep 3600` as a child of the other bash process:

```
PID   TTY     STAT    TIME COMMAND
4214 pts/1    Ss      0:00 bash
4262 pts/1    R+      0:00  \_ ps f
2430 pts/0    Ss      0:00 bash
4261 pts/0    S+      0:00  \_ sleep 3600
```

Now, still in the second terminal, let's commit a process crime—kill your poor sleep process:

```
pkill sleep
```

You will notice the sleep process die in the first terminal. It will print this output, and the prompt will become available again:

```
Terminated
```

This is useful to see, but most of the time, the processes you care about will die when you're not looking at them, and you'll be interested in gathering as much information about the circumstances of their death as possible. That's when the exit codes we covered before become handy. You can verify what exit code the sleep process returned before dying by using this familiar command:

```
echo $?
```

The exit code is 143. Similar to 136, it corresponds to 128 + 15, or SIGTERM, the default signal sent by the kill command. This is the same code that was displayed in the FizzBuzz logs, giving us an indication that their processes were being killed. This is an aha moment: a first piece to our puzzle!

If you chose a different signal, you would see a different exit code. To illustrate that, start the sleep process again from the first terminal by running the same command:

```
sleep 3600
```

To send a KILL signal, run the following command from the second terminal:

```
pkill -9 sleep
```

This will result in getting a different exit code. To see the exit code, run this command from the first terminal, the one in which the process died:

```
echo $?
```

You will see the following output:

```
137
```

As you might expect, the exit code is 137, or 128 + 9. Note that nothing prevents us from using kill -8, and getting the same exit code as in the previous example that had an arithmetic error in the program. All of this is just a convention, but most of the popular tooling will follow it.

So now you've covered another popular way for a process to die, by an explicit signal. It might be an administrator issuing a command, it might be the system detecting an arithmetic error, or it might be done by some kind of daemon managing the process. Of the latter category, an interesting example is the Out-Of-Memory (OOM) Killer. Let's take a look at the mighty killer.

Pop quiz: Return codes

Pick the false statement:

1 Linux processes provide a number that indicates the reason for exiting.
2 Number 0 means a successful exit.
3 Number 143 corresponds to SIGTERM.
4 There are 32 possible exit codes.

See appendix B for answers.

2.3.3   Out-Of-Memory Killer

The OOM Killer can be a surprise the first time you learn about it. If you haven't yet, I'd like you to experience it firsthand. Let's start with a little mystery to solve. To illustrate what OOM is all about, run the following program I've prepared for you from the command line:

```
~/src/examples/killer-whiles/mystery001
```

Can you find out what the program is doing? Where would you start? The source code is in the same folder as the executable, but stay with me for a few minutes before you read it. Let's try to first approach it as a black box.

After a minute or two of running the program, you might notice your VM getting a little sluggish, which is a good hint to check the memory utilization. You can see that by running the top command from the command line, as follows:

```
top -n1 -o+%MEM
```

Note the use of -n1 flag to print one output and exit, rather than update continuously, and -o+%MEM to sort the processes by their memory utilization.

Your output will be similar to the following:

Free memory at around 100 MB

```
top - 21:35:49 up  4:21,  1 user,  load average: 0.55, 0.46, 0.49
Tasks: 175 total,   3 running, 172 sleeping,   0 stopped,   0 zombie
%Cpu(s): 11.8 us, 29.4 sy,  0.0 ni, 35.3 id, 20.6 wa,  0.0 hi,  2.9 si,  0.0 st
MiB Mem :  3942.4 total,    98.9 free,    3745.5 used,     98.0 buff/cache   ◁──┐
MiB Swap:     0.0 total,     0.0 free,     0.0 used.      5.3 avail Mem

PID   USER   PR  NI    VIRT    RES     SHR  S  %CPU  %MEM  TIME+   COMMAND
5451  chaos  20   0  3017292   2.9g      0  S   0.0  74.7  0:07.95 mystery001  ◁──
5375  chaos  20   0  3319204 301960  50504  S  29.4   7.5  0:06.65 gnome-shell
1458  chaos  20   0   471964 110628  44780  S   0.0   2.7  0:42.32 Xorg
(...)
```

**Memory usage (RES and %MEM) and the
name of mystery001 process in bold font**

You can see that mystery001 is using 2.9 GB of memory, almost three-quarters for the VM, and the available memory hovers around 100 MB. Your top might start dying on you or struggle to allocate memory. Unless you're busy encoding videos or maxing out games, that's rarely a good sign. While you're trying to figure out what's going on, if my timing is any good, you should see your process die in the prompt (if you're running your VM with more RAM, it might take longer):

```
Killed
```

A murder! But what happened? Who killed it? The title of this section is a little bit of a giveaway, so let's check the kernel log to look for clues. To do that, you can use dmesg. It's a Linux utility that displays kernel messages. Let's search for our mystery001 by running the following in a terminal:

```
dmesg | grep -i mystery001
```

You will see something similar to the following output. As you read through these lines, the plot thickens. Something called oom_reaper just killed your mysterious process:

```
[14658.582932] Out of memory: Kill process 5451 (mystery001)
score 758 or sacrifice child
[14658.582939] Killed process 5451 (mystery001)
total-vm:3058268kB, anon-rss:3055776kB, file-rss:4kB, shmem-rss:0kB
[14658.644154] oom_reaper: reaped process 5451 (mystery001),
now anon-rss:0kB, file-rss:0kB, shmem-rss:0kB
```

What is that, and why is it claiming rights to your processes? If you browse through dmesg a bit more, you will see a little information about what OOM Killer did, including the list of processes it evaluated before sacrificing your program on the altar of RAM.

Here's an example, shortened for brevity. Notice the oom_score_adj column, which displays the scores of various processes from the OOM Killer's point of view (I put the name in bold for easier reading):

```
[14658.582809] Tasks state (memory values in pages):
[14658.582809] [pid ] uid tgid total_vm rss pgtables_bytes swapents
    oom_score_adj name
(...)
[14658.582912] [5451] 1000  5451 764567  763945  6164480  0   0 mystery001
(...)
[14658.582932] Out of memory: Kill process 5451 (mystery001) score 758 or
    sacrifice child
[14658.582939] Killed process 5451 (mystery001) total-vm:3058268kB, anon-
    rss:3055776kB, file-rss:4kB, shmem-rss:0kB
[14658.644154] oom_reaper: reaped process 5451 (mystery001), now anon-
    rss:0kB, file-rss:0kB, shmem-rss:0kB
```

The OOM Killer is one of the more interesting (and controversial) memory management features in the Linux kernel. Under low-memory conditions, the OOM Killer kicks in and tries to figure out which processes to kill in order to reclaim some memory and for the system to regain some stability. It uses heuristics (including niceness, how recent the process is and how much memory it uses—see https://linux-mm.org/OOM_Killer for more details) to score each process and pick the unlucky winner. If you're interested in how it came to be and why it was implemented the way it was, the best article on this subject that I know of is "Taming the OOM Killer" by Goldwyn Rodrigues (https://lwn.net/Articles/317814/).

So, there it is, the third popular reason for processes to die, one that often surprises newcomers. In the FizzBuzz logs sample, you know that the exit code you saw could be a result of either an explicit `kill` command or perhaps the OOM Killer. Unfortunately, unlike other exit codes that have a well-defined meaning, the one in the logs sample doesn't help you conclude the exact reason for the processes dying. Fortunately, chaos engineering allows you to make progress regardless of that. Let's go ahead and get busy applying some chaos engineering!

Pop quiz: What's OOM?

Pick one:

1 A mechanism regulating the amount of RAM any given process is given
2 A mechanism that kills processes when the system runs low on resources
3 A yoga mantra
4 The sound that Linux admins make when they see processes dying

See appendix B for answers.

OOM Killer settings

The OOM Killer behavior can be tweaked via flags exposed by the kernel. The following is from the kernel documentation, www.kernel.org/doc/Documentation/sysctl/vm.txt:

```
================================================================

oom_kill_allocating_task

This enables or disables killing the OOM-triggering task in
out-of-memory situations.

If this is set to zero, the OOM killer will scan through the entire
tasklist and select a task based on heuristics to kill.  This normally
selects a rogue memory-hogging task that frees up a large amount of
memory when killed.

If this is set to non-zero, the OOM killer simply kills the task that
triggered the out-of-memory condition.  This avoids the expensive
tasklist scan.

If panic_on_oom is selected, it takes precedence over whatever value
is used in oom_kill_allocating_task.

The default value is 0.
```

In addition, `oom_dump_tasks` will dump extra information when killing a process for easier debugging. In the provided VM based off Ubuntu Disco Dingo, you can see both flags defaulting to 0 and 1, respectively, meaning that the OOM Killer will attempt to use its heuristics to pick the victim and then dump extra information when killing processes. If you want to check the settings on your system, you can run the following commands:

```
cat /proc/sys/vm/oom_kill_allocating_task
cat /proc/sys/vm/oom_dump_tasks
```

2.4   *The first chaos experiment*

The exit codes from the logs didn't give you a good indication of what was causing FizzBuzz's API servers to die. While this might feel like an anticlimax, it is by design. Through that dead end, I want to lead you to a powerful aspect of chaos engineering: we work on hypotheses about the entire system as a whole.

As you'll recall (look at figure 2.2 for a refresher), the system is designed to handle API server instances dying through load balancing with automatic rerouting if one instance is down. Alas, the users are complaining that they are seeing errors!

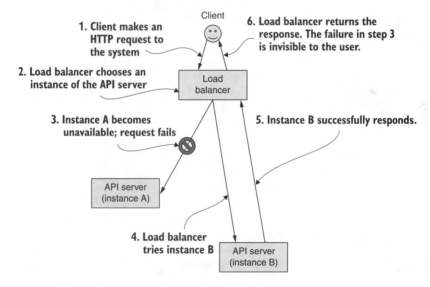

Figure 2.2   FizzBuzz as a Service technical architecture, repeated

While drilling down and fixing the reason that the API server instances get killed is important, from the perspective of the whole system, you should be more concerned that the clients are seeing the errors when they shouldn't. In other words, fixing the issue that gets the API server instances killed would "solve" the problem for now, until another bug, outage, or human error reintroduces it, and the end users are impacted. In our system, or any bigger distributed system, components dying is a norm, not an exception.

Take a look at figure 2.3, which illustrates the difference in thinking about the system's properties as whole, as compared to figure 2.2. The client interacts with the system, and for just a minute we stop thinking about the implementation and think about how the system should behave as a single unit.

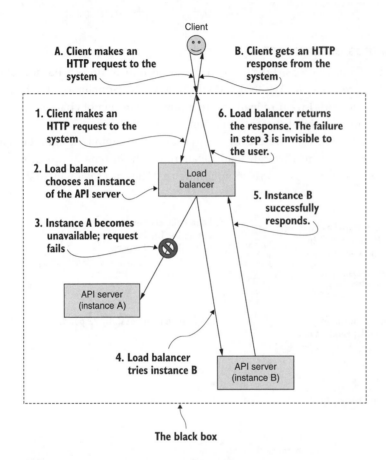

Figure 2.3   FizzBuzz as a Service whole system properties

Let's design our first chaos experiment to replicate the situation our clients are facing and see what happens for ourselves. The previous chapter presented the four steps to designing a chaos experiment:

1   Ensure observability.
2   Define a steady state.

3 Form a hypothesis.

4 Run the experiment!

It's best to start as simply as possible. You need a metric to work with (observability), preferably one you can produce easily. In this case, let's pick the number of failed HTTP responses that you receive from the system. You could write a script to make requests and count the failed ones for you, but existing tools can do that for you already.

To keep things simple, you'll use a tool that's well known: *Apache Bench.* You can use it to both produce the HTTP traffic for you to validate the steady state and to produce the statistics on the number of error responses encountered in the process. If the system behaves correctly, you should see no error responses, even if you kill an instance of the API server during the test. And that's going to be our hypothesis. Finally, implementing and running the experiment will also be simple, as we've just covered killing processes.

To sum it up, I've prepared figure 2.4, which should look familiar. It's the four-steps template from chapter 1, figure 1.2, with the details of our first experiment filled in. Please take a look.

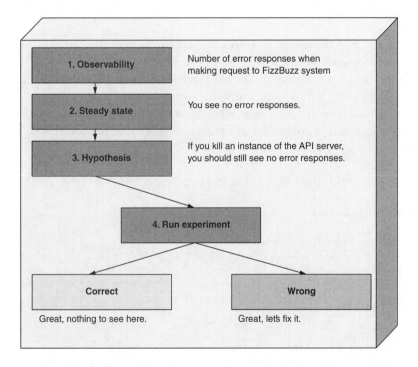

Figure 2.4 The four steps of our first chaos experiment

If this sounds like a plan to you, we're on the right track. It's finally time to get your hands dirty! Let's take a closer look at our application. Your VM comes with all the components preinstalled and all the source code can be found in the ~/src/examples/killer_whiles folder. The two instances of the API server are modeled as systemd services faas001_a and faas001_b. They come preinstalled (but disabled by default), so you can use systemctl to check their status. Use the command prompt to run this command for either faas001_a or faas001_b (and press Q to exit):

```
sudo systemctl status faas001_a
sudo systemctl status faas001_b
```

The output you see will look something like this:

```
● faas001_b.service - FizzBuzz as a Service API prototype - instance A
    Loaded: loaded (/home/chaos/src/examples/killer-
whiles/faas001_a.service; static; vendor preset: enabled)
    Active: inactive (dead)
```

As you can see, the API server instances are loaded but inactive. Let's go ahead and start them both via systemctl by issuing the following commands at the command line:

```
sudo systemctl start faas001_a
sudo systemctl start faas001_b
```

Note that these are configured to respond correctly to only the /api/v1/ endpoint. All other endpoints will return a 404 response code.

Now, onto the next component: the load balancer. The load balancer is an NGINX instance, configured to distribute traffic in a round-robin fashion between the two backend instances, and serve on port 8003. It should model the load balancer from our scenario accurately enough. It has a basic configuration that you can take a sneak peek into by issuing this at your command line:

```
cat ~/src/examples/killer-whiles/nginx.loadbalancer.conf | grep -v "#"
```

You will see the following:

```
    upstream backend {
        server 127.0.0.1:8001 max_fails=1 fail_timeout=1s;
        server 127.0.0.1:8002 max_fails=1 fail_timeout=1s;
    }
    server {
        listen 8003;

        location / {
            proxy_pass http://backend;
            proxy_set_header X-Forwarded-For $proxy_add_x_forwarded_for;
        }
    }
```

Configuring NGINX and its best practices are beyond the scope of this book. You won't need to know much more than that the server should behave like the one described in the scenario at the beginning of the chapter. The only thing worth mentioning might be the `fail_timeout` parameter set to 1 second, which means that after one of the servers returns an error (or doesn't respond), it will be taken away from the pool for 1 second, and then gracefully reintroduced. `max_fails` configures NGINX to consider a single error response enough to take the instance out of the pool. NGINX is configured to listen on port 8003 on localhost in your VM.

Let's make sure the load balancer is also up and running by running this at your command prompt:

```
sudo systemctl start nginx
```

To confirm that you can successfully reach the API servers through the load balancer, feel free to use `curl` to reach the load balancer. You can do that by making an HTTP request to localhost, on port 8003, requesting the only implemented endpoint /api/v1/. To do that, run the following command in your prompt:

```
curl 127.0.0.1:8003/api/v1/
```

You should see this amazing response:

```
{
    "FizzBuzz": true
}
```

If that's what you receive, we are good to go. If you're tempted to take a look at the source code now, I'm not going to stop you, but I recommend holding off and looking a bit later. That way, it's easier to think about these components as black boxes with certain behaviors you are interested in. OK, we're done here; it's time to make the system do some work by generating some load!

Pop quiz: Which step is not a part of the chaos experiment template?
Pick one:

1 Observability
2 Steady state
3 Hypothesis
4 Crying in the corner when an experiment fails

See appendix B for answers.

2.4.1 Ensure observability

There are many ways to generate HTTP loads. To keep things simple, let's use Apache Bench, preinstalled and accessible through the `ab` command. The usage is straightforward. For example, to run as many requests as you can to your load balancer with concurrency of 10 (-c 10) during a period of up to 30 seconds (-t 30) or up to 50,000 requests (whichever comes first), while ignoring the content length differences (-1), all you need to do is run this command at your prompt:

```
ab -t 30 -c 10 -l http://127.0.0.1:8003/api/v1/
```

The default output of ab is pretty informative. The bit of information that you are most interested in is Failed requests; you will use that as your success metric. Let's go ahead and take a look at what value it has in the steady state.

2.4.2   Define a steady state

To establish the steady state, or the normal behavior, execute the ab command in your terminal:

```
ab -t 30 -c 10 -l http://127.0.0.1:8003/api/v1/
```

You will see output similar to the following; it is a little verbose, so I removed the irrelevant parts:

```
(...)
Benchmarking 127.0.0.1 (be patient)
(...)
Concurrency Level:      10
Time taken for tests:   22.927 seconds
Complete requests:      50000
Failed requests:        0
(...)
```

As you can see, Failed requests is 0, and your two API servers are serving the load through the load balancer. The throughput itself is nothing to brag about, but since you're running all the components in the same VM anyway, you're going to ignore the performance aspect for the time being. You will use Failed requests as your single metric; it is all you need for now to monitor your steady state. It's time to write down your hypothesis.

2.4.3   Form a hypothesis

As I said before, you expect our system to handle a restart of one of the servers at a time. Your first hypothesis can therefore be written down as follows: "If we kill both instances, one at a time, the users won't receive any error responses from the load balancer." No need to make it any more complex than that; let's run it!

2.4.4   Run the experiment

The scene is now set, and you can go ahead and implement your very first experiment with some basic bash kung fu. You'll use ps to list the processes you're interested in, and then first kill instance A (port 8001), then add a small delay, and then kill instance B (port 8002), while running `ab` at the same time. I've prepared a simple script for you. Take a look by executing this command at your prompt:

```
cat ~/src/examples/killer-whiles/cereal_killer.sh
```

You will see the following output (shortened for brevity):

```
echo "Killing instance A (port 8001)"
ps auxf | grep 8001 | awk '{system("sudo kill " $2)}'   ⬅
(...)
```
Searches output of ps for a process with string "8001" (faas001_a) in it and kills it

```
echo "Wait some time in-between killings"
sleep 2                                                  ⬅
(...)
```
Waits 2 seconds to give NGINX enough time to detect the instance restarted by systemd

```
echo "Killing instance B (port 8002)"
ps auxf | grep 8002 | awk '{system("sudo kill " $2)}'   ⬅
```
Searches output of ps for a process with string "8002" (faas001_b) in it and kills it

The script first kills one instance, then waits some, and finally kills the other instance. The delay between killing instances is for `nginx` to have enough time to re-add the killed instance A to the pool before you kill instance B. With that, you should be ready to go! You can start the `ab` command in one window by running the following:

```
bash ~/src/examples/killer-whiles/run_ab.sh
```

And in another window, you can start killing the instances by using the `cereal_killer.sh` script you just looked at. To do that, run this command in your prompt:

```
bash ~/src/examples/killer-whiles/cereal_killer.sh
```

You should see something similar to this (I shortened the output by removing some less relevant bits):

```
Listing backend services
(...)

Killing instance A (port 8001)
● faas001_a.service - FizzBuzz as a Service API prototype - instance A
   Loaded: loaded (/home/chaos/src/examples/killer-
whiles/faas001_a.service; static; vendor preset: enabled)
   Active: active (running) since Sat 2019-12-28 21:33:00 UTC; 213ms ago
(...)

Wait some time in-between killings

Killing instance B (port 8002)
● faas001_b.service - FizzBuzz as a Service API prototype - instance B
   Loaded: loaded (/home/chaos/src/examples/killer-
whiles/faas001_b.service; static; vendor preset: enabled)
   Active: active (running) since Sat 2019-12-28 21:33:03 UTC; 260ms ago
(...)
```

```
Listing backend services
(...)

Done here!
```

Both instances are killed and restarted correctly—you can see their process ID (PID) change, and systemd reports them as active. In the first window, once finished, you should see no errors:

```
Complete requests:      50000
Failed requests:        0
```

You have successfully confirmed your hypothesis and thus concluded the experiment. Congratulations! You have just designed, implemented, and executed your very first chaos experiment. Give yourself a pat on the back!

It looks like our system can survive a succession of two failures of our API server instances. And it was pretty easy to do, too. You used ab to generate a reliable metric, established its normal value range, and then introduced failure in a simple bash script. And while the script is simple by design, I'm expecting that you thought I was being a little trigger-happy with the kill command—which brings me to a new concept called *blast radius.*

2.5   *Blast radius*

If you were paying attention, I'm pretty sure you noticed that my previous example cereal_killer.sh was a bit reckless. Take a look at the lines with sudo in them in our cereal_killer.sh script by running this command at the prompt:

```
grep sudo ~/src/examples/killer-whiles/cereal_killer.sh
```

You will see these two lines:

```
ps auxf | grep 8001 | awk '{system("sudo kill " $2)}'
ps auxf | grep 8002 | awk '{system("sudo kill " $2)}'
```

That implementation worked fine in the little test, but if any processes showed up with the string 8001 or 8002 in the output of ps, even just having such a PID, they would be killed. Innocent and without trial. Not a great look, and a tough one to explain to your supervisor at the nuclear power plant.

In this particular example, you could do many things to fix that, starting from narrowing your grep, to fetching PIDs from systemd, to using systemctl restart directly. But I just want you to keep this problem at the back of your mind as you go through the rest of the book. To drive the point home, figure 2.5 illustrates three possible blast radiuses, ranging from a broad grep from the example before to a more specific one, designed to affect only the targeted process.

That's what blast radius is all about: limiting the number of things our experiments can affect. You will see various examples of techniques used to limit the blast radius as we

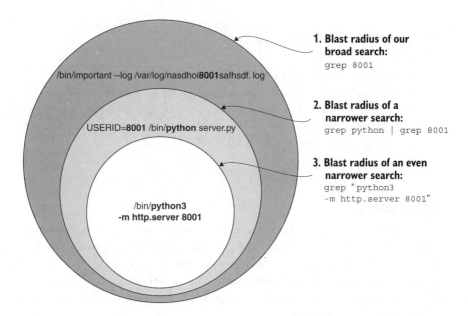

1. Blast radius of our broad search:
```
grep 8001
```

2. Blast radius of a narrower search:
```
grep python | grep 8001
```

3. Blast radius of an even narrower search:
```
grep "python3
-m http.server 8001"
```

Figure 2.5   Example of blast radiuses

cover various scenarios in the following chapters, but in general they fall into two categories: strategic and implementational.

The preceding situation falls into the latter category of an implementational approach. You can proactively look for ways to make the execution safer, but as with any code, you are bound to make mistakes.

The former category, strategic, is more about planning your experiments in a way so as to minimize the room for catastrophic events if your experiments go awry. Many good software deployment practices will apply. Here are a few examples:

- Roll out the experiment on a small subset of your traffic first, and expand later.
- Roll out the experiment in a quality assurance (QA) environment before going to production (we'll talk about testing in production later).
- Automate early, so that you can reproduce your findings more easily.
- Be careful with randomness; it's a double-edged sword. It can help find things like race conditions, but it might make things difficult to reproduce (we'll also come back to this a bit later).

All right, so knowing your blast radius is important. For this example, we're not going to change the script, but I'd like you to keep the blast radius at the back of your mind from now on. Our first experiment didn't detect any issues, and we've patted ourselves on the back, but wait! The FizzBuzz clients are still seeing errors, which indicates that we didn't go deep enough into the rabbit hole. Let's dig deeper!

Pop quiz: What's a blast radius?

Pick one:

1   The amount of stuff that can be affected by our actions
2   The amount of stuff that we want to damage during a chaos experiment
3   The radius, measured in meters, that's a minimal safe distance from coffee being spilled when the person sitting next to you realizes their chaos experiment went wrong and suddenly stands up and flips the table

See appendix B for answers.

2.6   *Digging deeper*

In our first experiment, we have been pretty conservative with our timing, allowing enough time for NGINX to re-add the previously killed server to the pool and gracefully start sending it requests. And by *conservative*, I mean to say that I put the sleep there to show you how a seemingly successful experiment might prove insufficient. Let's try to fix that. What would happen if the API server crashed more than once in succession? Would it continue to work?

Let's tweak our chaos experiment by changing our hypothesis with some concrete numbers: "If we kill an instance A six times in a row, spaced out by 1.25 seconds, and then do the same to instance B, we continue seeing no errors." Yes, these numbers are weirdly specific, and you're about to see why I picked these in just a second!

I wrote a script that does that for you: it's called `killer_while.sh`. Please take a look at the source code by running this in your prompt:

```
cat ~/src/examples/killer-whiles/killer_while.sh
```

You will see the body of the script, just like the following:

```
# restart instance A a few times, spaced out by 1.25 second delays
i="0"
while [ $i -le 5 ]                          ⟵─┤ Introduces a while loop to
do                                              │ repeat the killing six times
        echo "Killing faas001_a ${i}th time"
        ps auxf | grep killer-whiles | grep python | grep 8001 | awk
          '{system("sudo kill " $2)}'       ⟵─┐
        sleep 1.25                              │ Uses a slightly more conservative
        i=$[$i+1]                               │ series of grep commands to narrow
done                                            │ the target processes, and kills them

systemctl status faas001_a --no-pager       ⟵─┐ Displays status of the service
                                                │ faas001_a (--no-pager to prevent
(...)                                           │ piping the output to less)
```

Sleeps a little bit to give the service enough time to get restarted (annotation pointing to `sleep 1.25`)

This is essentially a variation of our previous script `cereal_killer.sh`, this time wrapped in a couple of while loops. (Yes, I did use while loops instead of for loops so that the killer "whiles" joke works. Worth it!).

What do you think will happen when you run it? Let's go ahead and find out by running the script at the command prompt like so:

```
bash ~/src/examples/killer-whiles/killer_while.sh
```

You should see output similar to this (again, shortened to show the most interesting bits):

```
Killing faas001_a 0th time
(...)
Killing faas001_a 5th time
● faas001_a.service - FizzBuzz as a Service API prototype - instance A
   Loaded: loaded (/home/chaos/src/examples/killer-
whiles/faas001_a.service; static; vendor preset: enabled)
   Active: failed (Result: start-limit-hit) since Sat 2019-12-28 22:44:04
UTC; 900ms ago
  Process: 3746 ExecStart=/usr/bin/python3 -m http.server 8001 --directory
/home/chaos/src/examples/killer-whiles/static (code=killed, signal=TERM)
 Main PID: 3746 (code=killed, signal=TERM)

Dec 28 22:44:04 linux systemd[1]: faas001_a.service: Service
RestartSec=100ms expired, scheduling restart.
Dec 28 22:44:04 linux systemd[1]: faas001_a.service: Scheduled restart job,
restart counter is at 6.
Dec 28 22:44:04 linux systemd[1]: Stopped FizzBuzz as a Service API
prototype - instance A.
Dec 28 22:44:04 linux systemd[1]: faas001_a.service: Start request repeated
too quickly.
Dec 28 22:44:04 linux systemd[1]: faas001_a.service: Failed with result
'start-limit-hit'.
Dec 28 22:44:04 linux systemd[1]: Failed to start FizzBuzz as a Service API
prototype - instance A.
Killing faas001_b 0th time
(...)
Killing faas001_b 5th time
● faas001_b.service - FizzBuzz as a Service API prototype - instance B
   Loaded: loaded (/home/chaos/src/examples/killer-
whiles/faas001_b.service; static; vendor preset: enabled)
   Active: failed (Result: start-limit-hit) since Sat 2019-12-28 22:44:12
UTC; 1s ago
  Process: 8864 ExecStart=/usr/bin/python3 -m http.server 8002 --directory
/home/chaos/src/examples/killer-whiles/static (code=killed, signal=TERM)
 Main PID: 8864 (code=killed, signal=TERM)

(...)
```

Not only do you end up with errors, but both of your instances end up being completely dead. How did that happen? It was restarting just fine a minute ago; what went wrong? Let's double-check that you didn't mess something up with the systemd service file. You can see it by running this command in your prompt:

```
cat ~/src/examples/killer-whiles/faas001_a.service
```

You will see this output:

```
[Unit]
Description=FizzBuzz as a Service API prototype - instance A

[Service]
ExecStart=python3 -m http.server 8001 --directory
/home/chaos/src/examples/killer-whiles/static
Restart=always
```

The `Restart=always` part sounds like it should always restart, but it clearly doesn't. Would you like to take a minute to try to figure it out by yourself? Did you notice any clues in the preceding output?

2.6.1   *Saving the world*

As it turns out, the devil is in the details. If you read the logs in the previous section carefully, `systemd` is complaining about the start request being repeated too quickly. From the `systemd` documentation (http://mng.bz/VdMO), you can get more details:

```
DefaultStartLimitIntervalSec=, DefaultStartLimitBurst=
Configure the default unit start rate limiting, as configured per-service
by StartLimitIntervalSec= and StartLimitBurst=. See systemd.service(5) for
details on the per-service settings. DefaultStartLimitIntervalSec= defaults
to 10s. DefaultStartLimitBurst= defaults to 5.
```

Unless `StartLimitIntervalSec` is specified, the default values allow only five restarts within a 10-second moving window and will stop restarting the service if that's ever exceeded. Which is both good news and bad news. Good news, because we're only two lines away from tweaking the `systemd` unit file to make it always restart. Bad, because once we fix it, the API itself might keep crashing, and our friends from Glanden might never fix it, because their clients are no longer complaining!

Let's fix it. Copy and paste the following command at your prompt to add the extra parameter `StartLimitIntervalSec` set to `0` to the service description (or use your favorite text editor to add it):

```
cat >> ~/src/examples/killer-whiles/faas001_a.service <<EOF
[Unit]
StartLimitIntervalSec=0
EOF
```

After that, you need to reload the `systemctl` daemon and start the two services again. You can do this by running the following command:

```
sudo systemctl daemon-reload
sudo systemctl start faas001_a
sudo systemctl start faas001_b
```

You should now be good to go. With this new parameter, instance A will be restarted indefinitely, thus surviving repeated errors, while instance B still fails. To test that, you can now run `killer_while.sh` again by executing the following command at your prompt:

```
bash ~/src/examples/killer-whiles/killer_while.sh
```

You will see output similar to this (again, shortened for brevity):

```
Killing faas001_a 0th time
(...)
Killing faas001_a 5th time
● faas001_a.service - FizzBuzz as a Service API prototype - instance A
   Loaded: loaded (/home/chaos/src/examples/killer-
whiles/faas001_a.service; static; vendor preset: enabled)
   Active: active (running) since Sat 2019-12-28 23:16:39 UTC; 197ms ago
(...)
Killing faas001_b 0th time
(...)
Killing faas001_b 5th time
● faas001_b.service - FizzBuzz as a Service API prototype - instance B
   Loaded: loaded (/home/chaos/src/examples/killer-
whiles/faas001_b.service; static; vendor preset: enabled)
   Active: failed (Result: start-limit-hit) since Sat 2019-12-28 23:16:44
UTC; 383ms ago
  Process: 9347 ExecStart=/usr/bin/python3 -m http.server 8002 --directory
/home/chaos/src/examples/killer-whiles/static (code=killed, signal=TERM)
 Main PID: 9347 (code=killed, signal=TERM)
(...)
```

Instance A now survives the restarts and reports as active, but instance B still fails. You made instance A immune to the condition you've discovered. You have successfully fixed the issue!

If you fix `faas001_b` the same way and then rerun the experiment with `killer_while.sh`, you will notice that you no longer see any error responses. The order of the universe is restored, and our friends in Glanden can carry on with their lives. You just used chaos engineering to test out the system without looking once into the actual implementation of the API servers, and you found a weakness that's easily fixed. Good job. Now you can pat yourself on the back, and I promise not to ruin that feeling for at least 7.5 minutes! Time for the next challenge!

Summary

- When performing chaos experiments, it's important to be able to observe why a process dies—from a crash, a kill signal, or the OOM Killer.
- The blast radius is the maximum number of things that can be affected by an action or an actor.

- Limiting the blast radius consists of using techniques that minimize the risk associated with running chaos experiments, and is an important aspect of planning the experiments.
- Useful chaos experiments can be implemented with a handful of bash commands, as illustrated in this chapter, by applying the simple four-step template that you saw in chapter 1.

Observability

This chapter covers

- Diagnosing system performance issues with the USE method
- Understanding basic system metrics used in chaos experiments
- Using Linux tools to check system metrics
- Using a time-series database to gain continuous insight into system performance

Strap in. We're about to tackle one of the more annoying situations you'll face when practicing chaos engineering: the infamous "my app is slow" complaint. If the piece of software in question went through all the stages of development and made it to production, chances are that it passed a decent number of tests and that multiple people signed off. If, later, for no obvious reason, the application begins to slow down, it tends to be a sign we're in for a long day at work.

"My app is slow" offers much more subtlety than an ordinary "my app doesn't work" and can sometimes be rather tricky to debug. In this chapter, you'll learn how to deal with one of the popular reasons for that: resource contention. We will cover tools necessary to detect and analyze this kind of issue.

A thin line separates chaos engineering, site reliability engineering (SRE), and system performance engineering in day-to-day life. In an ideal world, the job of a chaos engineer would only involve prevention. In practice, you will often need to debug, and then design an experiment to prevent the issue from happening again. Therefore, the purpose of this chapter is to give you just enough tools and the background you'll need in the practice of chaos engineering.

If I do my job well, by the end of the chapter, I expect you to feel comfortable discussing basic Linux performance-analysis tools with that slightly weird uncle at the next Thanksgiving dinner. Shoot me an email when you do! Let's set the scene with another helping of our dramatic friends from Glanden—the FaaS crowd. What are they up to?

3.1 *The app is slow*

It was a cold, windy, and exceptionally rainy November afternoon. The clouds were thick and heavy, ripping open with buckets of water pounding on the roof of the yellow cab stuck in traffic in Midtown Manhattan. Alice, the head of engineering (all five team members) at FaaS, trapped inside the cab, was making some last-minute changes to the presentation she was going to give to a client in a few minutes.

She had a bad feeling about it. Since the moment she flew in that day, she had been feeling like something was going to go terribly wrong—the feeling of impending doom. When she stepped out of the car into a wall of water, her phone started ringing. As she looked at her phone, lightning struck. It was the Big Client, accounting for most of her company's income. This client never called with good news.

Alice picked up. A cold shiver went down her spine. The wind wrestled away her umbrella and sent it flying away. Alice nodded a few times and hung up. The client said the four words that were about to shake her world: "The app is slow." Cue very loud thunder.

If you've ever had to deal with weird slowness issues in your system, I'm sure you can relate. They make for good stories and anecdotes later, but at the time they're anything but fun. Depending on the nature of the system, a little bit of slowness might go unnoticed (probably a bad thing anyway), but enough of it means that the system is as good as down. I'm sure you've heard stories about companies and products getting positive media attention only to succumb to the spike in traffic and receive negative coverage for unreliability shortly after. Slowness is dangerous for any business, and we need to be able to diagnose and fight it.

Great, but what does all of this have to do with chaos engineering? Plenty, as it turns out. When practicing chaos engineering, we often either try to actively prevent situations like this from happening (through simulating it and seeing what happens), or we're involved in debugging an ongoing situation and then trying to prevent it from happening again. Either way, in order to wreak havoc responsibly, we need to be able to have good insight (observability) into the system's performance metrics, and fast.

Typically, during problems like that, everyone is in panic mode, and you need to think quickly. In this chapter, I want to give you all the information you need to get started. Let's begin with a high-level overview of the methodology.

3.2 The USE method

Just like skinning a cat, there are many ways to go about debugging a server performance issue. My favorite, and the one we're going to cover, is called *USE*, which stands for *utilization, saturation, and errors* (see Brendan Gregg, www.brendangregg.com/usemethod.html). The idea is simple: for each type of resource, check for errors, utilization, and saturation to get a high-level idea of what might be going wrong.

> **DEFINITION** In this chapter, we're going to talk a lot about utilization and saturation of resources. A *resource* is any of the physical components making up a physical server, such as the CPU, disk, networking devices, and RAM. You may also have software resources, including threads, PIDs, or inode IDs. *Utilization* of a resource is indicated by an average time or proportion of the resource used. For example, for a CPU, a meaningful metric is the percentage of time spent doing work. For a disk, the percentage of the disk that is full can be a meaningful metric, but so can its throughput. Finally, *saturation* is the amount of work that the resource can't service at any given moment (often queued). A high saturation might be a sign of a problem, but also may very well be desirable (for example, in a batch processing system, where we want to use as close to 100% of the available processing power as possible).

Figure 3.1 shows a flowchart for applying the USE method. You start by identifying resources, and then for each one, you check for errors. If found, you investigate and try to fix them. Otherwise, you check the utilization level. If high, you investigate further. Otherwise, you look for saturation, and if that looks problematic, you dig deeper. If you don't find anything, at least you've reduced the number of unknown unknowns.

Known unknowns vs. unknown unknowns and the dark debt

Unknowns come in two flavors: known and unknown.

Known unknowns are the things we know we don't know. If I haven't opened the fridge, I can't be sure whether bacon is inside (please don't get me started on Schrödinger's bacon or smart fridges with cameras inside). Bacon is already on my radar. But what about things that aren't on my radar, and I don't know I should know?

These are the *unknown unknowns*, and every sufficiently complex computer system has some. These are harder to deal with, because usually by the time we realize we need to know about them, it's too late. For instance, after an incident, we might come up with some monitoring that would have alerted us to the problem. That's an unknown becoming a known unknown. Unknown unknowns are also often referred to as the *dark debt*. If that doesn't sound like something from a galaxy far, far away, then I don't know what does.

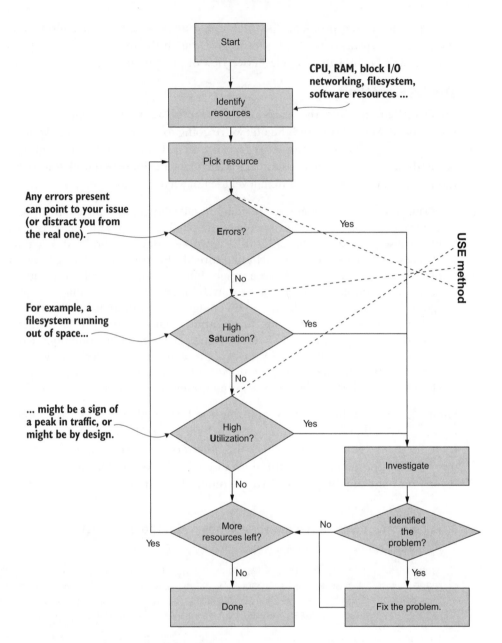

Figure 3.1 Flowchart of the USE method

This approach lets us quickly identify bottlenecks. It's worth noting that at the various steps of the flowchart, you will often find a problem, but not necessarily *the* problem causing the issue that prompted you to start the investigation. That is fine; you can add them to the to-do list and carry on with your investigation.

It also needs to be said that books have been (and will be) written about Linux performance observability, and in this chapter my goal is to give you just enough information to cover the useful types of issues in the context of chaos engineering. For those who are new to these Linux performance analysis tools, getting comfortable with the ones covered in this chapter will be left for you as an exercise. For others, please don't hate me for not including your favorite tool! With that asterisk out of the way, let's take a closer look, starting with the resources.

Pop quiz: What's USE?

Pick one:

1. A typo in USA
2. A method of debugging a performance issue, based around measuring utilization, severity, and exiting
3. A command showing you the usage of resources on a Linux machine
4. A method of debugging a performance issue, based around measuring utilization, saturation, and errors

See appendix B for answers.

3.3 Resources

Figure 3.2 illustrates the types of resources we will be looking into. It's a high-level overview, and we'll zoom in to the various sections later, but for now I would like you to take a look at the broad categories of resources we will be working with.

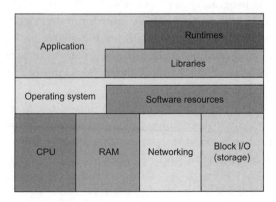

Figure 3.2 A simplified view of system resources

At the bottom sit four main logical components of a physical computer: CPU, RAM, networking, and block I/O. Above is an OS layer, which also provides software resources (such as file descriptors or threads). At the top we have an application layer, in which I included libraries and runtimes.

Now, going back to Alice and her terrible day, I would like you to put yourself in her shoes, and I'll guide you through the steps to finding out why her application was slow. We will use the USE method for that.

To make things more fun, I've prepared a simulation of Alice's situation for you. All of the commands we'll cover are already available in your VM, and the code snippets are to be executed inside a terminal in the VM. To start Alice's application in your VM, run the following command in your terminal:

```
~/src/examples/busy-neighbours/mystery002
```

You will see output similar to the following, calculating pi's digits in a loop. Notice the time it takes to do one set of calculations (bold font):

```
Press [CTRL+C] to stop..
Calculating pi's 3000 digits...
3.14159265358979323846264338327950288419716939937510582097494459 2307\

real    0m4.183s
user    0m4.124s
sys     0m0.022s
```

This is an approximation of what Alice was seeing when she logged in, running indefinitely.

> **NOTE**   This will run your CPUs hot (it's set up to use two cores), so if you're running this on modest hardware and don't want your laptop to work as a heater, you might want to switch it on and off as we go through the tools.

In the rest of the chapter, I'll assume that you have this running in a command-line window. When you're finished with the program, just press Ctrl-C to kill it. If you're curious about how it works, feel free to have a look, but it would be more fun if you tried to figure it out by letting me walk you through a collection of visibility tools available for Linux.

After the first few iterations, you should notice that the calculations of pi begin to take much longer, and with more variance in terms of time. This is going to be your "my app is slow" simulation. You'll feel some of Alice's pain.

Each of the following sections covers a subgroup of tools that you're going to be able to use when trying to gain visibility (observability) of your system, prompted by a slowness of the application. Let's dive in. First stop, "tools that apply to the system as a whole." I know, a pretty lousy name for a bus stop.

3.3.1   *System overview*

We'll begin by covering two basic tools that give us information about the whole system, uptime and dmesg. Let's start by looking at uptime.

UPTIME

uptime is often the first command you're going to run. Apart from telling you how long the system has been up (whether it has restarted recently), it gives you the load averages. *Load averages* are a quick way of seeing the direction (trend) in which your system is going in terms of load. Run the command `uptime` in your terminal window. You will see output similar to the following:

```
05:27:47 up 18 min,  1 user,  load average: 2.45, 1.00, 0.43
```

The three numbers represent a moving window sum average of processes competing over CPU time to run over 1, 5, and 15 minutes. The numbers are exponentially scaled, so a number twice as large doesn't mean twice as much load.

In this example, the 1-minute average is 2.45, 5-minute average is 1.00, and 15-minute average is 0.43, which indicates that the amount of load on the system is on the rise. It's an increasing trend. This is useful only for seeing the direction in which the load is going (increasing or decreasing), but the values don't paint the whole picture by themselves. In fact, don't worry about the values at all. Just remember that if the numbers are decreasing sharply, it might mean that we're too late and the program that was eating up all the resources went away. And if the numbers are increasing, it's a nice proxy for the rising load on the system.

And that's it for `uptime`. Let's take a look at `dmesg`.

Load averages

If you're ever interested in writing a program that uses load averages like the ones printed by `uptime`, you're in for a treat. Linux has you covered. All you need to do is read /proc/loadavg. If you print its contents by running the command `cat /proc/loadavg` in the terminal, the output you'll see is similar to this:

```
0.12 0.91 0.56 1/416 5313
```

The first three numbers are the 1-, 5-, and 15-minute moving window averages you saw previously in `uptime`. The fourth and fifth, separated by a slash, are the number of currently runnable, kernel schedulable entities (process, thread) and the total number of kernel schedulable entities currently existing, respectively. The last number is the PID of the most recently started program. To learn more, just run `man proc` in your terminal and search for *loadavg*.

DMESG

`dmesg` reads the message buffer of the kernel. Think of it as kernel and driver logs. You can read these logs by running the following command at your terminal prompt. Because there will be multiple pages of output, you're piping it to `less` for paging and easy searching:

```
dmesg | less
```

What are you looking for? Any errors and anomalies that can give you a clue about what's going on. Do you remember the OOM Killer from the previous chapter? You can search for *Kill* in the logs by typing /Kill and pressing Enter inside less. If your OOM Killer actually killed any processes, you should see output similar to the following:

```
[14658.582932] Out of memory: Kill process 5451 (mystery001)
score 758 or sacrifice child
[14658.582939] Killed process 5451 (mystery001) total-vm:3058268kB,
anon-rss:3055776kB, file-rss:4kB, shmem-rss:0kB
```

You want to give the output a quick glance to ensure that there isn't anything remarkable going on. If you see any error messages, they might or might not be related to what you're diagnosing. If the logs don't contain anything interesting, you can move on. The dmesg command also has a --human option, which makes the output slightly easier to read by displaying times in a human-readable format. You can run it with the following line at your command prompt:

```
dmesg --human
```

The output will then have relative times taken by each line, similar to this output (I've shortened the lines for brevity):

```
[Sep10 10:05] Linux version 5.4.0-42-generic (buildd@lgw01-amd64-038) (...)
[  +0.000000] Command line: BOOT_IMAGE=/boot/vmlinuz-5.4.0-42-generic (...)
```

The logs take a little while to get used to, but they are worth giving a quick check every time you want to debug a system performance issue. Don't worry if you're seeing things you don't understand in the logs; the kernel messages are pretty verbose. Most of the time, you can ignore anything that doesn't mention *error*.

That's all you need to know about dmesg for now. So far, so good. Let's segue into the next group of resources: the block I/O.

Pop quiz: Where can you find kernel logs?

Pick one:

1   /var/log/kernel
2   dmesg
3   kernel --logs

See appendix B for answers.

3.3.2   *Block I/O*

Let's take a closer look at block input/output (block I/O) devices, such as disks and other types of storage on your system. These have an interesting twist that can affect your system in two ways: they can be underperforming or they can be full. Thus, you'll need to look at their utilization from both of these perspectives: their throughput and their capacity.

Figure 3.3 shows what we are zooming in on, relative to the entire resource map from figure 3.2, including the tools we're going to use to get more information about the utilization and saturation.

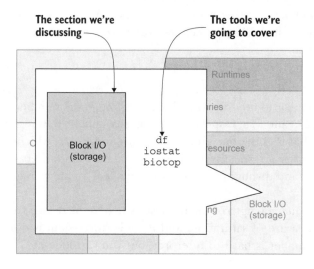

Figure 3.3   Zooming in to block I/O-related observability tools

Let's review some of the tools available for this investigation, starting with df.

DF

The definition of *utilization* is the percentage of the resource used. To assess that, you can use df, which reports filesystem disk space usage. Using it is straightforward: type the following command at your terminal prompt (-h here, sneakily, stands for *human readable*, not *help*) to list all the filesystems mounted and to show their size and used space:

```
df -h
```

You will see output similar to this (/dev/sda1, my main filesystem, in bold):

```
Filesystem     Size  Used Avail Use% Mounted on
udev           2.0G     0  2.0G   0% /dev
tmpfs          395M  7.9M  387M   2% /run
/dev/sda1       40G   13G   27G  33% /
tmpfs          2.0G     0  2.0G   0% /dev/shm
tmpfs          5.0M     0  5.0M   0% /run/lock
tmpfs          2.0G     0  2.0G   0% /sys/fs/cgroup
tmpfs          395M   24K  395M   1% /run/user/1000
```

For the device /dev/sda1, the utilization is at 33%. When the filesystem gets full, nothing more can be written to it, and it *will* become a problem. But how much data it can hold is just one of the two sides of utilization that a storage device provides. The other is how much it can write in a unit of time—the *throughput*. Let's investigate that part by using `iostat`.

IOSTAT

`iostat` is a great tool for looking into the performance and utilization (in terms of throughput) of block I/O devices such as disks. One flag you're going to use is `-x` to get the extended statistics, including percentage of utilization. Run the following command in your terminal:

```
iostat -x
```

You should see output similar to the following. In this example, the numbers of reads and writes per second (`r/s` and `w/s`, respectively) seem reasonable, but by themselves don't say much about what is going on. The fields `rkB/s` and `wkB/s`, which stand for *read* and *write kilobytes per second*, respectively, show the total throughput. Together, the two metrics (raw number and throughput) also give you a feel for an average size of a read or write.

aqu-sz is the average queue length of the requests issued to the device (nothing to do with Aquaman), a measure of saturation, and it shows the system is doing some work. Again, the bare number is hard to interpret, but you can look at whether it's increasing or decreasing.

Depending on the host system you use to run your VM, you might see very different values. My 2019 MacBook Pro is managing almost 750 MB/s, which is comfortably below the values set by online benchmarks:

```
Linux 5.0.0-38-generic (linux)    01/28/2020    _x86_64_    (2 CPU)

avg-cpu:  %user   %nice %system %iowait  %steal   %idle
          57.29    0.00   42.71    0.00    0.00    0.00

Device            r/s     w/s     rkB/s      wkB/s    rrqm/s   wrqm/s  %rrqm
%wrqm r_await w_await  aqu-sz rareq-sz wareq-sz  svctm   %util
loop0            0.00    0.00     0.00       0.00     0.00     0.00    0.00
0.00    0.00    0.00    0.00    0.00    0.00   0.00    0.00
sda              0.00  817.00     0.00  744492.00     0.00     0.00    0.00
0.00    0.00    3.44    1.29    0.00   911.25   0.56   46.00
```

Finally, the `%util` column shows the utilization, here defined as the percentage of time the device spent doing work. A high value *might* indicate saturation, but it's important to remember a couple of things. First, a logical device representing something more complex, like a RAID, might show a high saturation, whereas the underlying disks might actually be underused, so be careful when interpreting that. And second, a high saturation doesn't automatically translate into a performance bottleneck in the application, because various techniques are developed to try to do something productive while waiting for I/O.

All in all, in the preceding example, `iostat` shows some activity writing to my primary disk, but it seems to be comfortably within the range of what it should be able to do at around 740 MB/s writes and 46% utilization. Nothing really suspicious to see here, so let's move to the next tool: `biotop`.

BIOTOP

`biotop`, which stands for *block I/O top*, is part of the suite of tools called *BCC* (https://github.com/iovisor/bcc) that provides a toolkit for writing kernel monitoring and tracing programs. It leverages eBPF and provides example utilities, which are very useful in their own right, to show what you can do with it.

Berkeley Packet Filter

Berkeley Packet Filter (BPF), a powerful feature of the Linux kernel, allows a programmer to execute code inside the kernel in a way that guarantees safety *and* performance. It allows for a host of applications, most of which are beyond the scope of this book, but I strongly recommend you become familiar with it.

The BCC project builds on BPF and makes it much easier to work with BPF by providing wrappers and extra layers of abstraction. The official website of BCC (https://github.com/iovisor/bcc/tree/master/tools) has the source code of all the example applications, including `biotop`, `opensnoop`, and `execsnoop` that we'll cover in this chapter, and many more. The tools themselves are written in a manner that facilitates getting started with your own programs.

The *e* in *eBPF* stands for *extended*, a more modern version of BPF. However, *BPF* is often used to describe eBPF, and *classic BPF* to talk about the non-extended version.

The BCC tools are preinstalled on your VM, and you can install them from https://github.com/iovisor/bcc/blob/master/INSTALL.md. I would love to show you just how powerful eBPF is, and I recommend you get a book or two about it.[1] For now, let's just get a taste of a few example tools, starting with `biotop`.

On Ubuntu, which your VM is running, the tools come appended with `-bpfcc`. Run `biotop` by typing the following command into your terminal:

`sudo biotop-bpfcc`   ⟵ | **sudo is required here, because running BPF requires administrator privileges.**

You should see output similar to this, refreshed every second (pro tip: you can add `-C` if you'd like to prevent the command from clearing the screen every time):

```
06:49:44 loadavg: 2.70 1.24 0.47 6/426 5269

PID    COMM          D MAJ MIN DISK      I/O  Kbytes  AVGms
5137   kworker/u4:3  W 8   0   sda       677  611272  3.37
246    jbd2/sda1-8   W 8   0   sda         2     204  0.20
```

---

[1] You can start with *BPF Performance Tools* by Brendan Gregg (Addison-Wesley, 2019); http://mng.bz/aoA7.

`biotop` helps you identify where the load writing to the disk is coming from. In this case, you can see a process called `kworker`, which is writing more than 600 MB/s to the disk, and on occasion some other, less hungry processes. We've established that in our case this is fine, and you can let it carry on doing its thing. But if you are looking for the culprit eating up all the resources, this is the tool that will help you with that—good to remember when you're stressed out![2]

It's also worth noting that the tools installed by the `bpfcc-tool` package are written in Python, so if you're curious about what their source code looks like, you can take a sneak peek directly from your command line by running this command (replace `biotop-bpfcc` with the command you want to investigate) in your terminal:

```
less $(which biotop-bpfcc)
```

All right. So that covers what you're going to need for now in terms of finding out utilization and saturation of the block I/O. Let's take a look at the next section: networking!

Pop quiz: Which command does not help you see statistics about disks?
Pick one:

1 `df`
2 `du`
3 `iostat`
4 `biotop`
5 `top`

See appendix B for answers.

3.3.3   *Networking*

Networking in Linux can get pretty complex, and my assumption here is that you have an idea of how it works. In this section, we're going to focus on establishing the utilization and saturation of the network interfaces and on gaining insight into TCP. Figure 3.4 shows how the networking layer fits into our resource map and mentions the tools we're going to look into: `sar` and `tcptop`. Let's start by looking into the network interfaces utilization with `sar`.

---

[2] Brendan Gregg, the author of the BCC project, also maintains a set of graphics about Linux tooling that you can look into at www.brendangregg.com/linuxperf.html. They provide a memory aid of which tools you can use when you need to debug a particular part of the system and can be very valuable attached to the wall of your cubicle!

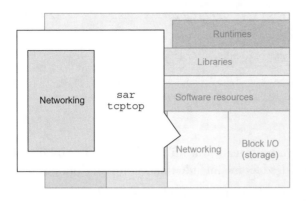

Figure 3.4 Zooming in to network-related observability tools

SAR

sar is a tool to collect, report, and save system metrics. I've preinstalled it into your VM, but in order for it to collect system metrics, you need to activate it. You can do that by editing the file /etc/default/sysstat to change ENABLED="false" to ENABLED= "true". In order for sysstat to pick up the changes, you also need to restart its service by running the following command at the prompt:

```
sudo service sysstat restart
```

sar provides various metrics around your system usage, but here we're going to focus on what it offers for networking. Let's start by checking the utilization. You can use the DEV keyword provided by sar, which provides a comprehensive overview of the network interfaces.

Interval and count

Note that sar, as well as many tools in the BCC suite, takes two optional, positional parameters at the end: [interval] [count]. They steer how often the output should be printed in seconds (interval) and how many times it should be printed before the program exits (count). Often, the default is 1 second and infinite count. In our examples, we'll often use 1 1 to print a single set of stats and exit.

Run the following command at your prompt:

```
sar -n DEV 1 1
```

You should see output similar to this (the utilization field and value are in bold font, and the output is shortened for easier reading). In this example (what you're likely to see when you run this command in your VM), nothing is really using networking, so all the stats are at 0. The sar command is showing two network interfaces—eth0 (the main network card) and lo (loopback):

```
Linux 5.0.0-38-generic (linux)      01/29/2020      _x86_64_     (2 CPU)

07:15:57 AM
IFACE  rxpck/s  txpck/s  rxkB/s  txkB/s  rxcmp/s  txcmp/s  rxmcst/s  %ifutil
07:15:58 AM
lo     0.00     0.00     0.00    0.00    0.00     0.00     0.00      0.00
07:15:58 AM
eth0   0.00     0.00     0.00    0.00    0.00     0.00     0.00      0.00
(...)
```

The %ifutil field is where you can read your utilization from. The other field names are not 100% straightforward, so let me include their definitions here from man sar:

- rxpck/s—Total number of packets received per second
- txpck/s—Total number of packets transmitted per second
- rxkB/s—Total number of kilobytes received per second
- txkB/s—Total number of kilobytes transmitted per second
- rxcmp/s—Number of compressed packets received per second (for cslip and so on)
- txcmp/s—Number of compressed packets transmitted per second
- rxmcst/s—Number of multicast packets received per second

To generate traffic, let's download a large file from the internet. You can download an ISO image with Ubuntu 19.10 from a relatively slow mirror by running this command from the prompt:

```
wget \
http://mirrors.us.kernel.org/ubuntu-releases/19.10/
ubuntu-19.10-desktop-amd64.iso
```

While that is downloading, you can use another terminal window to issue the same sar command you did before:

```
sar -n DEV 1 1
```

This time, the output should show the traffic going through on the eth0 interface (again, the utilization is in bold font):

```
07:29:44 AM
IFACE  rxpck/s  txpck/s  rxkB/s   txkB/s  rxcmp/s  txcmp/s  rxmcst/s  %ifutil
07:29:45 AM
lo     0.00     0.00     0.00     0.00    0.00     0.00     0.00      0.00
07:29:45 AM
eth0   1823.00  592.00   1616.29  34.69   0.00     0.00     0.00      1.32
```

The sar command also supports another keyword, EDEV, to display error statistics on the network. To do that, issue the following command at the prompt:

```
sar -n EDEV 1 1
```

You will see output similar to the following:

```
Linux 5.0.0-38-generic (linux)      01/29/2020    _x86_64_    (2 CPU)

07:33:53 AM
IFACE rxerr/s txerr/s coll/s rxdrop/s xdrop/s txcarr/s rxfram/s rxfifo/s txfifo/s
07:33:54 AM
lo    0.00    0.00   0.00   0.00     0.00    0.00     0.00     0.00     0.00
07:33:54 AM
eth0  0.00    0.00   0.00   0.00     0.00    0.00     0.00     0.00     0.00
(...)
```

As you can see, no errors are showing in our example. It doesn't look like Alice's problem lies here.

Again, the field names might seem a little confusing, especially at first, so let me include the definitions for your convenience:

- rxerr/s—Total number of bad packets received per second
- txerr/s—Total number of errors that happened per second while transmitting packets
- coll/s—Number of collisions that happened per second while transmitting packets
- rxdrop/s—Number of received packets dropped per second because of a lack of space in Linux buffers
- txdrop/s—Number of transmitted packets dropped per second because of a lack of space in Linux buffers
- txcarr/s—Number of carrier errors that happened per second while transmitting packets
- rxfram/s—Number of frame-alignment errors that happened per second on received packets
- rxfifo/s—Number of FIFO overrun errors that happened per second on received packets
- txfifo/s—Number of FIFO overrun errors that happened per second on transmitted packets

Finally, let's explore two keywords offered by sar: TCP (for TCP statistics) and ETCP (for errors in the TCP layer). You can run both at the same time by issuing the following command at your prompt:

```
sar -n TCP,ETCP 1 1
```

You will see output similar to this. No errors show up, which means it's not the source of Alice's trouble—not this time, at least. You can safely move on to the next tool:

```
Linux 5.0.0-38-generic (linux)      01/29/2020    _x86_64_    (2 CPU)

07:56:30 AM  active/s passive/s    iseg/s    oseg/s
07:56:31 AM      0.00      0.00   1023.00    853.00
```

```
07:56:30 AM  atmptf/s  estres/s  retrans/s  isegerr/s   orsts/s
07:56:31 AM      0.00      0.00       0.00       0.00      0.00

Average:     active/s passive/s     iseg/s      oseg/s
Average:         0.00      0.00    1023.00      853.00

Average:     atmptf/s  estres/s  retrans/s  isegerr/s   orsts/s
Average:         0.00      0.00       0.00       0.00      0.00
```

Again, for your convenience, here are the descriptions of the field names:

- `active/s`—The number of times TCP connections have made a direct transition to the `SYN-SENT` state from the `CLOSED` state per second [`tcpActiveOpens`].
- `passive/s`—The number of times TCP connections have made a direct transition to the `SYN-RCVD` state from the `LISTEN` state per second [`tcpPassiveOpens`].
- `iseg/s`—The total number of segments received per second, including those received in error [`tcpInSegs`]. This count includes segments received on currently established connections.
- `oseg/s`—The total number of segments sent per second, including those on current connections but excluding those containing only retransmitted octets [`tcpOutSegs`].
- `atmptf/s`—The number of times per second TCP connections have made a direct transition to the `CLOSED` state from either the `SYN-SENT` state or the `SYN-RCVD` state, plus the number of times per second TCP connections have made a direct transition to the `LISTEN` state from the `SYN-RCVD` state [`tcpAttemptFails`].
- `estres/s`—The number of times per second TCP connections have made a direct transition to the `CLOSED` state from either the `ESTABLISHED` state or the `CLOSE-WAIT` state [`tcpEstabResets`].
- `retrans/s`—The total number of segments retransmitted per second—that is, the number of TCP segments transmitted containing one or more previously transmitted octets [`tcpRetransSegs`].
- `isegerr/s`—The total number of segments received in error (for example, bad TCP checksums) per second [`tcpInErrs`].
- `orsts/s`—The number of TCP segments sent per second containing the `RST` flag [`tcpOutRsts`].

If the download hasn't finished, please keep it on for the next section. You'll still need to generate some traffic, while you're looking at `tcptop`!

TCPTOP

`tcptop` is part of the BCC project I mentioned earlier (https://github.com/iovisor/bcc). It shows the top (by default, 20) processes using TCP, sorted by bandwidth. You can run it from your command line like this:

```
sudo tcptop-bpfcc 1 1
```

You will see output similar to the following. `RX_KB` is the received traffic in kilobytes, `TX_KB` is the traffic sent (*t* is for *transmitted*). You can see the `wget` command, slowly downloading the Ubuntu image at just over 2 MB/s. You know that it's there, because you ran it on purpose to generate traffic, but `tcptop` can be an invaluable tool allowing you to track down what's using the bandwidth on the system. Isn't BPF pretty cool?

```
08:05:51 loadavg: 0.20 0.09 0.07 1/415 8210

PID     COMM    LADDR               RADDR               RX_KB  TX_KB
8142    wget    10.0.2.15:60080     149.20.37.36:80     2203   0
```

As you can see, the usage is really simple, and in certain circles might even earn you the title of the local computer magician (computer whisperer?) Make sure you remember about it in times of hardship!

OK, that's all you'll need to know about `tcptop` and hopefully enough to get you going using the USE method on the networking part of the system. Next stop: RAM.

Pop quiz: Which command does not help you see statistics about networking?
Pick one:

1 `sar`
2 `tcptop`
3 `free`

See appendix B for answers.

3.3.4 *RAM*

No program can run without random access memory, and RAM contention is often a problem you're going to have to deal with. It's paramount to be able to read the USE metrics of your system. Figure 3.5 shows where we are on our resource map and the tools we're going to cover: `free`, `top`, `vmstat`, and `oomkill`. Let's start with `free`.

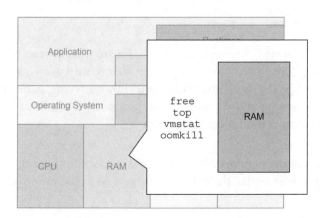

Figure 3.5 Zooming in to RAM-related observability tools

FREE

free is an equivalent of df for RAM: it shows utilization of RAM. It even accepts the same -h argument for human-readable output. You can run free from your command line like this:

```
free -h
```

You will see output similar to this, with the difference that I activated swap here, for it to show in the output, and yours will be disabled (discussed columns in bold font):

```
           total     used      free    shared   buff/cache   available
Mem:       3.8Gi     1.1Gi     121Mi   107Mi    2.7Gi        2.4Gi
Swap:      750Mi     3.0Mi     747Mi
```

If this is the first time you've seen this screen, I'd almost bet my breakfast that you're confused. If the total memory is 3.8 GB and you're using 1.1 GB, then why is only 121 MB free? If something smells fishy to you, you're not the only one. In fact, it's such a common reaction that it has its own website (www.linuxatemyram.com)!

So what's going on? The Linux kernel uses some of the available memory to speed things up for you (by maintaining disk caches), but it's perfectly happy to give it back to you (or any other user) anytime you ask for it. So that memory is technically not *free*, but it is indeed *available*. It's the equivalent of your younger brother borrowing your car when you're not using it, except that Linux always hands the memory back to you unscathed when you need it.

Fortunately, recent versions of free have the column available, just as in the preceding output. Versions not that long ago didn't have it, and instead provided an extra row called -/+ buffers/cache, which only added to the confusion.

If you are using an older version, you might see an extra row like the following one. This shows the values of used minus buffers and cache (so used, and can't be reclaimed), as well as free plus buffers and cache (free or can be reclaimed, so available). Also, in that version, used used to equal total minus free:

```
                   total    used     free    shared    buffers    cache
Mem:               3.8Gi    2.7Gi    121Mi   107Mi     1.1Gi      1.3Gi
-/+ buffers/cache:          302Mi    2.4Gi
```

So how do you know you've really run out of RAM? The surefire giveaways are the available column being close to zero, and (as you saw before with dmesg) the OOM Killer going wild (if active). If the available column is showing a reasonable amount left, you're all right. And looking at the preceding output, it looks like Alice is also all right. Let's move on to the next tool: the good old top.

TOP

top gives you an overview of the memory and CPU utilization of your system. Running top with default settings is easy. Strike the following three keys at the prompt:

```
top
```

You will see interactive output refreshing every 3 seconds, looking something like the following. Notice that by default, the output is sorted by the value of field %CPU, which is CPU usage of the program. You can exit by pressing Q on the keyboard, and again, I'm showing what it looks like with swap on; yours will be off. I've used bold font for columns corresponding to CPU utilization (%CPU) and memory utilization (%MEM), as well as the system CPU and memory overview rows:

```
Tasks: 177 total,    6 running, 171 sleeping,    0 stopped,    0 zombie
%Cpu(s): 53.3 us, 40.0 sy, 0.0 ni, 0.0 id, 0.0 wa, 0.0 hi,  6.7 si,  0.0 st
MiB Mem :   3942.4 total,    687.8 free,    1232.1 used,    2022.5 buff/cache
MiB Swap:    750.5 total,    750.5 free,       0.0 used.    2390.4 avail Mem

PID USER       PR  NI    VIRT    RES    SHR S   %CPU   %MEM    TIME+ COMMAND
3508 chaos      20   0  265960 229772    264 R   43.8    5.7  0:02.51 stress
3510 chaos      20   0    3812     96      0 R   43.8    0.0  0:02.72 stress
3507 chaos      20   0    3812     96      0 R   37.5    0.0  0:02.63 stress
3509 chaos      20   0    4716   1372    264 R   37.5    0.0  0:02.43 stress
   7 root       20   0       0      0      0 I   18.8    0.0  0:00.68 kworker/u4:0-
flush-8:0
1385 chaos      20   0  476172 146252  99008 S    6.2    3.6  0:01.95 Xorg
   1 root       20   0   99368  10056   7540 S    0.0    0.2  0:01.38 systemd
   2 root       20   0       0      0      0 S    0.0    0.0  0:00.00 kthreadd
```

I'll let you check the meaning of the other fields by using man top (which, by the way, is an amazing read; it explains everything from how the memory works, to some stupid tricks you can use to show off at the next team dinner).

You can see that my CPUs are working pretty hard, but more on that in a second. Also, notice the header, which gives you a quick overview of the CPU and memory utilization of the system as a whole. We'll cover what the different values mean in just a bit when we talk about CPUs. The memory summary should feel familiar to you, as it's similar to the output of free (minus the handy available field).

OK. Now, a show of hands of those who have never run top in their lives. Exactly, I see no hands up! So why are we even cutting down trees to talk about it? Well, the fun begins when you press the question mark (?) on the keyboard while running top. Do it, and you'll see something like this:

```
Help for Interactive Commands - procps-ng 3.3.15
Window 1:Def: Cumulative mode Off.  System: Delay 3.0 secs; Secure mode Off.

Z,B,E,e  Global: 'Z' colors; 'B' bold; 'E'/'e' summary/task memory scale
l,t,m    Toggle Summary: 'l' load avg; 't' task/cpu stats; 'm' memory info
0,1,2,3,I Toggle: '0' zeros; '1/2/3' cpus or numa node views; 'I' Irix mode
f,F,X    Fields: 'f'/'F' add/remove/order/sort; 'X' increase fixed-width

L,&,<,> . Locate: 'L'/'&' find/again; Move sort column: '<'/'>' left/right
R,H,V,J . Toggle: 'R' Sort; 'H' Threads; 'V' Forest view; 'J' Num justify
c,i,S,j . Toggle: 'c' Cmd name/line; 'i' Idle; 'S' Time; 'j' Str justify
x,y     . Toggle highlights: 'x' sort field; 'y' running tasks
z,b     . Toggle: 'z' color/mono; 'b' bold/reverse (only if 'x' or 'y')
u,U,o,O . Filter by: 'u'/'U' effective/any user; 'o'/'O' other criteria
```

```
n,#,^O   . Set: 'n'/'#' max tasks displayed; Show: Ctrl+'O' other filter(s)
C,...    . Toggle scroll coordinates msg for: up,down,left,right,home,end

k,r        Manipulate tasks: 'k' kill; 'r' renice
d or s     Set update interval
W,Y        Write configuration file 'W'; Inspect other output 'Y'
q          Quit
           ( commands shown with '.' require a visible task display window )
Press 'h' or '?' for help with Windows,
Type 'q' or <Esc> to continue
```

It's like accidentally walking into that weird wardrobe taking you to Narnia! Have a look through what that says when you have a minute, but let me highlight a few amazing features you'll love.

- *Toggle memory units*—By default, the memory usage is displayed in KB. If you want to toggle it through MB, GB, and so forth, type e (toggle in the list of processes) or E (toggle the summary).

- *Toggle memory (and CPU) summary*—Type m to change the view into progress bars if you don't fancy comparing numbers in your head. The same works with t for toggling CPU usage.

- *Hide clutter*—Type 0 (zero) to hide any zeros on the display.

- *Change and sort columns*—Typing f opens a new dialog box in which you can choose which columns to display, rearrange them, and choose which one to sort on. The dialog looks like the following output and lists all available options, along with the instructions on how to use them:

```
Fields Management for window 1:Def, whose current sort field is RES
      Navigate with Up/Dn, Right selects for move then <Enter> or Left commits,
      'd' or <Space> toggles display, 's' sets sort.  Use 'q' or <Esc> to end!

 * RES     = Resident Size (KiB)     nDRT    = Dirty Pages Count
 * PID     = Process Id              WCHAN   = Sleeping in Function
 * USER    = Effective User Name     Flags   = Task Flags <sched.h>
 * PR      = Priority                CGROUPS = Control Groups
 * NI      = Nice Value              SUPGIDS = Supp Groups IDs
 * VIRT    = Virtual Image (KiB)     SUPGRPS = Supp Groups Names
 * SHR     = Shared Memory (KiB)     TGID    = Thread Group Id
 * S       = Process Status          OOMa    = OOMEM Adjustment
 * %CPU    = CPU Usage               OOMs    = OOMEM Score current
 * %MEM    = Memory Usage (RES)      ENVIRON = Environment vars
 * TIME+   = CPU Time, hundredths    vMj     = Major Faults delta
 * COMMAND = Command Name/Line       vMn     = Minor Faults delta
   PPID    = Parent Process pid      USED    = Res+Swap Size (KiB)
   UID     = Effective User Id       nsIPC   = IPC namespace Inode
   RUID    = Real User Id            nsMNT   = MNT namespace Inode
   RUSER   = Real User Name          nsNET   = NET namespace Inode
   SUID    = Saved User Id           nsPID   = PID namespace Inode
   SUSER   = Saved User Name         nsUSER  = USER namespace Inode
   GID     = Group Id                nsUTS   = UTS namespace Inode
   GROUP   = Group Name              LXC     = LXC container name
```

```
PGRP    = Process Group Id       RSan    = RES Anonymous (KiB)
TTY     = Controlling Tty        RSfd    = RES File-based (KiB)
TPGID   = Tty Process Grp Id     RSlk    = RES Locked (KiB)
SID     = Session Id             RSsh    = RES Shared (KiB)
nTH     = Number of Threads      CGNAME  = Control Group name
P       = Last Used Cpu (SMP)    NU      = Last Used NUMA node
TIME    = CPU Time
SWAP    = Swapped Size (KiB)
CODE    = Code Size (KiB)
DATA    = Data+Stack (KiB)
nMaj    = Major Page Faults
nMin    = Minor Page Faults
```

Note that from the main screen of top, you can also change which column is used for sorting by using the < and > keys, but it's a little awkward, because there is no visual indication next to the column name. You can use x to toggle the sorted column to be in bold font, which helps with that.

- *Search (locate) a process name*—Type L to open a search dialog.
- *Show forest view*—Much like ps f, typing V shows which processes are children of which parents.
- *Save the view*—You can write the configuration file by typing w. This can be a real time-saver. Once you type w, top will write with all the interactive settings you've changed so that the next time you run it, it can pick up the same settings.

NOTE If you're running the Linux VM from a macOS host, you might be tempted to go and see what the built-in top on macOS offers by comparison. You will be disappointed, but fortunately, better alternatives (htop, glances, ...) are available through Homebrew and MacPorts.

OK, so that might feel a little off topic, but it really isn't. When practicing chaos engineering, I can't stress enough how important it is to understand your metrics and how to read them reliably. top is both powerful *and* pleasant to use, and knowing how to use it efficiently is crucial. If you've used top for years but still learned something new about it from this section, shoot me an email!

In the initial output, the memory utilization and saturation were pretty low, which indicates that it's not what we're looking for, so let's move on to the next tool. We'll get back to the busy CPUs in just a few moments. Next in line is vmstat.

VMSTAT

vmstat shows much more than just the virtual memory statistics its name implies. Run the vmstat command first without any arguments in your command prompt:

```
vmstat
```

You will see output similar to the following:

```
procs---------memory------------swap-- -----io---- -system-- ------cpu-----
 r  b   swpd   free    buff   cache   si   so    bi    bo   in    cs us sy id wa st
 5  0      0 1242808  47304 1643184    0    0  1866 53616  564   928 17 13 69  1  0
```

The values fit in a single row, which makes it practical to print them every *n* seconds (with vmstat n). The interesting columns include the memory (similar to free, with swpd showing used swap memory), r (the number of runnable processes, running or waiting to run), and b (the number of processes in uninterruptible sleep). The number of runnable processes gives an indication of the saturation of the system (the more processes competing for runtime, the busier the system—remember the load averages earlier in the chapter?). The columns in and cs stand for the total number of interrupts and context switches, respectively. We'll cover the breakdown of the CPU time in section 3.3.5.

As you can see, vmstat overlaps with the other tools like free and top. Among tools showing the same information, picking the one to use is largely a personal preference. But to help you make an informed decision, here are a few other things that vmstat can do for you:

- *Generate readable system usage stats*—If you run vmstat with the -s flag in your prompt, like this

```
vmstat -s
```

you will be presented a nicely readable list, just like the following:

```
    4037032 K total memory
    1134620 K used memory
     679320 K active memory
    1149236 K inactive memory
    2049752 K free memory
      17144 K buffer memory
     835516 K swap cache
     768476 K total swap
          0 K used swap
     768476 K free swap
      54159 non-nice user cpu ticks
        630 nice user cpu ticks
      45166 system cpu ticks
      25524 idle cpu ticks
        337 IO-wait cpu ticks
          0 IRQ cpu ticks
       3870 softirq cpu ticks
          0 stolen cpu ticks
    1010446 pages paged in
  255820616 pages paged out
          0 pages swapped in
          0 pages swapped out
    1363878 interrupts
    1140588 CPU context switches
 1580450660 boot time
       3541 forks
```

Notice the last row, forks. It's the number of forks executed since the boot— basically, the total number of processes that have run. It's yet another indication of the busyness of the system. You can even get just that piece of information by running vmstat -f directly.

- *Generate readable disk usage stats*—If you run vmstat -d, you will be presented with utilization/saturation statistics for the disks in your system. You can also run vmstat -D to get a one-off summary.

OK, enough about vmstat. Let's cover one last utility in the RAM department: oomkill.

OOMKILL

oomkill (part of the BCC project, https://github.com/iovisor/bcc) works by tracing kernel calls to oom_kill_process and printing to the screen information about it every time it happens.[3] Do you remember when we covered looking through dmesg output, searching for information about processes being killed by the OOM Killer? Well, this is the equivalent of plugging directly into the Matrix; you get the information from the source, and you can plug it into whatever system you are looking at.

To run oomkill, execute the following command in one terminal window:

```
sudo oomkill-bpfcc
```

It will start tracing OOM kills. You're now well equipped for dealing with a situation where a process gets killed by the OOM. Open another terminal window and run top in it, this time with -d 0.5 to refresh every half second:

```
top -d 0.5
```

You can type m a couple of times to get a nice progress bar showing the memory utilization of the system. Now, for the big finale: in a third terminal window, try to eat all the memory by using Perl (this actually comes directly from http://mng.bz/xmnY:

```
perl -e 'while (1) { $a .= "A" x 1024; }'
```

You should see top show more and more memory usage for a few seconds, and then go back to the previous state. In the first window with the oomkill, you should see the trace of the assassin:

```
06:49:11 Triggered by PID 3968 ("perl"), OOM kill of PID 3968 ("perl"),
1009258 pages, loadavg: 0.00 0.23 1.22 3/424 3987
```

Pretty neat, isn't it? If that was too quick, do you remember the mystery001 program you were debugging in the previous chapter? You can revisit that by running the following in the third terminal window:

```
./src/examples/killer-whiles/mystery001
```

---

[3] Look how simple BPF and BCC make it to attach a probe like that: http://mng.bz/A0y7. Isn't that amazing?

The memory usage bar in `top` should now be slowly creeping up, and in under a minute, you should see `oomkill` print another message, similar to the following:

```
07:09:20 Triggered by PID 4043 ("mystery001"), OOM kill of PID 4043
("mystery001"), 1009258 pages, loadavg: 0.22 0.10 0.36 4/405 4043
```

Sweet. Now you're fully armed to deal with OOM kills and read RAM utilization and saturation. Well done, detective. Time to move on to the next resource: the CPU.

Pop quiz: Which command does not help you see statistics about RAM?
Pick one:

1 `top`
2 `free`
3 `mpstat`

See appendix B for answers.

3.3.5   *CPU*

Time to talk about the workhorse of all the system resources: the CPU! Let's take a minute to appreciate all the hard work the processor is doing for us. I'm running my VM with two cores of my 2019 MacBook Pro. Let's take a sneak peek at what my Ubuntu sees about the processors, by running the following at your command prompt:

```
cat /proc/cpuinfo
```

You will see output similar to this (I removed most of it for brevity), containing the details of each processor, including the model and the CPU clock:

```
processor    : 0
(...)
model name   : Intel(R) Core(TM) i7-9750H CPU @ 2.60GHz
stepping     : 10
cpu MHz      : 2591.998
(...)
```

So during that minute we were appreciating its hard work, each of the two cores did about 2591.998 million cycles × 60 seconds in a minute = ~166 billion cycles total. If only our politicians were that hardworking! Now, what were the cores busy doing all that time? In this section, we'll take a look at that.

Figure 3.6 zooms in on our resource graph to show where we are, and lists the tools we're going to cover in this section: `top` and `mpstat`. We've already covered the memory-related aspects of `top`, so let's finish that one off by covering what it has to offer in the context of CPU!

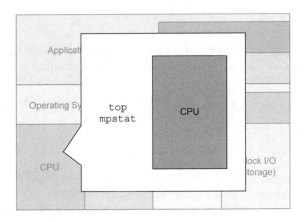

Figure 3.6 Zooming in to CPU observability tools

TOP

By now you're familiar with how to read top's memory usage, and how to use a few very cool features (if you're not, go back to section 3.3.4). Let's finally cover what a processor spends its time doing. Run top again from your terminal:

```
top
```

You will see output similar to the following. This time, let's focus on the %Cpu(s) row (bold font):

```
Tasks: 177 total,   6 running, 171 sleeping,   0 stopped,   0 zombie
%Cpu(s): 71.9 us, 25.0 sy, 0.0 ni, 0.0 id, 0.0 wa, 0.0 hi, 3.1 si, 0.0 st
```

What do all these numbers mean? Let's take a look:

- us (user time)—The percentage of time the CPU spent in user space.
- sy (system time)—The percentage of time the CPU spent in kernel space.
- ni (nice time)—The percentage of time spent on low-priority processes.
- id (idle time)—The percentage of time the CPU spent doing literally nothing. (It can't stop!)
- wa (I/O wait time)—The percentage of time the CPU spent waiting on I/O.
- hi (hardware interrupts)—The percentage of time the CPU spent servicing hardware interrupts.
- si (software interrupts)—The percentage of time the CPU spent servicing software interrupts.
- st (steal time)—The percentage of time a hypervisor stole the CPU to give it to someone else. This kicks in only in virtualized environments.

In the preceding output, you can see that you spend a majority of the time in user space (presumably running Alice's application), 25% in kernel space (probably executing system calls, or syscalls), and the remainder in software interrupts (most likely

Niceness

Niceness is an interesting concept in Linux. It's a numeric value, which shows how happy a process is to give CPU cycles to more high-priority neighbors (how *nice* it is with others). Allowed values range from –20 to 19.

A higher value means nicer, so happier to give CPU away (and so lower priority). A lower value means higher priority. See `man nice` and `man renice` for more info. These are the values you can see in the `ni` column in `top`.

handling the syscall invocations). There is no idle time at all, which means that whatever Alice's application is doing, it's using up all the available CPU!

Now, if you take a look at the rest of the output of the `top` command, you will see something similar to this (again, I've removed some output for brevity):

```
 PID USER      PR  NI    VIRT    RES    SHR S  %CPU  %MEM     TIME+ COMMAND
2893 chaos     20   0    3812    100      0 R  52.9   0.0   0:02.57 stress
2894 chaos     20   0  265960 183156    324 R  23.5   4.5   0:02.60 stress
2895 chaos     20   0    4712   1376    264 R  23.5   0.0   0:02.62 stress
2896 chaos     20   0    3812    100      0 R  17.6   0.0   0:02.64 stress
2902 chaos     20   0    3168   2000   1740 R  17.6   0.0   0:01.90 bc
```

(...)

You can see the `top` commands taking up pretty much all of the available two cores: `stress` and `bc`. It's now a good time to look under the covers of the simulation we've been investigating. Run this in your terminal to look at the `mystery002` command you've been running:

```
cat ~/src/examples/busy-neighbours/mystery002
```

You will see this output, which is a simple bash script, calculating pi's digits and running a totally benign script in the background:

```
#!/bin/bash
echo "Press [CTRL+C] to stop.."

# start some completely benign background daemon to do some
__lightweight__work
#     ^ this simulates Alice's server's environment
export dir=$(dirname "$(readlink -f "$0")")
(bash $dir/benign.sh)&          <-- This is the background
                                    process being started.
# do the actual work
while :
do
    echo "Calculating pi's 3000 digits..."        Here's our bc command,
    time echo "scale=3000; 4*a(1)" | bc -l | head -n1   <-- creatively used to
done                                                 calculate pi's digits!
```

So far, so good, but let's double-check how benign that background process really is by running this command at your prompt:

```
cat ~/src/examples/busy-neighbours/benign.sh
```

You will see the following output:

```
#!/bin/bash

# sleep a little, sneakily
sleep 20

# Just doing some lightweight background work
# Nothing to see here ;)
while :
do
    stress --cpu 2 -m 1 -d 1 --timeout 30 2>&1 > /dev/null
    sleep 5
done
```

Here's the stress command you were seeing in top!

There you go. Here's your problem: your app (bc command calculating pi) was competing for CPU time with the other commands in the system (stress), and as you can see in the output of top earlier in this section, it wasn't always winning (stress tended to get more %CPU allocated). For your convenience, let me repeat that output:

```
 PID  USER    PR  NI   VIRT    RES     SHR S  %CPU  %MEM   TIME+ COMMAND
2893 chaos    20   0   3812    100      0 R  52.9   0.0  0:02.57 stress
2894 chaos    20   0 265960 183156    324 R  23.5   4.5  0:02.60 stress
2895 chaos    20   0   4712   1376    264 R  23.5   0.0  0:02.62 stress
2896 chaos    20   0   3812    100      0 R  17.6   0.0  0:02.64 stress
2902 chaos    20   0   3168   2000   1740 R  17.6   0.0  0:01.90 bc
```

(...)

This is the source of our perceived slowness, your honor. The stress processes were a classic case of a busy neighbor. Case closed. Another mystery solved. Well done!

There should now be no *top* secrets anymore, and you're basically a certified *top* agent (I really can't help it). Hopefully, your computer hasn't overheated yet, but I do expect that your room temperature has risen since you started the chapter. We'll talk about how to deal with resource starvation and busy neighbors just a little later. Let's cover the last tool really quickly, and we'll be done with the CPU stuff!

MPSTAT –P ALL 1

mpstat is another tool that can show you the CPU utilization. The nice thing about it is that it can show you each CPU separately. Run the following in a terminal:

```
mpstat -P ALL 1
```

It will display output similar to this, printed every second:

```
01:14:08 PM CPU %usr %nice %sys %iowait %irq %soft %steal %guest %gnice %idle
01:14:09 PM all  60.10  0.00 33.33   0.00  0.00  6.57   0.00   0.00   0.00  0.00
01:14:09 PM 0    41.41  0.00 45.45   0.00  0.00 13.13   0.00   0.00   0.00  0.00
01:14:09 PM 1    78.79  0.00 21.21   0.00  0.00  0.00   0.00   0.00   0.00  0.00
```

The same statistics you were looking at with top are visible here, but now split separately for each CPU. This split is useful because you can see the distribution of load and analyze it. If you'd like to kill and restart the mystery002 process from the beginning of the chapter, you should see that for the first 20 seconds, the bc command is allowed to take as much CPU as it wants, but since it's single-threaded, it's scheduled on only a single CPU anyway. And then, after the initial 20 seconds, when the stress command starts running, it creates workers for both CPUs, and both of them become busy.

I like the output of mpstat, because the columns are more readable (nothing to do with the fact that it starts with my initials!). If you don't have mpstat available on your system, top also supports a split view similar to this one, and in the version available on our Ubuntu VM, you can toggle it by typing 1 (number one).

All right, so that puts mpstat on your radar. You have now more than enough tooling to detect what's going on, and to see when someone is eating up the CPU time you were hoping to get yourself. So, the question now becomes, how do you prevent that from happening? Let's take a look at your options.

MY DOG ATE MY CPU—HOW DO I FIX IT?

You found out that the app was slow for the simple reason that it was not getting enough CPU. This might sound pretty basic in our simulated environment, but in a larger, shared environment, it might be everything but obvious. A lot of serious production problems aren't rocket science, and that's fine.

I would like you to recall the four steps of the chaos experiment from the first chapter: ensure observability, define a steady state, form a hypothesis, and run the experiment. Let's look at what you have done so far:

1. You observed the times needed for your program to calculate the 3000 digits of pi—*your metric*.
2. You saw that initially an iteration was taking a certain time—*your steady state*.
3. You expected that the time per iteration would remain the same—*your hypothesis*.
4. But when you ran the experiment, the times were larger—*you were wrong*.

Look, ma, no hands! You've just applied what you learned in the previous chapters and conducted a reasonable chaos experiment. Take a look at figure 3.7, which sums all of it up in a format you should now find familiar.

Our experiment showed that the hypothesis was wrong; when the background processes were running, our application was slowing down considerably. How can you go about fixing it? One option would be to use *niceness*, a property you saw earlier in the

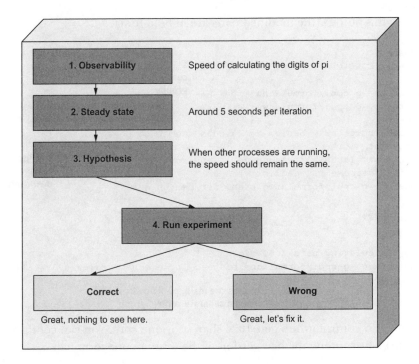

Figure 3.7 The four steps of our second chaos experiment

chapter, which allows you to set a higher relative priority for your process compared to other processes on the system to ensure it gets more CPU time. This could work, but it has one major drawback: it's hard to control precisely how much CPU they would get.

Linux offers another tool you can use in this situation: control groups. *Control groups* are a feature in the Linux kernel that allows the user to specify exact amounts of resources (CPU, memory, I/O) that the kernel should allocate to a group of processes. We will play with them a fair bit in chapter 5, but for now I want to give you a quick taste of what they can do.

Let's start by using `cgcreate` to create two control groups: `formulaone` and `formulatwo`. You can do that by running these commands at your prompt:

```
sudo cgcreate -g cpu:/formulaone
sudo cgcreate -g cpu:/formulatwo
```

Think of them as . . . Tupperware (oh my, was I just about to say *containers?*), in which you can put processes and have them share that space. You can put a process in one of these lunch boxes by starting it with `cgexec`. Let's tweak our initial `mystery002` script to use `cgcreate` and `cgexec`. I've included a modified version for you. You can see it by running this command at your prompt:

```
cat ~/src/examples/busy-neighbours/mystery002-cgroups.sh
```

You will see this output (the modified parts are in bold font):

```
#!/bin/bash
echo "Press [CTRL+C] to stop.."

sudo cgcreate -g cpu:/formulaone
sudo cgcreate -g cpu:/formulatwo

# start some completely benign background daemon to do some
  __lightweight__work
#    ^ this simulates Alice's server's environment
export dir=$(dirname "$(readlink -f "$0")")
(sudo cgexec -g cpu:/formulatwo bash $dir/benign.sh)&

# do the actual work
while :
do
    echo "Calculating pi's 3000 digits..."
    sudo cgexec -g cpu:/formulaone bash -c 'time echo "scale=3000; 4*a(1)"
| bc -l | head -n1'
done
```

Creates the CPU-controlled control groups

Executes the benign.sh script in its own control group

Executes the main, pi-digit-calculating code in a separate control group

By default, each control group gets 1024 shares, or one core. You can confirm that it works yourself by running the new version of the script in one terminal:

```
~/src/examples/busy-neighbours/mystery002-cgroups.sh
```

And in another terminal, running top, you should see output like the following, in which all the stress processes are sharing roughly one CPU, while the bc process is able to use another CPU:

```
Tasks: 187 total,   7 running, 180 sleeping,   0 stopped,   0 zombie
%Cpu(s): 72.7 us, 27.3 sy, 0.0 ni, 0.0 id, 0.0 wa, 0.0 hi,  0.0 si,  0.0 st
MiB Mem :   3942.4 total,    494.8 free,   1196.3 used,   2251.3 buff/cache
MiB Swap:      0.0 total,      0.0 free,      0.0 used.   2560.1 avail Mem

   PID  USER      PR  NI    VIRT    RES    SHR S  %CPU  %MEM     TIME+ COMMAND
  4888 chaos     20   0    3168   2132   1872 R  80.0   0.1   0:03.04 bc
  4823 root      20   0    3812    100      0 R  26.7   0.0   0:06.05 stress
  4824 root      20   0  265960 221860    268 R  26.7   5.5   0:06.13 stress
  4825 root      20   0    4712   1380    268 R  26.7   0.0   0:05.97 stress
  4826 root      20   0    3812    100      0 R  26.7   0.0   0:06.10 stress
```

We will look into that much more in later chapters. If you're curious to know now, run man cgroups in the terminal. Otherwise, we're done with the CPUs for now. Let's take a step up our resource map and visit the OS layer.

3.3.6 OS

We've already solved Alice's mystery with her app being slow, but before we go, I wanted to give you a few really powerful tools at the OS level—you know, for the next time the app is slow, but the CPU is not the issue.

Figure 3.8 shows where that fits on our resource map. The tools we'll take a look at are opensnoop and execsnoop, both coming from the BCC project. Let's start with opensnoop.

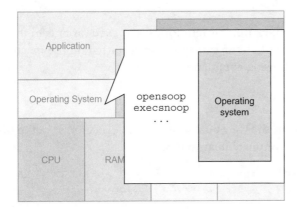

Figure 3.8   Zooming in to OS observability tools

OPENSNOOP

opensnoop allows you to see all the files being opened by all the processes on your system, in what's basically real time. BPF really is kind of like a Linux superpower, isn't it? To start it (again, remember about the postfix for the Ubuntu package), run this in your command line:

```
sudo opensnoop-bpfcc
```

You should start seeing files being opened by various processes on your system. If you want to get a sample of what it can do, try opening another terminal window, and do just one execution of top:

```
top -n1
```

You will see output similar to this (I've abbreviated most of it for you):

```
(...)
12396   top             6    0 /proc/sys/kernel/osrelease
12396   top             6    0 /proc/meminfo
12396   top             7    0 /sys/devices/system/cpu/online
12396   top             7    0 /proc
(...)
12396   top             8    0 /proc/12386/stat
12396   top             8    0 /proc/12386/statm
12396   top             7    0 /etc/localtime
```

```
12396   top                       7   0 /var/run/utmp
12396   top                       7   0 /proc/loadavg
(...)
```

This is how you know where top is getting all of its information from (feel free to explore what's in /proc). When practicing chaos engineering, you will often want to know what a particular application you didn't write is actually doing, in order to know how to design or implement your experiments. Knowing what files it opens is a really useful feature. Speaking of which, here's another one for you: execsnoop.

EXECSNOOP

execsnoop is similar to opensnoop, but it listens for calls to exec variants in the kernel, which means that you get a list of all the processes being started on the machine. You can start it by running the following command at a prompt:

```
sudo execsnoop-bpfcc
```

While that runs, try to open another terminal window, and execute ls. In the first window, execsnoop should print output similar to this:

```
PCOMM           PID   PPID   RET ARGS
ls              12419 2073     0 /usr/bin/ls --color=auto
```

Now, instead of ls, try running the mystery002 command we started the chapter with in the second terminal window, by running the following command at your prompt:

```
~/src/examples/busy-neighbours/mystery002
```

You will see all the commands being executed, just as in the following output. You should recognize all the auxiliary commands, like readlink, dirname, head, and sleep. You will also find the bc and stress commands starting.

```
PCOMM       PID     PPID   RET ARGS
mystery002 12426   2012   0 /home/chaos/src/examples/busy-
neighbours/mystery002
readlink    12428   12427 0 /usr/bin/readlink -f
/home/chaos/src/examples/busy-neighbours/mystery002
dirname     12427   12426 0
bash        12429   12426 0 /usr/bin/bash /home/chaos/src/examples/busy-
neighbours/benign.sh
bc          12431   12426 0 /usr/bin/bc -l
head        12432   12426 0 /usr/bin/head -n1
sleep       12433   12429 0 /usr/bin/sleep 20
(...)
stress      12462   12445 0 /usr/bin/stress --cpu 2 -m 1 -d 1 --timeout 30
(...)
```

This is an extremely convenient way of looking into what is being started on a Linux machine. Have I mentioned BFS was really awesome?

OTHER TOOLS

The OS level offers a large surface to cover, so the purpose of this section is not to give you a full list of all tools available, but rather to emphasize that you can (and should) consider all of that when you're doing chaos engineering.

I didn't include tools like `strace`, `dtrace`, and `perf`, which you might have expected to see here (if you don't know them, do look them up). Instead, I've opted to give you a taste of what BPF has to offer, because I believe that it will slowly replace the older technologies for this use case. I strongly recommend visiting https://github .com/iovisor/bcc and browsing through other available tools. We don't have room to cover them all here, but I hope that I've given you a taste, and I'll leave discovering others to you as an exercise. Let's take a look at the top level of our resource map.

3.4   *Application*

So here we are; we've reached the top layer of our resource map, the application layer. This is where the code is being written directly to implement what the clients want, whether it's a serious business app, video game, or bitcoin miner.

Every application is different, and it often makes sense to talk about high-level metrics provided directly by the application in the context of chaos experiments. For example, we could be looking into bank transaction latencies, the number of players able to play at the same time, or a number of hash processes per second. When doing chaos engineering, we will work with these on a case-by-case basis, because they have unique meanings.

But between the OS and the application, a lot of code is running that we don't always think about—the runtimes and libraries. And these are shared across applications and are therefore easier to look into and diagnose. In this section, we'll look into how to see what's going on inside a Python application. I'll show you how to use `cProfile`, `pythonstat`, and `pythonflow` to give you an idea of what you can easily do. Figure 3.9 is once again showing where all of this fits on the resource map.

Let's start with `cProfile`.

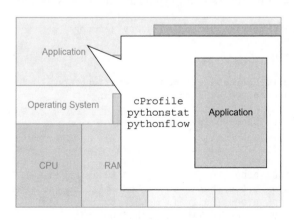

Figure 3.9   Zooming in to application observability tools

3.4.1   *cProfile*

Python, true to its "batteries included" motto, ships with two profiling modules: cProfile and profile (https://docs.python.org/3.7/library/profile.html). We will use the former, as it provides a lower overhead and is recommended for most use cases.

To play with it, let's start a Python read-eval-print loop (REPL) by running this in a command prompt:

```
python3.7
```

This will present you with some data on the Python binary and a blinking cursor where you can type your commands, much like the following output:

```
Python 3.7.0 (default, Feb  2 2020, 12:18:01)
[GCC 8.3.0] on linux
Type "help", "copyright", "credits" or "license" for more information.
>>>
```

Imagine that you are again trying to find out why a particular application is slow, and you want to check where it spends its time when executed by Python. That's where a profiler like cProfile can help. In its simplest form, cProfile can be used to analyze a snippet of code. Try running this in the interactive Python session you just started:

```
>>> import cProfile
>>> import re
>>> cProfile.run('re.compile("foo|bar")')
```

When you run the last line, you should see output similar to the following (output abbreviated for clarity). The output says that while running re.compile("foo|bar"), the program makes 243 function calls (236 primitive, or nonrecursive), and then lists all the calls. I used bold font to focus your attention on two columns: ncalls (total number of calls—if there are two numbers separated by slash, the second one is the number of primitive calls) and tottime (total time spent in there). cumtime is also noteworthy, as it gives a cumulative time spent in that call and all its subcalls:

```
    243 function calls (236 primitive calls) in 0.000 seconds

   Ordered by: standard name

ncalls tottime percall cumtime percall filename:lineno(function)
    1    0.000   0.000    0.000   0.000 <string>:1(<module>)
(...)
    1    0.000   0.000    0.000   0.000 re.py:232(compile)
(...)
    1    0.000   0.000    0.000   0.000 sre_compile.py:759(compile)
(...)
    1    0.000   0.000    0.000   0.000 {built-in method builtins.exec}
   26    0.000   0.000    0.000   0.000 {built-in method builtins.isinstance}
30/27    0.000   0.000    0.000   0.000 {built-in method builtins.len}
    2    0.000   0.000    0.000   0.000 {built-in method builtins.max}
```

```
       9   0.000   0.000   0.000   0.000 {built-in method builtins.min}
       6   0.000   0.000   0.000   0.000 {built-in method builtins.ord}
      48   0.000   0.000   0.000   0.000 {method 'append' of 'list' objects}
       1   0.000   0.000   0.000   0.000 {method 'disable' of '_lsprof.Profiler'
objects}
       5   0.000   0.000   0.000   0.000 {method 'find' of 'bytearray' objects}
       1   0.000   0.000   0.000   0.000 {method 'get' of 'dict' objects}
       2   0.000   0.000   0.000   0.000 {method 'items' of 'dict' objects}
       1   0.000   0.000   0.000   0.000 {method 'setdefault' of 'dict' objects}
       1   0.000   0.000   0.000   0.000 {method 'sort' of 'list' objects}
```

To make sense of this, a certain level of understanding of the source code is helpful, but by using this technique, you can at least get an indication of where the slowness might be happening.

If you'd like to run a module or a script, rather than just a snippet, you can run cProfile from the command line like this:

```
python -m cProfile [-o output_file] [-s sort_order] (-m module |
myscript.py)
```

For example, to run a simple HTTP server, you can run the following command at the prompt. It will wait until the program finishes, so when you're done with it, you can press Ctrl-C to kill it.

```
python3.7 -m cProfile -m http.server 8001
```

At another command prompt, make an HTTP call to the server to check that it works and to generate some more interesting stats:

```
curl localhost:8001
```

When you press Ctrl-C in the first prompt, cProfile will print the statistics. You should see a large amount of output, and among these lines, one line of particular interest. This is where our program spent most of its time—waiting to accept new requests:

```
36  17.682  0.491  17.682   0.491 {method 'poll' of 'select.poll' objects}
```

Hopefully, this gives you a taste of how easy it is to get started profiling Python programs and the kind of information you can get out of the box, with just the Python standard library. Other Python profilers (check https://github.com/benfred/py-spy, for example) offer more ease of use and visualization capabilities. Unfortunately, we don't have space to cover these. Let's take a quick look at another approach; let's leverage BPF.

3.4.2 BCC and Python

To use pythonstat and pythonflow, you'll need a Python binary that was compiled with --with-dtrace support to enable you to use the User Statically Defined Tracing (USDT) probes (read more at https://lwn.net/Articles/753601/). These probes are places in the code where authors of the software defined special endpoints to attach to with DTrace, to debug and trace their applications.

Many popular applications, like MySQL, Python, Java, PostgreSQL, Node.js, and many more can be compiled with these probes. BPF (and BCC) can also use these probes, and that's how the two tools we're going to use work.

I've precompiled a suitable Python binary for you in ~/Python3.7.0/python. It was built with --with-dtrace to enable support for the USDT probes. In a terminal window, run the following command to start a simple game:

```
~/Python-3.7.0/python -m freegames.life
```

It's a Conway's Game of Life implementation, which you can find at https://github .com/grantjenks/free-python-games. Now, in another terminal, start `pythonstat` by running this:

```
sudo pythonstat-bpfcc
```

You should see output similar to the following, showing the number of method invocations, garbage collections, new objects, classes loaded, exceptions, and new threads per second, respectively:

```
07:50:03 loadavg: 7.74 2.68 1.10 2/641 7492

PID     CMDLINE              METHOD/s  GC/s  OBJNEW/s  CLOAD/s  EXC/s  THR/s
7139    /home/chaos/Python-3 480906    3     0         0        0      0
7485    python /usr/sbin/lib 0         0     0         0        0      0
```

`pythonflow`, on the other hand, allows you to trace the beginning and end of execution of various functions in Python. Try it by starting an interactive session in one terminal by running this command:

```
~/Python-3.7.0/python
```

In another terminal, start `pythonflow` as follows:

```
sudo pythonflow-bpfcc $(pidof python)
```

Now, as you execute commands at the Python prompt, you will see the calls stack in the `pythonflow` window. For example, try running this:

```
>>> import this
The Zen of Python, by Tim Peters

Beautiful is better than ugly.
Explicit is better than implicit.
Simple is better than complex.
Complex is better than complicated.
Flat is better than nested.
Sparse is better than dense.
```

```
Readability counts.
Special cases aren't special enough to break the rules.
Although practicality beats purity.
Errors should never pass silently.
Unless explicitly silenced.
In the face of ambiguity, refuse the temptation to guess.
There should be one-- and preferably only one --obvious way to do it.
Although that way may not be obvious at first unless you're Dutch.
Now is better than never.
Although never is often better than *right* now.
If the implementation is hard to explain, it's a bad idea.
If the implementation is easy to explain, it may be a good idea.
Namespaces are one honking great idea -- let's do more of those!
```

In the `pythonflow` window, you will see the whole sequence needed to import that module:

```
Tracing method calls in python process 7539... Ctrl-C to quit.
CPU PID     TID     TIME(us) METHOD
1   7539    7539    4.547      -> <stdin>.<module>
1   7539    7539    4.547        -> <frozen importlib._bootstrap>._find_and_load
1   7539    7539    4.547          -> <frozen importlib._bootstrap>.__init__
1   7539    7539    4.547          <- <frozen importlib._bootstrap>.__init__
1   7539    7539    4.547          -> <frozen importlib._bootstrap>.__enter__
(...)
```

Try running other code in Python and see all the method invocations appear on your screen. Once again, when practicing chaos engineering, we will often work with other people's code, and being able to take a sneak peek into what it's doing is going to prove extremely valuable.

I picked Python as an example, but each language ecosystem has its own equivalent tools and methods. Each stack will let you profile and trace applications. We will cover a few more examples in the later chapters of this book. Let's move on to the last piece of this chapter's puzzle: the automation.

3.5 Automation: Using time series

All of the tools we've looked at so far are very useful. You've seen how to check which system resources are saturated, how to see system errors, how to look into what's going on at the system level, and even how to get insight into how various runtimes behave. But the tools also have one drawback: you need to sit down and execute each one. In this section, I'll discuss what you can do to automate getting this insight.

Various monitoring systems are available on the market right now. Popular ones include Datadog (www.datadoghq.com), New Relic (https://newrelic.com/), and Sysdig (https://sysdig.com/). They all provide some kind of agent you need to run on each of the machines you want to gain insight for, and then give you a way to browse through, visualize, and alert on the monitoring data. If you'd like to learn more about these commercial offerings, I'm sure their sales people will be delighted to give you a demo. In the context of this book, on the other hand, I'd like to focus on open source alternatives: Prometheus and Grafana.

3.5.1   *Prometheus and Grafana*

Prometheus (https://prometheus.io/) is an open source monitoring system and a time-series database. It provides everything you need to gather, store, query, and alert on monitoring data. *Grafana* (https://grafana.com/) is an analytics and visualization tool that works with various data sources, including Prometheus. A subproject of Prometheus called *Node Exporter* (https://github.com/prometheus/node_exporter) allows for exposing a large set of system metrics.

Together they make for a powerful monitoring stack. We won't cover setting up production Prometheus, but I want to show you how easily you can get the USE metrics into a time-series database by using this stack. To make things faster, we'll use Docker. Don't worry if you're not sure how it works; we'll cover that in later chapters. For now, just treat it as a program launcher.

Let's start by launching Node Exporter by executing this command at the prompt:

```
docker run -d \
  --net="host" \
  --pid="host" \
  -v "/:/host:ro,rslave" \
  quay.io/prometheus/node-exporter \
  --path.rootfs=/host
```

When it's finished, let's confirm it works by calling the default port, using the following command:

```
curl http://localhost:9100/metrics
```

You should see output similar to the following. This is the Prometheus format—one line per metric, in a simple, human-readable form:

```
promhttp_metric_handler_requests_total{code="200"} 0
promhttp_metric_handler_requests_total{code="500"} 0
promhttp_metric_handler_requests_total{code="503"} 0
```

Each line corresponds to a time series. In this example, the same name of the metric (promhttp_metric_handler_requests_total) has three values (200, 500, and 503) for the label code. That translates to three separate time series, each having some value at any point in time.

Now, Prometheus works by *scraping* metrics, which means making an HTTP call to an endpoint like the one you just called, interpreting the time-series data, and storing each value at the timestamp corresponding to the time of scraping. Let's start an instance of Prometheus and make it scrape the Node Exporter endpoint. You can do this by first creating a configuration file in your home directory, called prom.yml (/home/chaos/prom.yml) with the following content:

```
global:
  scrape_interval: 5s        ◁─┤ Sets scraping interval to 5 seconds
scrape_configs:                  so you get the metrics more quickly
- job_name: 'node'
  static_configs:               Tells Prometheus to scrape the
  - targets: ['localhost:9100']  ◁─ Node Exporter that runs on
                                     port 9100 (default port)
```

Then start Prometheus and pass this configuration file to it by running this command at your prompt:

```
docker run \
    -p 9090:9090 \
    --net="host" \
    -v /home/chaos/prom.yml:/etc/prometheus/prometheus.yml \
    prom/prometheus
```

When the container starts, open Firefox (or other browser) and navigate to http://127.0.0.1:9090/. You will see the Prometheus user interface (UI). The UI lets you see the configuration and status, and query various metrics. Go ahead and query for the CPU metric node_cpu_seconds_total in the query window and click Execute. You should see output similar to figure 3.10.

Notice the various values for the label mode: idle, user, system, steal, nice, and so on. These are the same categories you were looking at in top. But now, they are a time series, and you can plot over time, aggregate them, and alert on them easily.

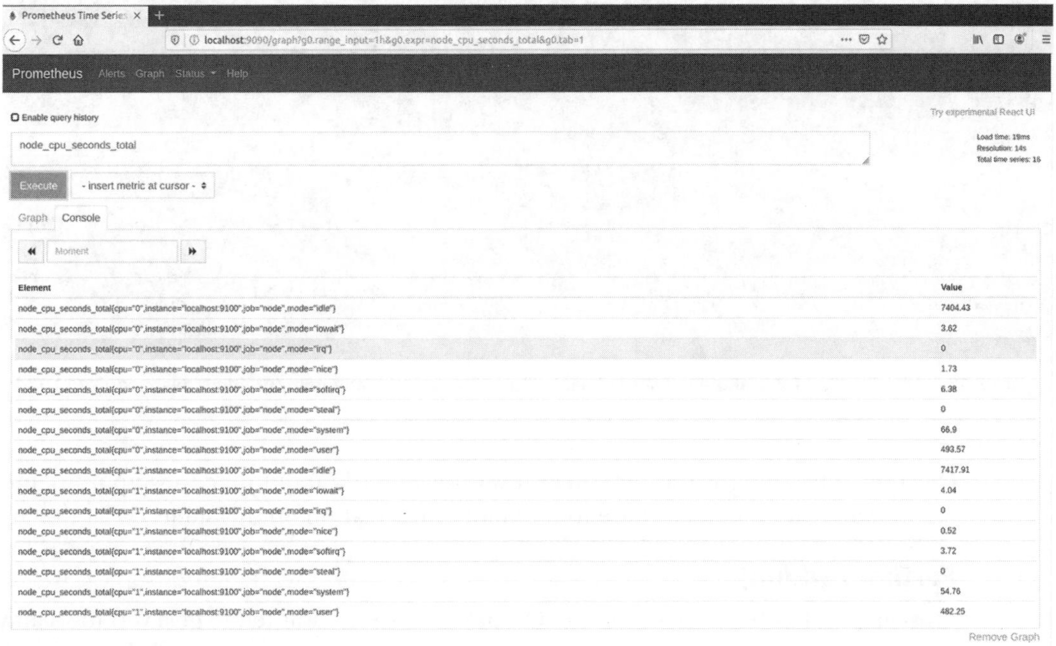

Figure 3.10 Prometheus UI in action, showing the node_cpu_seconds_total **metric**

We don't have space to cover querying Prometheus or building Grafana dashboards, so I leave that as an exercise for you. Go to http://mng.bz/go8V to learn more about Prometheus query language. If you'd like an inspiration for a Grafana dashboard, many are available at https://grafana.com/grafana/dashboards. Take a look at figure 3.11, which shows one of the dashboards available for download.

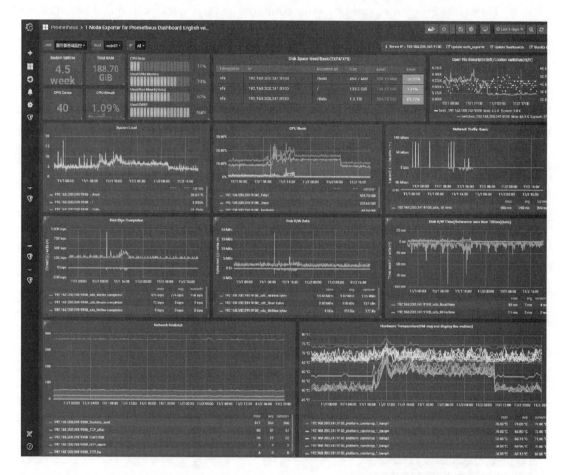

Figure 3.11   An example of a Grafana dashboard available at https://grafana.com/grafana/dashboards/11074

OK, hopefully it was as fun for you as it was for me. It's about time to wrap it up, but before we do, let's look at where to find more information on this subject.

3.6   *Further reading*

This chapter has been tricky for me. On the one hand, I wanted to give you tools and techniques you'll need in the following chapters to practice chaos engineering, so this section grew quickly. On the other hand, I wanted to keep the content to a minimum because it's not a system performance book. That means that I had to make some choices and to skip some great tools. If you'd like to delve deeper into the subject, I recommend the following books:

- *Systems Performance: Enterprise and the Cloud* by Brendan Gregg (Pearson, 2013), www.brendangregg.com/sysperfbook.html
- *BPF Performance Tools* by Brendan Gregg (Addison-Wesley, 2019), www.brendan-gregg.com/bpf-performance-tools-book.html
- *Linux Kernel Development* by Robert Love (Addison-Wesley Professional, 2010), https://rlove.org/

And that's a wrap!

Summary

- When debugging a slow application, you can use the USE method: check for utilization, saturation, and errors.
- Resources to analyze include physical devices (CPU, RAM, disk, network) as well as software resources (syscalls, file descriptors).
- Linux provides a rich ecosystem of tools available, including `free`, `df`, `top`, `sar`, `vmstat`, `iostat`, `mpstat`, and BPF.
- BCC makes it easy to leverage BPF to gain deep insights into the system with often negligible overheads.
- You can gain valuable insights at various levels: physical components, OS, library/runtime, application.

Database trouble and testing in production

This chapter covers
- Designing chaos experiments for open source software
- Adding network latency by using Traffic Control
- Understanding when testing in production might make sense and how to approach it

In this chapter, you will apply everything you've learned about chaos engineering so far in a real-world example of a common application you might be familiar with. Have you heard of WordPress? It's a popular blogging engine and content management system. According to some estimates, WordPress accounts for more than a third of all pages on the internet, and for most CMS-backed websites (http://mng .bz/e58Q). It's typically paired with a MySQL database, another popular piece of technology.

Let's take a vanilla instance of WordPress backed by MySQL and, using chaos engineering, try to gain confidence in how reliably you can run it. You'll try to preemptively guess what conditions might disturb it and design experiments to verify how it fares. Ready? Let's see what our friends from Glanden are up to these days.

4.1 We're doing WordPress

It's magical what VC dollars can do while they last. A lot has changed at our favorite startup from Glanden since we last saw them some 30-odd pages ago. The CEO read *The Lean Startup* by Eric Ries last weekend (http://theleanstartup.com/). That, coupled with mediocre FizzBuzz-as-a-Service sales, resulted in *pivoting*, or changing direction in *The Lean Startup* lingo. In practice, apart from a lot of talking, pivoting meant a personnel reshuffle (Alice is now leading a team of SREs, and engineering is led by a newcomer, Charlie), a new logo (Meower), and a complete change of business model ("Meower is like Uber for cats"). The details of the business model and demand for the feline transportation service remain a little fuzzy.

What's not fuzzy at all is the direct recommendation from the CEO: "We're doing WordPress now." Alice's team was tasked to take all the wisdom about running applications reliably from FizzBuzz as a Service and apply it to the new, WordPress-based *Meower*. No point arguing with the CEO, so let's get straight to work!

Here is where you come in. You will work with a vanilla installation of WordPress, which comes preinstalled in your Ubuntu VM. Let's take a look under the hood. Figure 4.1 shows an overview of the components of the system:

- *Apache2* (a popular HTTP server) is used to handle the incoming traffic.
- *WordPress*, written in PHP, processes the requests and generates responses.
- *MySQL* is used to store the data for the blog.

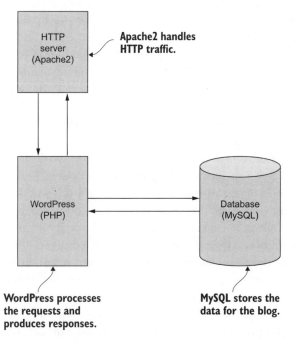

Figure 4.1 WordPress system setup

WordPress has packages readily available for a wide selection of Linux distributions. In the VM provided with this book, the software comes preinstalled through the default Ubuntu packages, and the remaining step is to start and configure it. You can start it by running the following commands at the terminal command prompt inside your VM. It will stop NGINX (if it is still running from previous chapters), and then start the database and the HTTP server:

```
sudo systemctl stop nginx        ◁──┐  Stops NGINX if it is running
sudo systemctl start mysql          │  from previous chapters
sudo systemctl start apache2
```

The Apache2 web server should now be serving WordPress on http://localhost/blog. To confirm it's working well, and to configure the WordPress application, open your browser and go to http://localhost/blog. You will see a configuration page. Please fill in the details with whatever you like (just remember the password, as you'll need it to log into WordPress later) and click Install WordPress. When the installation is finished, WordPress will allow you to log in, and you can start using your WordPress blog.

You should now be ready to roll! Time to put on your chaos engineer hat and generate ideas for a chaos experiment. In order to do that, let's identify some weak points of this simple setup.

4.2   Weak links

Let's look at the system again from the perspective of a chaos engineer. How does it work on a high level? Figure 4.2 provides an overview of the setup by showing what happens when a client makes a request to Meower.

Apache2 (a popular HTTP server) is used to handle the incoming HTTP traffic (1). Behind the scenes, Apache2 decodes HTTP, extracts the request, and calls out to the PHP interpreter running the WordPress application to generate the response (2). WordPress (PHP) connects to a MySQL database to fetch the data it needs to produce a response (3). The response is then fed back to Apache2 (4), which returns the data to the client as a valid HTTP response (5).

This is where the fun part of doing chaos engineering begins. With this high-level idea of how the system works, you can start looking into how it breaks. Let's try to predict the fragile points of the system, and how to experimentally test whether they are resilient to the type of failure you expect to see. Where would you start?

Finding weak links is often equal measures science and art. Based on an often-incomplete mental picture of how a system works, the starting points for chaos experiments are effectively educated guesses on where fragility might reside in a given system. By leveraging past experience and employing various heuristics, you can make guesses, which you'll then turn into actual science through chaos experiments. One of the heuristics is that often the parts of the system responsible for storing state are the most fragile ones. If you apply that to our simple example, you can see that the

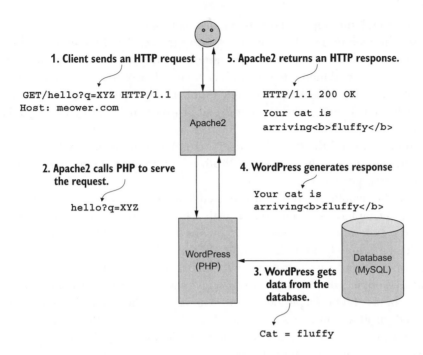

Figure 4.2 WordPress setup handling a user request

database might be the weak link. With that, here are two examples of educated guesses about a systemic weakness:

1 The database might require good disk I/O speeds. What happens when they slow down?
2 How much slowness can you accept in networking between the app server and the database?

They are both great learning opportunities, so let's try to develop them into full-featured chaos experiments, starting with the database disk I/O requirements.

4.2.1 Experiment 1: Slow disks

You suspect that disk I/O degradation might have a negative effect on your application's performance. Right now, it's just an educated guess. To confirm or deny, like any mad scientist, you turn to an experiment for answers! Luckily, by now you're familiar with the four steps to designing a chaos experiment introduced in chapter 1:

1 Ensure observability.
2 Define the steady state.
3 Form a hypothesis.
4 Run the experiment!

Let's go through the steps and design a real experiment!

First, you need to be able to reliably observe the results of the experiment. To do that, you need a reliable metric. You are interested in your website's performance, so an example of a good metric to start with is the number of successful requests per second (RPS). It's easy to work with (a single number), and you can easily measure it with the Apache Bench you saw in chapter 2—all of which makes it a good candidate for starters.

Second, you need to establish a steady state. You can do that by running Apache Bench on the system without any modifications and reading the normal range of successful requests per second.

Third, the hypothesis. You've just started learning about this system at the beginning of this chapter, so it's OK to start with a simple hypothesis and then refine it as you do the experiments and learn more about the characteristics of the system. One example of a simple hypothesis could be, "If the disk I/O is 95% used, the successful requests per second won't drop by more than 50%." It represents a potential real-world situation, in which another process, let's say a log cleaner/rotator, kicks in and uses a lot of disk I/O for a period of time. The values I chose here (95% and 50%) are completely arbitrary, just to get us started. In the real world, they would come from the SLOs you are trying to satisfy. Right now, you know very little about the system, so let's start somewhere and refine it later.

With these three elements, you're ready to implement our experiment. I'm sure you can't wait, so let's do this!

IMPLEMENTATION

Before making any change to the system, let's measure our baseline—define the steady state. The steady state is the value of your chosen metric during normal operation; that is, when you don't run any chaos experiments and the operation of the system is representative of its usual behavior. With the metric of successful RPS, it's simple to measure that steady state with Apache Bench. You used Apache Bench before in chapter 2, but if you need a refresher, you can run `man ab` at your command prompt.

When measuring the baseline, it's important to control all parameters so that later you can compare apples to apples, but right now the values themselves are completely arbitrary. Let's start by calling `ab` with a concurrency of 1 (`-c 1`) for a max of 30 seconds (`-t 30`), and let's remember to ignore the variable length of the response (`-l`) You can do that by running the following command at your command prompt. Be careful to add the trailing slash, because otherwise you'll get a redirect response, which is not what you are trying to test!

```
ab -t 30 -c 1 -l http://localhost/blog/
```

You will see output similar to the following (abbreviated for clarity). If you run the command multiple times, you will get slightly different values, but they should be similar. This example output has no failed requests, and the RPS value is `86.33`:

```
(...)
Concurrency Level:      1
Time taken for tests:   30.023 seconds
Complete requests:      2592
Failed requests:        0                    <-- Failed requests is none
Total transferred:      28843776 bytes
HTML transferred:       28206144 bytes
Requests per second:    86.33 [#/sec] (mean)     <-- RPS is around 86
Time per request:       11.583 [ms] (mean)
Time per request:       11.583 [ms] (mean, across all concurrent requests)
Transfer rate:          938.19 [Kbytes/sec] received
(...)
```

When I ran the command a dozen times, I received similar values. Remember that the output will depend entirely on your hardware and on how you configure your VM. In this example output, you can take the value of 86 RPS as your steady state.

Now, how do you implement the conditions for your hypothesis? In chapter 3, you were tracking a mysterious process called `stress`. It's a utility program designed to stress test your system, capable of generating load for CPU, RAM, and disks. You can use it to simulate a program hungry for disk I/O. The option `--hdd n` allows you to create *n* workers, each of which writes files to the disk and then removes them.

In our arbitrarily chosen value for the hypothesis, you used a percentage. To generate a load of 95%, you first need to see what your practical 100% is, so let's see how quickly you can write to disk. In one terminal window, start `iostat` by running the following command. You will use it to see the total throughput, updated every 3 seconds. You will use that to monitor the disk write speed:

```
iostat 3
```

In a second terminal window, let's run the `stress` command benchmarking disk with the `--hdd` option and start with a single disk-writing worker. Run the following command in the second terminal window, which will run as specified for 35 seconds:

```
stress --timeout 35 --hdd 1
```

In the first window, you will see output similar to the following. Depending on your PC configuration, the values will vary. In the following output, it tops at around 1 GB/s (in bold), and for the sake of simplicity, we'll assume that this is the practical 100% of our available throughput:

```
Device            tps    kB_read/s    kB_wrtn/s    kB_read    kB_wrtn
loop0            0.00         0.00         0.00          0          0
sda           1005.00         0.00   1017636.00          0    2035272
```

Depending on your setup, you might need to experiment with extra workers to see what your 100% throughput is like. Don't worry too much about the exact number, though; you are running all of this inside a VM, so there are going to be multiple levels of caches and platform-specific considerations to take into account that won't be discussed in this chapter. The goal here is to teach you how to design and implement your own experiments, but the low-level details need to be addressed case by case.

To double-check your numbers, you can run another test. dd is a utility for copying data from one source to another. If you copy enough data to stress test the system, it will give you an indication of how quickly you can go. To copy data from /dev/zero to a temporary file 15 times in blocks of 512 MB, run the following command at your prompt:

```
dd if=/dev/zero of=/tmp/file1 bs=512M count=15
```

The output will look similar to the following (the average write speed is in bold font). In this example, the speed was around 1 GB/s, similar to what you found with stress. Once again, to simplify, let's go with 1 GB/s write speed as our throughput:

```
15+0 records in
15+0 records out
8053063680 bytes (8.1 GB, 7.9 GiB) copied, 8.06192 s, 998 MB/s
```

Finally, you should compare your findings against the theoretical limits. Although Apple doesn't publish official numbers for its solid-state drives (SSDs), benchmarks on the internet put the value at about 2.5 GB/s. Therefore, the results you found at less than half that speed in your VM running with the default configuration sound plausible. So far, so good.

Now, in the initial hypothesis, you wanted to simulate 95% disk write utilization. As you saw earlier, a stress command with a single worker consumes just about 95% of that number. How convenient! It's almost like someone chose that value on purpose! Therefore, to generate the load you want, you can just reuse the same stress command as earlier. The scene is set!

Let's run the experiment. In one terminal window, start stress with a single worker for 35 seconds (giving you the extra 5 seconds to start ab in the other terminal), by running the following command:

```
stress --timeout 35 --hdd 1
```

In a second terminal window, rerun your initial benchmark with Apache Bench. Do that by running the following command:

```
ab -t 30 -c 10 -l http://localhost/blog/
```

When ab is finished, you should see output similar to the following. There are still no errors, and the RPS in this sample is 53.92, or a 38% decrease:

```
(...)
Concurrency Level:      1
Time taken for tests:   30.009 seconds
Complete requests:      1618
Failed requests:        0           ◁──┘
```

Failed requests is none

```
Total transferred:      18005104 bytes
HTML transferred:       17607076 bytes
Requests per second:    53.92 [#/sec] (mean)          ◁──┐ RPS is around 54
Time per request:       18.547 [ms] (mean)
Time per request:       18.547 [ms] (mean, across all concurrent requests)
Transfer rate:          585.92 [Kbytes/sec] received
(...)
```

Conveniently, this value fits comfortably within the 50% slowdown that your initial hypothesis allowed for and lets you conclude this experiment with success. Yes, if some other process on the same host as your database suddenly starts writing to the disk, taking 90% or more of the bandwidth, your blog continues working, and slows down by less than 50%. In absolute terms, the average time per request went from 12 ms to 19 ms, which is unlikely to be noticed by any human.

Deus ex machina

In this example, it is indeed convenient that you don't need to limit the writing speed of your `stress` command to another value, like 50%. If you did, one way of achieving the desired effect would be to calculate the maximum throughput that you want to allow as a percentage of the total throughput you discovered (for example, 50% of 1 GB/s would be 512 MB/s) and then leverage cgroups v2 (http://mng.bz/pVoz) to limit the `stress` command to that value.

Congrats, another chaos experiment under your belt! But before you pat yourself on the back, let's discuss the science.

DISCUSSION

One of the big limitations of this implementation is that all the processes involved—the application server, the application, the database, the `stress` command, and the `ab` command—run on the same host (and the same VM). While we were trying to simulate the disk writes, the action of writing to the disk requires CPU time, and that's what probably had a larger impact on the slowdown than the writing itself. And even if the writing is the main factor, which component does it affect the most?

These are all things we brushed aside here, but I want you to start being mindful of them because they will become relevant in the more serious applications of chaos engineering. When writing this book, I've tried to make following the examples as simple as possible so you can see things for yourself. In this case, I chose to sacrifice realism for ease of use to help the learning process. Please don't petition to kick me out of the Royal Society (I'm not a member) just yet!

Another thing worth noting is that average RPS, while a good starting point, is not a perfect metric, because like any average, it loses information about the distribution. For example, if you average two requests, one that took 1 ms and another that took 1 s, the average is ~0.5 s, but that doesn't say anything about the distribution. A much more useful metric would be a 90th, 95th, or 99th percentile. I chose the simple metric for learning purposes, and in later chapters we will look at the percentiles.

Also, in this example we chose to simulate using up the disk's throughput through writing. What would happen if you chose to do a lot of reading instead? How would the filesystem caching come into play? What filesystem should you use to optimize your results? Would it be the same if you had NVMe disks instead of SATA, which can do some of the reading and writing in parallel? What would happen if you did some writing and then some reading to try to use up the disk-writing bandwidth?

All of these are relevant questions, which you would need to consider when implementing a serious chaos experiment. And much as in this example, often you will be uncovering new layers as you implement the experiment and realize the importance of other variables. You will not have time to drill into any of these questions right now, but I do recommend that you try to research some of them as an exercise.

Finally, in both cases, you were running with a single request at a time. This made it easier to manage in your little VM, but in the real world, it's an unlikely scenario. Most traffic will be bursty. It's possible that a different usage pattern would put more stress on the disk and would yield different results.

With all these caveats out of the way, let's move on to the second experiment: What happens when networking slows down?

4.2.2   *Experiment 2: Slow connection*

Our second idea of what could go wrong with our application involved the networking being slow. How would that affect the end-user speed of the blog? To turn that idea into a real chaos experiment, you need to define what *being slow* means and how you expect it to affect your application. From there, you can follow the four steps to a chaos experiment.

The definition of *being slow* is wildly contextual. A person spending 45 minutes picking something to watch on Netflix will likely get offended by an accusation of being slow, but the same person waiting 45 minutes for a life-saving organ donation to be delivered from a different hospital will have a very different experience of time (unless they're in anesthesia). Time truly is relative.

Similarly, in the computer world, users of a high-frequency trading fund will care about every millisecond of latency, but let's be honest: the latest cat video on YouTube taking an extra second to load is hardly a deal breaker. In our case, Meower needs to become a commercial success, so you need the website to feel snappy for its users. Following the current best practices, it looks like the website needs to load for users in less than 3 seconds, or the probability of users leaving increases significantly (http:// mng.bz/ZPAa). You will need to account for the actual time it takes for the user to download your content, so let's start with a goal of not going more than 2.5 seconds in the average response time.

With that goal in mind, let's go through the steps of designing a chaos experiment:

1   Ensure observability.
2   Define the steady state.

3 Form a hypothesis.

4 Run the experiment!

First, observability. You care about the response time, so for your metric, you can stick with the number of successful requests per second—the same metric used in the previous chaos experiment. RPS is easy to use, and you already have tools to measure it. I mentioned the downsides of using averages in the previous section, but for our use in this example, the successful RPS will do just fine.

Second, the steady state. Because you're using the same metric, you can reuse the work you've done with ab to establish your baseline.

Third, the actual hypothesis. You already observed in the previous experiment that with a concurrency of 1, you were in double-digit milliseconds for average response time. Remember that all of your components are running on the same host, so the overhead of networking is much smaller than it would be if the traffic was going over an actual network. Let's see what happens if you add a 2-second delay in communicating to your database. Your hypothesis can therefore be, "If the networking between WordPress and MySQL experiences a delay of 2 seconds, the average response time remains less than 2.5 seconds." Again, these initial values are pretty arbitrary. The goal is to start somewhere and then refine as needed. With that, you can get your hands dirty with the implementation!

INTRODUCING LATENCY

How can you introduce latency to communications? Fortunately, you don't need to lay extra miles of cable (which is a viable solution). I recommend reading *Flash Boys* by Michael Lewis (W.W. Norton & Co., 2015) if you haven't already, because Linux comes with tools that can do that for you. One of the tools is tc.

tc, which stands for Traffic Control, is a tool used to show and manipulate traffic-control settings—to effectively change how the Linux kernel schedules packets. tc is many things, but easy to use is not one of them. If you type man tc at your terminal prompt inside the VM, you will be greeted with the output that follows (abbreviated). Note that the mysterious-sounding *qdisc* is a *queueing discipline* (scheduler), which has nothing to do with disks:

```
NAME
       tc - show / manipulate traffic control settings

SYNOPSIS
       tc  [ OPTIONS ] qdisc [ add | change | replace | link | delete ] dev
DEV [ parent qdisc-id | root ] [ handle qdisc-id ] [
       ingress_block BLOCK_INDEX ] [ egress_block BLOCK_INDEX ] qdisc [
qdisc specific parameters ]

(...)

       OPTIONS  := { [ -force ] -b[atch] [ filename ] | [ -n[etns] name ]
| [ -nm | -nam[es] ] | [ { -cf | -c[onf] } [ filename
       ] ] [ -t[imestamp] ] | [ -t[short] | -o[neline] ] }
```

```
        FORMAT := { -s[tatistics] | -d[etails] | -r[aw] | -i[ec] | -g[raph]
| -j[json] | -p[retty] | -col[or] }
```

Let's learn how to use `tc` by example and see how to add latency to something unrelated to our setup. Take a look at the `ping` command. `ping` is often used to see the connectivity (whether a certain host is reachable) and quality (the speed) of a connection. It uses the Internet Control Message Protocol (ICMP) and works by sending an `ECHO_REQUEST` datagram and expecting an `ECHO_RESPONSE` from a host or gateway in response. It's widely available in every Linux distro, as well as other operating systems.

Let's see how long it takes to ping google.com. Run the following command at your terminal prompt. It will try to execute three pings and then print statistics and exit:

```
ping -c 3 google.com
```

You will see output similar to the following (times are in bold). In this example, for the three pings, it took between 4.28 ms (minimum) and 28.263 ms (maximum), for an average of 14.292 ms. That's not too bad for free café Wi-Fi!

```
PING google.com (216.58.206.110) 56(84) bytes of data.
64 bytes from lhr25s14-in-f14.1e100.net (216.58.206.110):
icmp_seq=1 ttl=63 time=4.28 ms
64 bytes from lhr25s14-in-f14.1e100.net (216.58.206.110):
icmp_seq=2 ttl=63 time=28.3 ms
64 bytes from lhr25s14-in-f14.1e100.net (216.58.206.110):
icmp_seq=3 ttl=63 time=10.3 ms

--- google.com ping statistics ---
3 packets transmitted, 3 received, 0% packet loss, time 6ms
rtt min/avg/max/mdev = 4.281/14.292/28.263/10.183 ms
```

Now, let's use `tc` to add a static 500 ms delay to all connections across the board. You can do that by issuing the following command at the prompt. The command will add the delay to the device `eth0`, the main interface in our VM:

```
sudo tc qdisc add dev eth0 root netem delay 500ms
```

To confirm that it worked, let's rerun the `ping` command at the prompt:

```
ping -c 3 google.com
```

This time, the output looks different, similar to the following. Notice that the times are all greater than 500 ms, confirming that the `tc` command did its job. Once again, bold font highlights the times:

```
PING google.com (216.58.206.110) 56(84) bytes of data.
64 bytes from lhr25s14-in-f14.1e100.net (216.58.206.110):
icmp_seq=1 ttl=63 time=512 ms
64 bytes from lhr25s14-in-f14.1e100.net (216.58.206.110):
icmp_seq=2 ttl=63 time=528 ms
```

```
64 bytes from lhr25s14-in-f14.1e100.net (216.58.206.110):
icmp_seq=3 ttl=63 time=523 ms

--- google.com ping statistics ---
3 packets transmitted, 3 received, 0% packet loss, time 4ms
rtt min/avg/max/mdev = 512.369/521.219/527.814/6.503 ms
```

Finally, you can remove the latency by running the following command at the prompt:

```
sudo tc qdisc del dev eth0 root
```

Once that's done, it's worth confirming that it works as before by rerunning the ping command and verifying that the times are back to normal. Good—you have a new tool in the toolbox. Let's use it to implement our chaos experiment!

Pop quiz: What can Traffic Control (tc) not do for you?
Pick one:

1 Introduce all kinds of slowness on network devices
2 Introduce all kinds of failure on network devices
3 Give you permission for landing the aircraft

See appendix B for answers.

IMPLEMENTATION

You should now be well equipped to implement our chaos experiment. Let's start by reestablishing our steady state. As in the previous experiment, you can do that by using the ab command. Run the following command at the prompt:

```
ab -t 30 -c 1 -l http://localhost/blog/
```

You will see output similar to the following (again, abbreviated for clarity). The average time per request is 11.583 ms:

```
(...)
Time per request:        11.583 [ms] (mean, across all concurrent requests)
(...)
```

Let's now use tc to introduce the delay of 2000 ms, in a similar fashion to the previous example. But this time, instead of applying the delay to a whole interface, you'll target only a single program—the MySQL database. How can you add the latency to the database only? This is something that's going to be much easier to deal with after we cover Docker in chapter 5, but for now you're going to have to solve that manually.

The syntax of tc looks obscure at first. I would like you to see it so you can appreciate how much easier it will be when you use higher-level tools in later chapters. We won't go into much detail here (learn more at https://lartc.org/howto/lartc.qdisc .classful.html), but `tc` lets you build tree-like hierarchies, where packets are matched and routed using various queueing disciplines.

To apply the delay to only your database, the idea is to match the packets going there by destination port, and leave all others untouched. Figure 4.3 depicts the kind of structure we're going to build. The root (`1:`) is replaced with a `prio` qdisc, which has three *bands* (think of them as three possible ways a packet can go from there): `1:1`, `1:2`, and `1:3`. For the band `1:1`, you match IP traffic with only destination port 3306 (MySQL), and you attach the delay of 2000 ms to it. For the band `1:2`, you match everything else. Finally, for the band `1:3`, you completely ignore it.

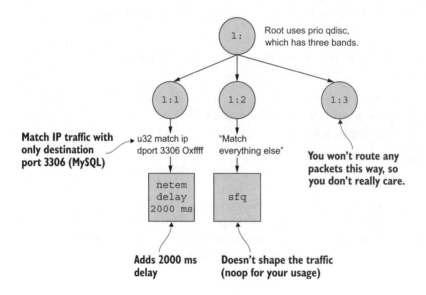

Figure 4.3   High-level hierarchy used to classify packets in `tc`

To set up this configuration, run the following commands at your prompt:

Adds a prio qdisc at the root to create the three bands: 1:1, 1:2, and 1:3

For the band 1:1, matches only IP traffic with port 3306 as the destination

```
sudo tc qdisc add dev lo root handle 1: prio
sudo tc filter add dev lo \
  protocol ip parent 1: prio 1 u32 \
  match ip dport 3306 0xffff flowid 1:1
sudo tc filter add dev lo \
  protocol all parent 1: prio 2 u32 \
  match ip dst 0.0.0.0/0 flowid 1:2
sudo tc qdisc add dev lo parent 1:1 handle 10: netem delay 2000ms
sudo tc qdisc add dev lo parent 1:2 handle 20: sfq
```

For the band 1:2, matches all other traffic

Adds 2000ms delay to band 1:1

Adds Stochastic Fairness Queueing (SFQ) qdisc (noop for our purposes) to band 1:2

That's the "meat" of our experiment. To check that it works, you can now use `telnet` to connect to localhost on port 80 (Apache2) by running the following command at your prompt:

```
telnet 127.0.0.1 80
```

You will notice no delay in establishing the connection. Similarly, run the following command at your prompt to test out connectivity to MySQL:

```
telnet 127.0.0.1 3306
```

You will notice that it takes 2 seconds to establish the connection. That's good news. You managed to successfully apply a selective delay to the database only. But if you try to rerun your benchmark, the results are not what you expect. Run the `ab` command again at the prompt to refresh your benchmark:

```
ab -t 30 -c 1 -l http://localhost/blog/
```

You will see an error message like the following. The program times out before it can produce any statistics:

```
apr_pollset_poll: The timeout specified has expired (70007)
```

You asked `ab` for a 30-second test, so a time-out means that it took longer than that to produce a response. Let's go ahead and check how much time it actually takes to generate a response with that delay. You can achieve that by issuing a single request with `curl` and timing it. Run the following command at the prompt:

```
time curl localhost/blog/
```

You should eventually get the response, and underneath see the output of the `time` command, similar to the following. It took more than 54 seconds to produce a response that used to take 11 ms on average without the delay!

```
(...)
real    0m54.330s
user    0m0.012s
sys     0m0.000s
```

To confirm that, let's remove the delay and try the `curl` command again by running the following in the terminal:

```
sudo tc qdisc del dev lo root
time curl localhost/blog/
```

The response will be immediate, similar to the times you were seeing before. What does it say about our experiment? Well, our hypothesis was just proven wrong. Adding a two-second delay in communications going to the database results in much more than a 2.5-second total response time. This is because WordPress communicates with the database multiple times, and with every communication, the delay is added. If you'd like to confirm it for yourself, rerun the `tc` commands, changing the delay to 100 ms. You will see that the total delay is a multiple of the 100 ms you add.

Don't worry, though; being wrong is good. This experiment shows that our initial conception of how the delay would work out was entirely wrong. And thanks to this experiment, you can either find the value you can withstand by playing around with different delays, or change the application to try to minimize the number of round trips and make it less fragile in the presence of delays.

I would like to plant one more thought in your head before we move on: that of testing in production.

4.3   Testing in production

I'm expecting that when you saw the delay of 54 seconds caused by the chaos experiment, you thought, "Fortunately, it's not in production." And that's a fair reaction; in many places, conducting an experiment like this in anything other than a test environment would cause a lot of pain. In fact, testing in production sounds so wrong that it's become an internet meme.

But the truth is that whatever testing we do *outside* the production environment is by definition incomplete. Despite our best efforts, the production environment will always differ from test environments:

- Data will almost always be different.
- Scale will almost invariably be different.
- User behavior will be different.
- Environment configurations will tend to drift away.

Therefore, we will never be able to produce 100% adequate tests outside production. How can we do better? In the practice of chaos engineering, working on (testing) a production system is a completely valid idea. In fact, we strive to do that. After all, it's the only place where the real system—with the real data and the real users—is. Of course, whether that's appropriate will depend on your use case, but it's something you should seriously consider. Let me show you why with an example.

Imagine you're running an internet bank and that you have an architecture consisting of various services communicating with each other. Your software goes through a simple software development life cycle:

1 Unit tests are written.
2 Feature code is written to comply with the unit tests.
3 Integration tests are run.
4 Code is deployed to a test stage.
5 More end-to-end testing is done by a QA team.
6 Code is promoted to production.

7 Traffic is progressively routed to the new software in increments of 5% of total traffic over a few days.

Now, imagine that a new release contains a bug that passes through all these stages, but will start manifesting itself only in rare network slowness conditions. This sounds like something chaos engineering was invented for, right? Yes, but if you do it only in test stages, potential issues arise:

- Test-stage hardware is using a previous generation of servers, with a different networking stack, so the same chaos experiment that would catch the bug in production wouldn't catch it in the test stage.
- Usage patterns in the test stage are different from the real user traffic, so the same chaos experiment might pass in test and fail in production.
- And so on . . .

The only way to be 100% sure something works with production traffic is to use production traffic. Should you test it in production? The decision boils down to whether you prefer the risk of hurting a portion of production traffic now, or potentially running into the bug later. And the answer to that will depend on how you see your risks. For example, it might be cheaper to uncover a problem sooner than later, even at the expense of a percentage of your users running into an issue. But equally, it might be unacceptable to fail on purpose for public image purposes. As with any sufficiently complex question, the answer is, "It depends."

Just to be perfectly clear: None of this is to say that you should skip testing your code and ship it directly in production. But with correct preemptive measures in place (to limit the blast radius), running a chaos experiment in production is a real option and can sometimes be tremendously beneficial. From now on, every time you design a chaos experiment, I would like you to ask yourself a question: "Should I do that in the production environment?"

Pop quiz: When should you test in production?
Pick one:

1 When you are short on time
2 When you want to get a promotion
3 When you've done your homework, tested in other stages, applied common sense, and see the benefits outweighing the potential problems
4 When it's failing in the test stages only intermittently, so it might just pass in production

See appendix B for answers.

Pop quiz: Which statement is true?

Pick one:

1   Chaos engineering renders other testing methods useless.
2   Chaos engineering makes sense only in production.
3   Chaos engineering is about randomly breaking things.
4   Chaos engineering is a methodology to improve your software beyond the existing testing methodologies.

See appendix B for answers.

Summary

- The Linux tool `tc` can be used to add latency to network communications.
- Network latencies between components can compound and slow the whole system significantly.
- A high-level understanding of a system is often enough to make educated guesses about useful chaos experiments.
- Experimenting (testing) in production is a real part of chaos engineering.
- Chaos engineering is not only about breaking things in production; it can be beneficial in every environment.

Part 2

Chaos engineering in action

This is where things really take off, and we start to have some real fun. Each chapter in this part zooms in on a particular stack, technology, or technique that's interesting for a chaos engineering practitioner. The chapters are reasonably independent, so you should be able to jump around as you please.

Chapter 5 takes you from a vague idea of what Docker is, to understanding how it works under the hood and testing its limitations by using chaos engineering. If you're new to Linux containers, brew double your usual amount of coffee, because we'll cover all you need to know. This is one of my favorite chapters of the book.

Chapter 6 demystifies system calls. It covers what they are, how to see applications make them, and how to block them to see how resistant to failure these applications are. This information is pretty low level, which makes it very powerful; it can be universally applied to any process.

Chapter 7 takes a stab at the Java Virtual Machine. With Java being one of the most popular programming languages ever, it's important for me to give you tools to deal with it. You'll learn how to inject code on the fly into the JVM, so that you can test how a complex application handles the types of failure you're interested in. It should super-charge your testing toolkit for the JVM.

Chapter 8 discusses when it's a good idea to bake failure directly into your application. We'll illustrate that by applying it to a very simple Python application.

Chapter 9 covers using the same chaos engineering principles at the top end of the stack—in the browser, using JavaScript. You'll take an existing open source application (pgweb) and experiment on it to see how it handles failure.

Poking Docker

This chapter covers

- What Docker is, how it works, and where it came from
- Designing chaos experiments for software running in Docker
- Performing chaos experiments on Docker itself
- Using tools like Pumba to implement chaos experiments in Docker

Oh, *Docker!* With its catchy name and lovely whale logo, Docker has become the public face of Linux containers in just a few short years since its first release in 2013. I now routinely hear things like, "Have you Dockerized it?" and, "Just build an image with that; I don't want to install the dependencies." And it's for a good reason. Docker capitalized on existing technology in the Linux kernel to offer a convenient and easy-to-use tool, ready for everyone to adopt. It played an important role in taking container technology from the arcane to the mainstream.

To be an effective chaos engineer in the containerized world, you need to understand what containers are, how to peek under the hood, and what new challenges (and wins) they present. In this chapter, we will focus on Docker, as it's the most popular container technology.

DEFINITION   What exactly is a *container*? I'll define this term shortly, but for now just know it's a construct designed to limit the resources that a particular program can access.

In this chapter, you will start by looking at a concrete example of an application running on Docker. I'll then give a brief refresher on what Docker and Linux containers are, where they came from, how to use them, and how to observe what's going on. Then you'll get your hands dirty to see what containers really contain through a series of experiments. Finally, armed with this knowledge, you'll execute chaos experiments on the application running in Docker to improve your grasp of how well it can withstand difficult conditions.

My goal is to help you demystify Docker, peek under its hood, and know how it might break. You'll even go as far as to reimplement a container solution from scratch by using what the kernel offers for free, because there is no better learning than through doing.

If this sounds exciting to you, that makes two of us! Let's get the ball rolling by looking at a concrete example of what an application running on Docker might look like.

5.1   *My (Dockerized) app is slow!*

Do you remember Meower from chapter 4, the feline transportation service? Turns out that it has been extremely successful and is now expanding to the United States, first targeting Silicon Valley. The local engineering team has been given a green light to redesign the product for US customers.

The team members decided that they wanted nothing to do with the decades-old WordPress and PHP, and decided to go down the fashionable route of Node.js. They picked Ghost (https://ghost.org/) as their new blogging engine, and decided they wanted to use Docker for its isolation properties and ease of use. Every developer can now run a mini Meower on their laptop without installing any nasty dependencies directly on the host (that's as long as you don't count Docker itself)—not even the Mac version running a Linux VM under the hood (https://docs.docker.com/docker-for-mac/docker-toolbox/)! After all, that's the least you are going to expect from a well-funded startup, now equipped with napping pods and serving free, organic, gluten-free, personalized quinoa salads to its engineers daily.

There is only one problem: just like the first version in chapter 4, the new and shiny setup has customers occasionally complaining about slowness, although from the engineering perspective, everything seems to be working fine! What's going on? Desperate for help, your manager offers you a bonus and a raise if you go to San Francisco to fix the slowness in Meower USA, just as you did in the previous chapter for Meower Glanden. SFO, here we come!

Upon arrival, having had an artisanal, responsibly sourced, quinoa sushi-burrito, you start the conversation with the engineering team by asking two pressing questions. First, how does all of it run?

5.1.1 Architecture

Ghost is a Node.js (https://nodejs.org/en/about/) application designed as a modern blogging engine. It's commonly published as a Docker image and accessible through Docker hub (https://hub.docker.com/_/ghost). It supports MySQL (www.mysql.com), as well as SQLite3 (www.sqlite.org) as the data backend.

Figure 5.1 shows the simple architecture that the Meower USA team has put in place. The team is using a third-party, enterprise-ready, cloud-certified load balancer, which is configured to hit in round-robin fashion the Ghost instances, all running on Docker. The MySQL database is also running on Docker and is used as the main datastore for Ghost to write to and read from. As you can see, the architecture is similar to the one covered in chapter 4, and in some ways simpler, because the load balancer has been outsourced to another company. But one new element is introducing its own complexity, and its name has been mentioned already multiple times in this short section: *Docker*.

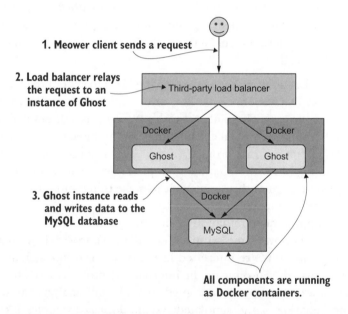

Figure 5.1 High-level overview of Meower USA technical architecture

This brings to mind your second pressing question: What's Docker again? To be able to debug and reason about any slowness of the system, you need to build an understanding of what Docker is, how it works, and what underlying technologies it leverages. So take a breath in and a step back, and let's build that knowledge right here, right now. You might want to refill your coffee first. And then let's see where Docker came from.

5.2   *A brief history of Docker*

When talking about Docker and containers, a bunch of connected (and exciting) concepts are useful to know. When speaking of them, a lot of information can get a bit fuzzy, depending on the context, so I'd like to spend a moment to layer the concepts in a logical order in your brain. Strap in; this is going to be fun. Let's start with emulation, simulation, and virtualization.

5.2.1   *Emulation, simulation, and virtualization*

An *emulator* is "hardware or software that enables one computer system (called the host) to behave like another computer system (called the guest)" (https://en.wikipedia .org/wiki/Emulator). Why would you want to do that? Well, as it turns out, it's extremely handy. Here are a few examples:

- Testing software designed for another platform without having to own the other platform (potentially rare, fragile, or expensive)
- Leveraging existing software designed for a different platform to make products backward-compatible (think new printers leveraging existing firmware)
- Running software (games, anyone?) from platforms that are no longer produced or available at all

I suspect that at least the last point might be close to the heart to a lot of readers. Emulators of consoles such as PlayStation, Game Boy, or operating systems like DOS help preserve old games and bring back good memories. When pushed, emulation also allows for more exotic applications, like emulating x86 architecture and running Linux on it . . . in JavaScript . . . in a browser (https://bellard.org/jslinux/). Emulation has a broad meaning, but without context people often mean "emulation done entirely in software" when they use this term. Now, to make things more exciting, how does emulation compare to simulation?

A *simulation* is "an approximate imitation of the operation of a process or system that represents its operation over time" (https://en.wikipedia.org/wiki/Simulation). The keyword here is *imitation*. We're interested in the behavior of the system we are simulating, but not necessarily reproducing the internals themselves, as we often do in emulation. Simulators are also typically designed to study and analyze, rather than simply replicate the behavior of the simulated system. Typical examples include a flight simulator, whereby the experience of flying a plane is approximated; or a physics simulation, in which the laws of physics are approximated to predict the way things will behave in the real world. Simulation is now so mainstream that films (*The Matrix*, anyone?) and even cartoons (*Rick and Morty*, episode 4—see http://mng.bz/YqzA) talk about it.

Finally, *virtualization* is defined as "the act of creating a virtual (rather than actual) version of something, including virtual computer hardware platforms, storage devices, and computer network resources" (https://en.wikipedia.org/wiki/Virtualization). Therefore, technically speaking, both emulation and simulation can be considered a means of achieving virtualization. A lot of amazing work has been done in this domain over the last few decades by companies such as Intel, VMware, Microsoft, Google, Sun Microsystems (now Oracle), and many more, and it's easily a topic for another book.

In the context of Docker and containers, we are most interested in *hardware virtualization* (or *platform virtualization*, which are often used interchangeably), wherein a whole hardware platform (for example, an x86 architecture computer) is virtualized. Of particular interest to us are the following two types of hardware virtualization:

- *Full virtualization* (virtual machines or VMs)—A complete simulation of the underlying hardware, which results in the creation of a virtual machine that acts like a real computer with an OS running on it.
- *OS-level virtualization* (containers)—The OS ensures isolation of various system resources from the point of view of the software, but in reality they all share the same kernel.

This is summarized by figure 5.2.

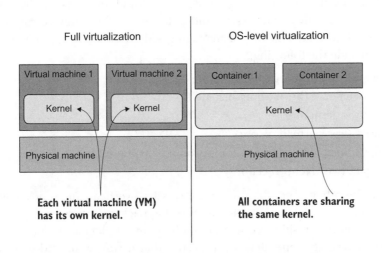

**Figure 5.2	Full virtualization versus OS-level virtualization**

Sometimes full virtualization is also referred to as *strong isolation*, and the OS-level virtualization as *lightweight isolation*. Let's take a look at how they compare side by side.

### 5.2.2	*Virtual machines and containers*

The industry uses both VMs and containers for different use cases. Either approach has its own pros and cons. For example, for a virtual machine, the pros are as follows:

- Fully isolated—more secure than containers.
- Can run a different operating system than the host.
- Can allow for better resource utilization. (The VM's unused resources can be given to another VM.)

The cons of a virtual machine include these:

- Higher overhead than a container because of operating systems running on top of each other.
- Longer startup time, due to the operating system needing to boot up.
- Typically, running a VM for a single application will result in unused resources.

In the same way, here are the pros for a container:

- Lower overhead, better performance—the kernel is shared.
- Quicker startup time.

A container has these cons:

- Bigger blast radius for security issues due to shared kernel.
- Can't run a different OS or even kernel version; it's shared across all containers.
- Often not all of the OS is virtualized, potentially resulting in weird edge cases.

Typically, VMs are used to partition larger physical machines into smaller chunks, and offer APIs to automatically create, resize, and delete VMs. The software running on the actual physical host, responsible for managing VMs, is called a *hypervisor*. Popular VM providers include the following:

- KVM (www.linux-kvm.org/page/Main_Page)
- Microsoft Hyper-V (http://mng.bz/DRD0)
- QEMU (www.qemu.org)
- VirtualBox (www.virtualbox.org)
- VMware vSphere (www.vmware.com/products/vsphere.html)
- Xen Project (www.xenproject.org)

Containers, on the other hand, thanks to their smaller overhead and quicker startup time, offer one more crucial benefit: they allow you to package and release software in a truly portable manner. Inside a container (we'll get to the details in a minute), you can add all the necessary dependencies to ensure that it runs well. And you can do that without worrying about conflicting versions or paths on filesystems. It's therefore useful to think of containers as a means of packaging software with extra benefits (we'll cover them extensively in the next section). Popular container providers include the following:

- Docker (www.docker.com)
- LXC (https://linuxcontainers.org/lxc/) and LXD (https://linuxcontainers.org/lxd/)
- Microsoft Windows containers (http://mng.bz/11Rz)

It's worth noting that VMs and containers are not necessarily exclusive; it's not unusual to run containers inside VMs. As you will see in chapter 10, it's a pretty common sight right now. In fact, we'll do exactly that later in this chapter!

Pop quiz: What's an example of OS-level virtualization?

Pick one:

1 Docker container
2 VMware virtual machine

See appendix B for answers.

Pop quiz: Which statement is true?

Pick one:

1 Containers are more secure than VMs.
2 VMs typically offer better security than containers.
3 Containers are equally secure as VMs.

See appendix B for answers.

Finally, virtualization of computer hardware has been around for a while, and various optimizations have been done. People now expect to have access to *hardware-assisted* virtualization: the hardware is designed specifically for virtualization, and the software executes approximately at the same speed as if it were run on the host directly.

VM, container, and everything in between

I've been trying to neatly categorize things, but the reality is often more complex. To quote a certain Jeff Goldblum in one of my favorite movies of all time, "Life finds a way." Here are some interesting projects on the verge of a VM and a container:

- Firecracker (https://firecracker-microvm.github.io/) used by Amazon, promises fast startup times and strong isolation microVMs, which would mean the best of both worlds.
- Kata Containers (https://github.com/kata-containers/runtime) offers hardware-virtualized Linux containers, supporting VT-x (Intel), HYP mode (ARM), and Power Systems and Z mainframes (IBM).
- UniK (https://github.com/solo-io/unik) builds applications into unikernels for building microVMs that can then be booted up on traditional hypervisors, but can boot quickly with low overhead.
- gVisor (https://github.com/google/gvisor) offers a user-space kernel, which implements only a subset of the Linux system interface, as a way of increasing the security level when running containers.

Thanks to all these amazing technologies, we now live in a world where Windows ships with a Linux kernel (http://mng.bz/BRZq), and no one bats an eye. I have to confess that I quite like this *Inception*-style reality, and I hope that I managed to get you excited as well!

Now, I'm sure you can't wait to dive deeper into the actual focus of this chapter. Time to sink our teeth into Docker.

5.3   *Linux containers and Docker*

Linux containers might look new and shiny, but the journey to where they are today took a little while. I've prepared a handy table for you to track the important events on the timeline (table 5.1). You don't have to remember these events to use containers, but it's helpful to be aware of the milestones in the context of their time, as these eventually led to (or inspired) what we call *Linux containers* today. Take a look.

Table 5.1   The chronology of events and ideas leading to the Linux containers we know today

Year	Isolation	Event
1979	Filesystem	UNIX v7 includes the chroot system call, which allows changing the root directory of a process and its children to a different location on the filesystem. Often considered the first step toward containers.
2000	Files, processes, users, networking	FreeBSD 4.0 introduces the `jail` system call, which allows for creation of mini-systems called *jails* that prevent processes from interacting with processes outside the jail they're in.
2001	Filesystems, networking, memory	Linux VServer offers a jail-like mechanism for Linux, through patching the kernel. Some system calls and parts of /proc and /sys filesystems are left not virtualized.
2002	Namespaces	Linux kernel 2.4.19 introduces *namespaces*, which control which set of resources is visible to each process. Initially just for mounts, other namespaces were gradually introduced in later versions (PID, network, cgroups, time . . .).
2004	Sandbox	Solaris releases *Solaris Containers* (also known as *Solaris Zones*), which provide isolated environments for processes within them.
2006	CPU, memory, disk I/O, network, . . .	Google launches *process containers* to limit, account for, and isolate the resource usage of groups of processes on Linux. These containers were later renamed *control groups* (or *cgroups* for short) and were merged into Linux kernel 2.6.24 in 2007.
2008	Containers	*LXC (Linux Containers)* offers the first implementation of a container manager for Linux, building on top of cgroups and namespaces.
2013	Containers	Google shares *lmctfy* (Let Me Contain That For You), its container abstraction through an API. Eventually parts of it end up being contributed to the libcontainer project.
2013	Containers	The first version of *Docker* is released, which builds on top of LXC and offers tools to build, manage, and share containers. Later, libcontainer is implemented to replace LXC (using cgroups, namespaces, and Linux capabilities). Containers start exploding in popularity as a convenient way of shipping software, with added resource management (and limited security) benefits.

Docker, through the use of libraries (previously LXC and now libcontainer), uses features of the Linux kernel to implement containers (with additions we'll look at later in the chapter). These features are as follows:

- *chroot*—Changes the root of the filesystem for a particular process
- *Namespaces*—Isolate what a container can "see" in terms of PIDs, mounts, networking, and more
- *cgroups*—Control and limit access to resources, such as CPU and RAM
- *Capabilities*—Grant subsets of superuser privileges to users, such as killing other users' processes
- *Networking*—Manages container networking through various tools
- *Filesystems*—Use Unionfs to create filesystems for containers to use
- *Security*—Uses mechanisms such as seccomp, SELinux, and AppArmor to further limit what a container can do

Figure 5.3 shows what happens when a user talks to Docker on a conceptual, simplified level.

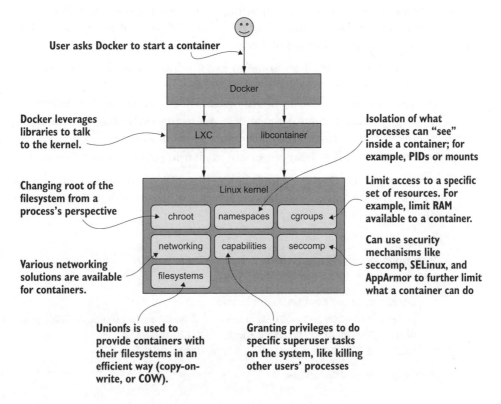

Figure 5.3 High-level overview of Docker interacting with the kernel

So if Docker relies on Linux kernel features for the heavy lifting, what does it actually offer? A whole lot of convenience, like the following:

- *Container runtime*—Program making the system calls to implement, modify, and delete containers, as well as creating filesystems and implementing networking for the containers
- dockerd—Daemon providing an API for interacting with the container runtime
- docker—Command-line client of dockerd API used by the end users
- *Dockerfile*—Format for describing how to build a container
- *Container image format*—Describing an archive containing all the files and metadata necessary to start a container based off that image
- *Docker Registry*—Hosting solution for images
- *A protocol*—For exporting (packaging into an archive), importing (pulling), and sharing (pushing) images to registries
- *Docker Hub*—Public registry where you can share your images for free

Basically, Docker made using Linux containers easy from the user's perspective by abstracting all the complicated bits away, smoothing out the rough edges, and offering standardized ways of building, importing, and exporting container images.

That's a lot of Docker lingo, so I've prepared figure 5.4 to represent that process. Let's just repeat that to let it sink in:

- A Dockerfile (you'll see some in just a minute) allows you to describe how to *build* a container.
- The container then can be exported (all its contents and metadata stored in a single archive) to an *image,* and *pushed* to the *Docker Registry*—for example, the *Docker Hub* (https://hub.docker.com/)—from where other people can *pull* it.
- Once they pull an image, they can *run* it using the command-line docker utility.

If you haven't used Docker before, don't worry. We're about to look into how all of this works and we'll also cover how to use it. And then break it. Ready to take a peek under the hood?

Pop quiz: Which statement is true?
Pick one:

1 Docker invented containers for Linux.
2 Docker is built on top of existing Linux technologies to provide an accessible way of using containers, rendering them much more popular.
3 Docker is the chosen one in *The Matrix* trilogy.

See appendix B for answers.

1. `docker build` **reads a Dockerfile and produces an image (archive with files and metadata).**

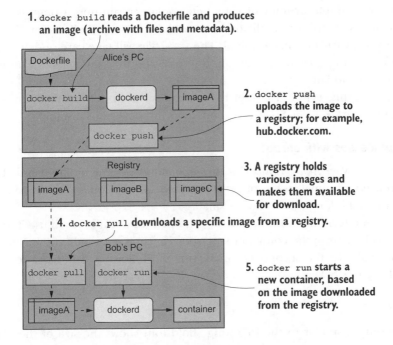

2. `docker push` **uploads the image to a registry; for example, hub.docker.com.**

3. A registry holds various images and makes them available for download.

4. `docker pull` **downloads a specific image from a registry.**

5. `docker run` **starts a new container, based on the image downloaded from the registry.**

Figure 5.4   Building, pushing, and pulling Docker images

5.4   Peeking under Docker's hood

It's time to get your hands dirty. In this section, you'll start a container and see how Docker implements the isolation and resource limits for the containers it runs. Using Docker is simple, but understanding what it does under the hood is essential for designing and executing meaningful chaos engineering experiments.

Let's begin by starting a Docker container! You can do that by running the following command in a terminal inside your VM. If you'd like to run it on a different system, you'll most likely need to prepend the following commands with sudo, since talking to the Docker daemon requires administrator privileges. The VM has been set up to not require that to save you some typing. To make things more interesting, let's start a different Linux distribution—Alpine Linux:

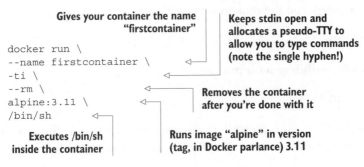

You should see a simple prompt of your new container running. Congrats! When you're done and want to stop it, all you need to do is exit the shell session. You can type exit or press Ctrl-D in this terminal. The --rm flag will take care of deleting the container after exiting, so you can start another one with the same name by using the exact same command later.

For the rest of this section, I'll refer to commands run in this terminal, inside the container, as the *first terminal*. So far, so good. Let's inspect what's inside!

5.4.1   *Uprooting processes with chroot*

What's Alpine, anyway? *Alpine Linux* (https://alpinelinux.org/) is a minimalistic Linux distro, geared for minimal usage of resources and quite popular in the container world. And I'm not joking when I say it's small.

Open a second terminal window and keep it open for a while; you'll use it to look at how things differ from the container's perspective (first terminal) and on the host (second terminal). In the second terminal, run the following command to list all images available to Docker:

```
docker images
```

You will see output similar to the following (bold font shows the size of the alpine image):

```
REPOSITORY        TAG        IMAGE ID        CREATED          SIZE
alpine            3.11       f70734b6a266    36 hours ago     5.61MB
(...)
```

As you can see, the alpine image is really small, clocking in at 5.6 MB. Now, don't take my word for it; let's confirm what we're running by checking how the distro identifies itself. You can do that by running the following command in the first terminal:

```
head -n1 /etc/issue
```

You will see the following output:

```
Welcome to Alpine Linux 3.11
```

In the second terminal, run the same command:

```
head -n1 /etc/issue
```

This time, you will see different output:

```
Ubuntu 20.04.1 LTS \n \l
```

The content of the file at the same path in the two terminals (inside the container and outside) is different. How come? In fact, the entire filesystem inside the container is *chroot'ed*, which means that the forward slash (/) inside a container is a different location on the host system.

Let me explain what I mean. Take a look at figure 5.5, which shows an example of a chroot'ed filesystem. On the left side is a host filesystem, with a folder called /fake-root-dir. On the right is an example of what the filesystem might look like from the perspective of a process chroot'ed to use /fake-root-dir as the root of its filesystem. This is exactly what you are seeing happen in the container you just started!

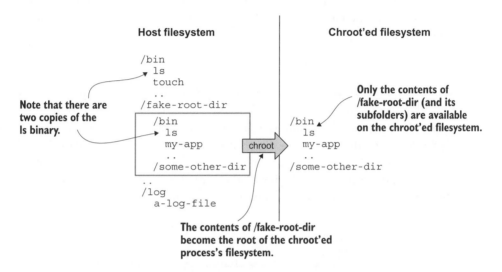

Figure 5.5 Visual example of a chroot'ed filesystem

Union filesystems, overlay2, layers, and Docker

An important part of implementing a container solution is to provide a robust mechanism for managing contents of the filesystems that the containers start with. One such mechanism, used by Docker, is a union filesystem.

In a *union filesystem*, two or more folders on a host can be transparently presented as a single, merged folder (called a *union mount*) for the user. These folders, arranged in a particular order, are called *layers*. Upper layers can "hide" lower layers' files by providing another file at the same path.

In a Docker container, by specifying the base image, you tell Docker to download all the layers that the image is made of, make a union of them, and start a container with a fresh layer on top of all of that. This allows for a reuse of these read-only layers in an efficient way, by having only a single file that can be read by all containers using that layer. Finally, if the process in the container needs to modify a file present on one of the lower layers, it is first copied in its entirety into the current layer (via copy-on-write, or COW).

> **(continued)**
>
> Overlay2 is a modern driver implementing this behavior. Learn more about how it works at http://mng.bz/rynE.

Where is the container, then? Depending on the storage settings of Docker, it might end up in different places on the host filesystem. To find out where it is, you can use a new command, `docker inspect`. It gives you all the information the Docker daemon has about a particular container. To do that, run the following command in the second terminal:

```
docker inspect firstcontainer
```

The output you're going to see is pretty long, but for now we're just interested in the `GraphDriver` section of it. See the following, abbreviated output showing just that section. The long IDs will be different in your case, but the structure and the `Name` member (overlay2, the default on the Ubuntu installation in your VM) will be the same. You will notice `LowerDir`, `UpperDir`, and `MergedDir` (bold font). These are, in respective order, the top layer of the image the container is based on, the read-write layer of the container, and the merged (union) view of the two:

```
...
      "GraphDriver": {
          "Data": {
              "LowerDir": "/var/lib/docker/overlay2/dc2…-
    init/diff:/var/lib/docker/overlay2/caf…/diff",
              "MergedDir": "/var/lib/docker/overlay2/dc2…9/merged",
              "UpperDir": "/var/lib/docker/overlay2/…/diff",
              "WorkDir": "/var/lib/docker/overlay2/dc2…/work"
          },
          "Name": "overlay2"
      },
...
```

In particular, we're interested in the `.GraphDriver.Data.MergedDir` path, which gives you the location of the container's merged filesystem. To confirm that you're looking at the same actual file, let's read the inode of the file from the outside.

To do that, still in the second terminal, run the following command. It uses the `-f` flag supported by Docker to access only a particular path in the output, as well as the `-i` flag in `ls` to print the inode number:

```
export CONTAINER_ROOT=$(docker inspect -f '{{ .GraphDriver.Data.MergedDir }}'
    firstcontainer)
sudo ls -i $CONTAINER_ROOT/etc/issue
```

You will see output similar to the following (bold font shows the inode number):

```
800436 /var/lib/docker/overlay2/dc2…/merged/etc/issue
```

Now, back in the first terminal, let's see the inode of the file from the container's perspective. Run the following command in the first terminal:

```
ls -i /etc/issue
```

The output will look similar to the following (again, bold font to show the inode):

```
800436 /etc/issue
```

As you can see, the inodes from the inside of the container and from the outside are the same; it's just that the file shows in different locations in the two scenarios. This is telling of the container's experience in general—the isolation is really thin. You'll see how that's important from the perspective of a chaos engineer in just a minute, but first, let's solidify your new knowledge about chroot by implementing a simple version of a container.

Pop quiz: What does chroot do?

Pick one:

1   Change the root user of the machine
2   Change permissions to access the root filesystem on a machine
3   Change the root of the filesystem from the perspective of a process

See appendix B for answers.

5.4.2   *Implementing a simple container(-ish) part 1: Using chroot*

I believe that there is no better way to really learn something than to try to build it yourself. Let's use what you learned about chroot and take a first step toward building a simple DIY container. Take a look at figure 5.6, which shows the parts of Docker's underlying technologies we're going to use.

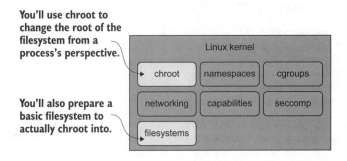

Figure 5.6   **DIY container part 1—chroot and filesystems**

As it turns out, changing the root of the filesystem for a new process is rather straightforward. In fact, you can do that with a single command, called—you guessed it— chroot.

I've prepared a simple script to demonstrate starting a process with the root of its filesystem pointing to a location of your choice. In your VM, open a terminal and type the following command to see the script:

```
cat ~/src/examples/poking-docker/new-filesystem.sh
```

You will see the following output. The command is creating a new folder, and copying over some tools and their dependencies, so that you can use it as a root filesystem. It's a very crude way of preparing a filesystem structure to be usable for a chroot'ed process. This is necessary so that you can execute something from inside the new filesystem. The only thing that you might not be familiar with here is the use of the `ldd` command, which prints shared object dependencies for binaries on Linux. These shared objects are necessary for the commands you're copying over to be able to start:

**Uses ldd to list shared libraries they need
and extract their locations to .deps**

```
#! /bin/bash

export NEW_FILESYSTEM_ROOT=${1:-~/new_filesystem}
export TOOLS="bash ls pwd mkdir ps touch rm cat vim mount"    ◁──┐ Lists some binaries
                                                                  │ you'll copy into the
echo "Step 1. Create a new folder for our new root"               │ new root
mkdir $NEW_FILESYSTEM_ROOT

echo "Step 2. Copy some (very) minimal binaries"
for tool in $TOOLS; do
    cp -v --parents `which $tool` $NEW_FILESYSTEM_ROOT;    ◁──┐ Copies the binaries,
done                                                          │ maintaining their
                                                             │ relative paths with
echo "Step 3. Copy over their libs"                          │ --parents
# use ldd to find the dependencies of the tools we've just copied
echo -n > ~/.deps
for tool in $TOOLS; do
    ldd `which $tool` | egrep -o '(/usr)?/lib.*\.[0-9][0-9]?' >> ~/.deps
done
# copy them over to our new filesystem
cp -v --parents `cat ~/.deps | sort | uniq | xargs` $NEW_FILESYSTEM_ROOT    ◁──┐

echo "Step 4. Home, sweet home"                           Copies the libraries,
NEW_HOME=$NEW_FILESYSTEM_ROOT/home/chaos                maintaining their structure
mkdir -p $NEW_HOME && echo $NEW_HOME created!
cat <<EOF > $NEW_HOME/.bashrc
echo "Welcome to the kind-of-container!"
EOF

echo "Done."                                              ┐ Prints usage
echo "To start, run: sudo chroot" $NEW_FILESYSTEM_ROOT    ◁──┘ instructions
```

Let's go ahead and run this script, passing as an argument the name of the new folder to create in your current working directory. Run the following command in your terminal:

```
bash ~/src/examples/poking-docker/new-filesystem.sh not-quite-docker
```

After it's done, you will see a new folder, not-quite-docker, with a minimal structure inside it. You can now start a chroot'ed bash session by running the following command in your terminal (sudo is required by chroot):

```
sudo chroot not-quite-docker
```

You will see a short welcome message, and you'll be in a new bash session. Go ahead and explore; you will find you can create folders and files (you copied vim over), but if you try to run ps, it will complain about the missing /proc. And it is right to complain; it's not there! The purpose here is to demonstrate to you the workings of chroot and to make you comfortable designing chaos experiments. But for the curious, you can go ahead and mount /proc inside your chrooted process by running the following commands in your terminal (outside chroot):

```
mkdir not-quite-docker/proc
sudo mount -t proc /proc/ not-quite-docker/proc
```

In the context of isolating processes, this is something you might or might not want to do. For now, treat this as an exercise or a party trick, whichever works best for you!

Now, with this new piece of knowledge that takes away some of the magic of Docker, you're probably itching to probe it a bit. If the containers are all sharing the same host filesystem and are just mounted in different locations, it should mean that one container can fill in the disk and prevent another one from writing, right? Let's design an experiment to find out!

5.4.3 Experiment 1: Can one container prevent another one from writing to disk?

Intuition hints that if all containers' filesystems are just chroot'ed locations on the host's filesystem, then one busy container filling up the host's storage can prevent all the other containers from writing to disk. But human intuition is fallible, so it's time to invite some science and design a chaos experiment.

First, you need to be able to observe a metric that quantifies "being able to write to disk." To keep it simple, I suggest you create a simple container that tries to write a file, erases it, and retries again every few seconds. You'll be able to see whether or not it can still write. Let's call that container control.

Second, define your steady state. Using your container, you'll first verify that it can write to disk.

Third, form your hypothesis. If another container (let's call it failure) consumes all available disk space until no more is left, then the control container will start failing to write.

To recap, here are the four steps to your chaos experiment:

1 Observability: a control container printing whether it can write every few seconds.
2 Steady state: the control container can write to disk.

3 Hypothesis: if another `failure` container writes to disk until it can't, the `control` container won't be able to write to disk anymore.

4 Run the experiment!

Implementation time! Let's start with the `control` container. I've prepared a small script continuously creating a 50 MB file on the disk, sleeping some, and then re-creating it indefinitely. To see it from your VM, run the following command in a terminal:

```
cat ~/src/examples/poking-docker/experiment1/control/run.sh
```

You will see the following content, a simple bash script calling out to `fallocate` to create a file:

```
#! /bin/bash
FILESIZE=$((50*1024*1024))          ⟵ Sets the size of the file
FILENAME=testfile                        to 50 MB in bytes
echo "Press [CTRL+C] to stop.."     ⟵ Gives the file you'll
while :                                  write a name
do
    fallocate -l $FILESIZE $FILENAME \
      && echo "OK wrote the file" `ls -alhi $FILENAME` \
      || echo "Couldn't write the file"          ⟵ Uses fallocate to create
    sleep 2                                          a new file of the desired
    rm $FILENAME || echo "Couldn't delete the file"  size, and prints success
done                                                 or failure messages
```

I've also prepared a sample Dockerfile to build that script into a container. You can see it by running the following command in a terminal:

```
cat ~/src/examples/poking-docker/experiment1/control/Dockerfile
```

You will see the following content. This very simple image starts from a base image of Ubuntu Focal, copies the script you've just seen, and sets that script as an entry point of the container, so that when you start it later, that script is run:

```
                    Starts from base image
                    ubuntu:focal-20200423        Copies the script run.sh
                                                 from the current working
FROM ubuntu:focal-20200423    ⟵                 directory into the container
COPY run.sh /run.sh           ⟵
ENTRYPOINT ["/run.sh"]        ⟵   Sets our newly copied script as the
                                  entry point of the container
```

The Dockerfile is a recipe for building a container. With just these two files, you can now build your first image by running the following command. Docker uses the current working directory to find files you point to in the Dockerfile, so you move to that directory first:

```
cd ~/src/examples/poking-docker/experiment1/control/
docker build \
```

```
-t experiment1-control \
.
```

Gives the container you'll build a tag, "experiment1-control"

Uses the Dockerfile in the current working directory

When you run this command, you will see the characteristic logs from Docker, in which it will pull the required base image from Docker Hub (separated in layers, the type we discussed earlier), and then run each command from the Dockerfile. Each command (or line in the Dockerfile) results in a new container. At the end, it will mark the last container with the tag you specified. You will see output similar to the following:

```
Sending build context to Docker daemon  4.608kB
Step 1/3 : FROM ubuntu:focal-20200423
focal-20200423: Pulling from library/ubuntu
d51af753c3d3: Pull complete
fc878cd0a91c: Pull complete
6154df8ff988: Pull complete
fee5db0ff82f: Pull complete
Digest:
      sha256:238e696992ba9913d24cfc3727034985abd136e08ee3067982401acdc30cbf3f
Status: Downloaded newer image for ubuntu:focal-20200423
 ---> 1d622ef86b13
Step 2/3 : COPY run.sh /run.sh
 ---> 67549ea9de18
Step 3/3 : ENTRYPOINT ["/run.sh"]
 ---> Running in e9b0ac1e77b4
Removing intermediate container e9b0ac1e77b4
 ---> c2829a258a07
Successfully built c2829a258a07
Successfully tagged experiment1-control:latest
```

Pulls the base image in the version (tag) you used as your base

Copies the script run.sh into the container's filesystem

Sets the newly copied script as the entry point of the container

Tags the built container

When that's finished, let's list the images available to Docker, which will now include our newly built image. You can list all tagged Docker images by running the following command in a terminal:

```
docker images
```

This will print output similar to the following (abbreviated to only show your new image and its base):

```
REPOSITORY            TAG              IMAGE ID       CREATED        SIZE
(...)
experiment1-control   latest           c2829a258a07   6 seconds ago  73.9MB
ubuntu                focal-20200423   1d622ef86b13   4 days ago     73.9MB
```

If this is the first Docker image you've built yourself, congratulations! Now, to our `failure` container. In a similar fashion, I've prepared another script, which tries to create as many 50 MB files as it can. You can see it by running the following command in the terminal:

```
cat ~/src/examples/poking-docker/experiment1/failure/consume.sh
```

You will see the following content, very similar to our previous script:

```
#! /bin/bash
FILESIZE=$((50*1024*1024))
FILENAME=testfile
echo "Press [CTRL+C] to stop.."
count=0
while :
do
    new_name=$FILENAME.$count
    fallocate -l $FILESIZE $new_name \
        && echo "OK wrote the file" `ls -alhi $new_name` \
        || (echo "Couldn't write " $new_name "Sleeping"; sleep 5)
    (( count++ ))
done
```

Tries to allocate a new file with a new name

On success prints a message showing the new file

On failure prints a failure message and sleeps a few seconds

Similarly, I've also prepared a Dockerfile for building the failure container in the same folder (~/src/examples/poking-docker/experiment1/failure/) with the following contents:

Starts from base image ubuntu:focal-20200423

Copies the script consume.sh from the current working directory into the container

```
FROM ubuntu:focal-20200423
COPY consume.sh /consume.sh
ENTRYPOINT ["/consume.sh"]
```

Sets our newly copied script as the entry point of the container

With that, you can go ahead and build the failure container by running the following command in a terminal window:

```
cd ~/src/examples/poking-docker/experiment1/failure/
docker build \
-t experiment1-failure \
.
```

Gives the container you'll build a tag, "experiment1-failure"

Uses the Dockerfile in the current working directory

When that's done, let's list the images available by running the following command again in a terminal:

```
docker images
```

You will see output similar to the following, once again abbreviated to show only the images relevant right now. Both our control and failure containers are present:

```
REPOSITORY            TAG             IMAGE ID       CREATED         SIZE
(...)
experiment1-failure   latest          001d2f541fb5   5 seconds ago   73.9MB
experiment1-control   latest          c2829a258a07   28 minutes ago  73.9MB
ubuntu                focal-20200423  1d622ef86b13   4 days ago      73.9MB
```

That's all you need to conduct your experiment. Now, let's prepare two terminal windows, preferably side by side, so that you can see what's happening in each window at the same time. In the first window, run your `control` container by issuing the following command:

```
docker run --rm -ti experiment1-control
```

You should see the container starting and printing a message, confirming it's able to write every couple of seconds, just like the following:

```
Press [CTRL+C] to stop..
OK wrote the file 919053 -rw-r--r-- 1 root root 50M Apr 28 09:13 testfile
OK wrote the file 919053 -rw-r--r-- 1 root root 50M Apr 28 09:13 testfile
OK wrote the file 919053 -rw-r--r-- 1 root root 50M Apr 28 09:13 testfile
(...)
```

That confirms our steady state: you are able to continuously write a 50 MB file to disk. Now, in the second window, start your `failure` container by running the following command from the second terminal window:

```
docker run --rm -ti experiment1-failure
```

You will see output similar to the following. For a few seconds, the container will be successful in writing the files, until it runs out of space and starts failing:

```
Press [CTRL+C] to stop..
OK wrote the file 919078 -rw-r--r-- 1 root root 50M Apr 28 09:21 testfile.0
OK wrote the file 919079 -rw-r--r-- 1 root root 50M Apr 28 09:21 testfile.1
(...)
OK wrote the file 919553 -rw-r--r-- 1 root root 50M Apr 28 09:21 testfile.475
fallocate: fallocate failed: No space left on device
Couldn't write the file testfile.476 Sleeping a bit
```

At the same time, in the first window, you will start seeing your `control` container failing with a message similar to the following:

```
(...)
OK wrote the file 919053 -rw-r--r-- 1 root root 50M Apr 28 09:21 testfile
OK wrote the file 919053 -rw-r--r-- 1 root root 50M Apr 28 09:21 testfile
fallocate: fallocate failed: No space left on device
Couldn't write the file
```

This confirms our hypothesis: one container can use up the space that another container would like to use in our environment. In fact, if you investigate the disk usage in your VM while the two containers are still running, you will see that the main disk is now 100% full. You can do that by running the following command in another terminal:

```
df -h
```

You will see output similar to the following (utilization of your main disk in bold):

```
Filesystem      Size  Used Avail Use% Mounted on
udev            2.0G     0  2.0G   0% /dev
tmpfs           395M  7.8M  387M   2% /run
/dev/sda1        32G   32G     0 100% /
(...)
```

If you now stop the `failure` container by pressing Ctrl-C in its window, you will see its storage removed (thanks to the `--rm` option), and in the first window, the `control` container will resume happily rewriting its file.

The takeaway here is that running programs in containers doesn't automatically prevent one process from stealing disk space from another. Fortunately, the authors of Docker thought about that, and exposed a flag called `--storage-opt size=X`. Unfortunately, when using the overlay2 storage driver, this option requires using an xfs filesystem with `pquota` option as the host filesystem (at least for the location where Docker stores its container data, which defaults to /var/lib/docker), which our VM running on default settings is not doing.

Therefore, allowing Docker containers to be limited in storage requires extra effort, which means that there is a good chance that many systems will not limit it at all. The storage driver setup requires careful consideration and will be important to the overall health of your systems.

Keeping that in mind, let's take a look at the next building block of a Docker container: the Linux namespaces.

5.4.4 *Isolating processes with Linux namespaces*

Namespaces, a feature of the Linux kernel, control which subset of resources is visible to certain processes. You can think of namespaces as filters, which control what a process can see. For example, as figure 5.7 illustrates, a resource can be visible to zero or more namespaces. But if it's not visible to the namespace, the kernel will make it look like it doesn't exist from the perspective of a process in that namespace.

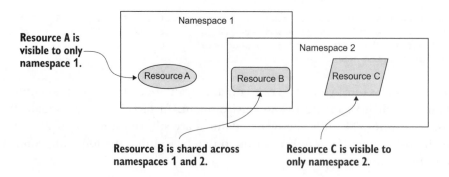

Figure 5.7 High-level idea of namespaces

Namespaces are a crucial part of the Linux container solutions, including Docker. Different types of namespaces deal with different resources. At the time of writing, the following namespaces are available:

- *Mounts* (mnt)—Controls which mounts are accessible within the namespace
- *Process ID* (pid)—Creates an independent set of PIDs for processes within the namespace
- *Network* (net)—Virtualizes the network stack, allows for network interfaces (physical or virtual) to be attached to network namespaces
- *Interprocess Communication* (ipc)—Isolates objects used for interprocess communication, System V IPC, and POSIX message queues (http://mng.bz/GxBO)
- *UTS* (uts)—Allows for different host and domain names in different namespaces
- *User ID* (user)—User identification and privilege isolation per namespace
- *Control group* (cname)—Hides the real identity of the control group the processes are a member of
- *Time* (time)—Shows different times for different namespaces

NOTE The Time namespace was introduced in version 5.6 of the Linux kernel in March 2020. Our VM, running kernel 4.18, doesn't have it yet.

By default, Linux starts with a single namespace of each type, and new namespaces can be created on the fly. You can list existing namespaces by typing the command lsns in a terminal window:

```
lsns
```

You will see output similar to the following. The command column, as well as PID, applies to the lowest PID that was started in that namespace. NPROCS shows the number of processes currently running in the namespace (from the current user perspective):

```
        NS TYPE    NPROCS   PID USER   COMMAND
4026531835 cgroup      69  2217 chaos  /lib/systemd/systemd --user
4026531836 pid         69  2217 chaos  /lib/systemd/systemd --user
4026531837 user        69  2217 chaos  /lib/systemd/systemd --user
4026531838 uts         69  2217 chaos  /lib/systemd/systemd --user
4026531839 ipc         69  2217 chaos  /lib/systemd/systemd --user
4026531840 mnt         69  2217 chaos  /lib/systemd/systemd --user
4026531993 net         69  2217 chaos  /lib/systemd/systemd --user
```

If you rerun the same command as the root user, you will see a larger set of namespaces, which are created by various components of the system. You can do that by running the following command in a terminal window:

```
sudo lsns
```

You will see output similar to the following. The important thing to note is that while there are other namespaces, the ones you saw previously are the same (they have a matching number in the column NS), although the number of processes and the lowest PID are different. In fact, you can see the PID of 1, the first process started on the host. By default, all users are sharing the same namespaces. I used bold font to point out the repeated ones.

```
        NS TYPE      NPROCS    PID USER              COMMAND
4026531835 cgroup       211      1 root              /sbin/init
4026531836 pid          210      1 root              /sbin/init
4026531837 user         211      1 root              /sbin/init
4026531838 uts          210      1 root              /sbin/init
4026531839 ipc          210      1 root              /sbin/init
4026531840 mnt          200      1 root              /sbin/init
4026531861 mnt            1     19 root              kdevtmpfs
4026531993 net          209      1 root              /sbin/init
4026532148 mnt            1    253 root              /lib/systemd/systemd-udevd
4026532158 mnt            1    343 systemd-resolve   /lib/systemd/systemd-resolved
4026532170 mnt            1    461 root              /usr/sbin/ModemManager…
4026532171 mnt            2    534 root              /usr/sbin/…
4026532238 net            1   1936 rtkit             /usr/lib/rtkit/rtkit-daemon
4026532292 mnt            1   1936 rtkit             /usr/lib/rtkit/rtkit-daemon
4026532349 mnt            1   2043 root              /usr/lib/x86_64-linux…
4026532350 mnt            1   2148 colord            /usr/lib/colord/colord
4026532351 mnt            1   3061 root              /usr/lib/fwupd/fwupd
```

lsns is pretty neat. It can do things like print out JSON (`--json` flag, good for consumption in scripts), look into only a particular type of namespace (`--type` flag), or give you the namespaces for a particular PID (`--task` flag). Under the hood, it reads from the /proc filesystem exposed by the Linux kernel—in particular, from /proc/<pid>/ns, a location that's good to know your way around.

To see what namespaces a particular process is in, you just need its PID. For the current bash session, you can access it via $$. You can check the namespaces that our bash session is in by running the following command in a terminal window:

```
ls -l /proc/$$/ns
```

You will see output similar to the following. For each type of namespace we just covered, you will see a symbolic link:

```
total 0
lrwxrwxrwx 1 chaos chaos 0 May  1 09:38 cgroup -> 'cgroup:[4026531835]'
lrwxrwxrwx 1 chaos chaos 0 May  1 09:38 ipc -> 'ipc:[4026531839]'
lrwxrwxrwx 1 chaos chaos 0 May  1 09:38 mnt -> 'mnt:[4026531840]'
lrwxrwxrwx 1 chaos chaos 0 May  1 09:38 net -> 'net:[4026531993]'
lrwxrwxrwx 1 chaos chaos 0 May  1 09:38 pid -> 'pid:[4026531836]'
lrwxrwxrwx 1 chaos chaos 0 May  1 10:11 pid_for_children -> 'pid:[…]'
lrwxrwxrwx 1 chaos chaos 0 May  1 09:38 user -> 'user:[4026531837]'
lrwxrwxrwx 1 chaos chaos 0 May  1 09:38 uts -> 'uts:[4026531838]'
```

These symbolic links are special. Try to probe them with the `file` utility by running the following command in your terminal:

```
file /proc/$$/ns/pid
```

You will see output similar to the following; it will complain that the symbolic link is broken:

```
/proc/3391/ns/pid: broken symbolic link to pid:[4026531836]
```

That's because the links have a special format: `<namespace type>:[<namespace number>]`. You can read the value of the link by running the `readlink` command in the terminal:

```
readlink /proc/$$/ns/pid
```

You will see output similar to the following. It's a namespace of type `pid` with the number `4026531836`. It's the same one you saw in the output of `lsns` earlier:

```
pid:[4026531836]
```

Now you know what namespaces are, what kinds are available, and how to see what processes belong to which namespaces. Let's take a look at how Docker uses them.

Pop quiz: What do namespaces do?

Pick one:

1 Limit what a process can see and access for a particular type of resource
2 Limit the resources that a process can consume (CPU, memory, and so forth)
3 Enforce naming conventions to avoid name clashes

See appendix B for answers.

5.4.5 Docker and namespaces

To see how Docker manages container namespaces, let's start a fresh container. You can do that by running the following command in a terminal window. Note that I'm again using a particular tag of the Ubuntu Focal image so that we use the exact same environment:

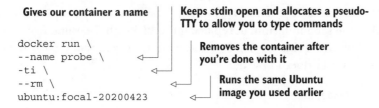

```
                                 Keeps stdin open and allocates a pseudo-
Gives our container a name       TTY to allow you to type commands

docker run \
--name probe \          ◁          Removes the container after
-ti \              ◁               you're done with it
--rm \        ◁                     Runs the same Ubuntu
ubuntu:focal-20200423  ◁           image you used earlier
```

You will enter into an interactive bash session in a new container. You can confirm that by checking the contents of /etc/issue as you did earlier in the chapter.

Now, let's see what namespaces Docker created for you. Open a second terminal window and inspect your Docker container. First, let's see the list of running containers by executing the following command in the second terminal:

```
docker ps
```

You will see output similar to the following. You are interested in the container ID (in bold font) of the container you just started (you name it probe):

```
CONTAINER ID   IMAGE                    COMMAND

91d17914dd23   ubuntu:focal-20200423    "/bin/bash"
CREATED          STATUS           PORTS     NAMES
48 seconds ago   Up 47 seconds              probe
```

Knowing its ID, let's inspect that container. Run the following command, still in the second terminal window, replacing the ID with the one you saw:

```
docker inspect 91d17914dd23
```

The output you see will be pretty long, but for now I'd like you to just focus on the State part, which will look similar to the following output. In particular, note the Pid (in bold font):

```
(...)
        "State": {
            "Status": "running",
            "Running": true,
            "Paused": false,
            "Restarting": false,
            "OOMKilled": false,
            "Dead": false,
            "Pid": 3603,
            "ExitCode": 0,
            "Error": "",
            "StartedAt": "2020-05-01T09:38:03.245673144Z",
            "FinishedAt": "0001-01-01T00:00:00Z"
        },
(...)
```

With that PID, you can list the namespaces the container is in by running the following command in the second terminal, replacing the PID with the value from your system (in bold). You are going to need to use sudo to access namespace data for a process the current user doesn't own:

```
sudo ls -l /proc/3603/ns
```

In the following output, you will see a few new namespaces, but not all of them:

```
total 0
lrwxrwxrwx 1 root root 0 May  1 09:38 cgroup -> 'cgroup:[4026531835]'
lrwxrwxrwx 1 root root 0 May  1 09:38 ipc -> 'ipc:[4026532357]'
lrwxrwxrwx 1 root root 0 May  1 09:38 mnt -> 'mnt:[4026532355]'
lrwxrwxrwx 1 root root 0 May  1 09:38 net -> 'net:[4026532360]'
lrwxrwxrwx 1 root root 0 May  1 09:38 pid -> 'pid:[4026532358]'
lrwxrwxrwx 1 root root 0 May  1 10:04 pid_for_children -> 'pid:[4026532358]'
lrwxrwxrwx 1 root root 0 May  1 09:38 user -> 'user:[4026531837]'
lrwxrwxrwx 1 root root 0 May  1 09:38 uts -> 'uts:[4026532356]'
```

You can match this output to the previous one to see which namespaces were created for the process, but that sounds laborious to me. Alternatively, you can also leverage the `lsns` command to give you output that's easier to read. Run the following command in the same terminal window (again, changing the value of the PID):

```
sudo lsns --task 3603
```

You can clearly see the new namespaces in the output, emphasized here in bold (the lowest PID is the one you are looking for):

```
        NS TYPE   NPROCS   PID USER COMMAND
4026531835 cgroup    210     1 root /sbin/init
4026531837 user      210     1 root /sbin/init
4026532355 mnt         1  3603 root /bin/bash
4026532356 uts         1  3603 root /bin/bash
4026532357 ipc         1  3603 root /bin/bash
4026532358 pid         1  3603 root /bin/bash
4026532360 net         1  3603 root /bin/bash
```

You can now kill that container (for example, by pressing Ctrl-D in the first window) because you won't be needing it anymore.

So Docker created a new namespace of each type, except for cgroup and user (we'll cover the former later in this chapter). In theory, then, from inside the container, you should be isolated from the host system in all aspects covered by the new namespaces. However, theory is often different from practice, so let's do what any self-proclaimed scientist should do; let's experiment and see how isolated we really are. Since we spoke a bit about PIDs, let's pick the pid namespace for the experiment.

5.5   *Experiment 2: Killing processes in a different PID namespace*

A fun experiment to confirm that the pid namespaces work (and that you understand how they're supposed to work!) is to start a container and try to kill a PID from outside its namespace. Observing it will be trivial (the process either gets killed or not), and our expectation is that it should not work. The whole experiment can be summarized in the following four steps:

1   Observability: checking whether the process is still running.

2   Steady state: the process is running.

3   Hypothesis: if we issue a kill command from inside the container, for a process outside the container, it should fail.

4   Run the experiment!

Easy peasy. To implement that, you'll need a practice target to kill. I've prepared one for you. You can see it by running the following command in a terminal window of your VM:

```
cat ~/src/examples/poking-docker/experiment2/pid-printer.sh
```

You will see the following output. It doesn't get much more basic than this:

```
#! /bin/bash
echo "Press [CTRL+C] to stop.."        Prints a message, includes its
while :                                 PID number, and sleeps
do
    echo `date` "Hi, I'm PID $$ and I'm feeling sleeeeeepy..." && sleep 2  ⊲
done
```

To run our experiment, you will use two terminal windows. In the first one, you'll run the target you're trying to kill, and in the second one, the container from which you'll issue the kill command. Let's start this script by running the following command in the first terminal window:

```
bash ~/src/examples/poking-docker/experiment2/pid-printer.sh
```

You will see output similar to the following, with the process printing its PID every few seconds. I used bold for the PID; copy it:

```
Press [CTRL+C] to stop..
Fri May 1 06:15:22 UTC 2020 Hi, I'm PID 9000 and I'm feeling sleeeeeepy...
Fri May 1 06:15:24 UTC 2020 Hi, I'm PID 9000 and I'm feeling sleeeeeepy...
Fri May 1 06:15:26 UTC 2020 Hi, I'm PID 9000 and I'm feeling sleeeeeepy...
```

Now, let's start a new container in a second terminal window. Start a new window and run the following command:

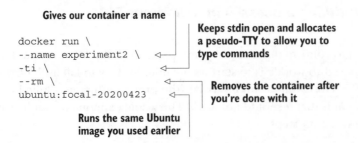

It looks like we're all set! From inside the container (the second terminal window), let's try to kill the PID that our target keeps printing. Run the following command (replace the PID with your value):

```
kill -9 9000
```

You will see in the output that the command did not find such a process:

```
bash: kill: (9000) - No such process
```

You can confirm that in the first window, your target is still running, which means that the experiment confirmed our hypothesis: trying to kill a process running outside a container's PID namespace did not work. But the error message you saw indicated that from inside the container, there was no process with a PID like that. Let's see what processes are listed from inside the container by running the following command from the second terminal window:

```
ps a
```

You will see output like the following. Only two processes are listed:

```
  PID TTY      STAT   TIME COMMAND
    1 pts/0    Ss     0:00 /bin/bash
   10 pts/0    R+     0:00 ps a
```

So as far as processes inside this container are concerned, there is no PID 9000. Or anything greater than 9000. You are done with the experiment, but I'm sure you're now curious about whether you could somehow enter the namespace of the container and start a process in there. The answer is yes.

To start a new process inside the existing container's namespace, you can use the nsenter command. It allows you to start a new process inside any of the namespaces on the host. Let's use that to attach to your container's PID namespace. I've prepared a little script for you. You can see it by running the following command inside a new terminal window (a third one):

```
cat ~/src/examples/poking-docker/experiment2/attach-pid-namespace.sh
```

You will see the following output, showcasing how to use the nsenter command:

```
#! /bin/bash
CONTAINER_PID=$(docker inspect -f '{{ .State.Pid }}' experiment2)    ◁──  Gets the PID of your container
                                                                          from 'docker inspect'
sudo nsenter \
   --pid \                                                           ... of the specified process
   --target $CONTAINER_PID \                                    ◁──  with the given PID
   /bin/bash /home/chaos/src/examples/poking-docker/experiment2/pid-
    printer.sh        ◁──
                          Executes the same bash script you previously
                          ran from the common namespace
```

Enters the pid namespace ... (arrow pointing to `--pid \` line)

Run the script with the following command:

```
bash ~/src/examples/poking-docker/experiment2/attach-pid-namespace.sh
```

You will see familiar output, similar to the following:

```
Press [CTRL+C] to stop..
Fri May 1 12:02:04 UTC 2020 Hi, I'm PID 15 and I'm feeling sleeeeeepy...
```

To confirm that you're in the same namespace, run ps again from inside the container (second terminal window):

```
ps a
```

You will now see output similar to the following, including your newly started script:

```
PID TTY       STAT    TIME COMMAND
1   pts/0     Ss      0:00 /bin/bash
15  ?         S+      0:00 /bin/bash /…/poking-docker/experiment2/pid-printer.sh
165 ?         S+      0:00 sleep 2
166 pts/0     R+      0:00 ps a
```

Finally, it's useful to know that the ps command supports printing namespaces too. You can add them by listing the desired namespaces in the -o flag. For example, to show the PID namespaces for processes on the host, run the following command from the first terminal window (from the host, not the container):

```
ps ao pid,pidns,command
```

You will see the PID namespaces along with the PID and command, similar to the following output:

```
PID    PIDNS       COMMAND
(...)
3505   4026531836  docker run --name experiment2 -ti --rm ubuntu:focal-20200423
4012   4026531836  bash /…/poking-docker/experiment2/attach-pid-namespace.sh
4039   4026531836  bash
4087   4026531836  ps o pid,pidns,command
```

> **NOTE** If you'd like to learn how to see the other namespaces a process belongs to, run the command man ps. For those of you not on Linux, man stands for *manual* and is a Linux command displaying help for different commands and system components. To use it, simply type man followed by the name of the item you're interested in (like man ps) to display help directly from the terminal. You can learn more at www.kernel.org/doc/man-pages/.

As you can see, PID namespaces are an efficient and simple-to-use way of tricking an application into thinking that it's the only thing running on the host and isolating it from seeing other processes at all. You're probably itching now to play around with it. And because I strongly believe playing is the best way to learn, let's add namespaces to our simple container(-ish) we started in section 5.4.2.

5.5.1 *Implementing a simple container(-ish) part 2: Namespaces*

It's time to upgrade your DIY container by leveraging what you've just learned—the Linux kernel namespaces. To refresh your memory on where namespaces fit, take a look at figure 5.8. We'll pick a single namespace, PID, to keep things simple and to make for nice demos.

You'll use namespaces to control what PIDs your container can see and access.

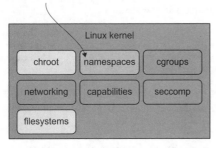

Figure 5.8   DIY container part 2—namespaces

In section 5.4.2, you used chroot to change the root mount from a process's perspective to a subfolder you've prepared that contained a basic structure of a Linux system. Let's leverage that script now and add a separate PID namespace. To create new namespaces and start processes in them, you can use the command unshare.

The syntax of unshare is straightforward: unshare [options] [program [arguments]]. It even comes with a useful example in its man pages (run man unshare in a terminal to display it), which shows you how to start a process in a new PID namespace. For example, if you want to start a new bash session, you can run the following command in a new terminal window:

```
sudo unshare --fork --pid --mount-proc /bin/bash
```

You will see a new bash session in a new PID namespace. To see what PID your bash (thinks it) has, run the following command in that new bash session:

```
ps
```

You will see output similar to the following. The bash command displays a PID of 1:

```
PID TTY          TIME CMD
  1 pts/3    00:00:00 bash
 18 pts/3    00:00:00 ps
```

Now, you can put together unshare and chroot (from section 5.4.2) to get closer to a real Linux container. I've prepared a script that does that for your convenience. You can see it by running the following command in a terminal window of your VM:

```
cat ~/src/examples/poking-docker/container-ish.sh
```

You will see the following output. It's a very basic script with essentially two important steps:

1 Call the previous new-filesystem.sh script to create your structure and copy some tools over to it.
2 Call the unshare command with the --pid flag, which calls chroot, which in turn calls bash. The bash program starts by mounting /proc from inside the container and then starts an interactive session.

The unshare command starts a process in a different namespace.

Runs the new-filesystem.sh script, which copies some basic binaries and their libraries

```
#! /bin/bash
CURRENT_DIRECTORY="$(dirname "${0}")"
FILESYSTEM_NAME=${1:-container-attempt-2}

# Step 1: execute our familiar new-filesystem script
bash $CURRENT_DIRECTORY/new-filesystem.sh $FILESYSTEM_NAME
cd $FILESYSTEM_NAME

# Step 2: create a new pid namespace, and start a chrooted bash session
sudo unshare \
    --fork \
    --pid \
    chroot . \
    /bin/bash -c "mkdir -p /proc && /bin/mount -t proc proc /proc &&
exec /bin/bash"
```

Forking is required for pid namespace change to work.

Creates a new pid namespace for the new process

Calls chroot to change the root of the filesystem for the new process you start

Mounts /proc from inside the container (for example, to make ps work) and runs bash

Let's use that script by running the following command in a new terminal window. The command will create a folder for the container(-ish) in the current directory:

```
bash ~/src/examples/poking-docker/container-ish.sh a-bit-closer-to-docker
```

You will see the greetings and a new bash session. To confirm that you successfully created a new namespace, let's see the output of ps. Run the following command from inside your new bash session:

```
ps aux
```

It will print the following list. Note that your bash claims to have the PID of 1 (bold).

USER	PID	%CPU	%MEM	VSZ	RSS	TTY	STAT	START	TIME	COMMAND
0	**1**	0.0	0.0	10052	3272	?	S	11:54	0:00	/bin/bash
0	4	0.0	0.0	25948	2568	?	R+	11:55	0:00	ps aux

Finally, while your kind-of-container is still running, open another terminal window and confirm that you can see the new namespace of type PID by running the following command:

```
sudo lsns -t pid
```

You will see output similar to the following (the new namespace is in bold font):

```
        NS TYPE NPROCS    PID USER COMMAND
4026531836 pid      211      1 root /sbin/init
4026532173 pid        1  24935 root /bin/bash
```

As you've seen before, Docker creates other types of namespaces for its containers, not just PID. In this example, we focus on the PID, because it's easy to demonstrate and helps with learning. I'm leaving tinkering with the other ones as an exercise for you.

Having demystified namespaces, let's now move on to the next piece of the puzzle. Let's take a look at how Docker restricts the amount of resources containers can use through cgroups.

5.5.2 Limiting resource use of a process with cgroups

Control groups, or *cgroups* for short, are a feature of the Linux kernel that allows for organizing processes into hierarchical groups and then limiting and monitoring their usage of various types of resources, such as CPU and RAM. Using cgroups allows you, for example, to tell the Linux kernel to give only a certain percentage of CPU to a particular process.

Figure 5.9 illustrates what limiting a process to 50% of a core looks like visually. On the left side, the process is allowed to use as much CPU as there is available. On the right side, a limit of 50% is enforced, and the process is throttled if it ever tries to use more than 50%.

How do you interact with cgroups? Kernel exposes a pseudo-filesystem called cgroupfs for managing the cgroups hierarchy, usually mounted at /sys/fs/cgroup.

> **NOTE** Two versions of cgroups are available, v1 and v2. V1 evolved over the years in a mostly uncoordinated, organic fashion, and v2 was introduced to reorganize, simplify, and remove some of the inconsistencies in v1. At the time of writing, most of the ecosystem still uses v1, or at least defaults to it, while support for v2 is being worked on (for example, the work for Docker via runc is tracked in this issue https://github.com/opencontainers/runc/issues/2315). You can read more about the differences between the two versions at http://mng.bz/zxeQ. We'll stick to v1 for the time being.

Cgroups have the concept of a controller for each type of supported resource. To check the currently mounted and available types of controllers, run the following command in a terminal inside your VM:

```
ls -al /sys/fs/cgroup/
```

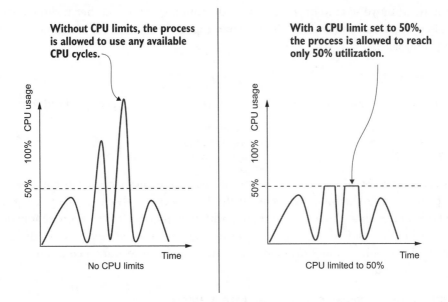

Figure 5.9   An example of CPU limiting possible with cgroups

You will see output similar to the following. We are going to cover two controllers: cpu and memory (in bold). Note that cpu is actually a link to cpu, cpuacct, a controller responsible for both limiting and accounting for CPU usage. Also, unified is where groups v2 are mounted, if you're curious to play with that as an exercise:

```
total 0
drwxr-xr-x 15 root root 380 May  2 14:23 .
drwxr-xr-x  9 root root   0 May  3 12:26 ..
dr-xr-xr-x  5 root root   0 May  3 12:26 blkio
lrwxrwxrwx  1 root root  11 May  2 14:23 cpu -> cpu,cpuacct
lrwxrwxrwx  1 root root  11 May  2 14:23 cpuacct -> cpu,cpuacct
dr-xr-xr-x  5 root root   0 May  3 12:26 cpu,cpuacct
dr-xr-xr-x  3 root root   0 May  3 12:26 cpuset
dr-xr-xr-x  5 root root   0 May  3 12:26 devices
dr-xr-xr-x  3 root root   0 May  3 12:26 freezer
dr-xr-xr-x  3 root root   0 May  3 12:26 hugetlb
dr-xr-xr-x  5 root root   0 May  3 12:26 memory
lrwxrwxrwx  1 root root  16 May  2 14:23 net_cls -> net_cls,net_prio
dr-xr-xr-x  3 root root   0 May  3 12:26 net_cls,net_prio
lrwxrwxrwx  1 root root  16 May  2 14:23 net_prio -> net_cls,net_prio
dr-xr-xr-x  3 root root   0 May  3 12:26 perf_event
dr-xr-xr-x  5 root root   0 May  3 12:26 pids
dr-xr-xr-x  2 root root   0 May  3 12:26 rdma
dr-xr-xr-x  6 root root   0 May  3 12:26 systemd
dr-xr-xr-x  5 root root   0 May  3 12:26 unified
```

You might recall two tools from chapter 3 that you can use to create cgroups and run programs within them: cgcreate and cgexec. These are convenient to use, but I'd like to show you how to interact with cgroupfs directly. When practicing chaos engineering on systems leveraging Docker, you must understand and be able to observe the limits that your applications are running with.

Creating a new cgroup of a particular type consists of creating a folder (or subfolder for nested cgroups) under /sys/fs/cgroup/<type of the resource>/. For example, Docker creates its parent cgroup, under which the containers are then nested. Let's take a look at the contents of the CPU cgroup. You can do that by running the following command in a terminal window:

```
ls -l /sys/fs/cgroup/cpu/docker
```

You will see a list just like the following one. For our needs, we'll pay attention to cpu.cfs_period_us, cpu.cfs_quota_us, and cpu.shares, which represent two ways cgroups offer to restrict CPU utilization of a process:

```
-rw-r--r-- 1 root root 0 May  3 12:44 cgroup.clone_children
-rw-r--r-- 1 root root 0 May  3 12:44 cgroup.procs
-r--r--r-- 1 root root 0 May  3 12:44 cpuacct.stat
-rw-r--r-- 1 root root 0 May  3 12:44 cpuacct.usage
-r--r--r-- 1 root root 0 May  3 12:44 cpuacct.usage_all
-r--r--r-- 1 root root 0 May  3 12:44 cpuacct.usage_percpu
-r--r--r-- 1 root root 0 May  3 12:44 cpuacct.usage_percpu_sys
-r--r--r-- 1 root root 0 May  3 12:44 cpuacct.usage_percpu_user
-r--r--r-- 1 root root 0 May  3 12:44 cpuacct.usage_sys
-r--r--r-- 1 root root 0 May  3 12:44 cpuacct.usage_user
-rw-r--r-- 1 root root 0 May  3 12:44 cpu.cfs_period_us
-rw-r--r-- 1 root root 0 May  3 12:44 cpu.cfs_quota_us
-rw-r--r-- 1 root root 0 May  3 12:44 cpu.shares
-r--r--r-- 1 root root 0 May  3 12:44 cpu.stat
-rw-r--r-- 1 root root 0 May  3 12:44 notify_on_release
-rw-r--r-- 1 root root 0 May  3 12:44 tasks
```

The first way is to set exactly the ceiling for the number of microseconds of CPU time that a particular process can get within a particular period of time. This is done by specifying the values for cpu.cfs_period_us (the period in microseconds) and cpu.cfs_quota_us (the number of microseconds within that period that the process can consume). For example, to allow a particular process to consume 50% of a CPU, you could give cpu.cfs_period_us a value of 1000, and cpu.cfs_quota_us a value of 500. A value of -1, which means no limitation, is the default. It's a hard limit.

The other way is through CPU shares (cpu.shares). The shares are arbitrary values representing a relative weight of the process. Thus, the same value means the same amount of CPU for every process, a higher value will increase the percentage of available time a process is allowed, and a lower value will decrease it. The value defaults to a rather arbitrary, round number of 1024. It's worth noting that the setting is enforced only when there isn't enough CPU time for everyone; otherwise, it has no effect. It's essentially a soft limit.

Now, let's see what Docker sets up for a new container. Start a container by running the following command in a terminal window:

```
docker run -ti --rm ubuntu:focal-20200423
```

Once inside the container, start a long-running process so that you can identify it easily later. Run the following command from inside the container to start a sleep process (doing nothing but existing) for 3600 seconds:

```
sleep 3600
```

While that container is running, let's use another terminal window to again check the cgroupfs folder that Docker maintains. Run the following command in that second terminal window:

```
ls -l /sys/fs/cgroup/cpu/docker
```

You will see familiar output, just like the following. Note that there is a new folder with a name corresponding to the container ID (in bold):

```
total 0
drwxr-xr-x 2 root root 0 May  3 22:21
      87a692e9f2b3bac1514428954fd2b8b80c681012d92d5ae095a10f81fb010450
-rw-r--r-- 1 root root 0 May  3 12:44 cgroup.clone_children
-rw-r--r-- 1 root root 0 May  3 12:44 cgroup.procs
-r--r--r-- 1 root root 0 May  3 12:44 cpuacct.stat
-rw-r--r-- 1 root root 0 May  3 12:44 cpuacct.usage
-r--r--r-- 1 root root 0 May  3 12:44 cpuacct.usage_all
-r--r--r-- 1 root root 0 May  3 12:44 cpuacct.usage_percpu
-r--r--r-- 1 root root 0 May  3 12:44 cpuacct.usage_percpu_sys
-r--r--r-- 1 root root 0 May  3 12:44 cpuacct.usage_percpu_user
-r--r--r-- 1 root root 0 May  3 12:44 cpuacct.usage_sys
-r--r--r-- 1 root root 0 May  3 12:44 cpuacct.usage_user
-rw-r--r-- 1 root root 0 May  3 12:44 cpu.cfs_period_us
-rw-r--r-- 1 root root 0 May  3 12:44 cpu.cfs_quota_us
-rw-r--r-- 1 root root 0 May  3 12:44 cpu.shares
-r--r--r-- 1 root root 0 May  3 12:44 cpu.stat
-rw-r--r-- 1 root root 0 May  3 12:44 notify_on_release
-rw-r--r-- 1 root root 0 May  3 12:44 tasks
```

To make things easier, let's just store that long container ID in an environment variable. Do that by running the following command:

```
export
CONTAINER_ID=87a692e9f2b3bac1514428954fd2b8b80c681012d92d5ae095a10f81fb010450
```

Now, list the contents of that new folder by running the following command:

```
ls -l /sys/fs/cgroup/cpu/docker/$CONTAINER_ID
```

You will see output similar to the following, with the now familiar structure. This time, I would like you to pay attention to cgroup.procs (in bold), which holds a list of PIDs of processes within this cgroup:

```
total 0
-rw-r--r-- 1 root root 0 May  3 22:43 cgroup.clone_children
-rw-r--r-- 1 root root 0 May  3 22:21 cgroup.procs
-r--r--r-- 1 root root 0 May  3 22:43 cpuacct.stat
-rw-r--r-- 1 root root 0 May  3 22:43 cpuacct.usage
-r--r--r-- 1 root root 0 May  3 22:43 cpuacct.usage_all
-r--r--r-- 1 root root 0 May  3 22:43 cpuacct.usage_percpu
-r--r--r-- 1 root root 0 May  3 22:43 cpuacct.usage_percpu_sys
-r--r--r-- 1 root root 0 May  3 22:43 cpuacct.usage_percpu_user
-r--r--r-- 1 root root 0 May  3 22:43 cpuacct.usage_sys
-r--r--r-- 1 root root 0 May  3 22:43 cpuacct.usage_user
-rw-r--r-- 1 root root 0 May  3 22:43 cpu.cfs_period_us
-rw-r--r-- 1 root root 0 May  3 22:43 cpu.cfs_quota_us
-rw-r--r-- 1 root root 0 May  3 22:43 cpu.shares
-r--r--r-- 1 root root 0 May  3 22:43 cpu.stat
-rw-r--r-- 1 root root 0 May  3 22:43 notify_on_release
-rw-r--r-- 1 root root 0 May  3 22:43 tasks
```

Let's investigate the processes contained in that cgroup.procs file. You can do that by running the following command in a terminal window:

```
ps -p $(cat /sys/fs/cgroup/cpu/docker/$CONTAINER_ID/cgroup.procs)
```

You will see the container's bash session, as well as the sleep you started earlier, just like the following:

```
  PID TTY      STAT   TIME COMMAND
28960 pts/0    Ss     0:00 /bin/bash
29199 pts/0    S+     0:00 sleep 3600
```

Let's also check the default values our container started with. In the same subdirectory, you will see the following default values. They indicate no hard limit and the default weight:

- cpu.cfs_period_us—Set to 100000.
- cpu.cfs_quota_us—Set to -1.
- cpu.shares—Set to 1024.

Similarly, you can peek into the default values set for memory usage. To do that, let's explore the memory part of the tree by running the following command:

```
ls -l /sys/fs/cgroup/memory/docker/$CONTAINER_ID/
```

This will print a list similar to the following. Note the memory.limit_in_bytes (which sets the hard limit of RAM accessible to the process) and memory.usage_in_bytes (which shows the current RAM utilization):

```
total 0
-rw-r--r-- 1 root root 0 May  3 23:04 cgroup.clone_children
--w--w--w- 1 root root 0 May  3 23:04 cgroup.event_control
-rw-r--r-- 1 root root 0 May  3 22:21 cgroup.procs
-rw-r--r-- 1 root root 0 May  3 23:04 memory.failcnt
--w------- 1 root root 0 May  3 23:04 memory.force_empty
-rw-r--r-- 1 root root 0 May  3 23:04 memory.kmem.failcnt
-rw-r--r-- 1 root root 0 May  3 23:04 memory.kmem.limit_in_bytes
-rw-r--r-- 1 root root 0 May  3 23:04 memory.kmem.max_usage_in_bytes
-r--r--r-- 1 root root 0 May  3 23:04 memory.kmem.slabinfo
-rw-r--r-- 1 root root 0 May  3 23:04 memory.kmem.tcp.failcnt
-rw-r--r-- 1 root root 0 May  3 23:04 memory.kmem.tcp.limit_in_bytes
-rw-r--r-- 1 root root 0 May  3 23:04 memory.kmem.tcp.max_usage_in_bytes
-r--r--r-- 1 root root 0 May  3 23:04 memory.kmem.tcp.usage_in_bytes
-r--r--r-- 1 root root 0 May  3 23:04 memory.kmem.usage_in_bytes
-rw-r--r-- 1 root root 0 May  3 23:04 memory.limit_in_bytes
-rw-r--r-- 1 root root 0 May  3 23:04 memory.max_usage_in_bytes
-rw-r--r-- 1 root root 0 May  3 23:04 memory.move_charge_at_immigrate
-r--r--r-- 1 root root 0 May  3 23:04 memory.numa_stat
-rw-r--r-- 1 root root 0 May  3 23:04 memory.oom_control
---------- 1 root root 0 May  3 23:04 memory.pressure_level
-rw-r--r-- 1 root root 0 May  3 23:04 memory.soft_limit_in_bytes
-r--r--r-- 1 root root 0 May  3 23:04 memory.stat
-rw-r--r-- 1 root root 0 May  3 23:04 memory.swappiness
-r--r--r-- 1 root root 0 May  3 23:04 memory.usage_in_bytes
-rw-r--r-- 1 root root 0 May  3 23:04 memory.use_hierarchy
-rw-r--r-- 1 root root 0 May  3 23:04 notify_on_release
-rw-r--r-- 1 root root 0 May  3 23:04 tasks
```

If you check the contents of these two files, you will see the following values:

- memory.limit_in_bytes set to 9223372036854771712, which seems to be a max number for a 64-bit int, minus a page size, or effectively representing infinity
- memory.usage_in_bytes, which happens to read 1445888 for me (or ~1.4 MB)

Although memory.usage_in_bytes is read-only, you can modify memory.limit_in_bytes by simply writing to it. For example, to impose a 20 MB memory limit on your container, run the following command:

```
echo 20971520 | sudo tee
/sys/fs/cgroup/memory/docker/$CONTAINER_ID/memory.limit_in_bytes
```

This covers what you need to know about cgroups for now. You can exit the container you were running by pressing Ctrl-D. For more detailed information about cgroups, you can always run man cgroups. Let's put this new knowledge to use and run some experiments!

Pop quiz: What do cgroups do?

Pick one:

1   Give extra control powers to groups of users
2   Limit what a process can see and access for a particular type of resource
3   Limit the resources that a process can consume (CPU, memory, and so forth)

See appendix B for answers.

5.6   *Experiment 3: Using all the CPU you can find!*

Docker offers two ways of controlling the amount of CPU a container gets to use, which are analogous to the approaches covered in the previous section. First, the `--cpus` flag controls the hard limit. Setting it to `--cpus=1.5` is equivalent to setting the period to 100,000 and the quota to 150,000. Second, through the `--cpu-shares`, we can give our process a relative weight.

Let's test the first one with the following experiment:

1   Observability: observe the amount of CPU used by the `stress` command, using `top` or `mpstat`.
2   Steady state: CPU utilization close to 0.
3   Hypothesis: if we run `stress` in CPU mode, in a container started with `--cpus =0.5`, it will use no more than 0.5 processor on average.
4   Run the experiment!

Let's start by building a container with the `stress` command inside it. I've prepared a simple Dockerfile for you that you can see by running the following command in a terminal window:

```
cat ~/src/examples/poking-docker/experiment3/Dockerfile
```

You will see the following output, a very basic Dockerfile containing a single command:

```
FROM ubuntu:focal-20200423

RUN apt-get update && apt-get install -y stress
```

Let's build a new image called `stressful` by using that Dockerfile. Run the following command in a terminal window:

```
cd ~/src/examples/poking-docker/experiment3/
docker build -t stressful .
```

After a few seconds, you should be able to see the new image in the list of Docker images. You can see it by running the following command:

```
docker images
```

You will see the new image (in bold) in the output, similar to the following:

```
REPOSITORY     AG          IMAGE ID          CREATED          SIZE
stressful      latest      9853a9f38f1c      5 seconds ago    95.9MB
(...)
```

Now, let's set up our working space. To make things easy, try to have two terminal windows open side by side. In the first one, start the container in which to use the `stress` command, as follows:

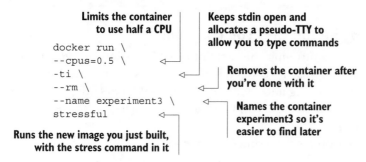

In the second terminal window, let's start monitoring the CPU usage of the system. Run the following command in the second window:

```
mpstat -u -P ALL 2
```

You should start seeing updates similar to the following, every 2 seconds. My VM is running with two CPUs, and so should yours if you're running the default values. Also, `%idle` is around 99.75%:

```
Linux 4.15.0-99-generic (linux)    05/04/2020    _x86_64_   (2 CPU)

12:22:22 AM CPU %usr   %nice %sys  %iowait %irq  %soft  %steal  %guest %gnice %idle
12:22:24 AM all 0.25   0.00  0.00  0.00    0.00  0.00   0.00    0.00   0.00   99.75
12:22:24 AM 0   0.50   0.00  0.00  0.00    0.00  0.00   0.00    0.00   0.00   99.50
12:22:24 AM 1   0.00   0.00  0.00  0.00    0.00  0.00   0.00    0.00   0.00   100.00
```

Showtime! In the first terminal, start the `stress` command:

```
stress --cpu 1 --timeout 30
```

In the second window running `mpstat`, you should start seeing one CPU at about 50% and the other one close to 0, resulting in total utilization of about 24.5%, similar to the following output:

```
12:27:21 AM  CPU  %usr   %nice %sys  %iowait %irq  %soft  %steal  %guest %gnice  %idle
12:27:23 AM  all  24.56  0.00  0.00  0.00    0.00  0.00   0.00    0.00   0.00    75.44
12:27:23 AM  0    0.00   0.00  0.00  0.00    0.00  0.00   0.00    0.00   0.00    100.00
12:27:23 AM  1    48.98  0.00  0.00  0.00    0.00  0.00   0.00    0.00   0.00    51.02
```

To confirm it in a different way, you can inspect the contents of the cpu.stat file in cgroupfs for that particular container:

```
CONTAINER_ID=$(docker inspect -f '{{ .Id }}' experiment3)
cat /sys/fs/cgroup/cpu/docker/$CONTAINER_ID/cpu.stat
```

You will see output similar to the following. Of particular interest, you will see an increasing throttled_time, which is the number of microseconds that processes in the cgroup were throttled, and nr_throttled, which is the number of periods in which throttling took place:

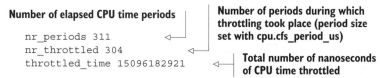

Number of elapsed CPU time periods

```
nr_periods 311
nr_throttled 304
throttled_time 15096182921
```

Number of periods during which throttling took place (period size set with cpu.cfs_period_us)

Total number of nanoseconds of CPU time throttled

That's another way of verifying that our setup worked. And work it did! Congratulations! The experiment worked; Docker did its job. If you used a higher value for the --cpu flag of the stress command, you would see the load spread across both CPUs, while still resulting in the same overall average. And if you check the cgroupfs metadata, you will see that Docker did indeed result in setting the cpu.cfs_period_us to 100000, cpu.cfs_quota_us to 50000, and cpu.shares to 1024. When you're done, you can exit the container by pressing Ctrl-D.

I wonder if it'll go as smoothly with limiting the RAM. Shall we find out?

5.7   *Experiment 4: Using too much RAM*

To limit the amount of RAM a container is allowed to use, you can use Docker's --memory flag. It accepts b (bytes), k (kilobytes), m (megabytes), and g (gigabytes) as suffixes. As an effective chaos engineering practitioner, you want to know what happens when a process reaches that limit.

Let's test it with the following experiment:

1 Observability: observe the amount of RAM used by the stress command, using top; monitor for OOM Killer logs in dmesg.
2 Steady state: no logs of killing in dmesg.
3 Hypothesis: if we run stress in RAM mode, trying to consume 512 MB, in a container started with --memory=128m, it will use no more than 128 MB of RAM.
4 Run the experiment!

Let's set up our working space again with two terminal windows open side by side. In the first one, start a container with the same image as for the previous experiment, but this time limiting the memory, not the CPU. Here is the command:

```
docker run \
--memory=128m \
-ti \
```

Limits the container to a max of 128 MB of RAM

Keeps stdin open and allocates a pseudo-TTY to allow you to type commands

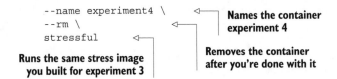

```
--name experiment4 \          ◁─┐    Names the container
--rm \                  ◁────┘ │    experiment 4
stressful      ◁──────┐        │
                      │        │
Runs the same stress image    │    Removes the container
you built for experiment 3    │    after you're done with it
```

In the second terminal window, let's first check the `dmesg` logs to see that there is nothing about OOM killing (if you've forgotten all about the OOM Killer, it's the Linux kernel feature that kills processes to recover RAM, covered in chapter 2). Run the following command in the second terminal window:

```
dmesg | egrep "Kill|oom"
```

Depending on the state of your VM machine, you might not get any results, but if you do, mark the timestamp, so that you can differentiate them from fresher logs. Now, let's start monitoring the RAM usage of the system. Run the following command in the second window:

```
top
```

You will start seeing updates of the `top` command. Observe and note the steady state levels of RAM utilization.

With that, the scene is set! Let's start the experiment by running the following command in the first terminal window, from within the container. It will run RAM workers, each allocating 512 MB of memory (bold):

```
stress \                      Runs one worker
--vm 1 \            ◁─────     allocating memory
--vm-bytes 512M \   ◁──────    Allocates 512 MB
--timeout 30        ◁─┐
                      │
                      Runs for 30 seconds
```

While that's running, you will see something interesting from the `top` command, similar to the following output. Notice that the container is using 528,152 KiB of virtual memory, and 127,400 KB of reserved memory, just under the 128 MB limit you gave to the container:

```
Tasks: 211 total,   1 running, 173 sleeping,   0 stopped,   0 zombie
%Cpu(s):  0.2 us,  0.1 sy,  0.0 ni, 99.6 id,  0.1 wa,  0.0 hi,  0.0 si,  0.0 st
KiB Mem :  4039228 total,  1235760 free,  1216416 used,  1587052 buff/cache
KiB Swap:  1539924 total,  1014380 free,   525544 used.  2526044 avail Mem

  PID USER      PR  NI    VIRT    RES    SHR S  %CPU %MEM     TIME+ COMMAND
32012 root      20   0  528152 127400    336 D  25.0  3.2   0:05.28 stress
(...)
```

After 30 seconds, the `stress` command will finish and print the following output. It happily concluded its run:

```
stress: info: [537] dispatching hogs: 0 cpu, 0 io, 1 vm, 0 hdd
stress: info: [537] successful run completed in 30s
```

Well, that's a fail for our experiment—and a learning opportunity! Things get even weirder if you rerun the `stress` command, but this time with `--vm 3`, to run three workers, each trying to allocate 512 MB. In the output of `top` (the second window), you will notice that all three workers have 512 MB of virtual memory allocated, but their total reserved memory adds up to about 115 MB, below our limit:

```
Tasks: 211 total,   1 running, 175 sleeping,   0 stopped,   0 zombie
%Cpu(s): 0.2 us, 0.1 sy, 0.0 ni, 99.6 id, 0.1 wa, 0.0 hi, 0.0 si, 0.0 st
KiB Mem :  4039228 total,  1224208 free,  1227832 used,  1587188 buff/cache
KiB Swap:  1539924 total,    80468 free,  1459456 used.  2514632 avail Mem

   PID USER       PR  NI    VIRT    RES    SHR S  %CPU %MEM     TIME+ COMMAND
 32040 root       20   0  528152  32432    336 D   6.2  0.8   0:02.22 stress
 32041 root       20   0  528152  23556    336 D   6.2  0.6   0:02.40 stress
 32042 root       20   0  528152  59480    336 D   6.2  1.5   0:02.25 stress
```

It looks like the kernel is doing something smart, because `stress` doesn't actually do anything with the allocated memory, so our initial idea for the experiment won't work. What can we do instead to see the kernel limit the amount of memory our container can use? Well, we could always use a good old fork bomb. It's for science!

Let's monitor the memory usage of the container. To do this, leverage the cgroupfs once again, this time to read the number of bytes of used memory, by running in a third terminal window the following command:

```
export CONTAINER_ID=$(docker inspect -f '{{ .Id }}' experiment4)
watch -n 1 sudo cat
    /sys/fs/cgroup/memory/docker/$CONTAINER_ID/memory.usage_in_bytes
```

And in the first terminal (inside your container) let's drop the fork bomb by running the following command. All it's doing is calling itself recursively to exhaust the available resources:

```
boom () {
  boom | boom &
}; boom
```

Now, in the third terminal, you will see that the number of bytes used is oscillating somewhere just above 128 MB, slightly more than the limit that you gave to the container. In the second window, running `top`, you're likely to see something similar to the following output. Note the very high CPU system time percentage (in bold).

```
Tasks: 1173 total, 131 running, 746 sleeping,   0 stopped, 260 zombie
%Cpu(s):  6.3 us, 89.3 sy,  0.0 ni,  0.0 id,  0.8 wa,  0.0 hi,  3.6 si,  0.0 st
```

In the first window, inside the container, you will see bash failing to allocate memory:

```
bash: fork: Cannot allocate memory
```

If the container hasn't been killed by the OOM Killer, you can stop it by running the following command in a terminal window:

```
docker stop experiment4
```

Finally, let's check the `dmesg` for OOM logs by running the following command:

```
dmesg | grep Kill
```

You will see output similar to the following. The kernel notices the cgroup is out of memory, and kicks in to kill some of the processes within it. But because our fork bomb managed to start a few thousand processes, it actually takes a non-negligible amount of CPU power for the OOM Killer to do its thing:

```
[133039.835606] Memory cgroup out of memory: Kill process 1929 (bash) score 2
    or sacrifice child
[133039.835700] Killed process 10298 (bash) total-vm:4244kB, anon-rss:0kB,
    file-rss:1596kB, shmem-rss:0kB
```

Once again a failed experiment teaches us more than a successful one. What did you learn? A few interesting bits of information:

- Just allocating the memory doesn't trigger the OOM Killer, and you can successfully allocate much more memory than the cgroup allows for.
- When using a fork bomb, the total of the memory used by your forks was slightly higher than the limit allocated to the container, which is useful when doing capacity planning.
- The cost of running the OOM Killer when dealing with a fork bomb is non-negligeable and can actually be pretty high. If you've done your math when allocating resources, it might be worth considering disabling OOM Killer for the container through the `--oom-kill-disable` flag.

Now, armed with that new knowledge, let's revisit for the third—and final—time our bare-bones container(-ish) implementation.

5.7.1 *Implementing a simple container(-ish) part 3: Cgroups*

In part 2 of the miniseries on a DIY container, you reused the script that prepared a filesystem, and you started chroot from within a new namespace. Now, to limit the amount of resources your container-ish can use, you can leverage the cgroups you just learned about.

To keep things simple, let's focus on just two cgroup types: memory and CPU. To refresh your memory on how this fits in the big picture, take a look at figure 5.10. It shows where cgroups fit with the other underlying technology in the Linux kernel that Docker leverages.

Now, let's put to use everything you've learned in the previous section. To create a new cgroup, all you need to do is create a new folder in the corresponding cgroupfs

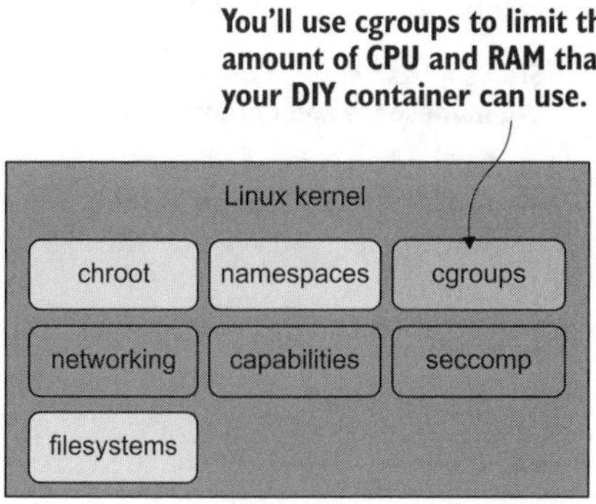

You'll use cgroups to limit the amount of CPU and RAM that your DIY container can use.

Figure 5.10　DIY container part 3—cgroups

filesystem. To configure the cgroup, you'll put the values you want in the files you've looked at in the previous section. And to add a new process to that filesystem, you'll add your bash process to it by writing to the tasks file. All the children of that process will then automatically be included in there. And voilà!

I've prepared a script that does that. You can see it by running the following command in a terminal window inside your VM:

```
cat ~/src/examples/poking-docker/container-ish-2.sh
```

You will see the following output. You reuse, once again, the filesystem prep script from part 1 of this series, and create and configure two new cgroups of type cpu and memory. Finally, we start the new process by using unshare and chroot, exactly the same way as in part 2:

```
#! /bin/bash
set +x

CURRENT_DIRECTORY="$(dirname "${0}")"
CPU_LIMIT=${1:-50000}
RAM_LIMIT=${2:-5242880}

echo "Step A: generate a unique ID (uuid)"
UUID=$(date | sha256sum | cut -f1 -d" ")

echo "Step B: create cpu and memory cgroups"
sudo mkdir /sys/fs/cgroup/{cpu,memory}/$UUID
echo $RAM_LIMIT | sudo tee /sys/fs/cgroup/memory/$UUID/memory.limit_in_bytes
echo 100000 | sudo tee /sys/fs/cgroup/cpu/$UUID/cpu.cfs_period_us
echo $CPU_LIMIT | sudo tee /sys/fs/cgroup/cpu/$UUID/cpu.cfs_quota_us

echo "Step C: prepare the folder structure to be our chroot"
bash $CURRENT_DIRECTORY/new-filesystem.sh $UUID > /dev/null && cd $UUID

echo "Step D: put the current process (PID $$) into the cgroups"
echo $$ | sudo tee /sys/fs/cgroup/{cpu,memory}/$UUID/tasks
```

Generates a nice-looking UUID

Writes the values you want to limit RAM and CPU usage

Creates cpu and memory cgroups using the UUID as the name

Prepares a filesystem to chroot into

Adds the current process to the cgroup

```
echo "Step E: start our namespaced chroot container-ish: $UUID"
sudo unshare \                          ◄───┐   Starts a bash session using a new
    --fork \                                 │   pid namespace and chroot
    --pid \
    chroot . \
    /bin/bash -c "mkdir -p /proc && /bin/mount -t proc proc /proc && exec
    /bin/bash"
```

You can now start your container-ish by running the following command in a terminal window:

```
~/src/examples/poking-docker/container-ish-2.sh
```

You will see the following output, and will be presented with an interactive bash session; note the container UUID (in bold):

```
Step A: generate a unique ID (uuid)
Step B: create cpu and memory cgroups
5242880
100000
50000
Step C: prepare the folder structure to be our chroot
Step D: put the current process (PID 10568) into the cgroups
10568
Step E: start our namespaced chroot container-ish:
169f4eb0dbd1c45fb2d353122431823f5b7b82795d06db0acf51ec476ff8b52d
Welcome to the kind-of-container!
bash-4.4#
```

Leave this session running and open another terminal window. In that window, let's investigate the cgroups our processes are running in:

```
ps -ao pid,command -f
```

You will see output similar to the following (I abbreviated it to show only the part we're interested in). Note the PID of the bash session "inside" your container(-ish):

```
  PID COMMAND
(...)
 4628 bash
10568 \_ /bin/bash /home/chaos/src/examples/poking-docker/container-ish-2.sh
10709     \_ sudo unshare --fork --pid chroot . /bin/bash -c mkdir -p /proc
    && /bin/mount -t
10717         \_ unshare --fork --pid chroot . /bin/bash -c mkdir -p /proc
    && /bin/mount -t
10718             \_ /bin/bash
```

With that PID, you can finally confirm the cgroups that processes ended up in. To do that, run the good old ps command in the second terminal window:

```
ps \                    │  Shows the process with
-p 10718 \         ◄────┤  the requested PID
```

```
-o pid,cgroup \          ◁─┐      Prints pid and cgroups
-ww                      ◁
                                  Doesn't shorten the output to fit the
                                  width of the terminal; prints all
```

You will see output just like the following. Note the cpu,cpuacct and memory cgroups (in bold), which should match the UUID you saw in the output when your container(-ish) started. In other aspects, it's using the default cgroups:

```
PID CGROUP
10718 12:pids:/user.slice/user-
1000.slice/user@1000.service,10:blkio:/user.slice,9:memory:/169f4eb0dbd1c45fb
2d353122431823f5b7b82795d06db0acf51ec476ff8b52d,6:devices:/user.slice,4:cpu,c
puacct:/169f4eb0dbd1c45fb2d353122431823f5b7b82795d06db0acf51ec476ff8b52d,1:na
me=systemd:/user.slice/user-1000.slice/user@1000.service/gnome-terminal-
server.service,0::/user.slice/user-1000.slice/user@1000.service/gnome-
terminal-server.service
```

I invite you to play around with the container and see for yourself how well the process is contained. With this short script slowly built over three parts of the series, you've contained the process in a few important aspects:

- The filesystem access
- PID namespace separation
- CPU and RAM limits

To aid visual memory, take a look at figure 5.11. It shows the elements we have covered (chroot, filesystems, namespaces, cgroups) and underlines the ones that remain to be covered (networking, capabilities, and seccomp).

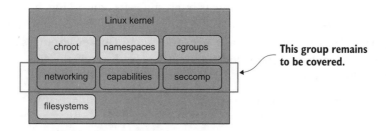

Figure 5.11   Coverage status after the DIY container part 3

It's beginning to look more like a real container, but with one large caveat: its networking access is still exactly the same as for any other process running on the host, and we haven't covered any security features at all. Let's look into how Docker does networking next.

5.8   *Docker and networking*

Docker allows you to explicitly manage networking through the use of the `docker network` subcommand. By default, Docker comes with three networking options for you to choose from when you're starting a container. Let's list the existing networks by running the following command in a terminal window:

```
docker network ls
```

As you can see, the output lists three options: `bridge`, `host`, and `none` (in bold). For now, you can safely ignore the `SCOPE` column:

```
NETWORK ID          NAME                DRIVER              SCOPE
130e904f5364        bridge              bridge              local
2ac4140a7b9d        host                host                local
278d7624eb4b        none                null                local
```

Let's start with the easy one: `none`. If you start a container with `--network none`, no networking will be set up. This is useful if you want to isolate your container from the network and make sure it can't be contacted. This is a runtime option; it doesn't affect how an image is built. You can build an image by downloading packages from the internet, but then run the finished product without access to any network. It uses a `null` driver.

The second option is also straightforward: `host`. If you start a container with `--network host`, the container will use the host's networking setup directly, without any special treatment or isolation. The ports you try to use from inside the container will be the same as if you did it from the outside. The driver for this mode is also called `host`.

Finally, the `bridge` mode is where it gets interesting. In networking, a *bridge* is an interface that connects multiple networks and forwards traffic between the interfaces it's connected to. You can think of it as a network switch. Docker leverages a bridge interface to provide network connectivity to containers through the use of virtual interfaces. It works like this:

1 Docker creates a bridge interface called `docker0` and connects it to the host's logical interface.
2 For each container, Docker creates a `net` namespace, which allows it to create network interfaces accessible to only processes in that namespace.
3 Inside that namespace, Docker creates the following:
   – A virtual interface connected to the `docker0` bridge
   – A local loopback device

When a process from within a container tries to connect to the outside world, the packets go through its virtual network interface and then the bridge, which routes it to where it should go. Figure 5.12 summarizes this architecture.

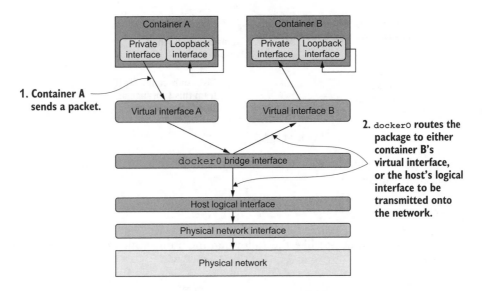

Figure 5.12 Docker networking running two containers in bridge mode

You can see the default Docker bridge device in your VM by running the following command in a terminal window:

```
ip addr
```

You will see output similar to the following (abbreviated for clarity). Note the local loopback device (lo), the ethernet device (eth0), and the Docker bridge (docker0):

```
1: lo: <LOOPBACK,UP,LOWER_UP> mtu 65536 qdisc noqueue state UNKNOWN group
default qlen 1000
(...)
2: eth0: <BROADCAST,MULTICAST,UP,LOWER_UP> mtu 1500 qdisc fq_codel state UP
group default qlen 1000
    link/ether 08:00:27:bd:ac:bf brd ff:ff:ff:ff:ff:ff
    inet 10.0.2.15/24 brd 10.0.2.255 scope global dynamic noprefixroute eth0
       valid_lft 84320sec preferred_lft 84320sec
(...)
3: docker0: <NO-CARRIER,BROADCAST,MULTICAST,UP> mtu 1500 qdisc noqueue state
DOWN group default
    link/ether 02:42:cd:4c:98:33 brd ff:ff:ff:ff:ff:ff
    inet 172.17.0.1/16 brd 172.17.255.255 scope global docker0
       valid_lft forever preferred_lft forever
```

So far, all of the containers you have started were running on the default network settings. Let's now go ahead and create a new network and inspect what happens. Creating a new Docker network is simple. To create a funky new network, run the following command in a terminal window:

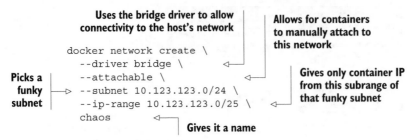

Once that's done, you can confirm the new network is there by running the following command again:

```
docker network ls
```

You will see output just like the following, including your new network called `chaos` (bold):

```
NETWORK ID          NAME                DRIVER              SCOPE
130e904f5364        bridge              bridge              local
b1ac9b3f5294        chaos               bridge              local
2ac4140a7b9d        host                host                local
278d7624eb4b        none                null                local
```

Let's now rerun the `ip` command to list all available network interfaces:

```
ip addr
```

In the following abbreviated output, you'll notice the new interface `br-b1ac9b3f5294` (bold), which has your funky IP range configured:

```
(...)
4: br-b1ac9b3f5294: <NO-CARRIER,BROADCAST,MULTICAST,UP> mtu 1500 qdisc
noqueue state DOWN group default
    link/ether 02:42:d8:f2:62:fb brd ff:ff:ff:ff:ff:ff
    inet 10.123.123.1/24 brd 10.123.123.255 scope global br-b1ac9b3f5294
       valid_lft forever preferred_lft forever
```

Let's now start a container using that new network by running the following command in a terminal window:

```
docker run \
    --name explorer \
    -ti \
    --rm \
    --network chaos \
    ubuntu:focal-20200423
```

The image you're running is pretty slim, so in order to look inside, you need to install the `ip` command. Run the following command from inside that container:

```
apt-get update
apt install -y iproute2
```

Now, let's investigate! From inside the container, run the following `ip` command to see what interfaces are available:

```
ip addr
```

You will see output just like the following. Note the interface with your funky range (in bold):

```
1: lo: <LOOPBACK,UP,LOWER_UP> mtu 65536 qdisc noqueue state UNKNOWN group
default qlen 1000
    link/loopback 00:00:00:00:00:00 brd 00:00:00:00:00:00
    inet 127.0.0.1/8 scope host lo
       valid_lft forever preferred_lft forever
5: eth0@if6: <BROADCAST,MULTICAST,UP,LOWER_UP> mtu 1500 qdisc noqueue state
UP group default
    link/ether 02:42:0a:7b:7b:02 brd ff:ff:ff:ff:ff:ff link-netnsid 0
    inet 10.123.123.2/24 brd 10.123.123.255 scope global eth0
       valid_lft forever preferred_lft forever
```

You can confirm you've gotten an IP address from within that funky range by running the following command inside the container:

```
hostname -I
```

Sure enough, it's what you'd expect it to be, just like the following:

```
10.123.123.2
```

Now, let's see how that plays with the `net` namespaces. You will remember from the previous sections that you can list namespaces by using `lsns`. Let's list the `net` namespaces by running the following command in a second terminal window on the host (not in the container you're running):

```
sudo lsns -t net
```

You will see the following output; I happen to have three `net` namespaces running:

```
        NS TYPE NPROCS   PID USER   COMMAND
4026531993 net     208     1 root   /sbin/init
4026532172 net       1 12543 rtkit  /usr/lib/rtkit/rtkit-daemon
4026532245 net       1 20829 root   /bin/bash
```

But which one is your container's? Let's leverage what you learned about the namespaces to track your container's net namespace by its PID. Run the following command in the second terminal window (not inside the container):

```
CONTAINER_PID=$(docker inspect -f '{{ .State.Pid }}' explorer)
sudo readlink /proc/$CONTAINER_PID/ns/net
```

You will see output similar to the following. In this example, the namespace is 4026532245:

```
net:[4026532245]
```

Now, for the grand finale, let's enter that namespace. In section 5.5, you used nsenter with the --target flag using a process's PID. You could do that here, but I'd like to show you another way of targeting a namespace. To directly use the namespace file, run the following command in the second terminal window (outside the container):

```
CONTAINER_PID=$(docker inspect -f '{{ .State.Pid }}' explorer)
sudo nsenter --net=/proc/$CONTAINER_PID/ns/net
```

You will notice that your prompt has changed: you are now root inside the net namespace 4026532245. Let's confirm that you are seeing the same set of network devices you saw from inside the container. Run the following command at this new prompt:

```
ip addr
```

You will see the same output you saw from inside the container, just as in the following output:

```
1: lo: <LOOPBACK,UP,LOWER_UP> mtu 65536 qdisc noqueue state UNKNOWN group
default qlen 1000
    link/loopback 00:00:00:00:00:00 brd 00:00:00:00:00:00
    inet 127.0.0.1/8 scope host lo
      valid_lft forever preferred_lft forever
5: eth0@if6: <BROADCAST,MULTICAST,UP,LOWER_UP> mtu 1500 qdisc noqueue state
UP group default
    link/ether 02:42:0a:7b:7b:02 brd ff:ff:ff:ff:ff:ff link-netnsid 0
    inet 10.123.123.2/24 brd 10.123.123.255 scope global eth0
      valid_lft forever preferred_lft forever
```

When you're done playing, you can type exit or press Ctrl-D to exit the shell session and therefore the namespace. Well done; we've just covered the basics you need to know about networking—the fourth pillar of how Docker implements the containers. Now for the last stop on this journey: capabilities and other security mechanisms.

5.8.1 *Capabilities and seccomp*

The final pillar of Docker is the use of *capabilities* and *seccomp*. For the final time, let me refresh your memory of where they fit in figure 5.13.

We'll cover capabilities and seccomp briefly, because they're necessary for the complete image of how Linux containers are implemented with Docker, but I couldn't do the content justice by trying to get into how they work under the hood in a single section. I'll leave that part as an exercise for you.

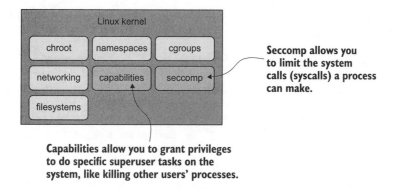

Figure 5.13 **Capabilities and seccomp**

CAPABILITIES

Let's start with capabilities. This Linux kernel feature splits superuser privileges (which skip all checks) into smaller, more granular units of permissions, with each unit called—you guessed it—a *capability*. So instead of a binary "all" or "nothing," you can grant users permissions to do specific tasks. For example, any user with the capability CAP_KILL bypasses permission checks for sending signals to processes. In the same way, any user with CAP_SYS_TIME can change the system clock.

By default, Docker grants every container a default set of capabilities. To find out what they are, let's start a container and use the getpcaps command to list its capabilities. Run the following command in a terminal window to start a fresh container with all the default settings:

```
docker run \
    --name cap_explorer \
    -ti --rm \
    ubuntu:focal-20200423
```

While that container is running, you can check its capabilities in another window by finding out its PID and using the getpcaps command:

```
CONTAINER_PID=$(docker inspect -f '{{ .State.Pid }}' cap_explorer)
getpcaps $CONTAINER_PID
```

You will see output similar to the following, listing all the capabilities a Docker container gets by default. Notice the cap_sys_chroot capability (bold font):

```
Capabilities for `4380': =
cap_chown,cap_dac_override,cap_fowner,cap_fsetid,cap_kill,cap_setgid,
cap_setuid,cap_setpcap,cap_net_bind_service,cap_net_raw,cap_sys_chroot,
cap_mknod,cap_audit_write,cap_setfcap+eip
```

To verify it works, let's have some *Inception*-style fun by chroot'ing inside the container's chroot! You can do that by running the following commands inside your container:

```
NEW_FS_FOLDER=new_fs
mkdir $NEW_FS_FOLDER
cp -v --parents `which bash` $NEW_FS_FOLDER
ldd `which bash` | egrep -o '(/usr)?/lib.*\.[0-9][0-9]?' \
| xargs -I {} cp -v --parents {} $NEW_FS_FOLDER
chroot $NEW_FS_FOLDER `which bash`
```

- Copies bash binary to the subfolder
- Finds out all the libraries bash needs
- Copies the libraries over into their respective locations
- Runs the actual chroot from the new subfolder and start bash

You will land in a new bash session (with not much to do, because you've copied only the bash binary itself). Now, to the twist: when starting a new container with docker run, you can use --cap-add and --cap-drop flags to add or remove any particular capability, respectively. A special keyword ALL allows for adding or dropping all available privileges.

Let's now kill the container (press Ctrl-D) and restart it with the --cap-drop ALL flag, using the following command:

```
docker run \
    --name cap_explorer \
    -ti --rm \
    --cap-drop ALL \
    ubuntu:focal-20200423
```

While that container is running, you can check its capabilities in another window by finding out its PID and using the getpcaps command. You can do that by running the following command:

```
CONTAINER_PID=$(docker inspect -f '{{ .State.Pid }}' cap_explorer)
getpcaps $CONTAINER_PID
```

You will see output similar to the following, this time listing no capabilities at all:

```
Capabilities for `4813': =
```

From inside the new container, retry the chroot snippet by running the following commands again:

```
NEW_FS_FOLDER=new_fs
mkdir $NEW_FS_FOLDER
cp -v --parents `which bash` $NEW_FS_FOLDER
ldd `which bash` | egrep -o '(/usr)?/lib.*\.[0-9][0-9]?' | xargs -I {} cp -v
    --parents {} $NEW_FS_FOLDER
chroot $NEW_FS_FOLDER `which bash`
```

This time you will see the following error:

```
chroot: cannot change root directory to 'new_fs': Operation not permitted
```

Docker leverages that (and so should you) to limit the actions the container can perform. It's always a good idea to give the container only what it really needs in terms of capabilities. And you have to admit that Docker makes it pretty easy. Now, let's take a look at seccomp.

SECCOMP

Seccomp is a Linux kernel feature that allows you to filter which syscalls a process can make. Interestingly, under the hood, seccomp uses Berkeley Packet Filter (BPF; for more information, see chapter 3) to implement the filtering. Docker leverages seccomp to limit the default set of syscalls that are allowed for containers (see more details about that set at https://docs.docker.com/engine/security/seccomp/).

Docker's seccomp profiles are stored in JSON files, which describe a series of rules to evaluate which syscalls to allow. You can see Docker's default profile at http://mng .bz/0mO6. To give you a preview of what a profile looks like, here's an extract from Docker's default:

```
{
    "defaultAction": "SCMP_ACT_ERRNO",        ⟵—  By default,
...                                               blocks all calls
    "syscalls": [
        {
                "names": [                    ⟵—  For the syscalls with the
                    "accept",                     following list of names
                    "accept4",
...
                    "write",
                    "writev"
                ],
                "action": "SCMP_ACT_ALLOW",   ⟵—  Allows them
...                                               to proceed
        },
...
    ]
}
```

To use a different profile than the default, use the `--security-opt seccomp=/my/ profile.json` flag when starting a new container. That's all we're going to cover about seccomp in the context of Docker. Right now, I just need you to know that it exists, that it limits the syscalls that are allowed, and that you can leverage that without using Docker because it's a Linux kernel feature. Let's go ahead and review what you've seen under Docker's hood.

5.9 *Docker demystified*

By now, you understand that containers are implemented with a collection of loosely connected technologies and that in order to know what to expect from a dish, you need to know the ingredients. We've covered chroot, namespaces, cgroups, networking, and briefly, capabilities, seccomp, and filesystems. Figure 5.14 shows once again what each of these technologies are for to drive the point home.

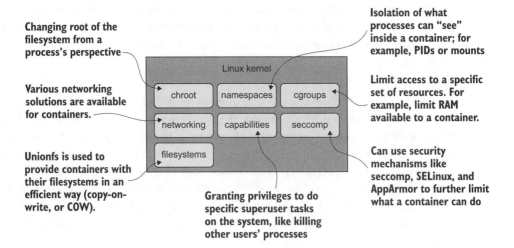

Changing root of the filesystem from a process's perspective

Various networking solutions are available for containers.

Unionfs is used to provide containers with their filesystems in an efficient way (copy-on-write, or COW).

Linux kernel

chroot   namespaces   cgroups

networking   capabilities   seccomp

filesystems

Isolation of what processes can "see" inside a container; for example, PIDs or mounts

Limit access to a specific set of resources. For example, limit RAM available to a container.

Can use security mechanisms like seccomp, SELinux, and AppArmor to further limit what a container can do

Granting privileges to do specific superuser tasks on the system, like killing other users' processes

Figure 5.14   High-level overview of Docker interacting with the kernel

This section showed you that Docker, as well as the Linux features that do the heavy lifting, are not that scary once you've checked what's under the hood. They are useful technologies and are fun to use! Understanding them is crucial to designing chaos engineering experiments in any system involving Linux containers.

Given the current state of the ecosystem, containers seem to be here to stay. To learn more about these technologies, I suggest starting with the man pages. Both man namespaces and man cgroups are pretty well written and accessible. Online documentation of Docker (https://docs.docker.com/) also provides a lot of useful information on Docker as well as the underlying kernel features.

I'm confident that you will be able to face whatever containerized challenges life throws at you when practicing chaos engineering. Now we're ready to fix our Dockerized Meower USA app that's being slow.

5.10   *Fixing my (Dockerized) app that's being slow*

Let's refresh your memory on how the app is deployed. Figure 5.15 shows a simplified overview of the app's architecture, from which I've removed the third-party load balancer; I'm showing only a single instance of Ghost, connecting to the MySQL database.

It's a simple setup—purposefully so, so that you can focus on the new element in the equation: Docker. Let's bring this up in your VM.

5.10.1   *Booting up Meower*

Now that you're comfortable running Docker commands, let's start up the Meower stack in the VM. You are going to use the functionality of Docker that allows you to describe a set of containers that need to be deployed together: docker stack deploy (see http://mng.bz/Vdyr for more information.) This command uses simple-to-understand

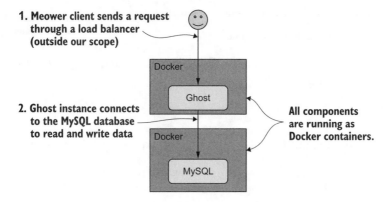

Figure 5.15 Simplified overview of Meower USA technical architecture

YAML files to describe sets of containers. This allows for a portable description of an application. You can see the description for the Meower stack by running the following command in a terminal in your VM:

```
cat ~/src/examples/poking-docker/meower-stack.yml
```

You will see the following output. It describes two containers, one for MySQL, and another one for Ghost. It also configures Ghost to use the MySQL database and takes care of things such as (very insecure) passwords:

```
version: '3.1'
services:
  ghost:                                    Runs the ghost container
    image: ghost:3.14.0-alpine              in a specific version
    ports:
      - 8368:2368                           Exposes port 8368 on the
    environment:                            host to route to port 2368
      database__client: mysql               in the ghost container
      database__connection__host: db
      database__connection__user: root
      database__connection__password: notverysafe    Specifies the
      database__connection__database: ghost          database password
      server__host: "0.0.0.0"                         for ghost to use
      server__port: "2368"
  db:                                       Runs the mysql container
    image: mysql:5.7
    environment:
      MYSQL_ROOT_PASSWORD: notverysafe      Specifies the same password
                                            for the mysql container to use
```

Let's start it! Run the following commands in a terminal window:

```
docker swarm init               You need to initialize your host to be
docker stack deploy \           able to run docker stack commands.
```

```
-c ~/src/examples/poking-docker/meower-stack.yml \
meower
```
⟵⟶ **Uses the stack file you saw earlier**

⟵⟶ **Gives the stack a name**

When that's done, you can confirm that the stack was created by running the following command in a terminal window:

```
docker stack ls
```

You will see the following output, showing a single stack, meower, with two services in it:

```
NAME                    SERVICES            ORCHESTRATOR
meower                  2                   Swarm
```

To confirm what Docker containers it started, run the following command in a terminal window:

```
docker ps
```

You will see output similar to the following. As expected, you can see two containers, one for MySQL and one for the Ghost application. If you're not seeing the containers start, you might want to wait a minute. The ghost container will crash and restart until the mysql container is actually ready, and that one takes longer to start:

```
CONTAINER ID   IMAGE                    COMMAND                  CREATED
STATUS         PORTS                    NAMES
72535692a9d7   ghost:3.14.0-alpine      "docker-entrypoint.s…"   39 seconds ago
Up 32 seconds  2368/tcp                 meower_ghost.1.4me3qjpcks6o8hvc19yp26svi
7d32d97aad37   mysql:5.7                "docker-entrypoint.s…"   51 seconds ago
Up 48 seconds  3306/tcp, 33060/tcp      meower_db.1.ol7vjhnnwhdx34ihpx54sfuia
```

To confirm that it worked, browse to http://127.0.0.1:8080/. If you feel like configuring the Ghost instance, feel free to go to http://127.0.0.1:8080/ghost/, but for our purposes it's fine to leave it unconfigured.

With the setup out of the way, we can now focus on the question that brought us here in the first place: Why is the app slow?

5.10.2 *Why is the app slow?*

So why might the app be slow? Given what you've learned so far in this chapter, there are at least two plausible explanations for the slowness of the Meower application.

One of the reasons might be that the process is starved for CPU time. It sounds obvious, but I've seen it happen a lot, when someone . . . else . . . typed one zero too few or too many. Fortunately, you now know that it's easy to check the cpu.stat of the underlying cgroup to see if any throttling took place at all, and take it from there.

Another reason, which we explored in chapter 4 with WordPress, is that the application is more fragile to the networking slowness of its database than we expected. It's a common gotcha to make assumptions based on the information from test environments and local databases, and then be surprised when networking slows down in the real world.

I'm confident that you can handle the first possibility with ease. I suggest, then, that we explore the second one now in the context of Docker, and using a more modern stack than that of chapter 4. Hakuna Matata!

5.11 Experiment 5: Network slowness for containers with Pumba

Let's conduct an experiment in which you add a certain amount of latency to the communications between Ghost and MySQL, and see how that affects the response time of the website. To do that, you can once again rely on ab to generate traffic and produce metrics about the website response time and error rate. Here are the four steps to one such experiment:

1 Observability: use ab to generate a certain amount of load; monitor for average response time and error rate.
2 Steady state: no errors arise, and you average X ms per request.
3 Hypothesis: if you introduce 100 ms latency to network connectivity between Ghost and MySQL, you should see the average website latency go up by 100 ms.
4 Run the experiment!

So the only question remaining now is this: What's the easiest way to inject latency into Docker containers?

5.11.1 Pumba: Docker chaos engineering tool

Pumba (https://github.com/alexei-led/pumba) is a really neat tool that helps conduct chaos experiments on Docker containers. It can kill containers, emulate network failures (using tc under the hood), and run stress tests (using Stress-ng, https://kernel .ubuntu.com/~cking/stress-ng/) from inside a particular container's cgroup.

> **NOTE** Pumba is preinstalled in the VM; for installation on your host, see appendix A.

Pumba is really convenient to use, because it operates on container names and saves a lot of typing. The syntax is straightforward. Take a look at this excerpt from running pumba help in a terminal window:

```
USAGE:
    pumba [global options] command [command options] containers (name, list
of names, RE2 regex)

COMMANDS:
    kill     kill specified containers
    netem    emulate the properties of wide area networks
    pause    pause all processes
    stop     stop containers
```

```
rm        remove containers
help, h   Shows a list of commands or help for one command
```

To introduce latency to a container's egress, you're interested in the netem subcommand. Under the hood, it uses the same tc command you used in chapter 4, section 4.2.2, but netem is much easier to use. There is one gotcha, though: the way it works by default is through executing a tc command from inside a container. That means that tc needs to be available, which is unlikely for anything other than a testing container.

Fortunately, there is a convenient workaround. Docker allows you to start a container in such a way that the networking configuration is shared with another, pre-existing container. By doing that, it is possible to start a container that has the tc command available, run it from there, and affect both containers' networking. Pumba conveniently allows for that through the --tc-image flag, which allows you to specify the image to use to create a new container (you can use gaiadocker/iproute2 as an example container that has tc installed). Putting it all together, you can add latency to a specific container called my_container by running the following command in the terminal:

```
pumba netem \
--duration 60s \           ◁  Duration of the experiment—
                              how long the delay should be
                              in there
--tc-image gaiadocker/iproute2 \  ◁  Specifies the image to run that
                                     has the tc command available
delay \                    ◁
--time 100 \               ◁  Uses the delay subcommand
"my_container"             ◁
                              Specifies the delay (ms)
Specifies the name of the
container to affect
```

Armed with that, you are ready to run the experiment!

5.11.2 Chaos experiment implementation

First things first: let's establish the steady state. To do that, let's run ab. You will need to be careful to run with the same settings later to compare apples to apples. Let's run for 30 seconds to give the command long enough to produce a meaningful number of responses, but not long enough to waste time. And let's start with a concurrency of 1, because in this setting, you're using the same CPUs to produce and serve the traffic, so it's a good idea to keep the number of variables to a minimum. Run the following command in your terminal:

```
ab -t 30 -c 1 -l http://127.0.0.1:8080/
```

You will see output similar to the following. I abbreviated it for clarity. Note the time per request at around 26 ms (in bold font) and failed requests at 0 (also bold font):

```
(...)
Complete requests:     1140
Failed requests:       0
(...)
```

```
Time per request:        26.328 [ms] (mean)
(...)
```

Now, let's run the actual experiment. Open another terminal window. Let's find the name of the Docker container running MySQL by running the following command in this second terminal window:

```
docker ps
```

You will see output similar to the following. Note the name of the MySQL container (bold font):

```
docker ps
CONTAINER ID   IMAGE                    COMMAND                CREATED       STATUS
PORTS                  NAMES
394666793a39   ghost:3.14.0-alpine      "docker-entrypoint.s…"  2 hours ago  Up 2
hours          2368/tcp                meower_ghost.1.svumole20gz4bkt7iccnbj8hn
a0b83af5b4f5   mysql:5.7                "docker-entrypoint.s…"  2 hours ago  Up 2
hours          3306/tcp, 33060/tcp     meower_db.1.v3jamilxm6wmptphbgqb8bung
```

Conveniently, Pumba allows you to use regular expressions by prepending the expression with re2:. So, to add 100 ms of latency to your MySQL container for 60 seconds, let's run the following command, still in the second terminal window (bold font for the regular expression prefix). Note that to simplify the analysis, you're disabling both random jitter and correlation between the events, to add the same delay to each call:

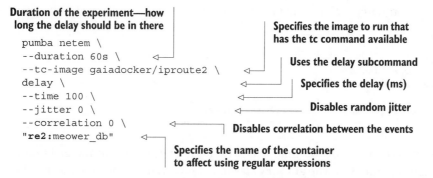

Duration of the experiment—how long the delay should be in there

Specifies the image to run that has the tc command available

Uses the delay subcommand

Specifies the delay (ms)

Disables random jitter

Disables correlation between the events

Specifies the name of the container to affect using regular expressions

```
pumba netem \
--duration 60s \
--tc-image gaiadocker/iproute2 \
delay \
--time 100 \
--jitter 0 \
--correlation 0 \
"re2:meower_db"
```

Now, while the delay is in place (you have 60 seconds!) switch back to the first terminal window, and rerun the same ab command as before:

```
ab -t 30 -c 1 -l http://127.0.0.1:8080/
```

The output you'll see will be rather different from the previous output and similar to the following (abbreviated for brevity, failed requests and time per request in bold font):

```
(...)
Complete requests:      62
```

```
Failed requests:        0
(...)
Time per request:       490.128 [ms] (mean)
(...)
```

Ouch. A "mere" 100 ms added latency to the MySQL database changes the average response time of Meower USA from 26 ms to 490 ms, or a factor of more than 18. If this sounds suspicious to you, that's the reaction I'm hoping for!. To confirm our findings, let's rerun the same experiment, but this time let's use 1 ms as the delay, the lowest that the tool will allow. To add the delay, run the following command in the second terminal window:

```
pumba netem \
--duration 60s \
--tc-image gaiadocker/iproute2 \
delay \
--time 1 \          ◁──┐  This time use a
--jitter 0 \           │  delay of just 1 ms.
--correlation 0 \
"re2:meower_db"
```

In the first terminal, while that's running, rerun the `ab` command once again with the following command:

```
ab -t 30 -c 1 -l http://127.0.0.1:8080/
```

It will print the output you're pretty familiar with by now, just like the following (once again, abbreviated). Notice that the result is a few milliseconds greater than our steady state:

```
(...)
Complete requests:      830
Failed requests:        0
(...)
Time per request:       36.212 [ms] (mean)
(...)
```

Back-of-a-napkin math warning: That result effectively puts an upper bound on the average amount of overhead your delay injector adds itself (36 ms – 26 ms = 10 ms per request). Assuming the worst-case scenario, in which the database sends a single packet delayed by 1 ms, that's a theoretical average overhead of 9 ms. The average time per request during the experiment was 490 ms, or 464 ms (490 – 26) larger than the steady state. Even assuming that worst-case scenario, 9 ms overhead, the result would not be significantly different (9 / 490 ~= 2%).

Long story short: these results are plausible, and that concludes our chaos experiment with a failure. The initial hypothesis was way off. Now, with the data, you have a much better idea of where the slowness might be coming from, and you can debug this further and hopefully fix the issue.

Just one last hint before we leave. List all containers, including the ones that are finished, by running the following command in a terminal window:

```
docker ps --all
```

You will see output similar to the following. Notice the pairs of containers started with the image `gaiadocker/iproute2` you specified earlier with the `--tc-image` flag:

```
CONTAINER ID   IMAGE                COMMAND               CREATED
STATUS                      PORTS             NAMES
9544354cdf9c   gaiadocker/iproute2  "tc qdisc del dev et…"  26 minutes ago
Exited (0) 26 minutes ago                     stoic_wozniak
8c975f610a29   gaiadocker/iproute2  "tc qdisc add dev et…"  27 minutes ago
Exited (0) 27 minutes ago                     quirky_shtern
(...)
```

These are the short-lived containers, which executed the `tc` command from inside the same networking configuration as your target container. You can even inspect one of them by running a command similar to the following:

```
docker inspect 9544354cdf9c
```

You will see a long JSON file, similar to the following output (abbreviated). Within this file, notice two members, `Entrypoint` and `Cmd`. They list the entry point binary and its arguments, respectively:

```
(...)
        "Cmd": [
            "qdisc",
            "del",
            "dev",
            "eth0",
            "root",
            "netem"
        ],
(...)
        "Entrypoint": [
            "tc"
        ],
(...)
```

So there you go, another chaos experiment under your belt and another tool in your toolbox. Let's finish by taking a tour of other mention-worthy aspects of chaos engineering relevant to Docker that we haven't covered.

Pop quiz: What is Pumba?

Pick one:

1   A really likable character from a movie
2   A handy wrapper around namespaces that facilitates working with Docker containers
3   A handy wrapper around cgroups that facilitates working with Docker containers
4   A handy wrapper around `tc` that facilitates working with Docker containers, and that also lets you kill containers

See appendix B for answers.

5.12   *Other parts of the puzzle*

I want to mention other topics that we haven't covered in detail in this chapter that are worth considering when designing your own chaos experiments. The list is potentially infinite, but let me present just a few common issues.

5.12.1   *Docker daemon restarts*

In its current model, a restart of the Docker daemon means a restart of all applications running on Docker on that host. This might sound obvious and trivial, but it can be a very real problem. Imagine a host running a few hundred containers and Docker crashing:

- How long is it going to take for all the applications to get started again?
- Do some containers depend on others, so the order of them starting is important?
- How do containers react to this situation, in which resources are used to start other containers (thundering herd problem)?
- Are you running infrastructure processes (say, an overlay network) on Docker? What happens if that container doesn't start before the other ones?
- If Docker crashes at the wrong moment, can it recover from any inconsistent state? Does any state get corrupted?
- Does your load balancer know when a service is really ready, rather than just starting, to know when to serve it traffic?

A simple chaos experiment restarting Docker mid-flight might help you answer all of these questions and many more.

5.12.2   *Storage for image layers*

Similarly, storage problems have a much larger scope for failure than we've covered. You saw earlier that a simple experiment showed that a default Docker installation on Ubuntu 18.04 doesn't allow for restricting the storage size that a container can use.

But in real life, a lot more can go wrong than a single container being unable to write to disk. For example, consider the following:

- What happens if an application doesn't know how to handle lack of space and crashes, and Docker is unable to restart it because of the lack of space?
- Will Docker have enough storage to download the layers necessary to start a new container you need to start? (It's difficult to predict the total amount of decompressed storage needed.)
- How much storage does Docker itself need to start if it crashes when a disk is full?

Again, this might sound basic, but a lot of damage can be caused by a single faulty loop writing too much data to the disk, and running processes in containers might give a false sense of safety in this respect.

5.12.3 *Advanced networking*

We covered the basics of Docker networking, as well using Pumba to issue `tc` commands to add delays to interfaces inside containers, but that's just the tip of the iceberg of what can go wrong. Although the defaults are not hard to wrap your head around, the complexity can grow quickly.

Docker is often used in conjunction with other networking elements such as overlay networks (for example, Flannel, https://github.com/coreos/flannel), cloud-aware networking solutions (such as Calico, www.projectcalico.org), and service meshes (such as Istio, https://istio.io/docs/concepts/what-is-istio/). These further add to the standard tools (for example, iptables, https://en.wikipedia.org/wiki/Iptables and IP Virtual Server, or IPVS, https://en.wikipedia.org/wiki/IP_Virtual_Server) to further increase the complexity.

We will touch upon some of these in the context of Kubernetes in chapter 12, but understanding how your networking stack works (and breaks) will always be important to anyone practicing chaos engineering.

5.12.4 *Security*

Finally, let's consider the security aspect of things. While security is typically the job of a dedicated team, using chaos engineering techniques to explore security problems is worthwhile. I briefly mentioned seccomp, SELinux, and AppArmor. Each provides layers of security, which can be tested against with an experiment.

Unfortunately, these are beyond the scope of this chapter, but a lot of low-hanging fruit still remains to look into. For example, all of the following situations can (and do) lead to security issues, and can usually be easily fixed:

- Containers running with the `--privileged` flag, often without a good reason
- Running as root inside the container (the default pretty much everywhere)
- Unused capabilities given to containers
- Using random Docker images from the internet, often without peeking inside

- Running ancient versions of Docker images containing known security flaws
- Running ancient versions of Docker itself containing known security flaws

Chaos engineering can help design and run experiments that reveal your level of exposure to the numerous threats out there. And if you tune in, you will notice that exploits do appear on a more or less regular basis (for example, see "Understanding Docker Container Escapes" at the Trail of Bits blog at http://mng.bz/xmMq).

Summary

- Docker builds on several decades of technology and leverages various Linux kernel functionalities (like chroot, namespaces, cgroups, and others) to make for a simple user experience.
- The same tools designed to operate on namespaces and cgroups apply equally to Docker containers.
- For effective chaos engineering in a containerized world, you need an understanding of how they work (and they're not that scary after you've seen them up close).
- Pumba is a convenient tool for injecting network problems, running stress tests from within a cgroup, and killing containers.
- Chaos engineering should be applied to applications running on Docker as well as to Docker itself to make both more resilient to failures.

6

Who you gonna call?
Syscall-busters!

This chapter covers

- Observing syscalls of a running process by using `strace` and BPF
- Working with black-box software
- Designing chaos experiments at the syscall level
- Blocking syscalls by using `strace` and seccomp

It's time to take a deep dive—all the way to the OS—to learn how to do chaos engineering at the syscall level. I want to show you that even in a simple system, like a single process running on a host, you can create plenty of value by applying chaos engineering and learning just how resilient that system is to failure. And, oh, it's good fun too!

This chapter starts with a brief refresher on syscalls. You'll then see how to do the following:

- Understand what a process does without looking at its source code
- List and block the syscalls that a process can make
- Experimentally test your assumptions about how a process deals with failure

If I do my job well, you'll finish this chapter with a realization that it's hard to find a piece of software that can't benefit from chaos engineering, even if it's closed source. Whoa, did I just say *closed source*? The same guy who always goes on about how great open source software is and who maintains some himself? Why would you do closed source? Well, sometimes it all starts with a promotion.

6.1   Scenario: Congratulations on your promotion!

Do you remember your last promotion? Perhaps a few nice words, some handshakes, and ego-friendly emails from your boss. And then, invariably, a bunch of surprises you hadn't thought of when you agreed to take on the new opportunity. A certain something somehow always appears in these conversations, but only after the deal is done: the maintenance of legacy systems.

Legacy systems, like potatoes, come in all shapes and sizes. And just as with potatoes, you often won't realize just how convoluted their shape really is until you dig them out of the ground. Things can get messy if you don't know what you're doing! What counts as legacy in one company might be considered pretty progressive in a different setting.

Sometimes there are good reasons to keep the same codebase for a long time (for example, the requirements haven't changed, it runs fine on modern hardware, and there is a talent pool), and other times software is kept in an archaic state for all the wrong reasons (sunk-cost fallacy, vendor lockdown, good old bad planning, and so on). Even modern code can be considered legacy if it's not well maintained.

But in this chapter, I'd like you to look at a particular type of legacy system—the kind that works, but no one really knows how. Let's take a look at an example of such a system.

6.1.1   System X: If everyone is using it, but no one maintains it, is it abandonware?

If you've been around for a while, you can probably name a few legacy systems that only certain people really understood inside out, but a lot of people use. Well, let's imagine that the last person knowing a certain system quits, and your promotion includes figuring out what to do with that system to maintain it. It's officially your problem now. Let's call that problem *System X.*

First things first—you check the documentation. Oops, there isn't any! Through a series of interviews of the more senior people in the organization, you find the executable binary and the source code. And thanks to tribal knowledge, you know that the binary provides an HTTP interface that everyone is using. Figure 6.1 summarizes this rather enigmatic description of the system.

Let's take a glance at the source code structure. If you're working inside the VM shipped with this book, you can find the source code by going to the following folder in a terminal window:

```
cd ~/src/examples/who-you-gonna-call/src/
```

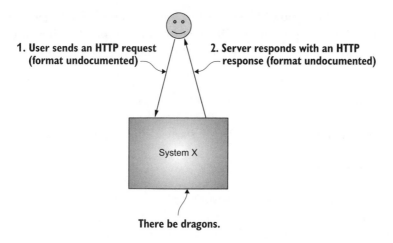

Figure 6.1　The (known part of the) architecture of the legacy System X

(Alternatively you can browse the code online on GitHub at http://mng.bz/A0VE). It's a simulated legacy application, written in C. To keep this as realistic as possible, don't dig too deep into how the application is written (it should appear to you to be awfully complicated for what it's doing). If you're really curious, this source code is generated through the generate_legacy.py script in the same folder, but I recommend you read it only after you're finished with this chapter.

I'm not going to walk you through what the code is doing, but let's just get a rough idea of how much code goes into the final product. To find all the files and sum up the lines of code, run the following command in a terminal window:

```
find ~/src/examples/who-you-gonna-call/src/ \
  -name "*.c" -o -name "*.h" \
  | sort | xargs wc -l
```

You will see output similar to the following (abbreviated). Note the total of 3128 lines of code (bold font):

```
   26 ./legacy/abandonware_0.c
  (...)
   26 ./legacy/web_scale_0.c
(...)
   79 ./main.c
 3128 total
```

Fortunately, the source code also comes with a Makefile, which allows you to build the binary. Run the following command in a terminal window, from the same directory, to build the binary called legacy_server. It will compile the application for you:

```
make
```

After it's done compiling, you will be left with a new executable file, legacy_server (if you're using the VM, the application will already be precompiled, so it won't do anything). You can now start the file by running the following command in a terminal window:

```
./legacy_server
```

It will print a single line to inform you that it started listening on port 8080:

```
Listening on port 8080, PID: 1649
```

You can now confirm that the server is working by opening a browser and going to http://127.0.0.1:8080/. You will see the web interface of the legacy System X. It doesn't keep the world spinning, but it's definitely an important aspect of the company culture. Make sure you investigate it thoroughly.

Now, this is the big question: Given that the legacy System X is a big, black box, how can you sleep well at night, not knowing how it might break? Well, as the title of this book might give away, a little bit of chaos engineering can help!

The purpose of this chapter is to show you how to inject failure on the boundary between the application and the system (something even the most basic of programs will need to do) and see how the application copes when it receives errors from the system. That boundary is defined by a set of syscalls. To make sure we're all on the same page, let's start with a quick refresher on syscalls.

6.2   *A brief refresher on syscalls*

System calls (more commonly abbreviated to *syscalls*) are the APIs of an OS, such as UNIX, Linux, or Windows. For a program running on an OS, syscalls are the way of communicating with the kernel of that OS. If you've ever written so much as a Hello World program, that program is using a syscall to print the message to your console.

What do syscalls do? They give programs access to resources managed by the kernel. Here are a few basic examples:

- open—Opens a file
- read—Reads from a file (or something file-like; for instance, a socket)
- write—Writes to a file (or something file-like)
- exec—Replaces the currently running process with another one, read from an executable file
- kill—Sends a signal to a running process

In a typical modern operating system like Linux, any code executed on a machine runs in either of the following:

- Kernel space
- User space (also called *userland*)

Inside the *kernel space*, as the name suggests, only the kernel code (with its subsystems and most drivers) is allowed, and access to the underlying hardware is granted. Anything else runs inside the *user space*, without direct access to the hardware.

So if you run a program as a user, it will be executed inside the user space; when it needs to access the hardware, it will make a syscall, which will be interpreted, validated, and executed by the kernel. The actual hardware access will be done by the kernel, and the results made available to the program in the user space. Figure 6.2 sums up this process.

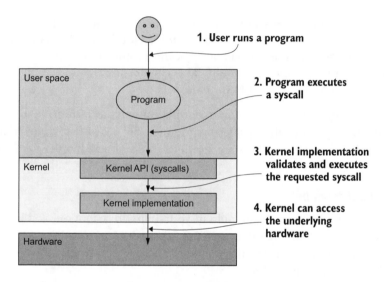

Figure 6.2   Division between kernel space, userland, and hardware

Why can't you write a program that directly uses the hardware? Well, nothing is stopping you from writing code directly for particular hardware, but in these modern times, it's not practical. Apart from specialized use cases, like embedded systems or unikernels (https://en.wikipedia.org/wiki/Unikernel; we touched upon this in chapter 5), it just makes more sense to program against a well-defined and documented API, like the Linux syscalls. All the usual arguments in favor of a well-defined API apply here. Here are a few advantages to this setup:

- *Portability*—An application written against the Linux kernel API will run on any hardware architecture supported by Linux.
- *Security*—The kernel will verify that the syscalls are legal and will prevent accidental damage to the hardware.
- *Not reinventing the wheel*—A lot of solutions to common problems (for example, virtual memory and filesystems) have already been implemented and thoroughly tested.

- *Rich features*—Linux comes with plenty of advanced features, which let the application developer focus on the application itself, rather than having to worry about the low-level, mundane stuff. These features include user management and privileges, and drivers for a lot of common hardware or advanced memory management.
- *Speed and reliability*—Chances are that the Linux kernel implementation of a particular feature, tested daily on millions of machines all over the world, will be of better quality than one that you'd need to write yourself to support your program.

NOTE Linux is POSIX-compliant (Portable Operating System Interface, https://en.wikipedia.org/wiki/POSIX). Therefore, a lot of its API is standardized, so you will find the same (or similar) syscalls in other UNIX-like operating systems; for example, the BSD family. This chapter focuses on Linux, the most popular representative of this group.

The downside is more overhead, compared with directly accessing the hardware, which is easily outweighed by the upsides for the majority of use cases. Now that you have a high-level idea of what syscalls are for, let's find out which ones are available to you!

6.2.1   *Finding out about syscalls*

To find out about all the syscalls available in your Linux distribution, you'll use the `man` command. This command has the concept of sections, numbered from 1 to 9; different sections can cover items with the same name. To see the sections, run the following command in a terminal window:

```
man man
```

You will see output similar to the following (abbreviated). Note that section 2 covers syscalls (bold font):

```
(...) A section, if provided, will direct man to look only in that section
of the manual. The default action is to search in all of the available
sections following a pre-defined order ("1 n  l  8  3  2 3posix  3pm  3perl
3am  5 4 9 6 7" by default, unless overridden by the SECTION directive in
/etc/manpath.config), and to show only the first page found, even if page
exists in several sections.

     The table below shows the section numbers of the manual followed by
the types of pages they contain.

1 Executable programs or shell commands
2 System calls (functions provided by the kernel)
3 Library calls (functions within program libraries)
4 Special files (usually found in /dev)
5 File formats and conventions eg /etc/passwd
6 Games
```

```
7 Miscellaneous (including macro packages and conventions)
8 System administration commands (usually only for root)
9 Kernel routines [Non standard]
```

Therefore, to list the available syscalls, run the following command:

```
man 2 syscalls
```

You will see a list of syscalls, along with the version of kernel they were introduced in, and notes, just like the following (abbreviated). The numbers in parentheses are the section numbers you can use with man:

```
        System call              Kernel         Notes
   _____

   (...)
        chroot(2)                1.0
   (...)
        read(2)                  1.0
   (...)
        write(2)                 1.0
```

Let's pick the read syscall as an example. To get more information about that syscall, run the man command in a terminal window, using section 2 (as instructed by the number in parentheses):

```
man 2 read
```

You will see the following output (abbreviated again for brevity). The synopsis contains a code sample in C (bold font), as well as a description of what the arguments and return values mean. This code sample (in C) describes the signature of the syscall in question, and you'll learn more about that later:

```
READ(2)                 Linux Programmer's Manual                 READ(2)

NAME
        read - read from a file descriptor

SYNOPSIS
        #include <unistd.h>

        ssize_t read(int fd, void *buf, size_t count);

DESCRIPTION
        read() attempts to read up to count bytes from file descriptor fd
into the buffer starting at buf.
```

Using the man command in section 2, you can learn about any and every syscall available on your machine. It will show you the signature, a description, possible error values, and any interesting caveats.

From the perspective of chaos engineering, if you want to inject failure into the syscalls a program is making, you first need to build a reasonable understanding of the purpose they serve. So now you know how to look them up. But how would you go about actually making a syscall? The answer to that question is most commonly glibc (www.gnu.org/software/libc/libc.html), and using one of the function-wrappers it provides for almost every syscall. Let's take a closer look at how it works.

6.2.2   *Using the standard C library and glibc*

A standard C library provides (among other things) an implementation of all the functions whose signatures you can see in section 2 of the man pages. These signatures are stored in unistd.h, which you have seen before. Let's look at a man page of read(2) once again, by running the following command:

```
man 2 read
```

You will see the following output in the synopsis section. Notice that the code sample in the synopsis includes a header file called unistd.h, as in the following output (in bold font):

```
#include <unistd.h>

ssize_t read(int fd, void *buf, size_t count);
```

How do you learn more about it? Once again, man pages to the rescue. Run the following statement in a terminal window:

```
man unistd.h
```

In the output of that command, you will learn about all of the functions that should be implemented by a standard C library. Note the signature of the read function (bold font):

```
(...)
NAME
       unistd.h — standard symbolic constants and types
(...)
   Declarations
       The following shall be declared as functions and may also be defined
as macros. Function prototypes shall be provided.
(...)
           ssize_t        read(int, void *, size_t);
(...)
```

This is the POSIX standard of what the signature of the syscall wrapper for read should look like. This begs the question: When you write a C program and use one of the wrappers, where is the implementation coming from? *glibc* (www.gnu.org/software/libc/libc.html) stands for the *GNU C Library* and is the most common C library implementation for Linux. It's been around for more than three decades, and a lot of software relies on it, despite being criticized for being bloated (http://mng.bz/ZPpj). Noteworthy alternatives include musl libc (https://musl.libc.org/) and diet libc (www .fefe.de/dietlibc/), both of which focus on reducing the footprint. To learn more, check out libc(7) man pages.

In theory, these wrappers provided by glibc invoke the syscall in question in the kernel and call it a day. In practice, a sizable portion of the wrappers adds code to make the syscalls easier to use. In fact, this is easy to check. The glibc source code includes a list of pass-through syscalls, for which the C code is automatically generated using a script. For example, for version 2.23, you can see the list at http://mng.bz/ RXvn. This list contains only 100 of the 380 or so, meaning that almost three-quarters of them contain auxiliary code.

A common example is the exit(3) glibc syscall, which adds the possibility to call any functions preregistered using atexit(3) before executing the actual _exit(2) syscall to terminate the process. So it's worth remembering that a one-to-one mapping doesn't necessarily exist between the functions in the C library and the syscalls they implement.

Finally, notice that the argument names might differ between the documentation of glibc and man pages in section 2. That doesn't matter in C, but you can use section 3 of the man pages (for example, man 3 read) to display the signatures from the C library, instead of unistd.h.

With this new information, it's time to upgrade figure 6.2. Figure 6.3 contains the updated version, with the addition of libc for a more complete image. The user runs a program, and the program executes a libc syscall wrapper, which in turns makes the syscall. The kernel then executes the requested syscall and accesses the hardware.

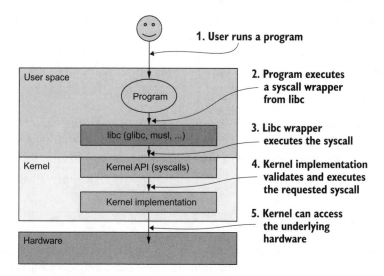

Figure 6.3 User space, libc, kernel space, and hardware

A final thought I'd like to plant in your brain is that libc isn't relevant only when writing software in C. In fact, it's likely to be relevant to you regardless of the programming language you use, and that's why using a Linux distribution relying on musl libc (like Alpine Linux) might sometimes bite you in the neck when you least expect it (for example, see http://mng.bz/opDp).

With that, I think that we've covered all the necessary theory, and it's time to get our chaos-engineering-wielding hands dirty! You know what syscalls are, how to look up their documentation, and what happens when a program makes one. The next question becomes, apart from reading through the entirety of the source code, how you know what syscalls a process is making. Let's cover two ways of achieving that: strace and BPF.

Pop quiz: What are syscalls?

Pick one:

1   A way for a process to request actions on physical devices, such as writing to disk or sending data on a network
2   A way for a process to communicate with the kernel of the operating system it runs on
3   A universal angle of attack for chaos experiments, because virtually every piece of software relies on syscalls
4   All of the above

See appendix B for answers.

6.3   *How to observe a process's syscalls*

For the purpose of chaos engineering, you need to first build a good understanding of what a process does before you can go and design experiments around it. Let's dive in and see what syscalls are being made by using the strace command (https://strace.io/). We'll go through a concrete example of what strace output looks like.

6.3.1   *strace and sleep*

Let's start with the simplest example I can think of; let's trace the syscalls that are made when you run sleep 1, a command that does nothing but sleep for 1 second. To do that, you can just prepend strace to the command you want to run. Run the following command in a terminal window (note that you'll need sudo privileges to use strace):

```
sudo strace sleep 1
```

The command you've just run starts a program you requested (sleep) and prints a line per syscall that is made by that program. In each line, the program prints the syscall name, the arguments, and the returned value after the equals sign (=). There are 12 unique syscalls executed, and nanosleep (providing the actual sleep) is the last one on the list. Let's walk through this output bit by bit (I used bold font for the first instance of a syscall in the output to make it easier to focus on the new syscalls each time).

You start with execve, which replaces the current process with another process from an executable file. Its three arguments are the path to the new binary, a list of command-line arguments, and the process environment, respectively. This is how the new program is started. It's then followed by the brk syscall, which reads (when the argument is NULL, as it is in this example) or sets the end of the process's data segment:

```
execve("/usr/bin/sleep", ["sleep", "1"], 0x7ffd215ca378 /* 16 vars */) = 0
brk(NULL)                            = 0x557cd8060000
```

To check user permissions to a file, you use the access syscall. If present, /etc/ld.so .preload is used to read the list of shared libraries to preload. Use man 8 ld.so for more details on these files. In this case, both calls return a value of -1, meaning that the files don't exist:

```
access("/etc/ld.so.preload", R_OK)   = -1 ENOENT (No such file or directory)
```

Next, you use openat to open a file (the at postfix indicates a variant that handles relative paths, which the regular open doesn't do) and return a file descriptor number 3. fstat is then used to get the file status, using that same file descriptor:

```
openat(AT_FDCWD, "/etc/ld.so.cache", O_RDONLY|O_CLOEXEC) = 3
fstat(3, {st_mode=S_IFREG|0644, st_size=69934, ...}) = 0
```

Next, the mmap syscall creates a map of the same file descriptor 3 into virtual memory of the process, and the file descriptor is closed using the close syscall. mmap is an advanced topic that is not relevant to our goal here; you can read more about how it works at https://en.wikipedia.org/wiki/Mmap:

```
mmap(NULL, 80887, PROT_READ, MAP_PRIVATE, 3, 0) = 0x7ffb65187000
close(3)                            = 0
```

Next, the program opens the libc shared object file at /lib/x86_64-linux-gnu/libc.so.6, with file descriptor 3 being reused:

```
openat(AT_FDCWD, "/lib/x86_64-linux-gnu/libc.so.6", O_RDONLY|O_CLOEXEC) = 3
```

It then reads from the libc shared object file (file descriptor 3) to a buffer using a read syscall. The display here is a bit confusing, because the second parameter is the buffer to which the read syscall will write, so displaying its contents doesn't make much sense. The returned value is the number of bytes read, in this case 832. fstat is used once again to get the file status:

```
read(3, "\177ELF\2\1\1\3\0\0\0\0\0\0\0\0\3\0>\0\1\0\0\0\260\34\2\0\0\0\0\0"...,
832) = 832
fstat(3, {st_mode=S_IFREG|0755, st_size=2030544, ...}) = 0
```

Then the code gets a little fuzzy. mmap is used again to map some virtual memory, including some of the libc shared object file (file descriptor 3). The mprotect syscall is used to protect a portion of that mapped memory from reading. The PROT_NONE flag means that the program can't access that memory at all. Finally, file descriptor 3 is closed with a close syscall. For our purposes, you can consider this boilerplate:

```
mmap(NULL, 8192, PROT_READ|PROT_WRITE, MAP_PRIVATE|MAP_ANONYMOUS, -1, 0) =
    0x7ffb65185000
mmap(NULL, 4131552, PROT_READ|PROT_EXEC, MAP_PRIVATE|MAP_DENYWRITE, 3, 0) =
    0x7ffb64b83000
mprotect(0x7ffb64d6a000, 2097152, PROT_NONE) = 0
mmap(0x7ffb64f6a000, 24576, PROT_READ|PROT_WRITE,
    MAP_PRIVATE|MAP_FIXED|MAP_DENYWRITE, 3, 0x1e7000) = 0x7ffb64f6a000
mmap(0x7ffb64f70000, 15072, PROT_READ|PROT_WRITE,
    MAP_PRIVATE|MAP_FIXED|MAP_ANONYMOUS, -1, 0) = 0x7ffb64f70000
close(3)                                   = 0
```

Next, arch_prctl is used to set an architecture-specific process state (you can ignore it), mprotect is used to make some virtual memory read-only (via the flag PROT_READ), and munmap is used to remove the mapping of the address 0x7ffb65187000, which was mapped to the file /etc/ld.so.cache earlier. All of these operations return value 0 (success):

```
arch_prctl(ARCH_SET_FS, 0x7ffb65186540) = 0
mprotect(0x7ffb64f6a000, 16384, PROT_READ) = 0
mprotect(0x557cd6c5e000, 4096, PROT_READ) = 0
mprotect(0x7ffb6519b000, 4096, PROT_READ) = 0
munmap(0x7ffb65187000, 80887)             = 0
```

The program first reads, and then tries to move, the end of the process's data segment, effectively increasing the memory allocated to the process, using brk:

```
brk(NULL)                               = 0x557cd8060000
brk(0x557cd8081000)                     = 0x557cd8081000
```

Next, it opens /usr/lib/locale/locale-archive, checks its stats, maps it to the virtual memory, and closes it:

```
openat(AT_FDCWD, "/usr/lib/locale/locale-archive", O_RDONLY|O_CLOEXEC) = 3
fstat(3, {st_mode=S_IFREG|0644, st_size=3004464, ...}) = 0
mmap(NULL, 3004464, PROT_READ, MAP_PRIVATE, 3, 0) = 0x7ffb648a5000
close(3)                                = 0
```

Then (finally!) you get to the actual meat of things, which is a single clock_nanosleep syscall, passing 1 second as an argument (tv_sec):

```
clock_nanosleep(CLOCK_REALTIME, 0, {tv_sec=1, tv_nsec=0}, NULL) = 0
```

Eventually, it closes file descriptors 1 (standard output, or stdout) and 2 (standard error, or stderr), just before the program terminates, specifying the exit code 0 (success) through exit_group:

```
close(1)                              = 0
close(2)                              = 0
exit_group(0)                         = ?
```

And you're through! As you can see, this simple program spent much longer doing things you didn't explicitly ask it to do, rather than what you asked (sleep). If you want to learn more about any of these syscalls, remember that you can run man 2 syscall-name in a terminal window.

One more thing I want to show you is the count summary that strace can produce. If you rerun the strace command, but this time add -C and -S count flags, it will produce a summary sorted by the count of each syscall. Run the following command in a terminal window:

```
sudo strace \          ┌── Produces a summary
-C \            ◁──┘   of syscalls
-S calls \      ◁──┐   Sorts that summary
sleep 1            └── by the count
```

After the previous output, you will see a summary similar to the following (your single call to clock_nanosleep in bold):

% time	seconds	usecs/call	calls	errors	syscall
0.00	0.000000	0	8		mmap
0.00	0.000000	0	6		pread64
0.00	0.000000	0	5		close
0.00	0.000000	0	4		mprotect
0.00	0.000000	0	3		fstat
0.00	0.000000	0	3		brk
0.00	0.000000	0	3		openat
0.00	0.000000	0	2	1	arch_prctl
0.00	0.000000	0	1		read
0.00	0.000000	0	1		munmap
0.00	0.000000	0	1	1	access
0.00	0.000000	0	1		execve
0.00	0.000000	0	1		**clock_nanosleep**
100.00	0.000000		39	2	total

This once again shows that the syscall you actually cared about is only 1 of 32. Equipped with this new toy, let's take a look at what our legacy System X does under the hood!

> **Pop quiz: What can strace do for you?**
> Pick one:
>
> 1   Show you what syscalls a process is making in real time
> 2   Show you what syscalls a process is making in real time, without incurring a performance penalty
> 3   List all the places in the source code of the application where a certain action, like reading from disk, is performed
>
> See appendix B for answers.

6.3.2   *strace and System X*

Let's use strace on the legacy System X binary to see what syscalls it makes. You know how to start a new process with strace; now you'll also learn how to attach to a process that's already running. You're going to use two terminal windows. In the first window, start the legacy_server binary you compiled earlier:

```
~/src/examples/who-you-gonna-call/src/legacy_server
```

You will see output similar to the following, printing the port number it listens on and its PID. Note the PID; you can use it to attach to the process with strace (bold font):

```
Listening on port 8080, PID: 6757
```

In a second terminal window, let's use strace to attach to that PID. Run the following command to attach to the legacy system:

```
sudo strace -C \
-p $(pidof legacy_server)        ◁──┐  Flag -p attaches to an existing
                                      │  process with the given PID
```

Now, back in the browser, go to (or refresh) http://127.0.0.1:8080/. Then go back to the second terminal window (the one with strace) and look at the output. You will see something similar to the following (abbreviated). This gives you a pretty good idea of what the program is doing. It accepts a connection with accept, writes a bunch of data with write, and closes the connection with close (all three in bold font):

```
accept(3, {sa_family=AF_INET, sin_port=htons(53698),
    sin_addr=inet_addr("127.0.0.1")}, [16]) = 4
read(4, "GET / HTTP/1.1\r\nHost: 127.0.0.1:"..., 2048) = 333
write(4, "HTTP/1.0 200 OK\r\nContent-Type: t"..., 122) = 122
write(4, "<", 1)                       = 1
write(4, "!", 1)                       = 1
write(4, "d", 1)
(...)
fsync(4)                               = -1 EINVAL (Invalid argument)
close(4)                               = 0
```

You might have noticed that this code has a bug: it tries to `fsync` a file (synchronize the file's in-core state with the storage device), and it gets back the error `EINVAL` (`Invalid argument`). You can now press Ctrl-C to detach `strace`, and print the summary, like the following one. You can also see that it does a whole lot of writes (292 to be precise), almost all of which write only a single character. More than 98% of the time is spent writing data (in bold font):

```
<detached ...>
% time     seconds  usecs/call     calls    errors syscall
------ ----------- ----------- --------- --------- ----------------
 98.34    0.002903          10       292           write
  0.68    0.000020          20         1           close
  0.61    0.000018          18         1           accept
  0.34    0.000010          10         1           read
  0.03    0.000001           1         1         1 fsync
------ ----------- ----------- --------- --------- ----------------
100.00    0.002952                   296         1 total
```

Notice that by attaching `strace` to a running process, you're sampling the syscalls that process made only while you were attached to it. This makes the method easier to work through, but will miss any potentially important initial setup the program might have done.

So far, so good! Using `strace` has been straightforward. Unfortunately, it also has its downsides, and the biggest one is overhead. Let's zoom in on that.

6.3.3　strace's problem: Overhead

The dark side of `strace` is the performance hit that it adds to the traced process. It's not really a secret—this comes directly from `man strace(1)` pages:

```
BUGS
        A traced process runs slowly.
```

Here's a good example I'm borrowing from Brendan Gregg's blog post that I recommend reading (it comes with a bunch of useful, accurately titled one-liners and it's overall hilarious): www.brendangregg.com/blog/2014-05-11/strace-wow-much-syscall.html.

dd is a simple Linux utility that copies a certain number of bytes from one file to another, using chunks of desired size. Its simplicity makes it a good candidate for testing the speed of syscalls; it does very little other than make `read` syscalls followed by `write` syscalls. Thus, by reading from an infinite source, like /dev/zero (returns zeros for every read) and writing to /dev/null (discards the written bytes), you can stress test the speed of `read` and `write` syscalls.

Let's do just that. First, let's see how quickly the program can go without `strace` attached to it. Let's make 500,000 operations (an arbitrary number that should be big enough to last a few hundred milliseconds, but small enough to not bore you to death) and writes of size 1 byte (the smallest amount we can write, for a maximum number of operations), by running the following command in a terminal window:

```
dd if=/dev/zero of=/dev/null bs=1 count=500k
```

You will see output similar to the following, taking about half a second (bold font) to perform that operation:

```
512000+0 records in
512000+0 records out
512000 bytes (512 kB, 500 KiB) copied, 0.509962 s, 1.0 MB/s
```

Now, let's rerun the same command, but trace it with strace. And let's use the -e flag to filter only the accept syscall, which dd doesn't even use (to show that just the action of attaching strace is already adding the overhead, even if it's on an unrelated syscall). Run the following command in a terminal window:

```
strace \
-e accept \          ◁──┐  Prints only the accept syscalls
dd if=/dev/zero of=/dev/null bs=1 count=500k   (which dd doesn't make)
```

You will see output similar to the following. In my example, it took 58.5 seconds (bold font), or a more than 100-fold slowdown, compared to the values without strace:

```
512000+0 records in
512000+0 records out
512000 bytes (512 kB, 500 KiB) copied, 58.4923 s, 8.8 kB/s
+++ exited with 0 +++
```

This means that it might be fine to use strace in a test environment, as you're doing now, but attaching it to a process running in production can have serious consequences. It also means that if you were looking into the performance of a program traced with strace, all your numbers would be off.

All of that limits the use cases for strace, but fortunately there are other options. Let's look at an alternative: the Berkeley Packet Filter.

---

ptrace syscall

I bet you're wondering about the underlying mechanism that allows strace to control and manipulate other processes. The answer is the ptrace syscall. You don't need to know how it works to get value out of using strace, but for those of you who are curious, check out the man page of ptrace(2). Wikipedia also has a good intro: https://en.wikipedia.org/wiki/Ptrace.

6.3.4   *BPF*

The *Berkeley Packet Filter* (*BPF*) was initially designed to filter network packets. It has since been extended (*extended Berkeley Packet Filter*, or *eBPF*) to become a generic Linux kernel execution engine, which allows for writing programs with guarantees of safety *and* performance. When talking about BPF, most people refer to the extended version. In the context of chaos engineering, BPF will often come in handy to produce metrics for our experiments.

One of the most exciting things about BPF is that it allows for writing very efficient programs executed during certain events in the Linux kernel. Together with the limits enforced on the time these programs can take and the memory they can access, as well as built-in efficient aggregation primitives, BPF is an amazing tool to gain visibility into what's going on at the kernel level. What is exciting for our chaos engineering needs is that unlike with `strace`, it is often possible to achieve that insight (for example, trace all the syscalls) with minimal overhead.

The downside of BPF is that the learning curve is pretty steep. To write a meaningful program looking into the Linux kernel internals, it's routinely necessary to look into how things are implemented in the kernel itself. Although the time investment pays off, it can be a little daunting at first. Fortunately, a few projects make that introduction much easier. Let's take a look at how one of those projects can help in the practice of chaos engineering.

BPF AND BCC

BPF Compiler Collection, or BCC (https://github.com/iovisor/bcc), is a framework that makes it easier to write and run BPF programs, providing wrappers in Python and Lua and many useful tools and examples. Reading through these tools and examples is currently the best way of starting with BPF that I can think of.

Chapter 3 covered a few of the BCC tools (`biotop`, `tcptop`, `oomkill`), and now I'd like to bring another one to your attention: `syscount`. Your VM comes with the tools preinstalled, but installing them on Ubuntu is as easy as running the following command from a terminal (check appendix A for more information):

```
sudo apt-get install bpfcc-tools linux-headers-$(uname -r)
```

In the previous section, you used `strace` to produce a list of syscalls made by a program. That approach worked well but had one serious problem: `strace` introduced a large amount of overhead to the program it was tracing. Let me show you how to get the same list without the overhead, by leveraging BPF and BCC through the tool `syscount`.

Let's start by getting used to using `syscount`. In its simplest form, it will count all syscalls of all the processes currently running and then print the top 10. Run the following command in a terminal window to count the syscalls (remember that on Ubuntu, the BCC tools are postfixed with `-bpfcc`):

```
sudo syscount-bpfcc
```

After a few seconds, press Ctrl-C to stop the process, and you will see output just like the following. You will recognize some of the syscalls on the list, like `write` and `read` (bold font). It's a list counting all syscalls made by all the processes on the host during the time `syscount` was running:

```
Tracing syscalls, printing top 10... Ctrl+C to quit.
^C[20:12:40]
SYSCALL               COUNT
recvmsg               42057
futex                 35200
poll                  12730
epoll_wait             6816
write                  6005
read                   5971
writev                 4200
setitimer              2957
mprotect               2748
sendmsg                2631
```

Now, let's verify this claim about low overhead. Remember that in the previous section, just using `strace` on the process slowed it down by a factor of 100, even though you were targeting a syscall that the program wasn't making? Let's compare how BPF fares. To do that, let's open two terminals. In the first one, you'll run the `syscount` command again, and in the other one, you'll rerun the same `dd` one-liner used earlier. Ready? Start by running the `syscount` in the first terminal:

```
sudo syscount-bpfcc
```

Then, from a second terminal window, run `dd` again:

```
dd if=/dev/zero of=/dev/null bs=1 count=500k
```

When the command is done, you will see output like the following in the second terminal. Notice that the total time of executing the half-million `read` and `write` syscalls took slightly longer than previously (0.509 seconds), 0.54 seconds in my example:

```
512000+0 records in
512000+0 records out
512000 bytes (512 kB, 500 KiB) copied, 0.541597 s, 945 kB/s
```

0.541597 seconds versus 0.509962 seconds is about 6% overhead, and that's for a close-to-worst-case scenario, where `dd` doesn't do much more than read and write. And you've been tracing everything that's happening on the kernel, not just a single PID.

Now that you've confirmed that the overhead is much more acceptable for BPF, compared to `strace`, let's go back to our chaos engineering use case: learning how to get a list of syscalls made by a process. Let's see how to use `syscount` to show the top syscalls for a specific PID, using the -p flag. To do that, let's once again use two terminal windows. In the first one, start legacy_server by running the following command:

```
~/src/examples/who-you-gonna-call/src/legacy_server
```

In a second terminal window, start the syscount command, but this time with the -p flag:

```
sudo syscount-bpfcc \
-p $(pidof legacy_server)
```
Traces only the calls for pid of our legacy server ◁──┘

You will see output like that shown in table 6.1. Note that it matches the summary of the output you've gotten from strace, with 292 calls to write, although it provides fewer details.

Table 6.1 Output of `syscount-bpfcc` side by side with the output of `strace`

syscount-bpfcc		strace					
Tracing syscalls, printing top 10... Ctrl+C to quit.		% time	seconds	usecs/call	calls	errors	syscall
^C[20:39:19]		98.34	0.002903	10		29	write
SYSCALL	COUNT	0.68	0.000020	20			close
write	292	0.61	0.000018	18			accept
accept	1	0.34	0.000010	10			read
read	1	0.03	0.000001	1		1	fsync
close	1						
fsync	1	100.00	0.002952	296		1	total

And voilà! Using this technique, you can now list syscalls that a process makes, without the overhead that strace introduces. Note that syscount-bpfcc gives you only a count, without the details that strace was printing for each syscall, but this will be sufficient if you need only a rough idea of what a process is doing. As always, when designing your chaos experiment, pick the right tool for the job.

I'd love to talk to you more about BPF (and I'm sure we will, if we bump into each other at the next conference), but it's time to move on. If you feel like you need more BPF in your life, read through the source code of syscount. It's only a single less $(which syscount-bpfcc) (or http://mng.bz/2erN) away! In the meantime, let's make a few other honorable mentions of alternative tools you might be able to use to get similar results.

6.3.5 *Other options*

I want to make you aware of other related technologies that are available to use to gain a similar level of visibility. Unfortunately, we won't get into the details, but having them on your radar is worthwhile. Let's take a look.

SYSTEMTAP

SystemTap (https://sourceware.org/systemtap/) is a tool for dynamically instrumenting running Linux systems. It uses a domain-specific language (which looks much like AWK or C; read more at https://sourceware.org/systemtap/man/stap.1.html) to describe various kinds of probes. The probes are then compiled and inserted into a running kernel. The original paper describing the motivations and architecture can be found at https://sourceware.org/systemtap/archpaper.pdf. SystemTap and BPF overlap, and there is even a BPF backend for SystemTap, called `stapbpf`.

FTRACE

Ftrace (www.kernel.org/doc/Documentation/trace/ftrace.txt) is another framework for tracing the Linux kernel. It allows for tracing many events happening in the kernel, both statically and dynamically defined. It requires a kernel built with ftracer support and has been part of the kernel codebase since 2008.

With that, we're ready to design some chaos experiments!

Pop quiz: What's BPF?

Pick one:

1 Berkeley Performance Filters: an arcane technology designed to limit the amount of resources a process can use, to avoid one client using all available resources
2 A part of the Linux kernel that allows you to filter network traffic
3 A part of the Linux kernel that allows you to execute special code directly inside the kernel to gain visibility into various kernel events
4 Options 2, 3, and much more!

See appendix B for answers.

Pop quiz: Is investing time into understanding BPF worthwhile if you're interested in system performance?

Pick one:

1 Yes
2 Definitely
3 Absolutely
4 Positively

See appendix B for answers.

6.4   *Blocking syscalls for fun and profit part 1: strace*

Let's put our chaos engineering hats on and design an experiment that will tell you how your legacy application fares when it gets errors while trying to make syscalls. So far you've looked under the hood to see what the black-box System X binary is doing, all without reading the source code. You've established that during an HTTP request from a browser, the binary makes a small number of syscalls, as in the following output:

```
% time     seconds  usecs/call     calls    errors syscall
------ ----------- ----------- --------- --------- ----------------
 98.34    0.002903          10       292           write
  0.68    0.000020          20         1           close
  0.61    0.000018          18         1           accept
  0.34    0.000010          10         1           read
  0.03    0.000001           1         1         1 fsync
------ ----------- ----------- --------- --------- ----------------
100.00    0.002952                   296         1 total
```

To warm up, let's start with something simple: pick the `close` syscall, which is called only a single time in our initial research, and see whether System X handles a situation in which `close` returns an error. What could possibly go wrong? Let's find out.

6.4.1 *Experiment 1: Breaking the close syscall*

As always, you'll start with the observability. Luckily, you can once again use the `ab` command, which will allow you to generate traffic and summarize statistics about the latencies, throughput, and number of failed requests. And because you have no information about it, except that the system has been running live for years, let's assume there will be no requests if you introduce failure on the `close` syscall. Therefore, you can devise the following four simple steps to run a chaos experiment:

1 Observability: use `ab` to generate traffic, read the number of failures and latencies.
2 Steady state: read `ab` numbers for System X under normal conditions.
3 Hypothesis: if you make calls to `close` fail for the System X binary, it will handle it gracefully, and transparently to the end user.
4 Run the experiment!

You're familiar with the `ab` command, and you know how to trace a process with `strace`, so the question now becomes how you introduce failure into a syscall for the System X binary. Fortunately, `strace` makes it easy through the use of the `-e` flag. Let's learn how to use the `-e` flag, by looking into the help of `strace`. To do that, run the `strace` command with the `-h` flag:

```
strace -h
```

You will see the following output (abbreviated); in particular, notice the `fault` option (bold font):

```
(...)
  -e expr  a qualifying expression: option=[!]all or option=[!]val1[,val2]...
     options:   trace, abbrev, verbose, raw, signal, read, write, fault
(...)
```

By default, running with the flag -e fault=<syscall name> returns an error (-1) on every call to the desired syscall. To inject failure into the close syscall, you can use the -e fault=close flag. This is the most popular form. But you can use another, more flexible flag (although, weirdly, it's not mentioned by strace -h), and that's -e inject. To learn about it, you need to read the man pages for strace by running the following command:

```
man strace
```

You will see much more detail on how to use strace. In particular, note the section describing the -e inject option (in bold font) and its syntax:

```
(...)
    -e inject=set[:error=errno|:retval=value][:signal=sig][:when=expr]
            Perform syscall tampering for the specified set of syscalls.

(...)
```

In fact, the flag is pretty powerful and supports the following arguments:

- fault=<syscall>—Injects a fault into a particular syscall
- error=<error name>—Specifies a particular error to return
- retval=<return code>—Overrides the actual syscall return value and sends the specified one instead
- signal=sig—Sends a particular signal to the traced process
- when=<expression>—Controls which calls are affected, and can take three forms:
  - when=<n>—Tampers with only the *n*th syscall
  - when=<n>+—Tampers with only the *n*th and all subsequent calls
  - when=<n>+<step>—Tampers with the *n*th, and every one in step occurrences after that

For example, the following flag fails every write syscall, starting with the second one, by injecting an EACCES error (permission denied) as the return value:

```
-e inject=write:error=EACCES:when=2+
```

The following flag, on the other hand, overrides the result of the first syscall to fsync (even if it is an error response) and returns a value of 0 instead:

```
-e inject=fsync:retval=0:when=1
```

All of this together gives you fairly fine-grained control over what happens to the process on the syscall level. The price? Well, once again, the overhead. You need to keep in mind that to compare apples to apples, you'll also need to establish your steady state, including the overhead of strace. But as long as you do that, you should be ready to implement the experiment. Let's do it!

EXPERIMENT 1 STEADY STATE

First, let's establish the steady state. You'll use three terminal windows: System X in the first one, `strace` in the second, and `ab` in the third. Let's start legacy_server (the System X binary) in the first window:

```
~/src/examples/who-you-gonna-call/src/legacy_server
```

Next, let's attach `strace` to legacy_server in the second terminal window, for now without any failures, and tracing only the `close` syscalls. Run the following command:

```
sudo strace \
-p $(pidof legacy_server) \        ┌ Displays only the
-e close                        ◄──┘ close syscall
```

Finally, let's start `ab` in the third window. You'll use a concurrency of 1 to keep things simple, and run for up to 30 seconds:

```
ab -c1 -t30 http://127.0.0.1:8080/
```

In the same third window, you will see results similar to the following. Of the ~3000 complete requests, none failed, and you achieve about 101 requests per second (all three in bold font):

```
(...)
Time taken for tests:    30.003 seconds
Complete requests:       3042
Failed requests:         0
(...)
Requests per second:     101.39 [#/sec] (mean)
(...)
```

So that's our steady state: no failures and about 100 requests per second. To be sure, you could run ab a few times and see how much the values vary between runs. Now, to the fun part: implementation time!

EXPERIMENT 1 IMPLEMENTATION

Let's see what happens when the legacy System X gets errors on the `close` syscall. To do that, let's keep the same setup with three terminal windows, but in the second one, close `strace` (press Ctrl-C) and restart it with `-e inject` option:

```
sudo strace \
-p $(pidof legacy_server) \
-e close \                         ┌ Adds failure to the close
-e inject=close:error=EIO       ◄──┘ syscall, uses error EIO
```

Now, in the third terminal window, start ab again with the same command:

```
ab -c1 -t30 http://127.0.0.1:8080/
```

This time, the output will be different. Your ab isn't even able to finish its run; it's getting an error (bold font):

```
(...)
Benchmarking 127.0.0.1 (be patient)
apr_socket_recv: Connection refused (111)
Total of 1 requests completed
```

If you switch back to the second window with strace, you will see that it injected the error you asked for, and that the application then exited with error code 1, just as in the following output. It also exited at the very first call to close (number of calls and errors in bold font):

```
close(4)                      = -1 EIO (Input/output error) (INJECTED)
+++ exited with 1 +++
% time     seconds  usecs/call     calls    errors syscall
------ ----------- ----------- --------- --------- ----------------
  0.00    0.000000           0         1         1 close
------ ----------- ----------- --------- --------- ----------------
100.00    0.000000                     1         1 total
```

And back in the first window, the application printed an error message and crashed with the following output:

```
legacy_server: error closing socket: Input/output error
```

What does it mean? Well, our experiment hypothesis was wrong. Let's analyze these findings.

EXPERIMENT 1 ANALYSIS

You've learned that the application doesn't handle failure gracefully when making the close syscall; it exits with an error code of 1, signaling a generic error. You still haven't looked into the source code, so you can't be sure why its authors decided to implement it that way, but using this simple experiment, you have already found a fragile point. How fragile? Let's see what the man pages tell us about the close syscall by running the following command in a terminal:

```
man 2 close
```

If you scroll to the ERRORS section, you will see the following output:

```
ERRORS
       EBADF  fd isn't a valid open file descriptor.

       EINTR  The close() call was interrupted by a signal; see signal(7).

       EIO    An I/O error occurred.

       ENOSPC, EDQUOT
              On NFS, these errors are not normally reported against the
```

```
                    first write which exceeds the available storage space, but instead against
                              a subsequent write(2), fsync(2), or close(2).
```

This information can be summarized as four possibilities:

1. The argument is not an open file descriptor.
2. The call was interrupted by a signal.
3. An I/O error occurred
4. A Network File System (NFS) write error is reported against a subsequent close, instead of a write.

Again, without even reading through the source code, you can make an educated guess that at least option 2 is possible, because any process could be interrupted by a signal. And now you know that this kind of interruption might cause the legacy System X to go down. Fortunately, you can test it by injecting that specific error code to see if the program handles it correctly.

Now that you know about this, you could try to find the place in the source code that handles this part and make it more resilient to failure. That would definitely help the newly promoted you sleep better. But let's not elect to rest on our laurels quite yet. I wonder what happens when failure occurs on one of the busier syscalls—for example, write?

6.4.2 Experiment 2: Breaking the write syscall

Recalling our handy table of syscalls, the legacy System X spent most of its time making write syscalls (in bold font), as shown in the following output:

```
% time     seconds  usecs/call     calls    errors syscall
------ ----------- ----------- --------- --------- ----------------
 98.34    0.002903          10       292           write
  0.68    0.000020          20         1           close
  0.61    0.000018          18         1           accept
  0.34    0.000010          10         1           read
  0.03    0.000001           1         1         1 fsync
------ ----------- ----------- --------- --------- ----------------
100.00    0.002952                   296         1 total
```

Surely, for a piece of software that might predate our tenure at the company, some kind of resilience and fault tolerance must be built in, right? Well, let's find out! Much as in the previous experiment, let's use ab and strace, but let's fail only every other call to write. Our experiment then becomes as follows:

1. Observability: use ab to generate traffic, and read the number of failures and latencies for System X.
2. Steady state: read ab numbers under normal conditions.
3. Hypothesis: if you make every other call to write fail for the System X binary, it will handle it gracefully, and transparently to the end user.
4. Run the experiment!

If this sounds like a plan, let's go and do it.

EXPERIMENT 2 STEADY STATE

Again, let's start by establishing the steady state. You'll use three terminal windows again: System X in the first one, `strace` in the second, and `ab` in the third. Let's start legacy_server (System X binary) in the first window by running the following command:

```
~/src/examples/who-you-gonna-call/src/legacy_server
```

Next, let's attach `strace` to legacy_server in the second terminal window, for now without any failures, and tracing only the `write` syscalls. Do that by running the following command:

```
sudo strace \
-p $(pidof legacy_server) \          Displays only the
-e write                    ◁⎦  write syscall
```

Finally, let's start `ab` in the third window. We'll use a concurrency of 1 to keep things simple, and run for up to 30 seconds:

```
ab -c1 -t30 http://127.0.0.1:8080/
```

In the same third window, you will see results similar to the following. Similar to the previous experiment, there should be no failures, but the throughput will be lower (bold font), due to more print operations at the terminal:

```
(...)
Complete requests:      1587
Failed requests:        0
(...)
```

Your steady state is similar to the one from the previous experiment; that shouldn't be a surprise. Let's now get to the fun part—the actual implementation of the failure injection for experiment 2.

EXPERIMENT 2 IMPLEMENTATION

The fun should start when the legacy System X gets errors on the `write` syscall. To do that, let's keep the same setup with three terminal windows. And just like the last time, in the second window, close `strace` (press Ctrl-C) and restart it with the `-e inject` option to add the failure you designed (fail every other `write` syscall):

```
sudo strace \                    Displays a           Adds failure to the close
-p $(pidof legacy_server) \      summary at the       syscall, uses error EIO, fails
   -C \                   ◁⎦    end of the session   on every other call starting
-e inject=write:error=EIO:when=1+2                    with the first one
                              ◁────────────
```

Now, in the third terminal window, let's start `ab` again with the same command:

```
ab -c1 -t10 http://127.0.0.1:8080/
```

This time, you're in for a pleasant surprise. You will see output similar to the following. Despite every other syscall failing, overall there are still no failed requests (bold font). But the throughput is roughly halved, at 570 requests in this example (also bold font):

```
(...)
Time taken for tests:    30.034 seconds
Complete requests:       570
Failed requests:         0
(...)
```

In the second window, you can now kill `strace` by pressing Ctrl-C. Take a look at the output. You will see a lot of lines similar to the following. You can clearly see that the program retries failed writes, because each write is done twice, first receiving the error you inject, and then succeeding:

```
(...)
write(4, "l", 1)                = -1 EIO (Input/output error) (INJECTED)
write(4, "l", 1)                = 1
write(4, ">", 1)                = -1 EIO (Input/output error) (INJECTED)
write(4, ">", 1)                = 1
(...)
```

The program implements some kind of algorithm to account for failed write syscalls, which is good news—one step closer to getting paged less at night. You can also see the cost of the additional operations: the throughput is roughly 50% of what it was without the retries. In real life, it's unlikely that every other `write` would fail, but even in this nightmarish scenario, System X turns out to not be as easy to break as it was with the `close` syscall.

And that concludes experiment 2. This time our hypothesis was correct. High five! You've learned how to discover which syscalls are made by a process and how to tamper with them to implement experiments using `strace`. And in this case, focusing on whether System X keeps working, rather than on how quickly it responds, it all worked out.

But we still have one skeleton in the closet: the overhead of `strace`. What can we do if we want to block some syscalls but can't accept the massive slowdown while doing the experiment? Before we wrap up this chapter, I'd like to point out an alternative solution for syscalls blocking: using seccomp.

6.5 *Blocking syscalls for fun and profit part 2: Seccomp*

You'll remember seccomp from chapter 5 as a way to harden containers by restricting the syscalls that they can make. I would like to show you how to use seccomp to implement experiments similar to what we've done with `strace` by blocking certain syscalls. You'll do it the easy way and the hard way, each covering a different use case. The easy way is quick but not very flexible. The hard way is more flexible but requires more work. Let's start with the easy way.

6.5.1   *Seccomp the easy way with Docker*

An easy way to block syscalls is to leverage a custom seccomp profile when starting a container. Probably the easiest way of achieving this is to download the default seccomp policy (http://mng.bz/1r9Z) and remove the syscall that you'd like to disable.

The profile has the following structure. It's a list of allowed calls; by default, all calls are blocked and return an error when called (the SCMP_ACT_ERRNO default action). Then a long list of names is explicitly allowed:

```
{
    "defaultAction": "SCMP_ACT_ERRNO",        ⟵  By default,
...                                              blocks all calls
    "syscalls": [
            {
                "names": [                    ⟵  For the syscalls with the
                    "accept",                     following list of names
                    "accept4",
...
                    "write",
                    "writev"
                ],
                "action": "SCMP_ACT_ALLOW",   ⟵  Allows them
...                                              to proceed
            },
...
...
        ]
}
```

Your System X binary uses the getpid syscall; let's try to block that. To construct a profile with getpid excluded, run the following commands in a terminal window. This will store the new profile in profile.json (or if you don't have internet access right now, you can find it in ~/src/examples/who-you-gonna-call/profile.json in the VM):

```
cd ~/src/examples/who-you-gonna-call/src
curl
https://raw.githubusercontent.com/moby/moby/master/profiles/seccomp/default.j
son \
| grep -v getpid > profile.json
```

I have also prepared a simple Dockerfile for you to package the System X binary into a container. You can see it by running the following command in the terminal:

```
cat ~/src/examples/who-you-gonna-call/src/Dockerfile
```

You will see the following output. You use the latest Ubuntu base image and just copy the binary from the host:

```
FROM ubuntu:focal-20200423
COPY ./legacy_server /legacy_server
ENTRYPOINT [ "/legacy_server" ]
```

With that, you can build a Docker image with your legacy software and start it. Do that by running the following commands from the same terminal window. The commands will build and run a new image called legacy, use the profile you just created, and expose port 8080 on the host:

```
cd ~/src/examples/who-you-gonna-call/src
make
docker build -t legacy .
docker run \
--rm \
-ti \
--name legacy \
--security-opt seccomp=./profile.json \     ◁─────  Uses the seccomp
-p 8080:8080 \                              ◁─────  profile just created
legacy
                                                    Exposes the container's
                                                    port 8080 on the host
```

You will see the process starting, but notice the PID equal to -1 (bold font). This is the seccomp blocking the getpid syscall, and returning an error code -1, just as you asked it to do:

```
Listening on port 8080, PID: -1
```

And voilà! You achieved blocking a particular syscall. That's the easy way! Unfortunately, doing it this way provides less flexibility than strace; you can't pick every other call and can't attach to a running process. You also need Docker to actually run it, which further limits suitable use cases.

On the bright side, you achieved blocking the syscall without incurring the harsh penalty introduced by strace. But don't just take my word for it; let's find out how it compares. While the container is running, let's rerun the same ab one-liner used to establish the steady state in our previous experiments:

```
ab -c1 -t30 http://127.0.0.1:8080/
```

You will see much more pleasant output, similar to the following. At 36,000 requests (bold font), you are at least 10 times faster than when tracing the close syscall (when you achieved 3042 requests per second):

```
(...)
Time taken for tests:    30.001 seconds
Complete requests:       36107
Failed requests:         0
Total transferred:       14912191 bytes
HTML transferred:        10507137 bytes
Requests per second:     1203.53 [#/sec]  (mean)
Time per request:        0.831 [ms]  (mean)
(...)
```

So there you have it: seccomp the easy way, leveraging Docker. But what if the easy way is not flexible enough? Or you can't or don't want to use Docker? If you need more flexibility, let's look at the level below—libseccomp, or seccomp the hard way.

6.5.2 *Seccomp the hard way with libseccomp*

Libseccomp (https://github.com/seccomp/libseccomp) is a higher-level, platform-independent library for managing seccomp in the Linux kernel that abstracts away the low-level syscalls and exposes easy-to-use functions for developers. It is leveraged by Docker to implement its seccomp profiles. The best place to start to learn how to use it is the tests (http://mng.bz/vzD4) and man pages, such as `seccomp_init(3)`, `seccomp_rule_add(3)`, and `seccomp_load(3)`. In this section, I'll show you a brief example of how you too can leverage libseccomp with just a few lines of C.

First, you need to install the dependencies from the package `libseccomp-dev` on Ubuntu/Debian or `libseccomp-devel` on RHEL/Centos. On Ubuntu, you can do that by running the following command (this step is already done for you if you're using the VM that comes with this book):

```
sudo apt-get install libseccomp-dev
```

This will allow you to include the `<seccomp.h>` header in your programs to link against the seccomp library (you'll do both in a second). Let me show you how to use libseccomp to limit the syscalls your program can make. I prepared a small example, which does a minimal amount of setup to change its permissions during the execution time to allow only a small number of syscalls to go through. To see the example, run the following command from a terminal window:

```
cat ~/src/examples/who-you-gonna-call/seccomp.c
```

You will see a simple C program. It uses four functions from libseccomp to limit the syscalls you're allowed to make:

- `seccomp_init`—Initializes the seccomp state and prepares it for usage; returns a context
- `seccomp_rule_add`—Adds a new filtering rule to the context
- `seccomp_load`—Loads the actual context into the kernel
- `seccomp_release`—Releases the filter context and frees memory when you're done with the context

You will see the following output (the four functions are in bold font). You start by initializing the context to block all syscalls and then explicitly allow two of them: `write` and `exit`. Then you load the context, execute one `getpid` syscall and one `write`, and release the context:

```
#include <stdio.h>
#include <unistd.h>
#include <seccomp.h>
#include <errno.h>
```

```
int main(void)                                    Initializes the context by defaulting
{                                                       to returning the EPERM error
    scmp_filter_ctx ctx;
    int rc; // note that we totally avoid any error handling here...

    // disable everything by default, by returning EPERM (not allowed)
    ctx = seccomp_init(SCMP_ACT_ERRNO(EPERM));
    // allow write...
    rc = seccomp_rule_add(ctx, SCMP_ACT_ALLOW, SCMP_SYS(write), 0);
    // and exit - otherwise it would segfault on exit
    rc = seccomp_rule_add(ctx, SCMP_ACT_ALLOW, SCMP_SYS(exit), 0);
    // load the profile
    rc = seccomp_load(ctx);                          Loads the context just
                                                     configured into the kernel

    // write should succeed, but the pid will not
    fprintf(stdout, "getpid() == %d\n", getpid());

    // release the seccomp context                   Releases the
    seccomp_release(ctx);                            context
}
```

Allows write → (points to `seccomp_rule_add(ctx, SCMP_ACT_ALLOW, SCMP_SYS(write), 0);`)

Allows exit → (points to `seccomp_rule_add(ctx, SCMP_ACT_ALLOW, SCMP_SYS(exit), 0);`)

Let's compile and start the program by running the following commands in the same terminal window:

```
cd ~/src/examples/who-you-gonna-call      You need to include the
cc seccomp.c \                            seccomp library, using
-lseccomp \                               the -l flag.
-o seccomp-example
./seccomp-example       Calls the output executable
                        "seccomp-example"
```

You will see the following output. The fact that you see the output at all proves that the write syscall was allowed. The program also finished without crashing, meaning that exit worked too. But as you can see, the result of getpid was -1 (bold font), just as you wanted:

```
getpid() == -1
```

And that's the hard way, which—thanks to libseccomp—is not that hard after all. You can now leverage this mechanism to block or allow syscalls as you see fit, and you can use it to implement chaos experiments. If you'd like to dig deeper into seccomp, I suggest checking the following resources:

- "A seccomp Overview," by Jake Edge, https://lwn.net/Articles/656307/
- "Using seccomp to Limit the Kernel Attack Surface" by Michael Kerrisk, http://mng.bz/4ZEj
- "Syscall Filtering and You" by Paul Moore, https://www.paul-moore.com/docs/devconf-syscall_filtering-pmoore-012014-r1.pdf

And with that, it's time to wrap it up!

Summary

- System calls (syscalls) are a way of communicating between userland programs and the operating system, allowing the programs to indirectly access system resources.

- Chaos engineering can produce value even for simple systems consisting of a single process, by testing their resilience to errors when making syscalls.

- strace is a flexible and easy-to-use tool that allows for detecting and manipulating syscalls made by any program on the host, but it incurs non-negligible overhead.

- BPF, made easier to use by projects like BCC, allows for much-lower-overhead insight into the running system, including listing syscalls made by processes.

- Seccomp can be leveraged to implement chaos experiments designed to block processes from making syscalls, and libseccomp makes it much easier to use seccomp.

7

Injecting failure into the JVM

This chapter covers

- Designing chaos experiments for applications written in Java

- Injecting failure into a JVM using the `java.lang.instrument` interface (`javaagent`)

- Using free, open source tools to implement chaos experiments

Java is one of the most popular programming languages on planet Earth; in fact, it is consistently placed in the top two or three of many popularity rankings.[1] When practicing chaos engineering, you are likely to work with systems written in Java. In this chapter, I'm going to focus on preparing you for that moment.

You'll start by looking at an existing Java application to come up with ideas for chaos experiments. Then you'll leverage a unique feature of the Java Virtual Machine (JVM) to inject failure into an existing codebase (without modifying the source code) to implement our experiments. Finally, you'll cover some existing tools that will allow you to make the whole process easier, as well as some further reading.

---

[1] Take, for example, the 2020 State of the Octoverse at https://octoverse.github.com/#top-languages or the Tiobe Index at www.tiobe.com/tiobe-index/, two popular rankings.

By the end of this chapter, you will have learned how to apply chaos engineering practices to any Java program you run into and understand the underlying mechanisms that make it possible to rewrite Java code on the fly. First stop: a scenario to put things in context.

7.1 Scenario

Your previous chapter's success in rendering the legacy System X less scary and more maintainable hasn't gone unnoticed. In fact, it's been the subject of many watercooler chats on every floor of the office and a source of many approving nods from strangers in the elevator. One interesting side effect is that people have started reaching out, asking for your help to make their projects more resilient to failure. Charming at first, it quickly turned into a "please pick a number and wait in the waiting room until your number appears on the screen" situation. Inevitably, a priority queue had to be introduced for the most important projects to be handled quickly.

One of these high-profile projects was called *FBEE*. At this stage, no one knew for sure what the acronym stood for, but everyone understood it was an enterprise-grade software solution, very expensive, and perhaps a tad overengineered. Helping make FBEE more resilient felt like the right thing to do, so you accepted the challenge. Let's see what's what.

7.1.1 Introducing FizzBuzzEnterpriseEdition

With a little bit of digging, you find out that *FBEE* stands for *FizzBuzzEnterpriseEdition*, and it certainly lives up to its name. It started as a simple programming game used to interview developer candidates and has evolved over time. The game itself is simple and goes like this—for each number between 1 and 100, do the following:

- If the number is divisible by 3, print *Fizz*.
- If the number if divisible by 5, print *Buzz*.
- If the number is divisible by both 3 and 5, print *FizzBuzz*.
- Otherwise, print the number itself.

Over time, however, some people felt that this simple algorithm wasn't enough to test enterprise-level programming skills, and decided to provide a reference implementation that was *really* solid. Hence, FizzBuzzEnterpriseEdition in its current form started to exist! Let's have a closer look at the application and how it works.

7.1.2 Looking around FizzBuzzEnterpriseEdition

If you're following along with the VM provided with this book, a Java Development Kit or JDK (OpenJDK) is preinstalled, and the FizzBuzzEnterpriseEdition source code, as well as JAR files, are ready to use (otherwise, refer to appendix A for installation instructions). In the VM, open a terminal window, and type the following command to go to the directory that contains the application:

```
cd ~/src/examples/jvm
```

In that directory, you'll see the FizzBuzzEnterpriseEdition/lib subfolder that contains a bunch of JAR files that together make the program. You can see the JAR files by running the following command from the same directory:

```
ls -al ./FizzBuzzEnterpriseEdition/lib/
```

You will see the following output. The main JAR file, called FizzBuzzEnterpriseEdition.jar, contains the `FizzBuzzEnterpriseEdition` main function (bold font), as well as some dependencies:

```
-rw-r--r-- 1 chaos chaos   4467 Jun  2 08:01 aopalliance-1.0.jar
-rw-r--r-- 1 chaos chaos  62050 Jun  2 08:01 commons-logging-1.1.3.jar
-rw-r--r-- 1 chaos chaos  76724 Jun  2 08:01 FizzBuzzEnterpriseEdition.jar
-rw-r--r-- 1 chaos chaos 338500 Jun  2 08:01 spring-aop-3.2.13.RELEASE.jar
-rw-r--r-- 1 chaos chaos 614483 Jun  2 08:01 spring-beans-3.2.13.RELEASE.jar
-rw-r--r-- 1 chaos chaos 868187 Jun  2 08:01 spring-context-3.2.13.RELEASE.jar
-rw-r--r-- 1 chaos chaos 885410 Jun  2 08:01 spring-core-3.2.13.RELEASE.jar
-rw-r--r-- 1 chaos chaos 196545 Jun  2 08:01 spring-expression-3.2.13.RELEASE.jar
```

If you're curious about how it works, you can browse through the source code, but that's not necessary. In fact, in the practice of chaos engineering, you're most likely to be working with someone else's code, and because it's often not feasible to become intimate with the entire codebase due to its size, it would be more realistic if you didn't look into that quite yet. The main function of the application is in com.seriouscompany .business.java.fizzbuzz.packagenamingpackage.impl.Main. With that information, you can now go ahead and start the application. Run the following command in a terminal window, still from the same directory:

Allows java to find the JAR files of the application by passing the directory with * wildcard　　　　　　　　**Specifies the path of the main function**

```
java \
-classpath "./FizzBuzzEnterpriseEdition/lib/*" \
com.seriouscompany.business.java.fizzbuzz.packagenamingpackage.impl.Main
```

After a moment, you will see the following output (abbreviated). Apart from the expected lines with numbers and words `Fizz` and `Buzz`, you'll also notice a few verbose log messages (they're safe to ignore):

```
(...)
1
2
Fizz
4
Buzz
Fizz
7
8
Fizz
Buzz
11
Fizz
```

```
13
14
FizzBuzz
(...)
```

That's great news, because it looks like FizzBuzzEnterpriseEdition is working as expected! It appears to correctly solve the problem at hand, and it would surely convey the message that we're doing serious business here to any new hires, killing two birds with one stone.

But the fact that it works in one use case doesn't tell you anything about how resilient the application is to failure, which is the very reason you agreed to look at this to begin with. You guessed it—chaos engineering to the rescue! Let's take a look at how to design an experiment that exposes this piece of software to failure to test how well it handles it.

7.2   Chaos engineering and Java

To design a meaningful chaos experiment, you need to start by making an educated guess about the kind of failure that might affect your application. Fortunately, over the course of the previous chapters, you've built a little arsenal of tools and techniques that can help. For example, you could treat this program as a black box, and apply the techniques you covered in chapter 6 to see what syscalls it's making, and then design experiments around blocking some of these syscalls.

You could also leverage the tools from the BCC project you saw earlier (https://github.com/iovisor/bcc), like `javacalls`, to gain insight into which methods are being called and devise an experiment around the most prominent ones. Or you could package the application in a Docker container and leverage what you learned in chapter 5. The point is that for the most part, the things you learned before will be applicable to a Java application as well.

But there is more, because Java and the JVM offer unique and interesting features that you can leverage for the practice of chaos engineering. I'll focus on those in this chapter. So instead of using one of the techniques you've learned before, let's approach the problem differently. Let's modify an existing method on the fly to throw an exception so that you can verify your assumptions about what happens to the system as a whole. Let me show you what I mean by that.

7.2.1   Experiment idea

The technique I want to teach you in this chapter boils down to these three steps:

1 Identify the class and method that might throw an exception in a real-world scenario.
2 Design an experiment that modifies that method on the fly to actually throw the exception in question.
3 Verify that the application behaves the way you expect it to behave (handles the exception) in the presence of the exception.

Steps 2 and 3 both depend on where you decide to inject the exception, so you're going to need to address that first. Let's find a good spot for the exception in the Fizz-BuzzEnterpriseEdition code now.

FINDING THE RIGHT EXCEPTION TO THROW

Finding the right place to inject failure requires building an understanding of how (a subset) of the application works. This is one of the things that makes chaos engineering both exciting (you get to learn about a lot of different software) and challenging (you get to learn about a lot of different software) at the same time.

It is possible to automate some of this discovery (see section 7.4), but the reality is that you will need to (quickly) build understanding of how things work. You learned techniques that can help with that in the previous chapters (for example, looking under the hood by observing syscalls, or the BCC tools that can give you visibility into methods being called). The right tool for the job will depend on the application itself, its complexity level, and the sheer amount of code it's built from. One simple yet useful technique is to search for the exceptions thrown.

As a reminder, in Java, every method needs to declare any exceptions that its code might throw through the use of the `throws` keyword. For example, a made-up method that might throw an `IOException` could look like the following:

```
public static void mightThrow(String someArgument) throws IOException {
  // definition here
}
```

You can find all the places in the source code where an exception might be thrown by simply searching for that keyword. From inside the VM, run the following commands in a terminal window to do just that:

```
cd ~/src/examples/jvm/src/src/main/java/com/seriouscompany/business/java/
fizzbuzz/packagenamingpackage/              Navigates to the folder to
grep \                                      avoid dealing with super-
    -n \          Prints the line           long paths in the output
    -r \          numbers
    ") throws" .
                  Recursively searches
                  in subfolders
```

You will see the following output, listing three locations with the `throws` keyword (in bold font). The last one is an interface, so let's ignore that one for now. Let's focus on the first two locations:

```
./impl/strategies/SystemOutFizzBuzzOutputStrategy.java:21:
public void output(final String output) throws IOException {

./impl/ApplicationContextHolder.java:41:
public void setApplicationContext(final ApplicationContext
applicationContext) throws BeansException {

./interfaces/strategies/FizzBuzzOutputStrategy.java:14:
public void output(String output) throws IOException;
```

Let's take a look at the first file from that list, SystemOutFizzBuzzOutputStrategy.java, by running the following command in a terminal window:

```
cat ~/src/examples/jvm/src/src/main/java/com/seriouscompany/business/java/
fizzbuzz/packagenamingpackage/impl/strategies/SystemOutFizzBuzzOutputStrategy
.java
```

You will see the following output (abbreviated), with a single method called `output`, capable of throwing `IOException`. The method is simple, printing to and flushing the standard output. This is the class and method that was used internally when you ran the application and saw all of the output in the console:

```
(...)
public class SystemOutFizzBuzzOutputStrategy implements
    FizzBuzzOutputStrategy {
(...)
    @Override
    public void output(final String output) throws IOException {
            System.out.write(output.getBytes());
            System.out.flush();
    }
}
```

This looks like a good starting point for an educational experiment:

- It's reasonably uncomplicated.
- It's used when you simply run the program.
- It has the potential to crash the program if the error handling is not done properly.

It's a decent candidate, so let's use it as a target for the experiment. You can go ahead and design the experiment. Let's do just that.

7.2.2   *Experiment plan*

Without looking at the rest of the source code, you can design a chaos experiment that injects an `IOException` into the `output` method of the `SystemOutFizzBuzzOutput-Strategy` class, to verify that the application as a whole can withstand that. If the error-handling logic is on point, it wouldn't be unreasonable to expect it to retry the failed write and at the very least to log an error message and signal a failed run. You can leverage the return code to know whether the application finished successfully.

Putting this all together into our usual four-step template, this is the plan of the experiment:

1 Observability: the return code and the standard output of the application.
2 Steady state: the application runs successfully and prints the correct output.
3 Hypothesis: if an `IOException` exception is thrown in the `output` method of the `SystemOutFizzBuzzOutputStrategy` class, the application returns an error code after its run.
4 Run the experiment!

The plan sounds straightforward, but to implement it, you need to know how to modify a method on the fly. This is made possible by a feature of the JVM often referred to as `javaagent`, which allows us to write a class that can rewrite the bytecode of any other Java class that is being loaded into the JVM. Bytecode? Don't worry, we'll cover that in a moment.

Modifying bytecode on the fly is an advanced topic that might be new to even a seasoned Java developer. It is of particular interest in the practice of chaos engineering; it allows you to inject failure into someone else's code to implement various chaos experiments. It's also easy to mess things up, because this technique gives you access to pretty much any and all code executed in the JVM, including built-in classes. It is therefore important to make sure that you understand what you're doing, and I'm going to take my time to guide you through this.

I want to give you all the tools you need in order to be able to implement this experiment:

- A quick refresher of what bytecode is, and how to peek into it, before you start modifying it
- An easy way to see the bytecode generated from Java code
- An overview of the `java.lang.instrument` interface, and how to use it to implement a class that can modify other classes
- A walk-through of how to implement our experiment with no external dependencies
- Finally, once you understand how modifying code on the fly works under the hood, some higher-level tools that can do some of the work for you

Let's start at the beginning by acquainting you with the bytecode.

7.2.3 Brief introduction to JVM bytecode

One of the key design goals of Java was to make it portable—the write once, run anywhere (WORA) principle. To that end, Java applications run inside a JVM. When you run an application, it's first compiled from the source code (.java) into Java bytecode (.class), which can then be executed by any compatible implementation of the JVM, on any platform that supports it. The bytecode is independent of the underlying hardware. This process is summed up in figure 7.1.

What does a JVM look like? You can see the formal specs for all Java versions for free at https://docs.oracle.com/javase/specs/, and they are pretty good. Take a look at the Java 8 JVM specification (that's the version you're running in the VM shipped with this book) at http://mng.bz/q9oK. It describes the format of a .class file, the instruction set of the VM (similar to an instruction set of a physical processor), and the structure of the JVM itself.

It's good to know that you can always look things up in the formal specification. But nothing teaches better than doing things ourselves, so let's get our hands dirty and look at what this process is like in practice. You want to modify other people's bytecode, so before you do that, let's peek into what the bytecode looks like.

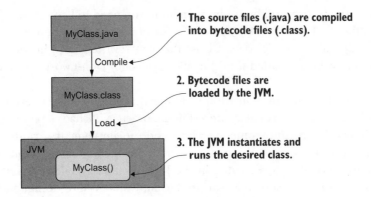

Figure 7.1 High-level overview of running Java code

READING THE BYTECODE

OK, so you want to modify someone else's code on the fly to inject failure for our chaos experiment. If you're serious about it (and want to be responsible), you need to become familiar with what bytecode actually looks like. Let's go through the whole process of compiling, running, and looking into the bytecode of a simple class.

To make things easy to start, I prepared a little sample application that you can work on. Let's start by opening a terminal window in your VM, and going to the location of the example by running the following command:

```
cd ~/src/examples/jvm/
```

From within that directory, you will find a subfolder structure (./org/my) with an example program (Example1.java). The directory structure is important, as this needs to match the package name, so let's stick to the same folder for the rest of this chapter. You can see the contents of the example program by running this command:

```
cat ./org/my/Example1.java
```

You will see the following Hello World program, a class called Example1. Note that it contains a main method that does a single call to println (both in bold font) to print a simple message to the standard output:

```
package org.my;

class Example1
{
    public static void main(String[] args)
    {
        System.out.println("Hello chaos!");
    }
}
```

Before you can run the program, it needs to be compiled into bytecode. You can do that using the `javac` command-line tool. In our simple example, you just need to specify the file path. Compile it by running the following command:

```
javac ./org/my/Example1.java
```

No output means that there were no errors.

> **TIP** If you'd like to learn more about what the compiler did there, run the same command with the `-verbose` flag added. Where did the bytecode file go? It will be sitting next to the source file, with the filename corresponding to the name of the class itself.

Let's take a look at that subfolder again by running the following command:

```
ls -l ./org/my/
```

You will see output just like the following; note the new file, Example1.class, the result of you compiling the java file (bold font):

```
(...)
-rw-r--r-- 1 chaos chaos 422 Jun  4 08:44 Example1.class
-rw-r--r-- 1 chaos chaos 128 Jun  3 10:43 Example1.java
(...)
```

To run it, you can use the `java` command and specify the fully qualified class name (with the package prefix); remember, you still need to be in the same directory:

```
java org.my.Example1
```

You will see output of the Hello World program:

```
Hello chaos!
```

The program runs, which is nice, but I bet this is all old news to you. Even if you are not very familiar with Java, the steps you took look pretty much like any other compiled language. What you might have not seen before is the bytecode it produces. Fortunately, JDK ships with another tool, `javap`, which allows us to print the bytecode contents of the class in a human-readable form. To do it to our `org.my.Example1` class, run the following command:

```
javap -c org.my.Example1
```

You will see output like the following (abbreviated to show just the `main` method), describing what JVM machine instructions were generated for our `Example1` class. You will see four instructions:

```
Compiled from "Example1.java"
class org.my.Example1 {
(...)
```

```
public static void main(java.lang.String[]);
  Code:
     0: getstatic     #2     // Field
  java/lang/System.out:Ljava/io/PrintStream;
     3: ldc           #3     // String Hello chaos!
     5: invokevirtual #4     // Method
  java/io/PrintStream.println:(Ljava/lang/String;)V
     8: return
}
```

Let's take a look at a single instruction to understand its format. For example, this one:

```
3: ldc           #3     // String Hello chaos!
```

The format is as follows:

- Relative address
- Colon
- Name of the instruction (you can look it up in the JVM spec document)
- Argument
- Comment describing the argument (human-readable format)

Translating the instructions making up the `main` method into English, you have a `getstatic` instruction that gets a static field out of type `java.io.PrintStream` from class `java.lang.System`,[2] and then an `ldc` instruction that loads a constant string "Hello chaos!" and pushes it onto what's called the *operand stack*. This is followed by the `invokevirtual` instruction, which invokes instance method `.println` and pops the value previously pushed to the operand stack. Finally, the `return` instruction ends the function call. And voilà! That's what is written in the Example1.java file, as far as the JVM is concerned.

This might feel a bit dry. Why is it important from the perspective of chaos engineering? Because this is what you're going to be modifying to inject failure in our chaos experiments.

You can look up all the details about these instructions from the docs I mentioned earlier (http://mng.bz/q9oK) but that's not necessary right now. As a practitioner of chaos engineering, I want you to know that you can easily access the bytecode, see it in a human-readable(-ish) form, and look up any definitions you might want to understand in more detail.

There are plenty of other interesting things about the JVM, but for this chapter, I just need to make you feel comfortable with some basic bytecode. This sneak peek of the JVM bytecode gives just enough of the information you need to understand the next step: instrumenting the bytecode on the fly. Let's take a look at that now.

---

[2] For documentation on out, see http://mng.bz/PPo2. For documentation on `java.io.Printstream`, see http://mng.bz/JDVp. For documentation on `java.lang.System`, see http://mng.bz/w9y7.

USING -JAVAAGENT TO INSTRUMENT THE JVM

OK, so you're on a quest to implement the chaos experiment you've designed, and to do that, you need to know how to modify the code on the fly. You can do that by leveraging a mechanism directly provided by the JVM.

This is going to get a little technical, so let me just say this: you will learn about higher-level tools that make it easier in section 7.3, but first it's important to learn what the JVM actually offers, in order to understand the limitations of this approach. Skipping straight to the higher-level stuff would be a little bit like driving a car without understanding how the gearbox works. It might be fine for most people, but it won't cut it for a race-car driver. When doing chaos engineering, I need you to be a race-car driver.

With that preamble out of the way, let's dive in and take a look at what the JVM has to offer. Java comes with instrumentation and code transformation capabilities built in, by means of the `java.lang.instrument` package that has been available since JDK version 1.5 (http://mng.bz/7VZx). People often refer to it as `javaagent`, because that's the name of the command-line argument that you use to attach the instrumentation. The package defines two interfaces, both of which are needed for you to inject failure into a class:

- `ClassFileTransformer`—Classes implementing this interface can be registered to transform class files of a JVM; it requires a single method called `transform`.
- `Instrumentation`—Allows for registering instances implementing the `ClassFileTransformer` interface with the JVM to receive classes for modification before they're used.

Together, they make it possible to inject code into the class, just as you need for the experiment. This setup allows you to register a class (implementing `ClassFileTransformer`) that will receive the bytecode of all other classes before they are used, and will be able to transform them. This is summarized in figure 7.2.

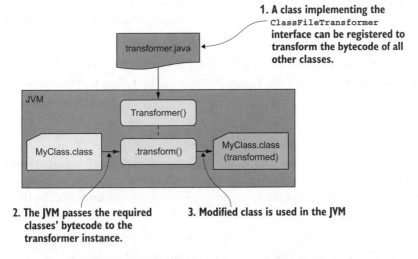

1. A class implementing the `ClassFileTransformer` **interface can be registered to transform the bytecode of all other classes.**

2. The JVM passes the required classes' bytecode to the transformer instance.

3. Modified class is used in the JVM

Figure 7.2 Instrumenting JVM with the `java.lang.instrument` package

Pop quiz: What's javaagent?
Pick one:

1   A secret service agent from Indonesia from a famous movie series
2   A flag used to specify a JAR that contains code to inspect and modify the code
    loaded into the JVM on the fly
3   Archnemesis of the main protagonist in a knockoff version of the movie *The Matrix*

See appendix B for answers.

Now, I know that this is a lot of new information, so I suggest absorbing that information in two steps:

1   Let's go through setting everything up with `javaagent`, but hold off from modifying any code.
2   Add the actual code to modify the bytecode of the classes you're interested in separately.

To implement the first part, you just need to follow the steps that the architects of the `java.lang.instrument` package came up with. To make your life easier, let me summarize it for you. It all boils down to these four steps:

1   Write a class implementing the `ClassFileTransformer` interface; let's call it `ClassPrinter`.
2   Implement another class with the special method called `premain` that will register an instance of `ClassPrinter`, so that the JVM knows to use it; let's call it `Agent`.
3   Package the `Agent` and `ClassPrinter` classes into a JAR file with an extra attribute, `Premain-Class`, pointing to the class with the `premain` method (`Agent`).
4   Run Java with an extra argument, `-javaagent:/path/to/agent.jar`, pointing to the JAR file created in the previous step.

Let's do that! I've prepared for you the three files that you need. First, you need the `ClassPrinter` class, which you can see by running the following command in a terminal window:

```
cat ~/src/examples/jvm/org/agent/ClassPrinter.java
```

You will see the contents of a class with a single method, `transform`, that is needed to satisfy the `ClassFileTransformer` interface (both in bold font). You'll notice that the method has a bunch of arguments that are required by the interface. In the use case of our chaos experiment, you'll need only two of them (both in bold font):

- `className`—The name of the class to transform
- `classfileBuffer`—The actual binary content of the class file

For now, as I suggested earlier, let's skip the modification part and instead just print the name and size for each class that the JVM will call the agent with, and return the class file buffer unchanged. This will effectively list all of the classes loaded by the JVM, in the order that they are loaded, showing you that the javaagent mechanism worked:

```
package org.agent;
import java.lang.instrument.ClassFileTransformer;
import java.lang.instrument.IllegalClassFormatException;
import java.security.ProtectionDomain;
class ClassPrinter implements ClassFileTransformer {
    public byte[] transform(ClassLoader loader,
                        String className,
                        Class<?> classBeingRedefined,
                        ProtectionDomain protectionDomain,
                        byte[] classfileBuffer)
            throws IllegalClassFormatException {
    System.out.println("Found class: " + className
    + " (" + classfileBuffer.length + " bytes)");
    return classfileBuffer;
    }
}
```

The name of the class brought by the JVM for transformation

The binary content of the class file for the class

Prints just the name of the class and its binary size

Returns the class unchanged

Now, you need to actually register that class so that the JVM uses it for instrumentation. This is straightforward too, and I prepared a sample class that does that for you. You can see it by running the following command in a terminal window:

```
cat ~/src/examples/jvm/org/agent/Agent.java
```

You will see the following Java class. It imports the Instrumentation package, and implements the special premain method (in bold font), which will be called by the JVM before the main method is executed. It uses the addTransformer method to register an instance of the ClassPrinter class (also in bold font). This is how you actually make the JVM take an instance of your class and allow it to modify the bytecode of all other classes:

```
package org.agent;

import java.lang.instrument.Instrumentation;

class Agent {
  public static void premain(String args,
                        Instrumentation instrumentation){
    ClassPrinter transformer = new ClassPrinter();
    instrumentation.addTransformer(transformer);
  }
}
```

The premain method needs to have this special signature.

An object implementing the Instrumentation interface will be passed by the JVM when the method is called.

Uses addTransformer method to register an instance of your ClassPrinter class

And finally, the pièce de résistance is a special attribute, Premain-Class, that needs to be set when packaging these two classes into a JAR file. The value of the attribute needs to point to the name of the class with the `premain` method (`org.agent.Agent` in this case) so that the JVM knows which class to call. The easiest way to do that is to create a manifest file. I prepared one for you. To see it, run the following command in a terminal window:

```
cat ~/src/examples/jvm/org/agent/manifest.mf
```

You will see the following output. Note the `Premain-Class` attribute, specifying the fully qualified class name of our `Agent` class, the one with the `premain` method. Once again, this is how you tell the JVM to use this particular class to attach the instrumentation.

```
Manifest-Version: 1.0
Premain-Class: org.agent.Agent
```

And that's all the ingredients you need. The last step is to package it all together in a format that's required by the JVM as the `-javaagent` argument, a simple JAR file with all the necessary classes and the special attribute you just covered. Let's now compile the two classes and build our JAR file into agent1.jar by running the following commands:

```
cd ~/src/examples/jvm
javac org/agent/Agent.java
javac org/agent/ClassPrinter.java
jar vcmf org/agent/manifest.mf agent1.jar org/agent
```

Once that's ready, you're all done. You can go ahead and leverage the `-javaagent` argument of the java command, to use our new instrumentation. Do that by running the following command in a terminal window:

```
cd ~/src/examples/jvm
java \
    -javaagent:./agent1.jar \        ◁───  Uses the -javaagent argument to specify
    org.my.Example1                         the path to your instrumentation JAR file
                        ◁───  Runs the Example1 class
                              you had looked at before
```

You will see the following output (abbreviated), with your instrumentation listing all the classes passed to it. There are a bunch of built-in classes, and then the name of your target class, `org/my/Example1` (bold font). Eventually, you can see the familiar `Hello chaos!` output of the main method of that target class (also bold font):

```
(...)
Found class: sun/launcher/LauncherHelper (14761 bytes)
Found class: java/util/concurrent/ConcurrentHashMap$ForwardingNode (1618 bytes)
Found class: org/my/Example1 (429 bytes)
Found class: sun/launcher/LauncherHelper$FXHelper (3224 bytes)
Found class: java/lang/Class$MethodArray (3642 bytes)
Found class: java/lang/Void (454 bytes)
Hello chaos!
(...)
```

So it worked; very nice! You have just instrumented your JVM and didn't even break a sweat in the process. You're getting really close to being able to implement our chaos experiment now, and I'm sure you can't wait to finish the job. Let's do it!

7.2.4 *Experiment implementation*

You are one step away from being able to implement our chaos experiment. You know how to attach your instrumentation to a JVM and get all the classes with their byte-code passed to you. Now you just need to figure out how to modify the bytecode to include the failure you need for the experiment. You want to inject code automatically into the class you're targeting, to simulate it throwing an exception. As a reminder, this is the class:

```
(...)
public class SystemOutFizzBuzzOutputStrategy implements
    FizzBuzzOutputStrategy {
(...)
    @Override
    public void output(final String output) throws IOException {
            System.out.write(output.getBytes());
            System.out.flush();
    }
}
```

For this experiment, it doesn't really matter where the exception is thrown in the body of this method, so you may as well add it at the beginning. But how do you know what bytecode instructions to add? Well, a simple way to figure that out is to copy some existing bytecode. Let's take a look at how to do that now.

WHAT INSTRUCTIONS SHOULD YOU INJECT?

Because the `javaagent` mechanism operates on bytecode, you need to know what bytecode instructions you want to inject. Fortunately, you now know how to look under the hood of a .class file, and you can leverage that to write the code you want to inject in Java, and then see what bytecode it produces. To do that, I prepared a simple class throwing an exception. Run the following command inside a terminal window in your VM to see it:

```
cat ~/src/examples/jvm/org/my/Example2.java
```

You will see the following code. It has two methods—a static `throwIOException` that does nothing but throw an `IOException`, and `main` that calls that same `throwIOException` method (both in bold font):

```
package org.my;
import java.io.IOException;
class Example2
{
    public static void main(String[] args) throws IOException
```

```
    {
        Example2.throwIOException();
    }

    public static void throwIOException() throws IOException
    {
        throw new IOException("Oops");
    }
}
```

I added this extra method to make things easier; calling a static method with no arguments is really simple in the bytecode. But don't take my word for it. You can check that by compiling the class and printing its bytecode. Run the following commands in the same terminal:

```
cd ~/src/examples/jvm/
javac org/my/Example2.java
javap -c org.my.Example2
```

You will see the following bytecode (abbreviated to show only the main method). Notice that it's a single invokestatic JVM instruction, specifying the method to call, as well as no arguments and no return value (which is represented by ()V in the comment). This is good news, because you're going to need to add only a single instruction injected into your target method:

```
(...)
  public static void main(java.lang.String[]) throws java.io.IOException;
    Code:
        0: invokestatic  #2                      // Method throwIOException:()V
        3: return
(...)
```

To make your target method SystemOutFizzBuzzOutputStrategy.output throw an exception, you can add a single invokestatic instruction to the beginning of it, pointing to any static method throwing the exception you want, and you're done! Let's finally take a look at how to put all of this together.

INJECTING CODE INTO JVM ON THE FLY

You know what instructions you want to inject, where to inject them, and how to use the instrumentation to achieve that. The last question is how to actually modify that bytecode that the JVM will pass to your class. You could go back to the JVM specs, open the chapter on the class file format, and implement code to parse and modify the instructions. Fortunately, you don't need to reinvent the wheel. The following are a few frameworks and libraries that you can use:

- ASM, https://asm.ow2.io/
- Javassist, www.javassist.org
- Byte Buddy, https://bytebuddy.net/

- The Byte Code Engineering Library, https://commons.apache.org/proper/commons-bcel/
- cglib, https://github.com/cglib/cglib

In the spirit of simplicity, I'll show you how to rewrite a method by using the ASM library, but you could probably pick any one of these frameworks. The point here is not to teach you how to become an expert at modifying Java classes. It's to give you just enough understanding of how that process works so you can design meaningful chaos experiments.

In your real-life experiments, you're probably going to use one of the higher-level tools detailed in section 7.3, but it is important to understand how to implement a complete example from scratch. Do you remember the race-car driver and gearbox analogy? When doing chaos engineering, you need to know the limitations of your methods, and that's harder to do when using tools that do things you don't understand. Let's dig in.

> ### Groovy and Kotlin
> If you've ever wondered how Apache Groovy (www.groovy-lang.org/) and Kotlin (https://kotlinlang.org/) languages were implemented to run in the JVM, the answer is that they use ASM to generate the bytecode. So do the higher-level libraries like Byte Buddy (https://bytebuddy.net/).

Remember that earlier I suggested splitting the implementation into two steps, the first being the `org.agent` package you used for printing classes passed to your instrumentation by the JVM? Let's take the second step now and build on top of that to add the bytecode-rewriting part.

I prepared another package, `org.agent2`, that implements the modification that you want to make using ASM. Note that ASM already ships with OpenJDK, so there is no need to install it. ASM is a large library with good documentation, but for our purposes you will use a very small subset of what it can do. To see it, run the following command from the terminal inside the VM:

```
cd ~/src/examples/jvm/
cat org/agent2/ClassInjector.java
```

You will see the following class, `org.agent2.ClassInjector`. It is Java, after all, so it's a little bit verbose. It implements the same `transform` method that needs to be registered for instrumenting the bytecode of classes inside the JVM, just as you saw before. It also implements another method, a static `throwIOException`, that prints a message to stderr and throws an exception. The `transform` method looks for the (very long) name of the class, and does any rewriting only if the class name matches. The method uses an ASM library `ClassReader` instance to read the bytecode of the class into an internal representation as an instance of the ClassNode class. That ClassNode instance allows you to do the following:

1 Iterate through the methods.
2 Select the one called output.
3 Inject a single invokestatic instruction as the first instruction, calling to your throwIOException static method.

This is depicted in figure 7.3.

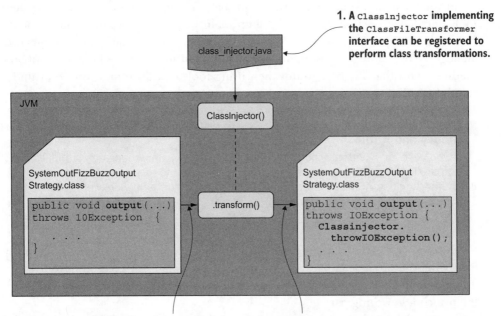

Figure 7.3   Instrumenting the JVM with the `java.lang.instrument` **package**

Take a look at the ClassInjector class in the following listing.

Listing 7.1   ClassInjector.java

```
package org.agent2;

import java.io.IOException;
import java.util.List;
import java.lang.instrument.ClassFileTransformer;
import java.lang.instrument.IllegalClassFormatException;
import java.security.ProtectionDomain;

import jdk.internal.org.objectweb.asm.ClassReader;
import jdk.internal.org.objectweb.asm.ClassWriter;
```

```
import jdk.internal.org.objectweb.asm.tree.*;
import jdk.internal.org.objectweb.asm.Opcodes;
public class ClassInjector implements ClassFileTransformer {
    public String targetClassName =
     "com/seriouscompany/business/java/fizzbuzz/packagenamingpackage/impl/
     strategies/SystemOutFizzBuzzOutputStrategy";

    public byte[] transform(ClassLoader loader, String className,
    Class<?> classBeingRedefined, ProtectionDomain protectionDomain,
    byte[] classfileBuffer) throws IllegalClassFormatException {

        if (className.equals(this.targetClassName)){

            ClassNode classNode = new ClassNode();
            new ClassReader(classfileBuffer).accept(classNode, 0);
            classNode.methods.stream()
             .filter(method -> method.name.equals("output"))
             .forEach(method -> {
                InsnList instructions = new InsnList();
                instructions.add(new MethodInsnNode(
                    Opcodes.INVOKESTATIC,
                    "org/agent2/ClassInjector",
                    "throwIOException",
                    "()V",
                    false // not a method
                ));
                method.maxStack += 1;
                method.instructions.insertBefore(
                method.instructions.getFirst(), instructions);
            });
            final ClassWriter classWriter = new ClassWriter(0);
            classNode.accept(classWriter);
            return classWriter.toByteArray();
        }
        return classfileBuffer;
    }
    public static void throwIOException() throws IOException
    {
        System.err.println("[CHAOS] BOOM! Throwing");
        throw new IOException("CHAOS");
    }
}
```

The same transform method needed to implement the ClassFileTransformer interface →

ClassReader reads and parses the bytecode into an internal representation of type ClassNode. ←

Filters only the method called "output" →

Creates a new instruction of type invokestatic, calling a static method throwIOException on the org/agent2/ClassInjector class with no arguments and no return value ←

To allow an extra instruction on the stack, you need to increase its size. →

Inserts the instructions at the beginning of the method ←

Generates the resulting bytecode by using a ClassWriter class

Once again, to satisfy the requirements of the format accepted by the javaagent argument in order for the JVM to use this class as instrumentation, you need the following:

- A class with a method called premain that creates and registers an instance of the ClassInjector class
- A manifest including the special attribute Premain-Class, pointing to the class with the premain method
- A JAR file packaging it all together, so you can pass in the javaagent argument

I wrote the simple premain class org.agent2.Agent for you, which you can see by running the following command from the same folder:

```
cat org/agent2/Agent.java
```

You will see the following class, implementing the premain method and using the same addTransformer method you used earlier to register an instance of the Class-Injector class with the JVM. Once again, this is how you tell the JVM to pass all the classes being loaded to ClassInjector for modifications:

```
package org.agent2;
import java.lang.instrument.Instrumentation;
class Agent {
  public static void premain(String args, Instrumentation instrumentation){
    ClassInjector transformer = new ClassInjector();
    instrumentation.addTransformer(transformer);
  }
}
```

I also prepared a manifest, very similar to the previous one, so that you can build the JAR the way it's required by the javaagent argument. You can see it by running the following command from the same directory:

```
cat org/agent2/manifest.mf
```

You'll see the following output. The only difference from the previous manifest is that it points to the new agent class (bold font):

```
Manifest-Version: 1.0
Premain-Class: org.agent2.Agent
```

The last part of the puzzle is that in order to have access to the internal.jdk packages, you need to add the -XDignore.symbol.file flag when compiling your classes. With that, you're ready to prepare a new agent JAR; let's call it agent2.jar. Create it by running the following commands, still from the same directory:

```
cd ~/src/examples/jvm/
javac -XDignore.symbol.file org/agent2/Agent.java
javac -XDignore.symbol.file org/agent2/ClassInjector.java
jar vcmf org/agent2/manifest.mf agent2.jar org/agent2
```

The resulting agent2.jar file will be created in the current directory and can be used to implement our experiment. Ready? Let's run it.

RUNNING THE EXPERIMENT

Finally, you have everything set up to run the experiment and see what happens. As a reminder, this is our experiment plan:

1 Observability: the return code and the standard output of the application.
2 Steady state: the application runs successfully and prints the correct output.

3 Hypothesis: if an `IOException` exception is thrown in the `output` method of the `SystemOutFizzBuzzOutputStrategy` class, the application returns an error code after it's run.

4 Run the experiment!

First, let's establish the steady state by running the application unmodified and inspecting the output and the return code. You can do that by running the following command in a terminal window:

```
                      Allows java to find the JAR files of the application,
                         by passing the directory with * wildcard          Specifies the path of
java \                                                                        the main function
-classpath "./FizzBuzzEnterpriseEdition/lib/*" \   ◄─┘
com.seriouscompany.business.java.fizzbuzz.packagenamingpackage.impl.Main \  ◄─┘
2> /dev/null      ◄─┐
                    Removes the noisy logging messages
```

After a few seconds, you will see the following output (abbreviated). The output is correct:

```
1
2
Fizz
4
Buzz
(...)
```

Let's verify the return code, by running the following command in the same terminal window:

```
echo $?
```

The output will be 0, indicating a successful run. So the steady state is satisfied: you have the correct output and a successful run. Let's now run the experiment! To run the same application, but this time using your instrumentation, run the following command:

```
java \                                        Adds the java agent instrumentation
-javaagent:./agent2.jar         ◄─┐           JAR you've just built
-classpath "./FizzBuzzEnterpriseEdition/lib/*" \
com.seriouscompany.business.java.fizzbuzz.packagenamingpackage.impl.Main \
2> /dev/null
```

This time, there will be no output, which is understandable, because you modified the function doing the printing to always throw an exception. Let's verify the other assumption of our hypothesis—namely, that the application handles it well by indicating an error as a return value. To check the return code, rerun the same command in the same terminal:

```
echo $?
```

The output is still 0, failing our experiment and showing a problem with the application. Turns out that the hypothesis about FizzBuzzEnterpriseEdition was wrong. Despite not printing anything, it doesn't indicate an error as its return code. Houston, we have a problem!

This has been a lot of learning, so I'd like you to appreciate what you just did:

- You started with an existing application you weren't familiar with.
- You found a place that throws an exception and designed a chaos experiment to test whether an exception thrown in that place is handled by the application in a reasonable way.
- You prepared and applied JVM instrumentation, with no magical tools and external dependencies.
- You prepared and applied automatic bytecode modifications, with no external dependencies other than the ASM library already provided by the OpenJDK.
- You ran the experiment, modified the code on the fly, and demonstrated scientifically that the application was not handling the failure well.

But once again, it's OK to be wrong. Experiments like this are supposed to help you find problems with software, as you just did. And it would make for a pretty boring chapter if you did all that work, and it turned out to be working just fine, wouldn't it?

The important thing here is that you added another tool to your toolbox and demystified another technology stack. Hopefully, this will come in handy sooner rather than later.

Now that you understand how the underlying mechanisms work, you're allowed to cheat a little bit—to take shortcuts. Let's take a look at some useful tools you can leverage to avoid doing so much typing in your next experiments to achieve the same effect.

Pop quiz: Which of the following is not built into the JVM?
Pick one:

1 A mechanism for inspecting classes as they are loaded
2 A mechanism for modifying classes as they are loaded
3 A mechanism for seeing performance metrics
4 A mechanism for generating enterprise-ready names from regular, boring names. For example: "butter knife" -> "professional, stainless-steel-enforced, dishwasher-safe, ethically sourced, low-maintenance butter-spreading device"

See appendix B for answers.

7.3   *Existing tools*

Although it's important to understand how the JVM `java.lang.instrument` package works in order to design meaningful chaos experiments, you don't need to reinvent the wheel every time. In this section, I'll show you a few free, open source tools that you can use to make your life easier. Let's start with Byteman.

7.3.1 *Byteman*

Byteman (https://byteman.jboss.org/) is a versatile tool that allows for modifying the bytecode of JVM classes on the fly (using the same instrumentation you learned in this chapter) to trace, monitor, and overall mess around with the behavior of your Java code.

Its differentiating factor is that it comes with a simple domain-specific language (DSL) that's very expressive and allows you to describe how you'd modify the source code of the Java class, mostly forgetting about the actual bytecode structure (you can afford to do that, because you already know how it works under the hood). Let's look at how to use it, starting by installing it.

INSTALLING BYTEMAN

You can get the binary releases, source code, and documentation for all versions of Byteman at https://byteman.jboss.org/downloads.html. At the time of writing, the latest version is 4.0.11. Inside your VM, that version is downloaded and unzipped to ~/src/examples/jvm/byteman-download-4.0.11. If you'd like to download it on a different host, you can do that by running the following command in a terminal:

```
wget https://downloads.jboss.org/byteman/4.0.11/byteman-download-4.0.11-bin.zip
unzip byteman-download-4.0.11-bin.zip
```

This will create a new folder called byteman-download-4.0.11, which contains Byteman and its docs. You're going to need the byteman.jar file, which can be found in the lib subfolder. To see it, run the following command in the same terminal:

```
ls -l byteman-download-4.0.11/lib/
```

You will see three JAR files, and you're interested in the byteman.jar (bold font), which you can use as a -javaagent argument:

```
-rw-rw-r-- 1 chaos chaos  10772 Feb 24 15:32 byteman-install.jar
-rw-rw-r-- 1 chaos chaos 848044 Feb 24 15:31 byteman.jar
-rw-rw-r-- 1 chaos chaos  15540 Feb 24 15:29 byteman-submit.jar
```

That's it. You're good to go. Let's use it.

USING BYTEMAN

To illustrate how much easier it is to use Byteman, let's reimplement the same modification you did for the chaos experiment from section 7.2.4. To do that, you need to follow three steps:

1. Prepare a Byteman script that throws an exception in the targeted method (let's call it throw.btm).
2. Run Java using byteman.jar as the -javaagent argument.
3. Point byteman.jar to use your throw.btm script.

Let's start with the first point. A Byteman script is a flat text file, with any number of rules, each of which follows this format (the programmer's guide is available at http://mng.bz/mg2n):

```
# rule skeleton
RULE <rule name>
CLASS <class name>
METHOD <method name>
BIND <bindings>
IF  <condition>
DO  <actions>
ENDRULE
```

I prepared a script that does exactly what the chaos experiment you implemented earlier does. You can see it by running the following command in a terminal window:

```
cd ~/src/examples/jvm/
cat throw.btm
```

You will see the following rule. It does exactly what you did before: it changes the method output in class `SystemOutFizzBuzzOutputStrategy` to throw a `java.io.IOException` exception at the entry into the method:

```
RULE throw an exception at output          Modifies the class
CLASS SystemOutFizzBuzzOutputStrategy   ◁   SystemOutFizzBuzzOutputStrategy
METHOD output                           ◁   Modifies the method output
AT ENTRY                                ◁
          IF true                       ◁   At the entry into the method
Throws    DO
a new       throw new java.io.IOException("BOOM");   Always executes (it's possible to add
exception ENDRULE                                    conditions here for the rule to trigger).
```

With that in place, let's handle steps 2 and 3. When using the `-javaagent` parameter with Java, it is possible to pass extra arguments after the equals sign (=). With Byteman, the only parameter supported is `script=<location of the script to execute>`. Therefore, to run the same `FizzBuzzEnterpriseEdition` class you did before, but have Byteman execute your script (bold font), all you need to do is run the following command:

Uses Byteman JAR file as a javaagent, and specifies your script after the "=" sign

```
cd ~/src/examples/jvm/
java \
  -javaagent:./byteman-download-4.0.11/lib/byteman.jar=script:throw.btm \   ◁
  -classpath "./FizzBuzzEnterpriseEdition/lib/*" \
  com.seriouscompany.business.java.fizzbuzz.packagenamingpackage.impl.Main \
  2>/dev/null    ◁   Discards the stderr to avoid
                     looking at the logging noise
```

You will see no output at all, just as in the experiment you ran before. You achieved the same result without writing or compiling any Java code or dealing with any bytecode.

Compared to writing your own instrumentation, using Byteman is simple, and the DSL makes it easy to quickly write rules, without having to worry about bytecode instructions at all. It also offers other advanced features, like attaching to a running JVM, triggering rules based on complex conditions, adding code at various points in methods, and much more.

It's definitely worth knowing about Byteman, but there are some other interesting alternatives. One of them is Byte-Monkey; let's take a closer look.

7.3.2 Byte-Monkey

Although not as versatile as Byteman, *Byte-Monkey* (https://github.com/mrwilson/byte -monkey) deserves a mention. It also works by leveraging the -javaagent option of the JVM and uses the ASM library to modify the bytecode. The unique proposition of Byte-Monkey is that it offers only actions useful for chaos engineering; namely, there are four modes you can use (verbatim from the README):

```
Fault: Throw exceptions from methods that declare those exceptions
Latency: Introduce latency on method-calls
Nullify: Replace the first non-primitive argument to the method with null
Short-circuit: Throw corresponding exceptions at the very beginning of try blocks
```

I'll show you how to use Byte-Monkey to achieve the same effect you did for the chaos experiment. But first, let's install it.

INSTALLING BYTE-MONKEY

You can get the binary releases and the Byte-Monkey source code from https://github .com/mrwilson/byte-monkey/releases. At the time of writing, the only version available is 1.0.0. Inside your VM, that version is downloaded to ~/src/examples/jvm/ byte-monkey.jar. If you'd like to download it on a different host, you can do that by running the following command in a terminal:

```
wget https://github.com/mrwilson/byte-monkey/releases/download/1.0.0/byte-
monkey.jar
```

That single file, byte-monkey.jar, is all you need. Let's see how to use it.

USING BYTE-MONKEY

Now, for the fun part. Let's reimplement the experiment once again, but this time with a small twist! Byte-Monkey makes it easy to throw the exceptions at only a particular rate, so to make things more interesting, let's modify the method to throw an exception only 50% of the time. This can be achieved by passing the rate argument when specifying the -javaagent JAR for the JVM.

Run the following command to use the byte-monkey.jar file as your javaagent, use the fault mode, rate of 0.5, and filter to only your fully qualified (and very long) name of the class and the method (all in bold font):

```
java \
-javaagent:byte-monkey.jar=mode:fault,rate:0.5,filter:com/seriouscompany/
business/java/fizzbuzz/packagenamingpackage/impl/strategies/SystemOutFizzBuzz
OutputStrategy/output \
-classpath "./FizzBuzzEnterpriseEdition/lib/*" \
com.seriouscompany.business.java.fizzbuzz.packagenamingpackage.impl.Main \
2>/dev/null
```

**Uses the fault mode (throwing exceptions), at a rate of 50%, and filters once again
to affect only the very long name of the class and method you're targeting.**

You will see output similar to the following, with about 50% of the lines printed, and
the other 50% skipped:

```
(...)
1314FizzBuzz1619
Buzz
22Fizz29Buzz

FizzBuzzFizz

38Buzz41Fizz43
FizzBuzz
4749
(...)
```

And voilà! Another day, another tool in your awesome toolbox. Give it a star on
GitHub (https://github.com/mrwilson/byte-monkey); it deserves one! When you're
back, let's take a look at Chaos Monkey for Spring Boot.

7.3.3   *Chaos Monkey for Spring Boot*

The final mention in this section goes to *Chaos Monkey for Spring Boot* (http://mng.bz/
5j14). I won't get into many details here, but if your application uses Spring Boot, you
might be interested in it. The documentation is pretty good and gives you a decent overview of how to get started (for the latest version 2.2.0, it's at http://mng.bz/6g1G).

In my opinion, the differentiating feature here is that it understands Spring Boot,
and offers failure (called *assaults*) on the high-level abstractions. It can also expose an
API, which allows you to add, remove, and reconfigure these assaults on the fly
through HTTP or Java Management Extensions (JMX). Currently supported are the
following:

- *Latency assault*—Injects latency to a request
- *Exception assault*—Throws exceptions at runtime
- *AppKiller assault*—Shuts down the app on a call to a particular method
- *Memory assault*—Uses up memory

If you're using Spring Boot, I recommend that you take a good look at this framework. That's the third and final tool I wanted to show you. Let's take a look at some
further reading.

7.4 Further reading

If you'd like to learn more about chaos engineering and JVM, I recommend a few pieces of further reading. First, two papers from the KTH Royal Institute of Technology in Stockholm. You can find them both, along with the source code, at https://github.com/KTH/royal-chaos:

- ChaosMachine (https://arxiv.org/pdf/1805.05246.pdf)—Analyzes the exception-handling hypotheses of three popular pieces of software written in Java (tTorrent, BroadleafCommerce, and XWiki) and produces actionable reports for the developers automatically. It leverages the same -javaagent mechanism you learned about in this chapter.
- TripleAgent (https://arxiv.org/pdf/1812.10706.pdf)—A system that automatically monitors, injects failure, and improves resilience of existing software running in the JVM. The paper evaluates BitTorrent and HedWig projects to demonstrate the feasibility of automatic resilience improvements.

Second, from the University of Lille and the National Institute for Research in Digital Science and Technology (INRIA) in Lille, the paper "Exception Handling Analysis and Transformation Using Fault Injection: Study of Resilience Against Unanticipated Exceptions" (https://hal.inria.fr/hal-01062969/document) analyzes nine open source projects and shows that 39% of catch blocks executed during test suite execution can be made more resilient.

Finally, I want to mention that when we covered the java.lang.instrument package (http://mng.bz/7VZx), I spoke only about instrumenting the classes when starting a JVM. It is also possible to attach to a running JVM and instrument classes that have already been loaded. Doing so involves implementing the agentmain method, and you can find all the details in the mentioned documentation page.

Summary

- The JVM allows you to instrument and modify code on the fly through the use of the java.lang.instrument package (part of the JDK).
- In Java programs, exception handling is often a weak spot, and it's a good starting point for chaos engineering experiments, even on a source codebase you're not very familiar with.
- Open source tools like Byteman, Byte-Monkey, and Chaos Monkey for Spring Boot make it easier to inject failure for your chaos experiments, and they run on top of the same java.lang.instrument package to achieve that.

Application-level
fault injection

This chapter covers

- Building chaos engineering capabilities directly into your application
- Ensuring that the extra code doesn't affect the application's performance
- More advanced usage of Apache Bench

So far, you've learned a variety of ways to apply chaos engineering to a selection of different systems. The languages, tools, and approaches varied, but they all had one thing in common: working with source code outside your control. If you're in a role like SRE or platform engineer, that's going to be your bread and butter. But sometimes you will have the luxury of applying chaos engineering to your own code.

This chapter focuses on baking chaos engineering options directly into your application for a quick, easy, and—dare I say it—fun way of increasing your confidence in the overall stability of the system as a whole. I'll guide you through designing and running two experiments: one injecting latency into functions responsible for communicating with an external cache, and another injecting intermittent failure through the simple means of raising an exception. The example code is written in Python, but don't worry if it's not your forte; I promise to keep it basic.

NOTE I chose Python for this chapter because it hovers at the top of the list in terms of popularity, and it allows for short, expressive examples. But what you learn here is universal and can be leveraged in any language. Yes, even Node.js.

If you like the sound of it, let's go for it. First things first: a scenario.

8.1 Scenario

Let's say that you work for an e-commerce company and you're designing a system for recommending new products to your customers, based on their previous queries. As a practitioner of chaos engineering, you're excited: this might be a perfect opportunity to add features allowing you to inject failure directly into the codebase.

To generate recommendations, you need to be able to track the queries your customers make, even if they are not logged in. The e-commerce store is a website, so you decide to simply use a cookie (https://en.wikipedia.org/wiki/HTTP_cookie) to store a session ID for each new user. This allows you to distinguish between the requests and attribute each search query to a particular session.

In your line of work, latency is important; if the website doesn't feel quick and responsive to customers, they will buy from your competitors. The latency therefore influences some of the implementation choices and becomes one of the targets for chaos experiments. To minimize the latency added by your system, you decide to use an in-memory key-value store, Redis (https://redis.io/), as your session cache and store only the last three queries the user made. These previous queries are then fed to the recommendation engine every time the user searches for a product, and come back with potentially interesting products to display in a You Might Be Interested In box.

So here's how it all works together. When a customer visits your e-commerce website, the system checks whether a session ID is already stored in a cookie in the browser. If it's not, a random session ID is generated and stored. As the customer searches through the website, the last three queries are saved in the session cache, and are used to generate a list of recommended products that is then presented to the user in the search results.

For example, after the first search query of "apple," the system might recommend "apple juice." After the second query for "laptop," given that the two consecutive queries were "apple" and "laptop," the system might recommend a "macbook pro." If you've worked in e-commerce before, you know this is a form of cross-selling (https://en.wikipedia.org/wiki/Cross-selling), a serious and powerful technique used by most online stores and beyond. Figure 8.1 summarizes this process.

Learning how to implement this system is not the point of this chapter. What I'm aiming at here is to show you a concrete, realistic example of how you can add minimal code directly into the application to make running chaos experiments on it easy. To do that, let me first walk you through a simple implementation of this system, for

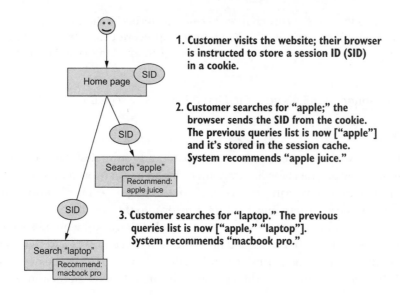

1. **Customer visits the website; their browser is instructed to store a session ID (SID) in a cookie.**

2. **Customer searches for "apple;" the browser sends the SID from the cookie. The previous queries list is now ["apple"] and it's stored in the session cache. System recommends "apple juice."**

3. **Customer searches for "laptop." The previous queries list is now ["apple," "laptop"]. System recommends "macbook pro."**

Figure 8.1   **High-level overview of the session-tracking system**

now without any chaos engineering changes, and then, once you're comfortable with it, I'll walk you through the process of building two chaos experiments into it.

8.1.1   *Implementation details: Before chaos*

I'm providing you with a bare-bones implementation of the relevant parts of this website, written in Python and using the Flask HTTP framework (https://flask.palletsprojects .com/). If you don't know Flask, don't worry; we'll walk through the implementation to make sure everything is clear.

Inside your VM, the source code can be found in ~/src/examples/app (for installation instructions outside the VM, refer to appendix A). The code doesn't implement any chaos experiments quite yet; we'll add that together. The main file, app.py, provides a single HTTP server, exposing three endpoints:

- Index page (at /) that displays the search form and sets the session ID cookie.
- Search page (at /search) that stores the queries in the session cache and displays the recommendations.
- Reset page (at /reset) that replaces the session ID cookie with a new one to make testing easier for you. (This endpoint is for your convenience only.)

Let's start with the index page route, the first one any customer will see. It's implemented in the index function and does exactly two things: returns some static HTML to render the search form, and sets a new session ID cookie, through the set_session_id function. The latter is made easy through Flask's built-in method of accessing cookies (flask.request.cookies.get) as well as setting new ones (response.set_cookie). After visiting this endpoint, the browser stores the random unique ID (UID) value in the sessionID cookie, and it sends that value with every subsequent request to the same host. That's how the system is able to attribute the further actions to a session ID. If you're not familiar with Flask, the @app.route("/") decorator tells Flask to serve the decorated function (in this case index) under the / endpoint.

Next, the search page is where the magic happens. It's implemented in the search function, decorated with @app.route("/search", methods=["POST", "GET"]), meaning that both GET and POST requests to /search will be routed to it. It reads the session ID from the cookie, the query sent from the search form on the home page (if any), and stores the query for that session by using the store_interests function. store_interests reads the previous queries from Redis, appends the new one, stores it back, and returns the new list of interests. Using that new list of interests, it calls the recommend_other_products function, that—for simplicity—returns a hardcoded list of products. Figure 8.2 summarizes this process.

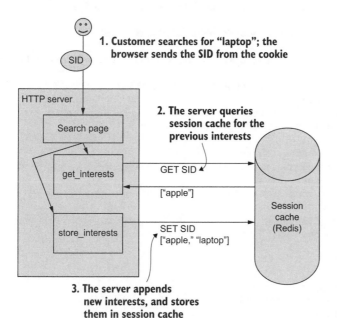

Figure 8.2 Search page and session cache interactions

When that's done, the search function renders an HTML page presenting the search results as well as the recommended items. Finally, the third endpoint, implemented in the reset function, replaces the session ID cookie with a new, random one and redirects the user to the home page.

The following listing provides the full source code for this application. For now, ignore the commented out section on chaos experiments.

Listing 8.1   app.py

```python
import uuid, json, redis, flask

COOKIE_NAME = "sessionID"

def get_session_id():
    """ Read session id from cookies, if present """
    return flask.request.cookies.get(COOKIE_NAME)

def set_session_id(response, override=False):
    """ Store session id in a cookie """
    session_id = get_session_id()
    if not session_id or override:
        session_id = uuid.uuid4()
    response.set_cookie(COOKIE_NAME, str(session_id))


CACHE_CLIENT = redis.Redis(host="localhost", port=6379, db=0)

# Chaos experiment 1 - uncomment this to add latency to Redis access
#import chaos
#CACHE_CLIENT = chaos.attach_chaos_if_enabled(CACHE_CLIENT)

# Chaos experiment 2 - uncomment this to raise an exception every other call
#import chaos2
#@chaos2.raise_rediserror_every_other_time_if_enabled
def get_interests(session):
    """ Retrieve interests stored in the cache for the session id """
    return json.loads(CACHE_CLIENT.get(session) or "[]")

def store_interests(session, query):
    """ Store last three queries in the cache backend """
    stored = get_interests(session)
    if query and query not in stored:
        stored.append(query)
    stored = stored[-3:]
    CACHE_CLIENT.set(session, json.dumps(stored))
    return stored


def recommend_other_products(query, interests):
    """ Return a list of recommended products for a user,
    based on interests """
    if interests:
        return {"this amazing product":
     "https://youtube.com/watch?v=dQw4w9WgXcQ"}
    return {}


app = flask.Flask(__name__)

@app.route("/")
def index():
    """ Handle the home page, search form """
```

```python
    resp = flask.make_response("""
<html><body>
    <form action="/search" method="POST">
        <p><h3>What would you like to buy today?</h3></p>
        <p><input type='text' name='query'/>
        <input type='submit' value='Search'/></p>
    </form>
    <p><a href="/search">Recommendations</a>. <a href="/reset">Reset</a>.
 </p>
</body></html>
""")
    set_session_id(resp)
    return resp


@app.route("/search", methods=["POST", "GET"])
def search():
    """ Handle search, suggest other products """
    session_id = get_session_id()
    query = flask.request.form.get("query")
    try:
        new_interests = store_interests(session_id, query)
    except redis.exceptions.RedisError as exc:
        print("LOG: redis error %s", str(exc))
        new_interests = None
    recommendations = recommend_other_products(query, new_interests)
    return flask.make_response(flask.render_template_string("""
<html><body>
    {% if query %}<h3>I didn't find anything for "{{ query }}"</h3>{%
 endif %}
    <p>Since you're interested in {{ new_interests }}, why don't you
 try...
    {% for k, v in recommendations.items() %} <a href="{{ v }}">{{ k
 }}</a>{% endfor %}!</p>
    <p>Session ID: {{ session_id }}. <a href="/">Go back.</a></p>
</body></html>
""",
        session_id=session_id,
        query=query,
        new_interests=new_interests,
        recommendations=recommendations,
    ))


@app.route("/reset")
def reset():
    """ Reset the session ID cookie """
    resp = flask.make_response(flask.redirect("/"))
    set_session_id(resp, override=True)
    return resp
```

Let's now see how to start the application. It has two external dependencies:

- Flask (https://flask.palletsprojects.com/)
- redis-py (https://github.com/andymccurdy/redis-py)

You can install both in the versions that were tested with this book by running the following command in your terminal window:

```
sudo pip3 install redis==3.5.3 Flask==1.1.2
```

You also need an actual instance of Redis running on the same host, listening for new connections on the default port 6379. If you're using the VM, Redis is preinstalled (consult appendix A for installation instructions if you're not using the VM). Open another terminal window, and start a Redis server by running the following command:

```
redis-server
```

You will see the characteristic output of Redis, similar to the following:

```
54608:C 28 Jun 2020 18:32:12.616 # oO0OoO0OoO0Oo Redis is starting oO0OoO0OoO0Oo
54608:C 28 Jun 2020 18:32:12.616 # Redis version=6.0.5, bits=64,
    commit=00000000, modified=0, pid=54608, just started
54608:C 28 Jun 2020 18:32:12.616 # Warning: no config file specified, using the
    default config. In order to specify a config file use ./redis-server
    /path/to/redis.conf
54608:M 28 Jun 2020 18:32:12.618 * Increased maximum number of open files to
    10032 (it was originally set to 8192).
```

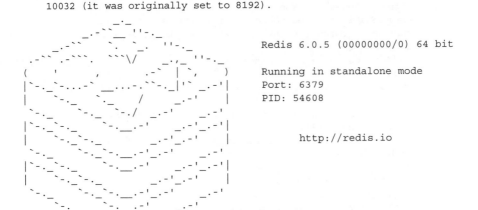

With that, you are ready to start the application! While Redis is running in the second terminal window, go back to the first one and run the following command, still from ~/src/examples/app. It will start the application in development mode, with detailed error stacktraces and automatic reload on changes to the source code:

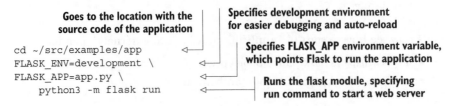

Goes to the location with the source code of the application

Specifies development environment for easier debugging and auto-reload

```
cd ~/src/examples/app
FLASK_ENV=development \
FLASK_APP=app.py \
    python3 -m flask run
```

Specifies FLASK_APP environment variable, which points Flask to run the application

Runs the flask module, specifying run command to start a web server

The application will start, and you'll see output just like the following, specifying the app it's running, the host and port where the application is accessible, and the environment (all in bold font):

```
* Serving Flask app "app.py" (lazy loading)
* Environment: development
* Debug mode: on
* Running on http://127.0.0.1:5000/ (Press CTRL+C to quit)
* Restarting with stat
* Debugger is active!
* Debugger PIN: 289-495-131
```

You can now browse to http://127.0.0.1:5000/ to confirm it's working. You will see a simple search form, asking you to type the name of the product you're interested in. Try searching for "apple." You are taken to a second page, where you will be able to see your previous queries as well as the recommendations. Be absolutely sure to click the recommendations; they are great! If you repeat this process a few times, you will notice that the page retains the last three search queries. Finally, note that the page also prints the session ID, and if you're curious, you can see it in the cookies section in your browser.

OK, so now you have a simple, yet functional application that we'll pretend you wrote. Time to have some fun with it! Let's do some chaos engineering.

8.2 Experiment 1: Redis latency

In the e-commerce store scenario I described at the beginning of the chapter, the overall latency of the website is paramount: you know that if you slow the system down too much, customers will start leaving the website and buying from your competitors. It's therefore important that you understand how the latency communicating with the session cache (Redis) affects the overall speed of the website. And that's where chaos engineering shines: we can simulate some latency and measure how much it affects the system as a whole.

You have injected latency before in different ways. In chapter 4, you used Traffic Control (`tc`) to add latency to a database, and in chapter 5 you leveraged Docker and Pumba to do the same. So how is this different this time? In the previous scenarios, we tried hard to modify the behavior of the system without modifying the source code. This time, I want to add to that by showing you how easy it is to add chaos engineering when you *are* in control of the application's design. Everyone can do that—you just need to have a little bit of imagination! Let's design a simple experiment around the latency.

8.2.1 Experiment 1 plan

In the example application, it's easy to establish that for each request, the session cache is accessed twice: first to read the previous queries, and second to store the new set. You can therefore hypothesize that you will see a double of any latency added to the Redis calls in the overall latency figure for the website.

Let's find out whether that's true. By now, you're well versed in using Apache Bench (ab) for generating traffic and observing latencies, so let's leverage that once again. Here's one possible version of a chaos experiment that will help test that theory:

1 Observability: generate traffic and observe the latency by using ab.
2 Steady state: observe latency without any chaos changes.
3 Hypothesis: if you add a 100 ms latency to each interaction with the session cache (reads and writes), the overall latency of the /search page should increase by 200 ms.
4 Run the experiment!

That's it! Now, all you need to do is follow this plan, starting with the steady state.

8.2.2 Experiment 1 steady state

So far, you've used ab to generate GET requests. This time, you have a good opportunity to learn how to use it to send POST requests, like the ones sent from the search form on the index page that the browser sends to the /search page. To do that, you need to do the following:

1 Use the POST method, instead of GET.
2 Use the `Content-type` header to specify the value used by the browser when sending an HTML form (`application/x-www-form-urlencoded`).
3 Pass the actual form data as the body of the request to simulate the value from a form.
4 Pass the session ID (you can make it up) in a cookie in another header, just as the browser does with every request.

Fortunately, this all can be done with ab by using the following arguments:

- `-H "Header: value"` to set custom headers, one for the cookie with the session ID and one for the content type. This flag can be used multiple times to set multiple headers.
- `-p post-file` to send the contents of the specified file as the body of the request. It also automatically assumes the POST method. That file needs to follow the HTML form format, but don't worry if you don't know it. In this simple use case, I'll show you a body you can use: `query=TEST` to query for "TEST." The actual query in this case doesn't matter.

Putting this all together, and using our typical concurrency of 1 (`-c 1`) and runtime of 10 seconds (`-t 10`), you end up with the following command. Assuming that the server is still running, open another terminal window and run the following:

Creates a simple file with the query content

Sends a header with the cookie specifying the sessionID

Sends a header specifying the content type to a simple HTML form

```
echo "query=Apples" > query.txt
ab -c 1 -t 10 \
    -H "Cookie: sessionID=something" \
    -H "Content-type: application/x-www-form-urlencoded" \
```

```
-p query.txt \
http://127.0.0.1:5000/search
```

◁──┐ **Uses the previously created file
with the simple query in it**

You will see the familiar output of ab, similar to the following (abbreviated). My VM managed to do 1673 requests, or about 167 requests per second (5.98 ms per request) with no errors (all four in bold font):

```
Server Software:        Werkzeug/1.0.1
Server Hostname:        127.0.0.1
Server Port:            5000
(...)
Complete requests:      1673
Failed requests:        0
(...)
Requests per second:    167.27 [#/sec] (mean)
Time per request:       5.978 [ms] (mean)
```

So far, so good. These numbers represent your steady state, the baseline. Let's implement some actual chaos and see how these change.

8.2.3 *Experiment 1 implementation*

It's time to implement the core of your experiment. This is the cool part: because you own the code, there are a million and one ways of implementing the chaos experiment, and you're free to pick whichever works best for you! I'm going to guide you through just one example of what that could look like, focusing on three things:

- Keep it simple.
- Make the chaos experiment parts optional for your application and disabled by default.
- Be mindful of the performance impact the extra code has on the whole application.

These are good guidelines for any chaos experiments, but as I said before, you will pick the right implementation based on the actual application you're working on. This example application relies on a Redis client accessible through the CACHE_CLIENT variable, and then the two functions using it, get_interests and store_interest, use the get and set methods on that cache client, respectively (all in bold font):

**An instance of Redis client is created and
accessible through the CACHE_CLIENT variable.**

```
CACHE_CLIENT = redis.Redis(host="localhost", port=6379, db=0)    ◁──┘

def get_interests(session):
    """ Retrieve interests stored in the cache for the session id """
    return json.loads(CACHE_CLIENT.get(session) or "[]")    ◁──┐  get_interests is
                                                                 using the get
def store_interests(session, query):                             method of
    """ Store last three queries in the cache backend """        CACHE_CLIENT.
    stored = get_interests(session)
```

```
if query and query not in stored:
    stored.append(query)
stored = stored[-3:]
CACHE_CLIENT.set(session, json.dumps(stored))
return stored
```

stores_interests is using the set method of CACHE_CLIENT (and get by transition, through the call to get_interests).

All you need to do to implement the experiment is to modify CACHE_CLIENT to inject latency into both of the get and set methods. There are plenty of ways of doing that, but the one I suggest is to write a simple wrapper class.

The wrapper class would have the two required methods (get and set) and rely on the wrapped class for the actual logic. Before calling the wrapped class, it would sleep for the desired time. And then, based on an environment variable, you'd need to optionally replace CACHE_CLIENT with an instance of the wrapper class.

Still with me? I prepared a simple wrapper class for you (ChaosClient), along with a function to attach it (attach_chaos_if_enabled) in another file called chaos.py, in the same folder (~/src/examples/app). The attach_chaos_if_enabled function is written in a way so as to inject the experiment only if an environment variable called CHAOS is set. That's to satisfy the "disabled by default" expectation. The amount of time to inject is controlled by another environment variable called CHAOS_DELAY_SECONDS and defaults to 750 ms. The following listing is an example implementation.

Listing 8.2   chaos.py

```
import time
import os


class ChaosClient:
    def __init__(self, client, delay):
        self.client = client
        self.delay = delay
    def get(self, *args, **kwargs):
        time.sleep(self.delay)
        return self.client.get(*args, **kwargs)
    def set(self, *args, **kwargs):
        time.sleep(self.delay)
        return self.client.set(*args, **kwargs)
def attach_chaos_if_enabled(cache_client):
    """ creates a wrapper class that delays calls to get and set methods """
    if os.environ.get("CHAOS"):
        return ChaosClient(cache_client,
    float(os.environ.get("CHAOS_DELAY_SECONDS", 0.75)))
    return cache_client
```

The wrapper class stores a reference to the original cache client.

The wrapper class provides the get method, expected on the cache client, that wraps the client's method of the same name.

Before the method relays to the original get method, it waits for a certain amount of time.

The wrapper class also provides the set method, exactly like the get method.

Returns the wrapper class only if the CHAOS environment variable is set

Now, equipped with this, you can modify the application (app.py) to make use of this new functionality. You can import it and use it to conditionally replace CACHE_CLIENT, provided that the right environment is set. All you need to do is find the line where you instantiate the cache client inside the app.py file:

```
CACHE_CLIENT = redis.Redis(host="localhost", port=6379, db=0)
```

Add two lines after it, importing and calling the `attach_chaos_if_enabled` function, passing the `CACHE_CLIENT` variable as an argument. Together, they will look like the following:

```
CACHE_CLIENT = redis.Redis(host="localhost", port=6379, db=0)
import chaos
CACHE_CLIENT = chaos.attach_chaos_if_enabled(CACHE_CLIENT)
```

With that, the scene is set and ready for the grand finale. Let's run the experiment!

8.2.4 *Experiment 1 execution*

To activate the chaos experiment, you need to restart the application with the new environment variables. You can do that by stopping the previously run instance (press Ctrl-C) and running the following command:

Activates the conditional chaos experiment code by setting the CHAOS environment variable

Specifies chaos delay injected as 0.1 second, or 100 ms

Specifies the Flask development env for better error messages

```
CHAOS=true \
CHAOS_DELAY_SECONDS=0.1 \
FLASK_ENV=development \
FLASK_APP=app.py \
python3 -m flask run
```

Specifies the same app.py application

Runs Flask

Once the application is up and running, you're good to go to rerun the same ab command you used to establish the steady state once again. To do that, run the following command in another terminal window:

Creates a simple file with the query content

Sends a header with the cookie specifying the sessionID

```
echo "query=Apples" > query.txt && \
ab -c 1 -t 10 \
    -H "Cookie: sessionID=something" \
    -H "Content-type: application/x-www-form-urlencoded" \
    -p query.txt \
http://127.0.0.1:5000/search
```

Uses the previously created file with the simple query in it

Sends a header specifying the content type to a simple HTML form

After the 10-second wait, when the dust settles, you will see the ab output, much like the following. This time, my setup managed to complete only 48 requests (208 ms per request), still without errors (all three in bold font):

```
(...)
Complete requests:      48
Failed requests:         0
```

```
(...)
Requests per second:    4.80 [#/sec]  (mean)
Time per request:       208.395 [ms]  (mean)
(...)
```

That's consistent with our expectations. The initial hypothesis was that adding 100 ms to every interaction with the session cache should result in an extra 200 ms additional latency overall. And as it turns out, for once, our hypothesis was correct! It took a few chapters, but that's a bucket list item checked off! Now, before we get too narcissistic, let's discuss a few pros and cons of running chaos experiments this way.

8.2.5 *Experiment 1 discussion*

Adding chaos engineering code directly to the source code of the application is a double-edged sword: it's often easier to do, but it also increases the scope of things that can go wrong. For example, if your code introduces a bug that breaks your program, instead of increasing the confidence in the system, you've decreased it. Or, if you added latency to the wrong part of the codebase, your experiments might yield results that don't match reality, giving you false confidence (which is arguably even worse).

You might also think, "Duh, I added code to sleep for *X* seconds; of course it's slowed down by that amount." And yes, you're right. But now imagine that this application is larger than the few dozen lines we looked at. It might be much harder to be sure about how latencies in different components affect the system as a whole. But if the argument of human fallibility doesn't convince you, here's a more pragmatic one: doing an experiment and confirming even the simple assumptions is often quicker than analyzing the results and reaching meaningful conclusions.

I'm also sure you noticed that reading and writing to Redis in two separate actions is not going to work with any kind of concurrent access and can lose writes. Instead, it could be implemented using a Redis set and atomic add operation, fixing this problem as well as the double penalty for any network latency. My focus here was to keep it as simple as possible, but thanks for pointing that out!

Finally, there is always the question of performance: if you add extra code to the application, you might make it slower. Fortunately, because you are free to write the code whatever way you please, there are ways around that. In the preceding example, the extra code is applied only if the corresponding environment variables are set during startup. Apart from the extra if statement, there is no overhead when running the application without the chaos experiment. And when it's on, the penalty is the cost of an extra function call to our wrapper class. Given that we're waiting for times at a scale of milliseconds, that overhead is negligible.

That's what my lawyers advised me to tell you, anyway. With all these caveats out of the way, let's do another experiment, this time injecting failure, rather than slowness.

8.3   *Experiment 2: Failing requests*

Let's focus on what happens when things fail rather than slow down. Let's take a look at the function get_interests again. As a reminder, it looks like the following. (Note that there is no exception handling whatsoever.) If the CACHE_CLIENT throws any exceptions (bold font), they will just bubble up further up the stack:

```
def get_interests(session):
    """ Retrieve interests stored in the cache for the session id """
    return json.loads(CACHE_CLIENT.get(session) or "[]")
```

To test the exception handling of this function, you'd typically write unit tests and aim to cover all legal exceptions that can be thrown. That will cover this bit, but will tell you little about how the entire application behaves when these exceptions arise. To test the whole application, you'd need to set up some kind of *integration* or *end-to-end* (*e2e*) tests, whereby an instance of the application is stood up along with its dependencies, and some client traffic is created. By working on that level, you can verify things from the user's perspective (what error will the user see, as opposed to what kind of exception some underlying function returns), test for regressions, and more. It's another step toward reliable software.

And this is where applying chaos engineering can create even more value. You can think of it as the next step in that evolution—a kind of end-to-end testing, while injecting failure into the system to verify that the whole reacts the way you expect. Let me show you what I mean: let's design another experiment to test whether an exception in the get_interests function is handled in a reasonable manner.

8.3.1   *Experiment 2 plan*

What should happen if get_interests receives an exception when trying to read from the session store? That depends on the type of page you're serving. For example, if you're using that session date to list recommendations in a sidebar to the results of a search query, it might make more economic sense to skip the sidebar and allow the user to at least click on other products. If, on the other hand, we are talking about the checkout page, then not being able to access the session data might make it impossible to finish the transaction, so it makes sense to return an error and ask the user to try again.

In our case, we don't even have a buy page, so let's focus on the first type of scenario: if the get_interests function throws an exception, it will bubble up in the store_interests function, which is called from our search website with the following code. Note the except block, which catches RedisError, the type of error that might be thrown by our session cache client (in bold font):

```
try:
    new_interests = store_interests(session_id, query)
except redis.exceptions.RedisError:          ◁─┐  The type of exception thrown
    print("LOG: redis error %s", str(exc))      │  by the Redis client you use is
    new_interests = None                         │  caught and logged here.
```

That error handling should result in the exception in get_interests being transparent to the user; they just won't see any recommendations. You can create a simple experiment to test that out:

1 Observability: browse to the application and see the recommended products.
2 Steady state: the recommended products are displayed in the search results.
3 Hypothesis: if you add a redis.exceptions.RedisError exception every other time get_interests is called, you should see the recommended products every other time you refresh the page.
4 Run the experiment!

You've already seen that the recommended products are there, so you can jump directly to the implementation!

8.3.2   *Experiment 2 implementation*

Similar to the first experiment, there are plenty of ways to implement this. And just as in the first experiment, let me suggest a simple example. Since we're using Python, let's write a simple decorator that we can apply to the get_interests function. As before, you want to activate this behavior only when the CHAOS environment variable is set.

I prepared another file in the same folder, called chaos2.py, that implements a single function, raise_rediserror_every_other_time_if_enabled, that's designed to be used as a Python decorator (https://wiki.python.org/moin/PythonDecorators). This rather verbosely named function takes another function as a parameter and implements the desired logic: return the function if the chaos experiment is not active, and return a wrapper function if it is active. The wrapper function tracks the number of times it's called and raises an exception on every other call. On the other calls, it relays to the original function with no modifications. The following listing provides the source code of one possible implementation.

Listing 8.3   chaos2.py

```python
import os
import redis


def raise_rediserror_every_other_time_if_enabled(func):
    """ Decorator, raises an exception every other call to the wrapped
      function """
    if not os.environ.get("CHAOS"):          # If the special environment
        return func                          # variable CHAOS is not set,
    counter = 0                              # returns the original function
    def wrapped(*args, **kwargs):
        nonlocal counter
        counter += 1
        if counter % 2 == 0:                                        # Raises an exception
            raise redis.exceptions.RedisError("CHAOS")              # on every other call
        return func(*args, **kwargs)                                # to this method
    return wrapped                           # Relays the call to the
                                             # original function
```

Now you just need to actually use it. Similar to the first experiment, you'll modify the app.py file to add the call to this new function. Find the definition of the get_inster-ests function, and prepend it with a call to the decorator you just saw. It should look like the following (the decorator is in bold font):

```
import chaos2
@chaos2.raise_rediserror_every_other_time_if_enabled
def get_interests(session):
    """ Retrieve interests stored in the cache for the session id """
    return json.loads(CACHE_CLIENT.get(session) or "[]")
```

Also, make sure that you undid the previous changes, or you'll be running two experiments at the same time! If you did, then that's all you need to implement for experiment 2. You're ready to roll. Let's run the experiment!

8.3.3 Experiment 2 execution

Let's make sure the application is running. If you still have it running from the previous sections, you can keep it; otherwise, start it by running the following command:

Activates the conditional chaos experiment code by setting the CHAOS environment variable

Specifies the Flask development env for better error messages

```
CHAOS=true \
FLASK_ENV=development \
FLASK_APP=app.py \
python3 -m flask run
```

Specifies the same app.py application

Runs Flask

This time, the actual experiment execution step is really simple: browse to the application (http://127.0.0.1:5000/) and refresh it a few times. You will see the recommendations every other time, and no recommendations the other times, just as we predicted, proving our hypothesis! Also, in the terminal window running the application, you will see logs similar to the following, showing an error on every other call. That's another confirmation that what you did worked:

```
127.0.0.1 - - [07/Jul/2020 22:06:16] "POST /search HTTP/1.0" 200 -
127.0.0.1 - - [07/Jul/2020 22:06:16] "POST /search HTTP/1.0" 200 -
LOG: redis error CHAOS
```

And that's a wrap. Two more experiments under your belt. Pat yourself on the back, and let's take a look at some pros and cons of the approach presented in this chapter.

8.4 Application vs. infrastructure

When should you bake the chaos engineering directly into your application, as opposed to doing that on the underlying layers? Like most things in life, that choice is a trade-off.

Incorporating chaos engineering directly in your application can be much easier and has the advantage of using the same tools that you're already familiar with. You can also get creative about the way you structure the code for the experiments, and implementing sophisticated scenarios tends to not be a problem.

The flip side is that since you're writing code, all the problems you have writing any code apply: you can introduce bugs, you can test something other than what you intend, or you can break the application altogether. In some cases (for example, if you wanted to restrict all outbound traffic from your application), a lot of places in your code might need changes, so a platform-level approach might be more suitable.

The goal of this chapter is to show you that both approaches can be useful and to demonstrate that chaos engineering is not only for SREs; everyone can do chaos engineering, even if it's only on a single application

Pop quiz: When is it a good idea to build chaos engineering into the application?

Pick one:

1   When you can't get it right on the lower levels, such as infrastructure or syscalls
2   When it's more convenient, easier, safer, or you have access to only the application level
3   When you haven't been certified as a chaos engineer yet
4   When you downloaded only this chapter instead of getting the full book!

See appendix B for answers.

Pop quiz: What is not that important when building chaos experiments into the application itself?

Pick one:

1   Making sure the code implementing the experiment is executed only when switched on
2   Following the best practices of software deployment to roll out your changes
3   Rubbing the ingenuity of your design into everyone else's faces
4   Making sure you can reliably measure the effects of your changes

See appendix B for answers.

Summary

- Building fault injection directly into an application can be an easy way of practicing chaos engineering.
- Working on an application, rather than at the infrastructure level, can be a good first step into chaos engineering, because it often requires no extra tooling.

- Although applying chaos engineering at the application level might require less work to set up, it also carries higher risks; the added code might contain bugs or introduce unexpected changes in behavior.
- *With great power comes great responsibility*—the Peter Parker principle (http://mng .bz/Xdya).

There's a monkey in my browser!

This chapter covers

- Applying chaos engineering to frontend code
- Overriding browser JavaScript requests to inject failure, with no source code changes

The time has come for us to visit the weird and wonderful world of JavaScript (JS). Regardless of what stage of the love-hate relationship you two are at right now, there is no escaping JavaScript in one form or another. If you're part of the 4.5 billion people using the internet, you're almost certainly running JS, and the applications keep getting more and more sophisticated. If the recent explosion in popularity of frameworks for building rich frontends, like React (https://github.com/facebook/react) and Vue.js (https://github.com/vuejs/vue) is anything to go by, it doesn't look like that situation is about to change.

The ubiquitous nature of JavaScript makes for an interesting angle for chaos engineering experiments. On top of the layers covered in the previous chapters (from the infrastructure level to the application level), there is another layer where failure can occur (and therefore can be injected): the frontend JavaScript. It's the proverbial cherry on the equally proverbial cake.

In this chapter, you'll take a real, open source application and learn to inject slowness and failure into it with just a few lines of extra code that can be added to a running application on the fly. If you love JavaScript, come and learn new ways it can be awesome. If you hate it, come and see how it can be used as a force for good. And to make it more real, let's start with a scenario.

9.1 Scenario

One of the neighboring teams is looking for a better way of managing its PostgreSQL (www.postgresql.org) databases. The team evaluated a bunch of free, open source options, and suggested a PostgreSQL database UI called *pgweb* (https://github.com/sosedoff/pgweb) as the way forward. The only problem is that the manager of that team is pretty old-school. He reads Hacker News (https://news.ycombinator.com/news) through a plugin in his Emacs, programs his microwave directly in Assembly, has JavaScript disabled on all his kids' browsers, and uses a Nokia 3310 (2000 was the last year they made a proper phone) to avoid being hacked.

To resolve the conflict between the team members and their manager, both parties turn to you, asking you to take a look at pgweb from the chaos engineering perspective and see how reliable it is—and in particular, at the JavaScript that the manager is so distrustful of. Not too sure what you're getting yourself into, you accept, of course.

To help them, you'll need to understand what pgweb is doing, and then design and run meaningful experiments. Let's start by looking into how pgweb actually works.

9.1.1 Pgweb

Pgweb, which is written in Go, lets you connect to any PostgreSQL 9.1+ database and manage all the usual aspects of it, such as browsing and exporting data, executing queries, and inserting new data.

It's distributed as a simple binary, and it's preinstalled, ready to use inside the VM shipped with this book. The same goes for an example PostgreSQL installation, without which you wouldn't have anything to browse (as always, refer to appendix A for installation instructions if you don't want to use the VM). Let's bring it all up.

First, start the database by running the following command:

```
sudo service postgresql start
```

The database is prepopulated with example data. The credentials and data needed for this installation are the following:

- User: `chaos`
- Password: `chaos`
- Some example data in a database called `booktown`

To start pgweb using these credentials, all you need to do is run the following command:

```
pgweb --user=chaos --pass=chaos --db=booktown
```

And voilà! You will see output similar to the following, inviting you to open a browser (bold font):

```
Pgweb v0.11.6 (git: 3e4e9c30c947ce1384c49e4257c9a3cc9dc97876)
(go: go1.13.7)
Connecting to server…
Connected to PostgreSQL 10.12
Checking database objects…
Starting server…
To view database open http://localhost:8081/ in browser
```

Go ahead and browse to http://localhost:8081. You will see the neat pgweb UI. On the left are the available tables that you can click to start browsing the data. The UI will look similar to figure 9.1.

1. Click a table name to display its contents.

2. The contents will be displayed in the main table.

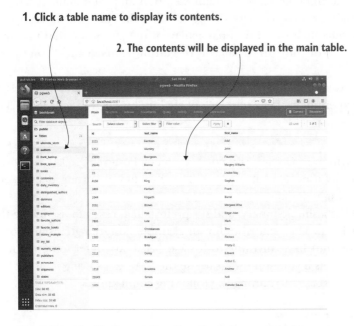

Figure 9.1   The UI of pgweb in action, displaying example data

As you click around the website, you will see new data being loaded. From the chaos engineering perspective, every time data is being loaded, it means an opportunity for failure. Let's see what is happening behind the scenes to populate the screen with that new data.

9.1.2 Pgweb implementation details

To design a chaos experiment, you first need to understand how the data is loaded. Let's see how it is populated. Modern browsers make it easy to look at what's going on under the hood. I'm going to use Firefox, which is open source and accessible in your VM, but the same thing can be done in all major browsers.

While browsing the pgweb UI, open the Web Developer tools on the Network tab by pressing Ctrl-Shift-E (or choosing Tools > Web Developer > Network from the Firefox menu). You will see a new pane open at the bottom of the screen. It will initially be empty.

Now, click to select another table on the pgweb menu on the left. You will see the Network pane populate with three requests. For each request, you will see the status (HTTP response code), method (GET), domain (localhost:8081), the file requested (endpoint), a link to the code that made the request, and other details. Figure 9.2 shows what it looks like in my VM.

All requests are shown in the table in the Network pane of the developer tools (Tools > Web Developer in Firefox).

Figure 9.2 Network view in Firefox, showing requests made by pgweb from JavaScript

The cool stuff doesn't end here, either: you can now click any of these three requests, and an extra pane, this time on the right, shows more details about it. Click the request to the *info* endpoint. A new pane opens, with extra details, just as in figure 9.3. You can see the headers sent and received, cookies, the parameters sent, response received, and more.

Looking at these three requests gives you a lot of information about how the UI is implemented. For every action the user takes, you can see in the Initiator column that

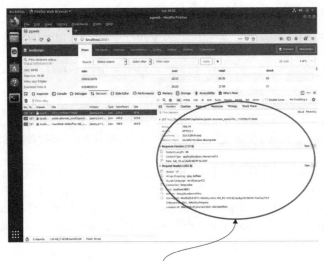

Figure 9.3   Request details view in Network tab of Web Developer tools in Firefox, displaying a request made by pgweb UI

The details of each request can be seen, including request, response, headers, times, and more.

the UI leverages *jQuery* (https://jquery.com/), a popular JavaScript library, to make requests to the backend. And you can see all of that before you even look at any source code. The browsers we have today have sure come a long way from the days of IE6!

So let's put all of this together:

1   When you browse to see the pgweb UI, your browser connects to the HTTP server built into the pgweb application. It sends back the basic web page, and the JavaScript code that together make the UI.

2   When you click something in the UI, the JavaScript code makes a request to the pgweb HTTP server to load the new data, like the contents of a table, and displays the data it receives in the browser, by rendering it as part of the web page.

3   To return that data to the UI, the pgweb HTTP server reads the data from the PostgreSQL database.

4   Finally, the browser receives and displays the new data.

Figure 9.4 summarizes this process. This is a pretty common sight among recent web applications, and it's often referred to as a *single-page application*, or SPA (http://mng.bz/yYDd), because only the initial "traditional" web page is served, and all the content is then displayed through JavaScript code manipulating it.

Feel free to poke around some more. When you're done, let's design a chaos experiment.

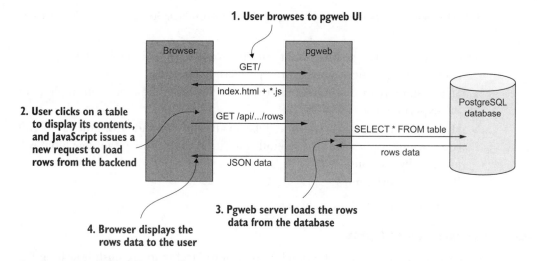

Figure 9.4 Events that happen when users browse the pgweb UI to display table contents

9.2 Experiment 1: Adding latency

You're running pgweb and PostgreSQL locally, so you're not exposed to any networking latencies while using it. The first idea you might have is to check how the application copes with such latencies. Let's explore that idea.

In the previous chapters, you saw how to introduce latencies on various levels, and you could use that knowledge to add latency between the pgweb server and the database. But you're here to learn, so this time, let's focus on how to do that in the JavaScript application itself. This way, you add yet another tool to your chaos engineering toolbox.

You saw that three requests were made when you clicked a table to display. They were all made in quick succession, so it's not clear whether they're prone to cascading delays (whereby requests are made in a sequence, so all the delays add up), and that's something that's probably worth investigating. And as usual, the chaos engineering way to do that is to add the latency and see what happens. Let's turn this idea into a chaos experiment.

9.2.1 Experiment 1 plan

Let's say that you would like to add a 1-second delay to all the requests that are made by the JavaScript code of the application, when the user selects a new table to display. An educated guess is that all three requests you saw earlier were done in parallel, rather than sequentially, because there don't seem to be any dependencies between them. Therefore, you expect the overall action to take about 1 second longer than before. In terms of observability, you should be able to leverage the built-in timers that the browser offers to see how long each request takes. So the plan for the experiment is as follows:

1   Observability: use the timer built into the browser to read the time taken to execute all three requests made by the JavaScript code.
2   Steady state: read the measurements from the browser before you implement the experiment.
3   Hypothesis: if you add a 1-second delay to all requests made from the JavaScript code of the application, the overall time it takes to display the new table will increase by 1 second.
4   Run the experiment!

As always, let's start with the steady state.

9.2.2   *Experiment 1 steady state*

Let me show you how to use the timeline built into Firefox to establish how long the requests made by clicking a table name really take. In the browser with the pgweb UI, with the Network tab still open (press Ctrl-Shift-E to reopen it, if you closed it before), let's clean the inputs. You can do that by clicking the trashcan icon in the top-left corner of the Network pane. It should wipe the list.

With this clean slate, select a table in the left menu of the UI by clicking its name. You will see another three requests made, just as you did before. But this time, I'd like to focus your attention on two things. First, the rightmost columns in the list display a timeline; each request is represented by a bar, starting at the time the request was issued, and ending when it was resolved. The longer the request takes, the longer the bar. The timeline looks like figure 9.5.

Each of these bars represents a duration of the request on the timeline. The longer the bar, the longer the request took to execute.

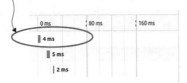

Figure 9.5   Firefox's timeline showing three requests issued and the times they took to complete

Second, at the bottom of the page is a line saying "Finish" that displays the total time between the first request started and the last event finished, within the ones you captured. In my test runs, the number seemed to hover around the 25 ms mark.

So there's your steady state. You don't have an exact number from between the user click action and the data being visible, but you have the time from the beginning of the first request to the end of the last one, and that number is around 25 ms. That should be good enough for our use. Let's see how to add the actual implementation!

9.2.3 *Experiment 1 implementation*

One of the reasons people dislike JavaScript is that it's really easy to shoot yourself in the foot; for example, by accidentally overriding a method or using an undefined variable. Very few things are prohibited. And while that is a valid criticism, it also makes it fun to implement chaos experiments.

You want to add latency to requests, so you need to find the place in the code that makes the requests. As it turns out, JavaScript can make requests in two main ways:

- XMLHttpRequest built-in class (http://mng.bz/opJN)
- Fetch API (http://mng.bz/nMJv)

jQuery (and therefore by extension pgweb, which uses jQuery) uses XMLHttpRequest, so we'll focus on it here (don't worry—we'll look into the Fetch API later in this chapter).

To avoid disturbing the learning flow from the chaos engineering perspective, I'm going to make an exception here, skip directly to the code snippet, and add the explanation in the sidebar. If you're interested in JavaScript, read the sidebar now, but if you're here for chaos engineering, let's get straight to the point.

Overriding XMLHttpRequest.send()

To make a request, you first create an instance of the XMLHttpRequest class, set all the parameters you care about, and then call the parameterless send method that does the actual sending of the request. The documentation referenced earlier gives the following description of send:

```
XMLHttpRequest.send()
Sends the request. If the request is asynchronous (which is the default),
this method returns as soon as the request is sent.
```

This means that if you can find a way to somehow modify that method, you can add an artificial 1-second delay. If only JavaScript was permissive enough to do that, and preferably do that on the fly, after all the other code was already set up, so that you could conveniently affect only the part of the execution flow you care about. But surely, something this fundamental to the correct functioning of the application must not be easily changeable, right? Any serious language would try to protect it from accidental overwriting, and so would JavaScript.

Just kidding! JavaScript won't bat an eye at you doing that. Let me show you how.

Back in the pgweb UI, open a console (in Firefox press Ctrl-Shift-K or choose Tools >Web Developer >Web Console from the menu). For those of you unfamiliar with the console, it lets you execute arbitrary JavaScript. You can execute any valid code you want at any time in the console, and if you break something, you can just refresh the page and all changes will be gone. That's going to be the injection mechanism: just copy and paste the code that you want to inject in the console.

What would the code look like? If you're not familiar with JavaScript, you're going to have to trust me that this is not straying too far out of the ordinary. Strap in.

(continued)

First, you need to access the `XMLHttpRequest` object. In the browser, the global scope is called `window`, so to access `XMLHttpRequest`, you'll write `window.XMLHttpRequest`. OK, makes sense.

Next, JavaScript is a prototype-based language (http://mng.bz/vz1x), which means that for an object A to inherit a method from another object B, object A can set object B as its prototype. The `send` method is not defined on the `XMLHttpRequest` object itself, but on its prototype. So to access the method, you need to use the following mouthful: `window.XMLHttpRequest.prototype.send`. With this, you can store a reference to the original method as well as replace the original method with a brand-new function. This way, the next time the pgweb UI code creates an instance of `XMLHttpRequest` and calls its `send` method, it's the overwritten function that will get called. A bit weirder, but JavaScript is still only warming up.

Now, what would that new function look like? To make sure that things continue working, it'll need to call the original `send` method after the 1-second delay. The mechanics of calling a method with the right context are a bit colorful (http://mng.bz/4Z1B), but for the purposes of this experiment, just know that any function can be invoked with the `.apply(this, arguments)` method, which takes a reference to the object to call the function as a method of, and a list of arguments to pass to it. And to make it easy to observe that the overwritten function was actually called, let's use a `console.log` statement to print a message to the console.

Finally, to introduce an artificial delay, you can use a built-in `setTimeout` function that takes two arguments: a function to call and a time-out to wait before doing that (in milliseconds). Note that `setTimeout` isn't accessed through the `window` variable. Well, JavaScript is like that.

Putting this all together, you can construct the seven lines of weird that make up listing 9.1, which is ready to be copied and pasted into the console window.

Listing 9.1 contains a snippet of code that you can copy and paste directly into the console (to open it in Firefox, press Ctrl-Shift-K or choose Tools >Web Developer >Web Console from the menu) to add a 1-second delay to the `send` method of `XMLHttpRequest`.

Listing 9.1   XMLHttpRequest-3.js

Stores a reference to the original send method for later use

Overrides the send method in XMLHttpRequest's prototype with a new function

Prints a message to show that the function was called

setTimeout to execute the function after a delay

```
const originalSend = window.XMLHttpRequest.prototype.send;
window.XMLHttpRequest.prototype.send = function(){
    console.log("Chaos calling", new Date());
    let that = this;
    setTimeout(function() {
        return originalSend.apply(that);
    }, 1000);
}
```

Stores the context of the original call to later use when calling the original send

Uses the delay of 1000 ms

Returns the result of the call to the original send method, with the stored context

If this is your first encounter with JavaScript, I apologize. You might want to take a walk, but make it quick, because we're ready to run the experiment!

Pop quiz: What is XMLHttpRequest?

Pick one:

1   A JavaScript class that generates XML code that can be sent in HTTP requests
2   An acronym standing for *Xeno-Morph! Little Help to them please Request*, which is horribly inconsistent with the timeline in the original movie *Alien*
3   One of the two main ways for JavaScript code to make requests, along with the Fetch API

See appendix B for answers.

9.2.4   *Experiment 1 run*

Showtime! Go back to the pgweb UI, refresh it if you've made any changes in the console, and wait for it to load. Select a table from the menu on the left. Make sure the Network tab is open (Ctrl-Shift-E on Firefox) and empty (use the trash bin icon to clean it up). You're ready to go:

1   Copy the code from listing 9.1.
2   Go back to the browser, open the console (Ctrl-Shift-K), paste the snippet, and press Enter.
3   Now go back to the Network tab and select another table. It will take a bit longer this time, and you will see the familiar three requests made.
4   Focus on the timeline, on the rightmost column of the Network tab. You will notice that the spacing (time) between the three requests is similar to what you observed in our steady state. It will look something like figure 9.6.

Note that the requests are not spaced out by 1 second, meaning that they are done in parallel.

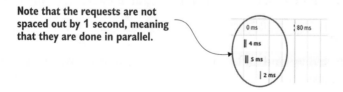

Figure 9.6   Firefox's timeline showing three requests made from JavaScript

What does this timeline mean? You added the same 1-second delay to each call of the send method. Because the requests on the timeline are not spaced by 1 second, you can conclude that they're not made in a sequence, but rather all in parallel. This is good news, because it means that with a slower connection, the overall application should slow down in a linear fashion. In other words, there doesn't seem to be a bottleneck in this part of the application.

But the hypothesis was about the entire time it takes to execute the three requests, so let's confirm whether that's the case. We can't read it directly from the timeline, because we added the artificial delay before the request is issued, and the timeline begins only at the time the first request actually starts. If we wanted to go deep down the rabbit hole, we could override more functions to print different times and calculate the overall time it took.

But because our main goal here is just to confirm that the requests aren't waiting for one another without actually reading the source code, we can do something much simpler. Go back to the console. You will see three lines starting with *Chaos calling*, printed by the snippet of code you used to inject the delay. They also print the time of the call. Now, back in the Network tab, select the last request, and look at the response headers. One of them will have the date of the request. Compare the two and note that they are 1 second apart. In fact, you can compare the other requests, and they'll all be 1 second apart from the time our overwritten function was called. The hypothesis was correct; case closed!

This was fun. Ready for another experiment?

9.3   *Experiment 2: Adding failure*

Since we're at it, let's do another experiment, this time focusing on the error handling that pgweb implements. Running pgweb locally, you're not going to experience any connectivity issues, but in the real world you definitely will. How do you expect the application to behave in face of such networking issues? Ideally, it would have a retry mechanism where applicable, and if that fails, it would present the user with a clear error message and avoid showing stale or inconsistent data. A simple experiment basically designs itself:

1 Observability: observe whether the UI shows any errors or stale data.
2 Steady state: no errors or stale data.
3 Hypothesis: if we add an error on every other request that the JavaScript UI is making, you should see an error and no inconsistent data every time you select a new table.
4 Run the experiment!

You have already clicked around and confirmed the steady state (no errors), so let's jump directly to the implementation.

9.3.1   *Experiment 2 implementation*

To implement this experiment, you can use the same injection mechanism from experiment 1 (paste a code snippet in the browser console) and even override the same method (send). The only new piece of information you need is this: How does XMLHttpRequest fail in normal conditions?

To find out, you need to look up XMLHttpRequest in the documentation at http://mng.bz/opJN. As it turns out, it uses *events*. For those of you unfamiliar with events in JavaScript, they provide a simple but flexible mechanism for communicating between objects. An object can emit (dispatch) events (simple objects with a name and optionally a payload with extra data). When that happens, the dispatching object checks whether functions are registered to receive that name, and if there are, they're all called with the event. Any function can be registered to receive (listen to) any events on an object emitting objects. Figure 9.7 presents a visual summary. This paradigm is used extensively in web applications to handle asynchronous events; for example, those generated by user interaction (click, keypress, and so forth).

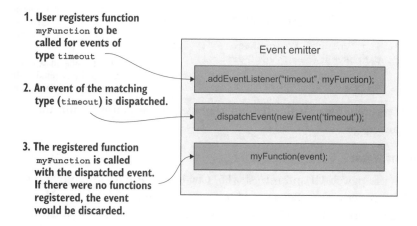

Figure 9.7   High-level overview of events in JavaScript

The Events section of the XMLHttpRequest documentation lists all the events that an instance of XMLHttpRequest can dispatch. One event looks particularly promising—the error event, which is described like this:

```
error
Fired when the request encountered an error.
Also available via the onerror property.
```

It's a legal event that can be emitted by an instance of XMLHttpRequest, and it's one that should be handled gracefully by the pgweb application, which makes it a good candidate for our experiment!

Now that you have all the elements, let's assemble them into a code snippet. Just as before, you need to override the window.XMLHttpRequest.prototype.send but keep a reference to the original method. You need a counter to keep track of which call is "every other one." And you can use the dispatchEvent method directly on the XML-HttpRequest instance to dispatch a new event that you can create with a simple new Event('timeout'). Finally, you want to either dispatch the event or do nothing (just call the original method), based on the value of the counter. You can see a snippet doing just that in the following listing.

Listing 9.2   XMLHttpRequest-4.js

Overrides the send method in XMLHttpRequest's prototype with a new function   Stores a reference to the original send method for later use

```
const originalSend = window.XMLHttpRequest.prototype.send;
var counter = 0;
window.XMLHttpRequest.prototype.send = function(){
    counter++;
    if (counter % 2 == 1){
        return originalSend.apply(this, [...arguments]);
    }
    console.log("Unlucky " + counter + "!", new Date());
    this.dispatchEvent(new Event('error'));
}
```

Keeps a counter to act on only every other call

On even calls, relays directly to the original method, noop

On odd calls, instead of calling the original method, dispatches an "error" event

With that, you're all set to run the experiment. The suspense is unbearable, so let's not waste any more time and do it!

9.3.2   *Experiment 2 run*

Go back to the pgweb UI and refresh (F5, Ctrl-R, or Cmd-R) to erase any artifacts of the previous experiments. Select a table from the menu on the left. Make sure the Network tab is open (Ctrl-Shift-E on Firefox) and empty (use the trash bin icon to clean it up). Copy the code from listing 9.2, go back to the browser, open the console (Ctrl-Shift-K), paste the snippet, and hit Enter.

Now, try selecting three different tables in a row by clicking their names in the pgweb menu on the left. What do you notice? You will see that rows of data, as well as the table information, are not refreshed every time you click, but only every other time. What's worse, no visual error message pops up to tell you there was an error. So you can select a table, see incorrect data, and not know that anything went wrong.

Fortunately, if you look into the console, you're going to see an error message like the following for every other request:

```
Uncaught SyntaxError: JSON.parse:
unexpected character at line 1 column 1 of the JSON data
```

Although you didn't get a visual presentation of the error in the UI, you can still use the information from the console to dig down and uncover the underlying issue. If you're curious, this is because the error handler used in the pgweb UI for all the requests accesses a property that is not available when there was an error before the response was received. It tries to parse it as JSON, which results in an exception being thrown and the user getting stale data and no visible mention of the error, as in the following line:

```
parseJSON(xhr.responseText)
```

NOTE Thanks to the open source nature of the project, you can see the line in the project's repo on GitHub: http://mng.bz/Xd5Y. Technically, with a GUI implemented in JavaScript, you could always take a peek into what's running in the browser, but having it out in the open for everyone to see is pretty neat.

So there you have it. With a grand total of 10 lines of (verbose) code and about 1 minute of testing, you were able to find issues with the error handling of a popular, good-quality open source project. It goes without saying that it doesn't take away from the awesomeness of the project itself. Rather, this is an illustration of how little effort it sometimes takes to benefit from doing chaos engineering.

JavaScript overdose can have a lot of serious side effects, so I'm going to keep the remaining content short. One last pit stop to show you two more neat tricks, and we're done.

9.4   Other good-to-know topics

Before we wrap up the chapter, I want to give you a bit more information on two more things that might be useful for implementing your JavaScript-based chaos experiments. Let's start with the Fetch API.

9.4.1   Fetch API

The *Fetch API* (http://mng.bz/nMJv) is a more modern replacement for XMLHttp-Request. Like XMLHttpRequest, it allows you to send requests and fetch resources. The main interaction point is through the function fetch accessible in the global scope. Unlike XMLHttpRequest, it returns a Promise object (http://mng.bz/MXl2). In its basic form, you can just call fetch with a URL, and then attach the .then and .catch handlers, as you would with any other promise. To try this, go back to the pgweb UI, open a console, and run the following snippet (fetch, then, and catch methods in bold) to try to fetch a nonexistent endpoint, /api/does-not-exist:

```
fetch("/api/does-not-exist").then(function(resp) {
    // deal with the fetched data
    console.log(resp);
}).catch(function(error) {
    // do something on failure
    console.error(error);
});
```

It will print the response as expected, complaining about the status code 404 (Not Found). Now, you must be thinking, "Surely, this time, with a modern codebase, the authors of the API designed it to be harder to override." Nope. You can use the exact same technique from the previous experiments to override it. The following listing puts it all together.

Listing 9.3   fetch.js

Stores a reference to the
original fetch function

Overrides the
fetch function in
the global scope

Calls the original fetch
function after printing
something

```
const original = window.fetch;
window.fetch = function(){
    console.log("Hello chaos");
    return original.apply(this, [...arguments]);
}
```

To test it, copy the code from listing 9.3, paste it in the console, and press Enter. Then paste the previous snippet once again. It will run the same way it did before, but this time it will print the Hello chaos message.

That's it. Worth knowing, in case the application you work with is using this API, rather than XMLHttpRequest, which is increasingly more likely every day. OK, one last step and we're done. Let's take a look at the built-in throttling.

9.4.2   Throttling

One last tidbit I want to leave you with is the built-in throttling capacity that browsers like Firefox and Chrome offer these days. If you've worked with frontend code before, you're definitely familiar with it, but if you're coming from a more low-level background, it might be a neat surprise to you!

Go back to the pgweb UI in the browser. When you open the Web Developer tools on the Network tab by pressing Ctrl-Shift-E (or choosing Tools > Web Developer > Network), on the right side, just above the list of calls is a little drop-down menu that defaults to No Throttling. You can change that to the various presets listed, like GPRS, Good 2G, or DSL, which emulate the networking speed that these connections offer (figure 9.8).

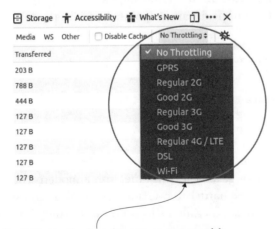

By clicking on the drop-down menu, you can pick
throttling options from a variety of presets.

**Figure 9.8   Networking throttling
options built into Firefox**

If you want to inspect how the application performs on a slower connection, try setting this to GPRS! It's a neat trick to know and might come in handy during your chaos engineering adventures. And that's a JavaScript wrap!

Pop quiz: To simulate a frontend application loading slowly, which one of the following is the best option?
Pick one:

1 Expensive, patented software from a large vendor
2 An extensive, two-week-long training session
3 A modern browser, like Firefox or Chrome

See appendix B for answers.

Pop quiz: Pick the true statement
Pick one:

1 JavaScript is a widely respected programming language, famous for its consistency and intuitive design that allows even beginner programmers to avoid pitfalls.
2 Chaos engineering applies to only the backend code.
3 JavaScript's ubiquitous nature combined with its lack of safeguards makes it very easy to inject code to implement chaos experiments on the fly into existing applications.

See appendix B for answers.

9.4.3   *Tooling: Greasemonkey and Tampermonkey*

Just before you wrap up this chapter, I want to mention two tools that you might find convenient. So far, you've been pasting scripts directly into the console, which is nice, because it has no dependencies. But it might get tedious if you do a lot of it.

   If that's the case, check out Greasemonkey (https://github.com/greasemonkey/greasemonkey) or Tampermonkey (https://www.tampermonkey.net/). Both offer a similar feature, allowing you to inject scripts to specific websites more easily.

Summary

- JavaScript's malleable nature makes it easy to inject code into applications running in the browser.
- There are currently two main ways of making requests (XMLHttpRequest and the Fetch API), and both lend themselves well to code injection in order to introduce failure.

- Modern browsers offer a lot of useful tools through their Developer Tools, including insight into the requests made to the backend, as well as the console, which allows for executing arbitrary code.

Part 3

Chaos engineering in Kubernetes

Kubernetes has taken the deployment world by storm. If you're reading this online, chances are that this text is sent to you from a Kubernetes cluster. It's so significant that it gets its own part in the book!

Chapter 10 introduces Kubernetes, where it came from, and what it can do for you. If you're not familiar with Kubernetes, this introduction should give you enough information to benefit from the following two chapters. It also covers setting two chaos experiments (crashing and network latency) manually.

Chapter 11 speeds things up a notch by introducing you to some higher-level tools (PowerfulSeal) that let you implement sophisticated chaos engineering experiments with simple YAML files. We also cover testing SLOs and chaos engineering at the cloud provider level.

Chapter 12 takes you deep down the rabbit hole of Kubernetes under the hood. To understand its weak points, you need to know how it works. This chapter covers all the components that together make Kubernetes tick, along with ideas on how to identify resiliency problems by using chaos engineering.

Finally, chapter 13 wraps up the book by showing you that the same principles also apply to the other complex distributed systems that you deal with on a daily basis—human teams. It covers the chaos engineering mindset, gives you ideas for games you can use to make your teams more reliable, and discusses how to get buy-in from stakeholders.

Chaos in Kubernetes

10

This chapter covers

- Quick introduction to Kubernetes
- Designing chaos experiments for software running on Kubernetes
- Killing subsets of applications running on Kubernetes to test their resilience
- Injecting network slowness using a proxy

It's time to cover Kubernetes (https://kubernetes.io/). Anyone working in software engineering would have a hard time not hearing it mentioned, at the very least. I have never seen an open source project become so popular so quickly. I remember going to one of the first editions of KubeCon in London in 2016 to try to evaluate whether investing any time into this entire Kubernetes thing was worth it. Fast-forward to 2020, and Kubernetes expertise is now one of the most demanded skills!

Kubernetes solves (or at least makes it easier to solve) a lot of problems that arise when running software across a fleet of machines. Its wide adoption indicates that it might be doing something right. But, like everything else, it's not perfect, and it adds its own complexity to the system—complexity that needs to be managed and understood, and that lends well to the practices of chaos engineering.

Kubernetes is a big topic, so I've split it into three chapters:

1 This chapter: Chaos in Kubernetes
   – Quick introduction to Kubernetes, where it came from, and what it does.
   – Setting up a test Kubernetes cluster. We'll cover getting a mini cluster up and running because there is nothing like working on the real thing. If you have your own clusters you want to use, that's perfectly fine too.
   – Testing a real project's resilience to failure. We'll first apply chaos engineering to the application itself to see how it copes with the basic types of failure we expect it to handle. We'll set things up manually.

2 Chapter 11: Automating Kubernetes experiments
   – Introducing a high-level tool for chaos engineering on Kubernetes.
   – Using that tool to reimplement the experiments we set up manually in chapter 10 to teach you how to do it more easily.
   – Designing experiments for an ongoing verification of SLOs. You'll see how to set up experiments to automatically detect problems on live systems—for example, when an SLO is breached.
   – Designing experiments for the cloud layer. You'll see how to use cloud APIs to test systems' behavior when machines go down.

3 Chapter 12: Under the hood of Kubernetes
   – Understanding how Kubernetes works and how to break it. This is where we dig deeper and test the actual Kubernetes components. We'll cover the anatomy of a Kubernetes cluster and discuss various ideas for chaos experiments to verify our assumptions about how it handles failure.

My goal with these three chapters is to take you from a basic understanding of what Kubernetes is and how it works, all the way to knowing how things tick under the hood, where the fragile points are, and how chaos engineering can help with understanding and managing the way the system handles failure.

> **NOTE**   The point of this trio is not to teach you how to use Kubernetes. I'll cover all you need to follow, but if you're looking for a more comprehensive Kubernetes learning experience, check out *Kubernetes in Action* by Marko Luksa (Manning, 2018, www.manning.com/books/kubernetes-in-action).

This is pretty exciting stuff, and I can't wait to show you around! Like every good journey, let's start ours with a story.

10.1 *Porting things onto Kubernetes*

"It's technically a promotion, and Kubernetes is really hot right now, so that's going to be great for your career! So you're in, right?" said Alice as she walked out of the room. As the door closed, it finally hit you that even though what she said was phrased as a question, in her mind, there wasn't much uncertainty about the outcome: you must save that High-Profile Project, period.

The project was weird from the beginning. Upper management announced it to a lot of fanfare and red-ribbon cutting, but never made quite clear the function it was supposed to serve—apart from "solving a lot of problems" by doing things like "getting rid of the monolith" and leveraging "the power of microservices" and the "amazing features of Kubernetes." And—as if this wasn't mysterious enough—the previous technical lead of the team just left the company. He *really* left. The last time someone was in contact with him, he was on his way to the Himalayas to start a new life as a llama breeder.

Truth be told, you are the person for this job. People know you're into chaos engineering, and they've heard about the problems you've uncovered with your experiments. If anyone can pick up where the llama-breeder-to-be left off and turn the existing system into a reliable system, it's you! You just need to learn how this entire Kubernetes thing works and what the High-Profile Project is supposed to do, and then come up with a plan of attack. Lucky for you, this chapter will teach you exactly that. What a coincidence! Also, the documentation you inherited reveals some useful details. Let's take a look at it.

10.1.1 *High-Profile Project documentation*

There is little documentation for the High-Profile Project, so I'll just paste it verbatim for you to get the full experience. Turns out that, rather suitably, the project is called *ICANT*. Here's how the document describes this acronym:

> ICANT: International, Crypto-fueled, AI-powered, Next-generation market Tracking

A little cryptic, isn't it? It's almost like someone designed it to be confusing to raise more funds. Something to do with AI and cryptocurrencies. But wait, there is a mission statement too; maybe this clears things up a little bit:

> Build a massively scalable, distributed system for tracking cryptocurrency flows with cutting-edge AI for technologically advanced clients all over the world.

No, not really; that doesn't help much. Fortunately, there is more. The section on current status reveals that you don't need to worry about the AI, crypto, or market stuff—that's all on the to-do list. This is what it says:

> Current status: First we approached the "distributed" part. We're running Kubernetes, so we set up Goldpinger, which makes connections between all the nodes to simulate the crypto traffic.

> To do: The AI stuff, the crypto stuff, and market stuff.

All of a sudden, starting a new life in the Himalayas makes much more sense! The previous technical lead took the network diagnostic tool Goldpinger (https://github.com/bloomberg/goldpinger), by yours truly, deployed it on their Kubernetes cluster, put all the actual work in the to-do, and left the company. And now it's your problem!

10.1.2   *What's Goldpinger?*

What does Goldpinger actually do? It produces a full graph of Kubernetes cluster connectivity by calling all instances of itself, measuring the times, and producing reports based on that data. Typically, you'd run an instance of Goldpinger per node in the cluster to detect any networking issues across nodes.

Figure 10.1 shows an example of a graph of a single node having connectivity issues. The Goldpinger UI uses colors (green for OK, red for trouble), and I marked the affected link in the screenshot.

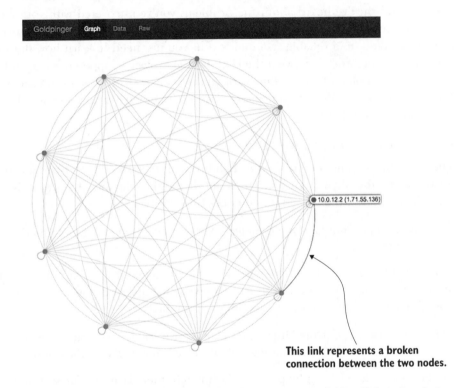

This link represents a broken connection between the two nodes.

Figure 10.1   Goldpinger graph showing connectivity between nodes in a Kubernetes cluster

For any crypto-AI-market-tracking enthusiast, this is going to be an anticlimax. But from our point of view, it makes the job easier: we have a single component to work with that doesn't require any buzzword knowledge. We can do it. First stop: a quick intro to Kubernetes. Start your stopwatch.

10.2   *What's Kubernetes (in 7 minutes)?*

Kubernetes (*K8s* for short) describes itself as "an open source system for automating deployment, scaling, and management of containerized applications" (https://kubernetes.io/). That sounds great, but what does that really mean?

Let's start simple. Let's say you have a piece of software that you need to run on your computer. You can start your laptop, log in, and run the program. Congratulations, you just did a manual deployment of your software! So far, so good.

Now imagine that you need the same piece of software to run not on 1, but on 10 computers. All of a sudden, logging into 10 computers doesn't sound so attractive, so you begin to think about automating that deployment. You could hack together a script that uses Secure Shell (SSH) to remotely log in to the 10 computers and start your program. Or you could use one of the many existing configuration management tools, like Ansible (https://github.com/ansible/ansible) or Chef (www.chef.io/). With 10 computers to take care of, it might just work.

Unfortunately, it turns out that the program you started on these machines sometimes crashes. The problem might not even be a bug, but something else—for example, insufficient disk storage. So you need something to supervise the process and to try to bring it back up when it crashes. You could achieve that by making your configuration management tool configure a `systemd` service (http://mng.bz/BRlq) so that the process gets restarted automatically every time it dies.

The software also needs to be upgraded. Every time you want to deploy a new version, you need to rerun your configuration management solution to stop and uninstall the previous version, and then install and start the new one. Also, the new version has different dependencies, so you need to take care of that too, during the update. Oh, and now your cluster contains 200 machines, because other people like your program and want you to run their software too (no need to reinvent the wheel for each piece of software you want to deploy, right?), so it's beginning to take a long time to roll out a new version.

Every machine has limited resources (CPU, RAM, disk space), so you now have this massive spreadsheet to keep track of what software should run on which machine, so that the machines don't run out of resources. When you onboard a new project, you allocate resources to it and mark where it should run in the spreadsheet. And when one of the machines goes down, you look for available room elsewhere and migrate the software from the affected machine onto another one. It's hard work, but people keep coming, so you must be doing something right!

Wouldn't it be great if a program could do all this for you? Well, yes, you guessed it, it's called Kubernetes; it does all this and more. Where did it come from?

10.2.1 *A very brief history of Kubernetes*

Kubernetes, from a Greek word meaning *helmsman* or *governor,* is an open source project released by Google in 2015 as a reimplementation of its internal scheduler system called Borg (https://research.google/pubs/pub43438/). Google donated Kubernetes to a newly formed foundation called Cloud Native Computing Foundation (or CNCF for short; www.cncf.io), which created a neutral home for the project and encouraged a massive influx of investment from other companies.

It worked. In the short five years since the project's creation, it has become a de facto API for scheduling containers. As companies adopted the open source project,

Google managed to pull people away from investing more into solutions specific to Amazon Web Services (AWS), and its cloud offering has gained more clout.

Along the way, the CNCF also gained many auxiliary projects that work with Kubernetes, like the monitoring system Prometheus (https://prometheus.io/), container runtime containerd (https://containerd.io/) and figuratively tons more.

It all sounds great, but the real question that leads to a wide adoption is this: What can it do for you? Let me show you.

10.2.2 *What can Kubernetes do for you?*

Kubernetes works *declaratively*, rather than imperatively. What I mean by that is that it lets you describe the software you want to run on your cluster, and it continuously tries to converge the current cluster state into the one you requested. It also lets you read the current state at any given time. Conceptually, it's an API for herding cats (https://en.wiktionary.org/wiki/herd_cats).

To use Kubernetes, you need a Kubernetes cluster. A *Kubernetes cluster* is a set of machines that run the Kubernetes components, and that make their resources (CPU, RAM, disk space) available to be allocated and used by your software. These machines are typically called *worker nodes*. A single Kubernetes cluster can have thousands of worker nodes.

Let's say you have a cluster, and you want to run new software on that cluster. Your cluster has three working nodes, each containing a certain amount of resources available. Imagine that one of your workers has a moderate amount of resources available, a second one has plenty available, and the third one is entirely used. Depending on the resources that the new piece of software needs, your cluster might be able to run it on the first or the second, but not the third, worker node. Visually, it could look like figure 10.2. Note that it's possible (and sometimes pretty useful) to have heterogeneous nodes, with various configurations of resources available.

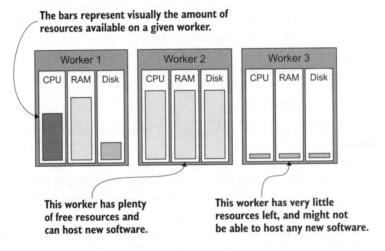

The bars represent visually the amount of resources available on a given worker.

This worker has plenty of free resources and can host new software.

This worker has very little resources left, and might not be able to host any new software.

Figure 10.2   Resources available in a small Kubernetes cluster

What would starting new software on this cluster look like? All you need to do is *tell* your cluster what your software looks like (the container image to run, any configuration like environment variables or secrets), the amount of resources you want to give it (CPU, RAM, disk space), and how to run it (the number of copies, any constraints on where it should run). You do that by making an HTTP request to the Kubernetes API—or by using a tool, like the official command-line interface (CLI) called kubectl. The part of the cluster that receives the request, stores it as the desired state, and immediately goes to work in the background on converging the current state of the cluster to the desired state is often referred to as *the control plane*.

Let's say you want to deploy version v1.0 of *mysoftware*. You need to allocate one core and 1 GB of RAM for each copy, and you need to run two copies for high availability. To make sure that one worker going down doesn't take both copies down with it, you add a constraint that the two copies shouldn't run on the same worker node. You send this request to the control plane, which stores it and returns OK. In the background, the same control plane calculates where to schedule the new software, finds two workers with enough available resources, and notifies these workers to start your software. Figure 10.3 illustrates this process.

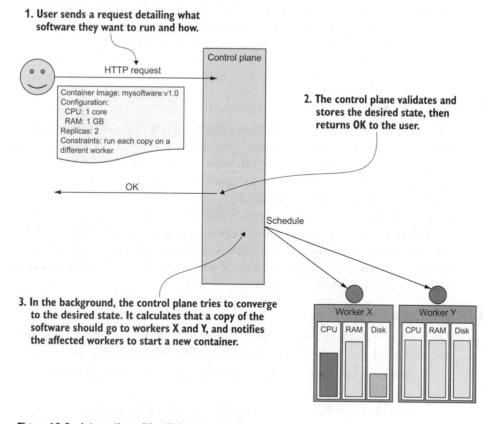

Figure 10.3 Interacting with a Kubernetes cluster

And voilà! That's what Kubernetes can do for you. Instead of making your machines do specific, low-level tasks like starting a process, you can tell your cluster to figure out how to do what you need it to do. This is a 10,000-feet aerial view, but don't worry, we'll get into the nitty-gritty later in the chapter. Right now, I bet you can't wait for some hands-on experience. Let's get to that by setting up a test cluster.

Pop quiz: What's Kubernetes?

Pick one:

1   A solution to all of your problems
2   Software that automatically renders the system running on it immune to failure
3   A container orchestrator that can manage thousands of VMs and will continuously try to converge the current state into the desired state
4   A thing for sailors

See appendix B for answers.

10.3 Setting up a Kubernetes cluster

Before we can continue with our scenario, you need access to a working Kubernetes cluster. The beauty of Kubernetes is that you can get the cluster from various providers, and it should behave exactly the same! All the examples in this chapter will work on any conforming clusters, and I will mention any potential caveats. Therefore, you're free to pick whatever installation of Kubernetes is the most convenient for you.

10.3.1 Using Minikube

For those who don't have a Kubernetes cluster handy, the easiest way to get started is to deploy a single-node, local mini-cluster on your local machine with Minikube (https://github.com/kubernetes/minikube). *Minikube* is an official part of Kubernetes itself, and allows you to deploy a single node with single instances of all the Kubernetes control-plane components inside a virtual machine. It also takes care of the little yet crucial things like helping you easily access processes running inside the cluster.

Before continuing, please follow appendix A to install Minikube. In this chapter, I'll assume you're following along with a Minikube installation on your laptop. I'll also mention whatever might be different if you're not. Everything in this chapter was tested on Minikube 1.12.3 and Kubernetes 1.18.3.

10.3.2 Starting a cluster

Depending on the platform, Minikube supports multiple virtualization options to run the actual VM with Kubernetes. The options differ for each platform:

- *Linux*—KVM or VirtualBox (running processes directly on the host is also supported)
- *macOS*—HyperKit, VMware Fusion, Parallels, or VirtualBox
- *Windows*—Hyper-V or VirtualBox

For our purposes, you can pick any of the supported options, and Kubernetes should work the same. But because I already made you install VirtualBox for the previous chapters and it's a common denominator of all three supported platforms, I recommend you stick with VirtualBox.

To start a cluster, all you need is the `minikube start` command. To specify the VirtualBox driver, use the `--driver` flag. Run the following command from a terminal to start a new cluster using VirtualBox:

```
minikube start --driver=virtualbox
```

The command might take a minute, because Minikube needs to download the VM image for your cluster and then start a VM with that image. When the command is done, you will see output similar to the following. Someone took the time to pick relevant emoticons for each log message, so I took the time to respect that and copy verbatim. You can see that the command uses the VirtualBox driver as I requested and defaults to give the VM two CPUs, 4 GB of RAM, and 2 GB of storage. It's also running Kubernetes v1.18.3 on Docker 19.03.12 (all in bold font).

```
☺    minikube v1.12.3 on Darwin 10.14.6
✌    Using the virtualbox driver based on user configuration
👍   Starting control plane node minikube in cluster minikube
💧    Creating virtualbox VM (CPUs=2, Memory=4000MB, Disk=20000MB) …
🐳    Preparing Kubernetes v1.18.3 on Docker 19.03.12 …
🔎    Verifying Kubernetes components…
🌟    Enabled addons: default-storageclass, storage-provisioner
🏄    Done! kubectl is now configured to use "minikube"
```

To confirm that the cluster started OK, try to list all pods running on the cluster. Run the following command in a terminal:

```
kubectl get pods -A
```

You will see output just like the following, listing the various components that together make the Kubernetes control plane. We will cover in detail how they work later in this chapter. For now, this command working at all proves that the control plane works:

```
NAMESPACE     NAME                                 READY   STATUS    RESTARTS   AGE
kube-system   coredns-66bff467f8-62g9p             1/1     Running   0          5m44s
kube-system   etcd-minikube                        1/1     Running   0          5m49s
kube-system   kube-apiserver-minikube              1/1     Running   0          5m49s
kube-system   kube-controller-manager-minikube     1/1     Running   0          5m49s
kube-system   kube-proxy-bwzcf                      1/1     Running   0          5m44s
kube-system   kube-scheduler-minikube              1/1     Running   0          5m49s
kube-system   storage-provisioner                  1/1     Running   0          5m49s
```

You're now ready to go. When you're done for the day and want to stop the cluster, use `minikube stop`, and to resume the cluster, use `minikube start`.

TIP You can use the command `kubectl --help` to get help on all available commands in `kubectl`. If you'd like more details on a particular command, use `--help` on that command. For example, to get help concerning the available options of the `get` command, just run `kubectl get --help`.

It's time to get our hands dirty with the High-Profile Project.

10.4 *Testing out software running on Kubernetes*

With a functional Kubernetes cluster at your disposal, you're now ready to start working on the High-Profile Project, aka ICANT. The pressure is on; you have a project to save!

As always, the first step is to build an understanding of how things work before you can reason about how they break. You'll do that by kicking the tires and looking at how ICANT is deployed and configured. You'll then conduct two experiments and finish this section by seeing how to make things easier for the next time. Let's start at the beginning by running the actual project

10.4.1 *Running the ICANT Project*

As you discovered earlier when reading the documentation you inherited, the project didn't get very far. The original team took an off-the-shelf component (Goldpinger), deployed it, and called it a day. All of this is bad news for the project, but good news to me; I have less explaining to do!

Goldpinger works by querying Kubernetes for all the instances of itself, and then periodically calling each of these instances and measuring the response time. It then uses that data to generate statistics (metrics) and plot a pretty connectivity graph. Each instance works in the same way: it periodically gets the address of its peers and makes a request to each one. Figure 10.4 illustrates this process. Goldpinger was invented to detect network slowdowns and problems, especially in larger clusters. It's really simple and effective.

How do you go about running it? You'll do it in two steps:

1 Set up the right permissions so Goldpinger can query Kubernetes for its peer.
2 Deploy the Goldpinger deployment on the cluster.

You're about to step into Kubernetes Wonderland, so let me introduce you to some Kubernetes lingo.

UNDERSTANDING KUBERNETES TERMINOLOGY

The documentation often mentions *resources* to mean the objects representing various abstractions that Kubernetes offers. For now, I'm going to introduce you to three basic building blocks used to describe software on Kubernetes:

- *Pod*—A collection of containers that are grouped together, run on the same host, and share some system resources (for example, an IP address). This is the unit of software that you can schedule on Kubernetes. You can schedule pods

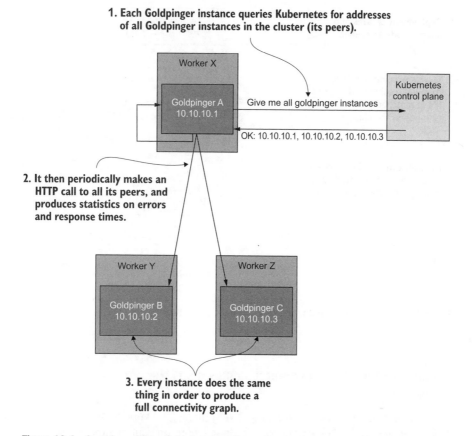

1. Each Goldpinger instance queries Kubernetes for addresses of all Goldpinger instances in the cluster (its peers).

2. It then periodically makes an HTTP call to all its peers, and produces statistics on errors and response times.

3. Every instance does the same thing in order to produce a full connectivity graph.

Figure 10.4 Overview of how Goldpinger works

directly, but most of the time you will be using a higher-level abstraction, such as a deployment.

- *Deployment*—A blueprint for creating pods, along with extra metadata, such as the number of replicas to run. Importantly, it also manages the life cycle of pods that it creates. For example, if you modify a deployment to update a version of the image you want to run, the deployment can handle a rollout, deleting old pods and creating new ones one by one to avoid an outage. It also offers other options, like rollback in case the rollout ever fails.

- *Service*—A service matches an arbitrary set of pods and provides a single IP address that resolves to the matched pods. That IP is kept up-to-date with the changes made to the cluster. For example, if a pod goes down, it will be taken out of the pool.

You can see a visual representation of how these fit together in figure 10.5. Another thing you need to know in order to understand how Goldpinger works is that to query Kubernetes, you need the right permissions.

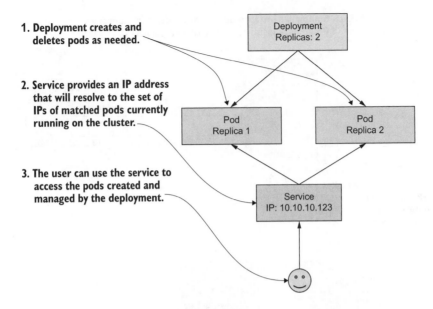

1. Deployment creates and deletes pods as needed.

2. Service provides an IP address that will resolve to the set of IPs of matched pods currently running on the cluster.

3. The user can use the service to access the pods created and managed by the deployment.

Figure 10.5   Pods, deployments, and services example in Kubernetes

Pop quiz: What's a Kubernetes deployment?

Pick one:

1   A description of how to reach software running on your cluster
2   A description of how to deploy some software on your cluster
3   A description of how to build a container

See appendix B for answers.

SETTING PERMISSIONS

Kubernetes has an elegant way of managing permissions. First, it has *ClusterRoles*, which allow you to define a role and a corresponding set of permissions to execute verbs (create, get, delete, list, . . .) on various resources. Second, it has *ServiceAccounts*, which can be linked to any software running on Kubernetes, so that it inherits all the permissions that the ServiceAccount was granted. And finally, to make a link between a ServiceAccount and a ClusterRole, you can use a ClusterRoleBinding, which does exactly what it says.

If you're new to permissioning, this might sound a little bit abstract, so take a look at figure 10.6 to see how all of this comes together.

In this case, you want to allow Goldpinger pods to list their peers, so all you need is a single ClusterRole and the corresponding ServiceAccount and ClusterRoleBinding. Later, you will use that ServiceAccount to permission the Goldpinger pods.

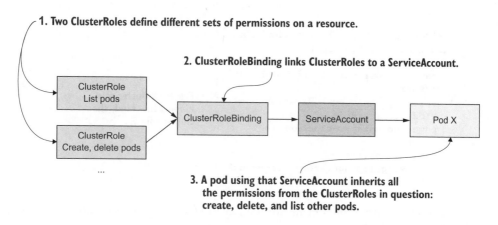

1. Two ClusterRoles define different sets of permissions on a resource.

2. ClusterRoleBinding links ClusterRoles to a ServiceAccount.

3. A pod using that ServiceAccount inherits all the permissions from the ClusterRoles in question: create, delete, and list other pods.

Figure 10.6 Kubernetes permissioning example

CREATING THE RESOURCES

It's time for some code! In Kubernetes, you can describe all the resources you want to create by using a YAML (.yml) file (https://yaml.org/) that follows the specific format that Kubernetes accepts. Listing 10.1 shows how all of this permissioning translates into YAML.

For each element described, there is a YAML object, specifying the corresponding type (kind) and the expected parameters. First, a ClusterRole called `goldpinger-clusterrole` allows for listing pods (bold font). Then you have a ServiceAccount called `goldpinger-serviceaccount` (bold font). And finally, a ClusterRoleBinding links the ClusterRole to the ServiceAccount. If you're new to YAML, note that the `---` separators allow for describing multiple resources in a single file.

Listing 10.1 Setting up permission peers (goldpinger-rbac.yaml)

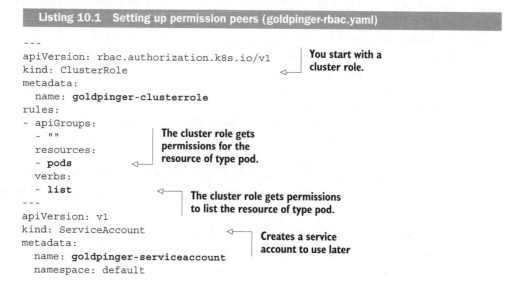

```
---
apiVersion: rbac.authorization.k8s.io/v1        You start with a
kind: ClusterRole                               cluster role.
metadata:
  name: goldpinger-clusterrole
rules:
- apiGroups:
  - ""                    The cluster role gets
  resources:             permissions for the
  - pods                 resource of type pod.
  verbs:
  - list           The cluster role gets permissions
---                to list the resource of type pod.
apiVersion: v1
kind: ServiceAccount            Creates a service
metadata:                       account to use later
  name: goldpinger-serviceaccount
  namespace: default
```

```
---
apiVersion: rbac.authorization.k8s.io/v1
kind: ClusterRoleBinding
metadata:
  name: goldpinger-clusterrolebinding
roleRef:
    apiGroup: rbac.authorization.k8s.io         Creates a cluster role
    kind: ClusterRole                           binding that binds the
    name: goldpinger-clusterrole   ◁──┘         cluster role . . .
subjects:
                                                 . . . to the service
  - kind: ServiceAccount                         account
    name: goldpinger-serviceaccount   ◁──┘
    namespace: default
```

This takes care of the permissioning part. Let's now go ahead and see what deploying the actual Goldpinger looks like.

CREATING GOLDPINGER YAML FILES

To make sense of deploying Goldpinger, I need to explain more details that I've skipped over so far: labels and matching.

Kubernetes makes extensive use of *labels*, which are simple key-value pairs of type string. Every resource can have arbitrary metadata attached to it, including labels. They are used by Kubernetes to match sets of resources, and are fairly flexible and easy to use.

For example, let's say that you have two pods with the following labels:

- Pod A, with labels app=goldpinger and stage=dev
- Pod B, with labels app=goldpinger and stage=prod

If you match (select) all pods with label app=goldpinger, you will get both pods. But if you match with label stage=dev, you will get only pod A. You can also query by multiple labels, and in that case Kubernetes will return pods matching all requested labels (a logical AND).

Labels are useful for manually grouping resources, but they're also leveraged by Kubernetes; for example, to implement deployments. When you create a deployment, you need to specify the *selector* (a set of labels to match), and that selector needs to match the pods created by the deployment. The connection between the deployment and the pods it manages relies on labels.

Label matching is also the same mechanism that Goldpinger leverages to query for its peers: it just asks Kubernetes for all pods with a specific label (by default, app=goldpinger). Figure 10.7 shows that graphically.

Putting this all together, you can finally write a YAML file with two resource descriptors: a deployment and a matching service. Inside the deployment, you need to specify the following:

- The number of replicas (we'll go with three for demonstration purposes)
- The selector (again, the default app=goldpinger)
- The actual template of pods to create

1. Each Goldpinger instance queries Kubernetes for its peers.

2. It receives a list of peers to test connectivity with.

Figure 10.7   Kubernetes permissioning for Goldpinger

In the pod template, you will specify the container image to run, some environment values required for Goldpinger to work, and ports to expose so that other instances can reach it. The important bit is that you need to specify an arbitrary port that matches the PORT environment variable (this is what Goldpinger uses to know which port to listen on). You'll go with 8080. Finally, you also specify the service account you created earlier to permission the Goldpinger pods to query Kubernetes for their peers.

Inside the service, you once again use the same selector (app=goldpinger) so that the service matches the pods created by the deployment, and the same port 8080 that you specified on the deployment.

> **NOTE**   In a typical installation, you would like to have one Goldpinger pod per node (physical machine, VM) in your cluster. That can easily be achieved by using a *DaemonSet*. It works a lot like a deployment, but instead of specifying the number of replicas, it assumes one replica per node (learn more at http://mng.bz/d4Jz). In our example setup, you will use a deployment instead, because with only one node, you would only have a single pod of Goldpinger, which defeats the purpose of this demonstration.

The following listing contains the YAML file you can use to create the deployment and the service. Take a look.

Listing 10.2   Creating a Goldpinger deployment (goldpinger.yml)

```
---
apiVersion: apps/v1
kind: Deployment
metadata:
  name: goldpinger
  namespace: default
  labels:
    app: goldpinger
spec:
  replicas: 3
  selector:
```

The deployment will create three replicas of the pods (three pods).

The deployment is configured to match pods with label app=goldpinger.

```
      matchLabels:
        app: goldpinger          The pods template
  template:                      actually gets the label
    metadata:                ◄──┘ app=goldpinger.
      labels:
        app: goldpinger
    spec:
      serviceAccount: "goldpinger-serviceaccount"
      containers:
      - name: goldpinger
        image: "docker.io/bloomberg/goldpinger:v3.0.0"
        env:
        - name: REFRESH_INTERVAL
          value: "2"
        - name: HOST             Configures the
          value: "0.0.0.0"       Goldpinger pods to
        - name: PORT             run on port 8080
          value: "8080"      ◄──┘
        # injecting real pod IP will make things easier to understand
        - name: POD_IP
          valueFrom:
            fieldRef:
              fieldPath: status.podIP
        ports:
        - containerPort: 8080  ◄──   Exposes port 8080 on the
          name: http                 pod so it's reachable
---
apiVersion: v1
kind: Service
metadata:
  name: goldpinger
  namespace: default
  labels:
    app: goldpinger          In the service, targets
spec:                        port 8080 that you made
  type: LoadBalancer         available on the pods
  ports:
    - port: 8080      ◄──┐
      name: http          │ The service will target
  selector:               │ pods based on the label
    app: goldpinger    ◄──┘ app=goldpinger.
```

With that, you're now ready to actually start the program! If you're following along, you can find the source code for both of these files (goldpinger-rbac.yml and gold-pinger.yml) at http://mng.bz/rydE. Let's make sure that both files are in the same folder, and let's go ahead and run them.

DEPLOYING GOLDPINGER

Start by creating the permissioning resources (the goldpinger-rbac.yml file) by running the following command:

```
kubectl apply -f goldpinger-rbac.yml
```

You will see Kubernetes confirming that the three resources were created successfully, with the following output:

```
clusterrole.rbac.authorization.k8s.io/goldpinger-clusterrole created
serviceaccount/goldpinger-serviceaccount created
clusterrolebinding.rbac.authorization.k8s.io/goldpinger-clusterrolebinding
    created
```

Then, create the actual deployment and a service:

```
kubectl apply -f goldpinger.yml
```

Just as before, you will see the confirmation that the resources were created:

```
deployment.apps/goldpinger created
service/goldpinger created
```

Once that's done, let's confirm that pods are running as expected. To do that, list the pods:

```
kubectl get pods
```

You should see output similar to the following, with three pods in status `Running` (bold font). If they're not, you might need to give it a few seconds to start:

```
NAME                             READY   STATUS    RESTARTS   AGE
goldpinger-c86c78448-5kwpp       1/1     Running   0          1m4s
goldpinger-c86c78448-gtbvv       1/1     Running   0          1m4s
goldpinger-c86c78448-vcwx2       1/1     Running   0          1m4s
```

The pods are running, meaning that the deployment did its job. Goldpinger crashes if it can't list its peers, which means that the permissioning you set up also works as expected. The last thing to check is that the service was configured correctly. You can do that by running the following command, specifying the name of the service you created (`goldpinger`):

```
kubectl describe svc goldpinger
```

You will see the details of the service, just as in the following output (abbreviated). Note the `Endpoints` field, specifying three IP addresses, for the three pods that it's configured to match.

```
Name:            goldpinger
Namespace:       default
Labels:          app=goldpinger
(...)
Endpoints:       172.17.0.3:8080,172.17.0.4:8080,172.17.0.5:8080
(...)
```

If you want to be 100% sure that the IPs are correct, you can compare them to the IPs of Goldpinger pods. You can display the IPs easily by appending `-o wide` (for wide output) to the `kubectl get pods` command:

```
kubectl get pods -o wide
```

You will see the same list as before, but this time with extra details, including the IP (bold font). These details should correspond to the list specified in the service. Any mismatch between the IP addresses matched by the service and the IP addresses of the pods would point to misconfigured labels. Depending on your internet connection speed and your setup, the pods might take a little bit of time to start. If you see pods in Pending state, give it an extra minute:

```
NAME                        READY STATUS   RESTARTS AGE IP         NODE
      NOMINATED NODE    READINESS GATES
goldpinger-c86c78448-5kwpp 1/1  Running 0      15m 172.17.0.4 minikube <none>
      <none>
goldpinger-c86c78448-gtbvv 1/1  Running 0      15m 172.17.0.3 minikube <none>
      <none>
goldpinger-c86c78448-vcwx2 1/1  Running 0      15m 172.17.0.5 minikube <none>
      <none>
```

Everything's up and running, so let's access Goldpinger to see what it's really doing. To do that, you need to access the service you created.

> **NOTE** Kubernetes does a great job of standardizing the way people run their software. Unfortunately, not everything is easily standardized. Although every Kubernetes cluster supports services, the way you access the cluster, and therefore its services, depends on the way the cluster was set up. This chapter sticks to Minikube because it's simple and easily accessible to anyone. If you're running your own Kubernetes cluster, or use a managed solution from a cloud provider, accessing software running on the cluster might require extra setup (for example, setting up an ingress; http://mng.bz/Vdpr). Refer to the relevant documentation.

On Minikube, you can leverage the command `minikube service`, which will figure out a way to access the service directly from your host machine and open the browser for you. To do that, run the following command:

```
minikube service goldpinger
```

You will see output similar to the following specifying the special URL that Minikube prepared for you (bold font). Your default browser will be launched to open that URL:

```
|-----------|-------------|--------------|----------------------------|
| NAMESPACE |    NAME     | TARGET PORT  |            URL             |
|-----------|-------------|--------------|----------------------------|
| default   | goldpinger  | http/8080    | http://192.168.99.100:30426 |
|-----------|-------------|--------------|----------------------------|
  Opening service default/goldpinger in default browser…
```

Inside the newly launched browser window, you will see the Goldpinger UI. It will look similar to what's shown in figure 10.8. It's a graph, on which every point represents an instance of Goldpinger, and every arrow represents the last connectivity check (an HTTP request) between the instances. You can click a node to select it and display extra information.

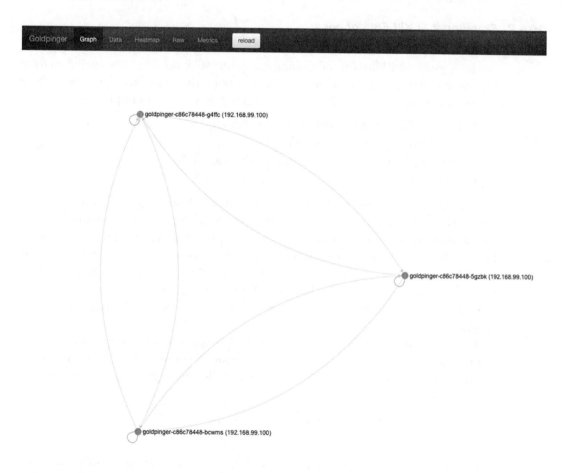

Figure 10.8 Goldpinger UI in action

The graph also provides other functionality, such as a heatmap, showing hotspots of any potential networking slowness, and metrics, providing statistics that can be used to generate alerts and pretty dashboards. Goldpinger is a really handy tool for detecting any network issues, downloaded more than a million times from Docker Hub!

Feel free to take some time to play around, but otherwise you're done setting it all up. You have a running application that you can interact with, deployed with just two kubectl commands.

Unfortunately, on our little test cluster, all three instances are running on the same host, so you're unlikely to see any network slowness, which is pretty boring. Fortunately, as chaos engineering practitioners, we're well equipped to introduce failure and make things interesting again. Let's start with the basics—an experiment to kill some pods.

10.4.2 *Experiment 1: Kill 50% of pods*

Much like a villain from a comic book movie, you might be interested in seeing what happens when you kill 50% of Goldpinger pods. Why do that? It's an inexpensive experiment that can answer a lot of questions about what happens when one of these instances goes down (simulating a machine going down). For example

- Do the other instances detect that to begin with?
- If so, how long before they detect it?
- How does Goldpinger configuration affect all of that?
- If you had an alert set up, would it get triggered?

How should you go about implementing this? The previous chapters covered different ways this could be addressed. For example, you could log into the machine running the Goldpinger process you want to kill, and simply run a `kill` command, as you did before. Or, if your cluster uses Docker to run the containers (more on that soon), you could leverage the tools covered in chapter 5. All of the techniques you learned in the previous chapters still apply. That said, Kubernetes gives you other options, like directly deleting pods. It's definitely the most convenient way of achieving that, so let's go with that option.

Our experiment has another crucial detail: Goldpinger works by periodically making HTTP requests to all of its peers. That period is controlled by the environment variable REFRESH_PERIOD. In the goldpinger.yml file you deployed, that value was set to 2 seconds:

```
- name: REFRESH_INTERVAL
  value: "2"
```

This means that the maximum time it takes for an instance to notice another instance being down is 2 seconds. This is pretty aggressive, and in a large cluster would result in a lot of traffic and CPU time spent on this, but I chose that value for demonstration purposes. It will be handy to see the changes detected quickly. With that, you now have all the elements, so let's turn this into a concrete plan for an experiment.

EXPERIMENT 1 PLAN

If you take the first question (Do other Goldpinger instances detect a peer down?), you can design a simple experiment plan like so:

1. Observability: use the Goldpinger UI to see whether any pods are marked as inaccessible; use `kubectl` to see new pods come and go.
2. Steady state: all nodes are healthy.

3 Hypothesis: if you delete one pod, you should see it marked as failed in the Goldpinger UI, and then be replaced by a new, healthy pod.

4 Run the experiment!

That's it! Let's see how to implement it.

EXPERIMENT 1 IMPLEMENTATION

To implement this experiment, the pod labels come in useful once again. All you need to do is leverage `kubectl get pods` to get all pods with label `app=goldpinger`, and then pick a random pod and kill it, using `kubectl delete`. To make things easy, you can also leverage `kubectl`'s `-o name` flag to display only the pod names, and use a combination of `sort --random-sort` and `head -n1` to pick a random line of the output.

Put all of this together, and you get a script like `kube-thanos.sh` in the following listing. Store the script somewhere on your system (or clone it from the GitHub repo).

Listing 10.3   Killing pods randomly (kube-thanos.sh)

```
#!/bin/bash

kubectl get pods \          Uses kubectl
  -l app=goldpinger \       to list pods
  -o name \                 Lists only pods with
    | sort --random-sort \  label app=goldpinger
    | head -n 1 \           Displays the name
    | xargs kubectl delete  as the output
                            Sorts in random order
            Deletes the pod  Picks the first one
```

Armed with that, you're ready to rock. Let's run the experiment.

EXPERIMENT 1 RUN!

Let's start by double-checking the steady state. Your Goldpinger installation should still be running, and you should have the UI open in a browser window. If it's not, you can bring both back up by running the following commands:

```
kubectl apply -f goldpinger-rbac.yml
kubectl apply -f goldpinger.yml
minikube service goldpinger
```

To confirm that all nodes are OK, simply refresh the graph by clicking the Reload button, and verify that all three nodes are showing in green. So far, so good.

To confirm that the script works, let's also set up some observability for the pods being deleted and created. You can leverage the `--watch` flag of the `kubectl get` command to print the names of all pods coming and going to the console. You can do that by opening a new terminal window and running the following command:

```
kubectl get pods --watch
```

You will see the familiar output, showing all the Goldpinger pods, but this time the command will stay active, blocking the terminal. You can use Ctrl-C to exit at any time if needed:

```
NAME                          READY   STATUS    RESTARTS   AGE
goldpinger-c86c78448-6rtw4    1/1     Running   0          20h
goldpinger-c86c78448-mj76q    1/1     Running   0          19h
goldpinger-c86c78448-xbj7s    1/1     Running   0          19h
```

Now, to the fun part! To conduct our experiment, you'll open another terminal window for the `kube-thanos.sh` script, run it to kill a random pod, and then quickly go to the Goldpinger UI to observe what the Goldpinger pods saw. Bear in mind that in the local setup, the pods will recover rapidly, so you might need to be quick to actually observe the pod becoming unavailable and then healing. In the meantime, the `kubectl get pods --watch` command will record the pod going down and a replacement coming up. Let's do that!

Open a new terminal window and run the script to kill a random pod:

```
bash kube-thanos.sh
```

You will see output showing the name of the pod being deleted:

```
pod "goldpinger-c86c78448-shtdq" deleted
```

Go quickly to the Goldpinger UI and click Refresh. You should see some failure, as in figure 10.9. Nodes that can't be reached by at least one other node will be marked as unhealthy. I marked the unhealthy node in the figure. The live UI also uses a red color to differentiate them. You will also notice four nodes showing up. This is because after the pod is deleted, Kubernetes tries to reconverge to the desired state (three replicas), so it creates a new pod to replace the one you deleted.

> **NOTE** If you're not seeing any errors, the pods probably recovered before you switched to the UI window, because your computer is quicker than mine when I was writing this and chose the parameters. If you rerun the command and refresh the UI more quickly, you should be able to see it.

Now, go back to the terminal window that is running `kubectl get pods --watch`. You will see output similar to the following. Note the pod that you killed (`-shtdq`) goes into `Terminating` state, and a new pod (`-lwxrq`) takes its place (both in bold font). You will also notice that the new pod goes through a life cycle of `Pending` to `Container-Creating` to `Running`, while the old one goes to `Terminating`:

```
NAME                          READY   STATUS        RESTARTS   AGE
goldpinger-c86c78448-pfqmc    1/1     Running       0          47s
goldpinger-c86c78448-shtdq    1/1     Running       0          22s
goldpinger-c86c78448-xbj7s    1/1     Running       0          20h
```

goldpinger-c86c78448-shtdq	**1/1**	**Terminating**	**0**	**38s**
goldpinger-c86c78448-lwxrq	**0/1**	**Pending**	**0**	**0s**
goldpinger-c86c78448-lwxrq	0/1	Pending	0	0s
goldpinger-c86c78448-lwxrq	**0/1**	**ContainerCreating**	**0**	**0s**
goldpinger-c86c78448-shtdq	0/1	Terminating	0	39s
goldpinger-c86c78448-lwxrq	**1/1**	**Running**	**0**	**2s**
goldpinger-c86c78448-shtdq	0/1	Terminating	0	43s
goldpinger-c86c78448-shtdq	0/1	Terminating	0	43s

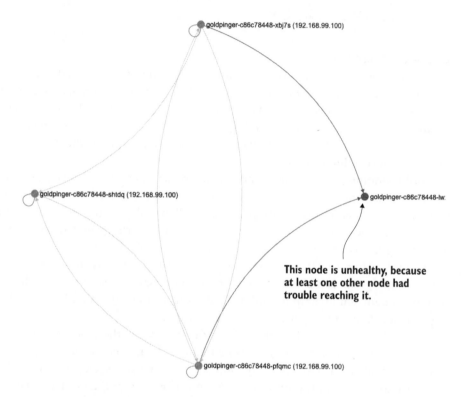

Figure 10.9 Goldpinger UI showing an unavailable pod being replaced by a new one.

Finally, let's check that everything recovered smoothly. To do that, go back to the browser window with Goldpinger UI, and refresh once more. You should now see the three new pods happily pinging each other, all in green. This means that our hypothesis was correct on both fronts.

Nice job. Another one bites the dust another experiment under your belt. But before we move on, let's discuss a few points.

Pop quiz: What happens when a pod dies on a Kubernetes cluster?

Pick one:

1   Kubernetes detects it and sends you an alert.
2   Kubernetes detects it and will restart it as necessary to make sure the expected number of replicas are running.
3   Nothing.

See appendix B for answers.

EXPERIMENT 1 DISCUSSION

For the sake of teaching, I took a few shortcuts here that I want to make you aware of. First, when accessing the pods through the UI, you're using a service, which resolves to a pseudorandom instance of Goldpinger every time you make a new call. This means it's possible to get routed to the instance you just killed and get an error in the UI. It also means that every time you refresh the view, you get the reality from the point of view of a different pod.

For illustration purposes, that's not a deal breaker on a small test cluster, but if you run a large cluster and want to make sure that a network partition doesn't obscure your view, you need to make sure you consult all available instances, or at least a reasonable subset. Goldpinger addresses that issue with metrics, and you can learn more at https://github.com/bloomberg/goldpinger#prometheus.

Second, using a GUI-based tool this way is a bit awkward. If you see what you expect, that's great. But if you don't, it doesn't necessarily mean the event didn't happen; you might simply have missed it. Again, this can be alleviated by using the metrics, which I skipped here for the sake of simplicity.

Third, if you look closely at the failures that you see in the graph, you will see that the pods sometimes start receiving traffic before they are actually up. This is because, again for simplicity, I skipped the readiness probe that serves exactly that purpose. If set, a readiness probe prevents a pod from receiving any traffic until a certain condition is met (see the documentation at http://mng.bz/xmdq). For an example of how to use a readiness probe, see the installation docs of Goldpinger (https://github.com/bloomberg/goldpinger#installation).

Finally, remember that depending on the refresh period you're running Goldpinger with, the data you're looking at is up to that many seconds stale, which means that for the pods you killed, you'll keep seeing them for an extra number of seconds equal to the refresh period (2 seconds in this setup).

These are the caveats my lawyers advised me to clarify before this goes to print. In case that makes you think I'm not fun at parties, let me prove you wrong. Let's play some *Invaders*, like it's 1978.

10.4.3 *Party trick: Kill pods in style*

If you really want to make a point that chaos engineering is fun, I have two tools for you.

First, let's look at *KubeInvaders* (https://github.com/lucky-sideburn/KubeInvaders). It gamifies the process of killing pods by starting a clone of *Space Invaders*; the aliens are pods in the specified namespace. You guessed it: the aliens you shoot down are deleted in Kubernetes. Installation involves deploying Kubernetes on a cluster, and then connecting a local client that actually displays the game content. See figure 10.10 to see what KubeInvaders looks like in action.

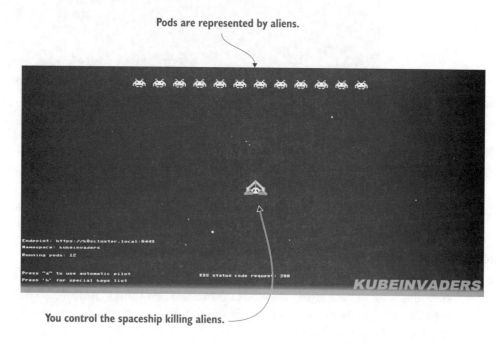

Figure 10.10   KubeInvaders: https://github.com/lucky-sideburn/KubeInvaders

The second tool is for fans of the first-person shooter genre: Kube DOOM (https://github.com/storax/kubedoom). Similar to KubeInvaders, it represents pods as enemies, and kills in Kubernetes the ones that die in the game. Here's a tip to justify using it: playing the game is often much quicker than copying and pasting the name of a pod, saving so much time (mandatory reference: https://xkcd.com/303/). See figure 10.11 for a screenshot.

For Kube DOOM, the installation is pretty straightforward: you run a pod on the host, pass a `kubectl` configuration file to it, and then use a desktop-sharing client to connect to the game. After a long day of debugging, it might be just what you need. I'll just leave it there.

Pods represent the enemies.

Figure 10.11   Kube DOOM: https://github.com/storax/kubedoom

I'm sure that will help with your next house party. When you finish the game, let's take a look at another experiment—some good old network slowness.

10.4.4 Experiment 2: Introduce network slowness

Slowness, my nemesis, we meet again. If you're a software engineer, chances are you're spending a lot of time trying to outwit slowness. When things go wrong, actual failure is often easier to debug than situations where things *mostly* work. And slowness tends to fall into the latter category.

Slowness is such an important topic that we touch upon it in nearly every chapter of this book. I introduced some slowness using tc in chapter 4, and then again using Pumba in Docker in chapter 5. You've used some in the context of the JVM, application level, and even browser in other chapters. It's time to take a look at what's different when running on Kubernetes.

It's worth mentioning that everything we covered before still applies here. You could very well use tc or Pumba directly on one of the machines running the processes you're interested in, and modify them to introduce the failure you care about. In fact, using kubectl cp and kubectl exec, you could upload and execute tc commands directly in a pod, without even worrying about accessing the host. Or you could even add a second container to the Goldpinger pod that would execute the necessary tc commands.

All of these options are viable but share one downside: they modify the existing software that's running on your cluster, and so by definition carry risks of messing things up. A convenient alternative is to add *extra* software, tweaked to implement the failure you care about, but otherwise identical to the original, and introduce the extra software in a way that will integrate with the rest of the system. Kubernetes makes it really easy. Let me show you what I mean; let's design an experiment around simulated network slowness.

EXPERIMENT 2 PLAN

Let's say that you want to see what happens when one instance of Goldpinger is slow to respond to queries of its peers. After all, this is what this piece of software was designed to help with, so before you rely on it, you should test that it works as expected.

A convenient way of doing that is to deploy a copy of Goldpinger that you can modify to add a delay. Once again, you could do it with `tc`, but to show you some new tools, let's use a standalone network proxy instead. That proxy will sit in front of that new Goldpinger instance, receive the calls from its peers, add the delay, and relay the calls to Goldpinger. Thanks to Kubernetes, setting it all up is pretty straightforward.

Let's iron out some details. Goldpinger's default time-out for all calls is 300 ms, so let's pick an arbitrary value of 250 ms for our delay: enough to be clearly seen, but not enough to cause a time-out. And thanks to the built-in heatmap, you will be able to visually show the connections that take longer than others, so the observability aspect is taken care of. The plan of the experiment figuratively writes itself:

1 Observability: use the Goldpinger UI's graph and heatmap to read delays.
2 Steady state: all existing Goldpinger instances report healthy.
3 Hypothesis: if you add a new instance that has a 250 ms delay, the connectivity graph will show all four instances healthy, and the 250 ms delay will be visible in the heatmap.
4 Run the experiment!

Sound good? Let's see how to implement it.

EXPERIMENT 2 IMPLEMENTATION

Time to dig into what the implementation will look like. Do you remember figure 10.4 that showed how Goldpinger worked? Let me copy it for your convenience in figure 10.12. Every instance asks Kubernetes for all its peers, and then periodically makes calls to them to measure latency and detect problems.

Now, what you want to do is add a copy of the Goldpinger pod that has the extra proxy we just discussed in front of it. A pod in Kubernetes can have multiple containers running alongside each other and able to communicate via localhost. If you use the same label `app=goldpinger`, the other instances will detect the new pod and start calling. But you will configure the ports in such a way that instead of directly reaching the new instance, the peers will first reach the proxy (in port 8080). And the proxy will add the desired latency. The extra Goldpinger instance

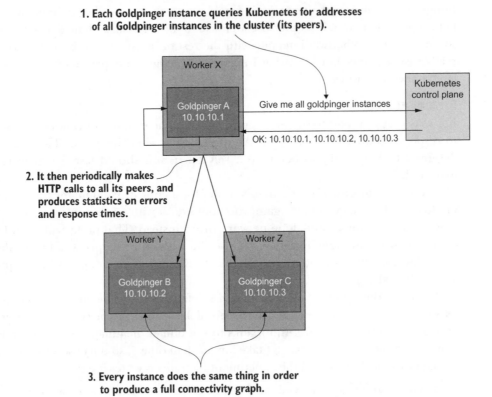

1. Each Goldpinger instance queries Kubernetes for addresses of all Goldpinger instances in the cluster (its peers).

2. It then periodically makes HTTP calls to all its peers, and produces statistics on errors and response times.

3. Every instance does the same thing in order to produce a full connectivity graph.

Figure 10.12 Overview of how Goldpinger works (again)

will be able to ping the other hosts freely, like a regular instance. This is summarized in figure 10.13.

You get the idea of what the setup will look like; now you need the actual networking proxy. Goldpinger communicates via HTTP/1.1, so you're in luck. It's a text-based, reasonably simple protocol running on top of TCP. All you need is the protocol specification (RFC 7230, RFC 7231, RFC 7232, RFC 7233 and RFC 7234), and you should be able to implement a quick proxy in no time.[1] Dust off your C compiler, stretch your arms, and let's do it!

EXPERIMENT 2 TOXIPROXY

Just kidding! You'll use an existing, open source project designed for this kind of thing, called Toxiproxy (https://github.com/shopify/toxiproxy). It works as a proxy on the TCP level (Level 4 of the Open Systems Interconnection, or OSI, model),

---

[1] The specifications are available online at the IETF Tools pages: RFC 7230 at https://tools.ietf.org/html/rfc7230, RFC 7231 at https://tools.ietf.org/html/rfc7231, RFC 7232 at https://tools.ietf.org/html/rfc7232, RFC 7233 at https://tools.ietf.org/html/rfc7233, and RFC 7234 at https://tools.ietf.org/html/rfc7234.

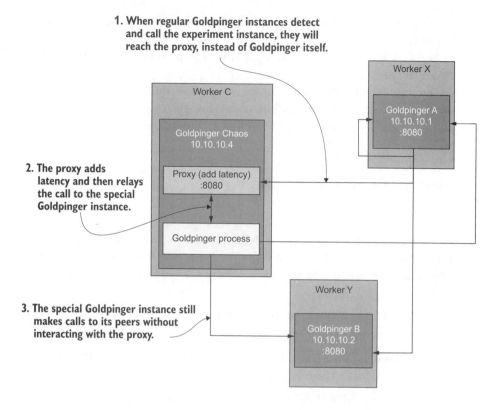

1. When regular Goldpinger instances detect and call the experiment instance, they will reach the proxy, instead of Goldpinger itself.

2. The proxy adds latency and then relays the call to the special Goldpinger instance.

3. The special Goldpinger instance still makes calls to its peers without interacting with the proxy.

Figure 10.13 A modified copy of Goldpinger with an extra proxy in front of it

which is fine, because you don't actually need to understand anything about what's going on at the HTTP level (Level 7) to introduce a simple latency. The added benefit is that you can use the same tool for any other TCP-based protocol in the exact same way, so what you're about to do will be equally applicable to a lot of other popular software, like Redis, MySQL, PostgreSQL, and many more.

Toxiproxy consists of two pieces:

- The actual proxy server, which exposes an API you can use to configure what should be proxied where and the kind of failure that you expect
- A CLI client that connects to that API and can change the configuration live

NOTE   Instead of using the CLI, you can also talk to the API directly, and Toxiproxy offers ready-to-use clients in a variety of languages.

The dynamic nature of Toxiproxy makes it really useful when used in unit and integration testing. For example, your integration test could start by configuring the proxy to add latency when connecting to a database, and then your test could verify that time-outs are triggered accordingly. It's also going to be handy in implementing our experiment.

The version you'll use, 2.1.4, is the latest available release at the time of writing. You'll run the proxy server as part of the extra Goldpinger pod by using a prebuilt, publicly available image from Docker Hub. You'll also need to use the CLI locally on your machine.

To install it, download the CLI executable for your system (Ubuntu/Debian, Windows, macOS) from https://github.com/Shopify/toxiproxy/releases/tag/v2.1.4 and add it to your PATH. To confirm it works, run the following command:

```
toxiproxy-cli --version
```

You should see version 2.1.4 displayed:

```
toxiproxy-cli version 2.1.4
```

When a Toxiproxy server starts, by default it doesn't do anything apart from running its HTTP API. By calling the API, you can configure and dynamically change the behavior of the proxy server. You can define arbitrary configurations by the following:

- A unique name
- A host and port to bind to and listen for connections
- A destination server to proxy to

For every configuration like this, you can attach failures. In Toxiproxy lingo, these failures are called *toxics*. Currently, the following toxics are available:

- latency—Adds arbitrary latency to the connection (in either direction)
- down—Takes down the connection
- bandwidth—Throttles the connection to the desired speed
- slow close—Delays the TCP socket from closing for an arbitrary time
- timeout—Waits for an arbitrary time and then closes the connection
- slicer—Slices the received data into smaller bits before sending it to the destination

You can attach an arbitrary combination of failures to every proxy configuration you define. For our needs, the latency toxic will do exactly what you want it to. Let's see how all of this fits together.

Pop quiz: What's Toxiproxy?

Pick one:

1 A configurable TCP proxy that can simulate various problems such as dropped packets or network slowness
2 A K-pop band singing about the environmental consequences of dumping large amounts of toxic waste sent to developing countries through the use of proxy and shell companies

See appendix B for answers.

To sum it all up, you want to create a new pod with two containers: one for Goldpinger and one for Toxiproxy. You need to configure Goldpinger to run on a different port so that the proxy can listen on the default port 8080 that the other Goldpinger instances will try to connect to. You'll also create a service that routes connections to the proxy API on port 8474, so you can use `toxiproxy-cli` commands to configure the proxy and add the latency that you want, just as in figure 10.14.

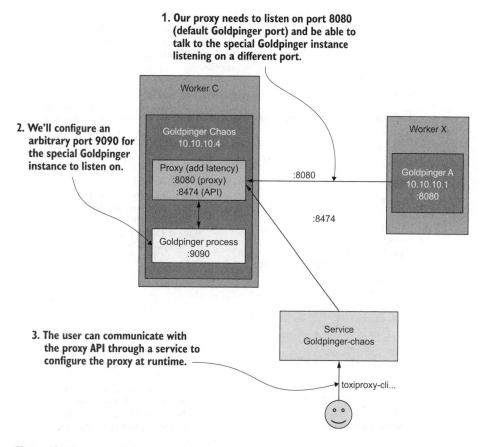

Figure 10.14   Interacting with the modified version of Goldpinger using `toxiproxy-cli`

Let's now translate this into a Kubernetes YAML file. You can see the resulting gold-pinger-chaos.yml in listing 10.4. You will see two resource descriptions, a pod (with two containers) and a service. You use the same service account you created before, to give Goldpinger the same permissions. You're also using two environment variables, `PORT` and `CLIENT_PORT_OVERRIDE`, to make Goldpinger listen on port 9090, but call its peers on port 8080, respectively. This is because, by default, Goldpinger calls its peers on the same port that it runs itself.

Finally, notice that the service is using the label `chaos=absolutely` to match to the new pod you created. It's important that the Goldpinger pod has the label `app=gold-pinger` so that it can be found by its peers, but you also need another label in order to route connections to the proxy API.

Listing 10.4   Goldpinger deployment (goldpinger-chaos.yml)

```
---
apiVersion: v1
kind: Pod
metadata:
  name: goldpinger-chaos
  namespace: default
  labels:
    app: goldpinger              ◁
    chaos: absolutely
spec:
  serviceAccount: "goldpinger-serviceaccount"    ◁
  containers:
  - name: goldpinger
    image: docker.io/bloomberg/goldpinger:v3.0.0
    env:
    - name: REFRESH_INTERVAL
      value: "2"
    - name: HOST
      value: "0.0.0.0"
    - name: PORT
      value: "9090"              ◁
    - name: CLIENT_PORT_OVERRIDE
      value: "8080"
    - name: POD_IP
      valueFrom:
        fieldRef:
          fieldPath: status.podIP
  - name: toxiproxy
    image: docker.io/shopify/toxiproxy:2.1.4
    ports:
    - containerPort: 8474         ◁
      name: toxiproxy-api
    - containerPort: 8080
      name: goldpinger
---
apiVersion: v1
kind: Service
metadata:
  name: goldpinger-chaos
  namespace: default
spec:
  type: LoadBalancer
  ports:
    - port: 8474                  ◁
      name: toxiproxy-api
  selector:
    chaos: absolutely             ◁
```

The new pod has the same label app=goldpinger to be detected by its peers, but also chaos=absolutely to be matched by the proxy api service.

Uses the same service account as other instances to give Goldpinger permission to list its peers

Uses HOST envvar to make Goldpinger listen on port 9090, and CLIENT_PORT_OVERRIDE to make it call its peers on the default port 8080

Toxiproxy container exposes two ports: 8474 with the Toxiproxy API, and 8080 to proxy through to Goldpinger

Service routes traffic to port 8474 (Toxiproxy API)

Service uses label chaos=absolutely to select the pods running Toxiproxy

And that's all you need. Make sure you have this file handy (or clone it from the repo as before). Ready to rock? Let the games begin!

EXPERIMENT 2 RUN!

To run this experiment, you're going to use the Goldpinger UI. If you closed the browser window before, restart it by running the following command in the terminal:

```
minikube service goldpinger
```

Let's start with the steady state, and confirm that all three nodes are visible and report as healthy. In the top bar, click Heatmap. You will see a heatmap similar to the one in figure 10.15. Each square represents connectivity between nodes and is color-coded based on the time it took to execute a request:

- Columns represent source (from).
- Rows represent destinations (to).
- The legend clarifies which number corresponds to which pod.

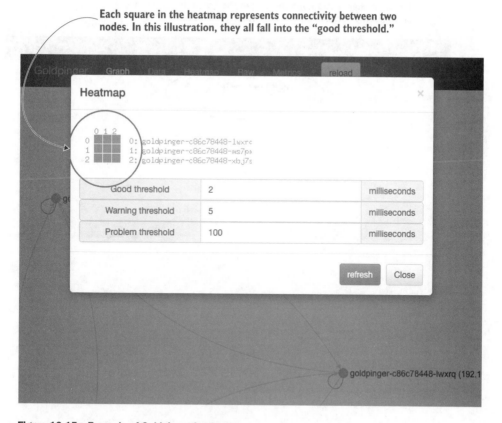

Figure 10.15   Example of Goldpinger heatmap

In this example, all squares are the same color and shade, meaning that all requests take below 2 ms, which is to be expected when all instances run on the same host. You can also tweak the values to your liking and click Refresh to show a new heatmap. Close it when you're ready.

Let's introduce our new pod! To do that, you'll `kubectl apply` the goldpinger-chaos.yml file from listing 10.4. Run the following command:

```
kubectl apply -f goldpinger-chaos.yml
```

You will see output confirming creation of a pod and service:

```
pod/goldpinger-chaos created
service/goldpinger-chaos created
```

Let's confirm it's running by going to the UI. You will now see an extra node, just as in figure 10.16. But notice that the new pod is marked as unhealthy; all of its peers are failing to connect to it. In the live UI, the node is marked in red, and in figure 10.16

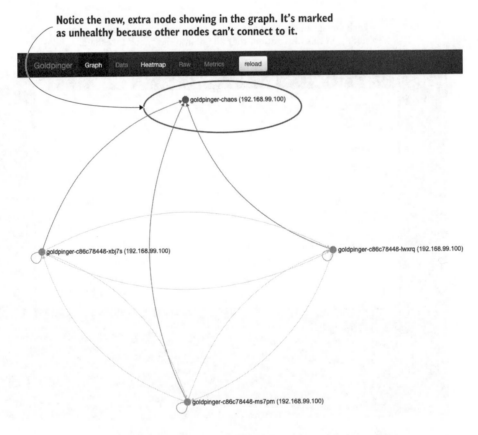

Figure 10.16   Extra Goldpinger instance, detected by its peers, but inaccessible

I annotated the new, unhealthy node for you. This is because you haven't configured the proxy to pass the traffic yet.

Let's address that by configuring the Toxiproxy. This is where the extra service you deployed comes in handy: you will use it to connect to the Toxiproxy API using `toxiproxy-cli`. Do you remember how you used `minikube service` to get a special URL to access the Goldpinger service? You'll leverage that again, but this time with the `--url` flag, to print only the URL itself. Run the following command in a bash session to store the URL in a variable:

```
TOXIPROXY_URL=$(minikube service --url goldpinger-chaos)
```

You can now use the variable to point `toxiproxy-cli` to the right Toxiproxy API. That's done using the `-h` flag. Confusingly, `-h` is not for *help*; it's for *host*. Let's confirm it works by listing the existing proxy configuration:

```
toxiproxy-cli -h $TOXIPROXY_URL list
```

You will see the following output, saying no proxies are configured. It even goes so far as to hint that you should create some proxies (bold font):

```
Name           Listen           Upstream           Enabled      Toxics
================================================================================
no proxies

Hint: create a proxy with `toxiproxy-cli create`
```

Let's configure one. You'll call it `chaos`, make it route to localhost:9090 (where you configured Goldpinger to listen to), and listen on 0.0.0.0:8080 to make it accessible to its peers to call. Run the following command to make that happen:

```
                Connects to a specific proxy          Creates a new proxy
toxiproxy-cli \                                       configuration called "chaos"
    -h $TOXIPROXY_URL \
    create chaos \                                    Listens on 0.0.0.0:8080
        -l 0.0.0.0:8080 \                             (default Goldpinger port)
        -u localhost:9090
                                                      Relays connections to localhost:9090
                                                      (where you configured Goldpinger to run)
```

You will see a simple confirmation that the proxy was created:

```
Created new proxy chaos
```

Rerun the `toxiproxy-cli list` command to see the new proxy appear this time:

```
toxiproxy-cli -h $TOXIPROXY_URL list
```

You will see the following output, listing a new proxy configuration called `chaos` (bold font):

```
Name          Listen         Upstream            Enabled        Toxics
=================================================================
chaos       [::]:8080      localhost:9090      enabled        None
```

Hint: inspect toxics with `toxiproxy-cli inspect <proxyName>`

If you go back to the UI and click Refresh, you will see that the `goldpinger-chaos` extra instance is now green, and all instances happily report healthy state in all directions. If you check the heatmap, it will also show all green.

Let's change that. Using the command `toxiproxy-cli toxic add`, let's add a single toxic with 250 ms latency:

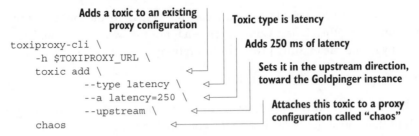

You will see a confirmation:

```
Added upstream latency toxic 'latency_upstream' on proxy 'chaos'
```

To confirm that the proxy got it right, you can inspect your `chaos` proxy. To do that, run the following command:

```
toxiproxy-cli -h $TOXIPROXY_URL inspect chaos
```

You will see output just like the following, listing your brand-new toxic (bold font):

```
Name: chaos      Listen: [::]:8080      Upstream: localhost:9090
=======================================================================
Upstream toxics:
latency_upstream:          type=latency      stream=upstream toxicity=1.00
attributes=[    jitter=0         latency=250      ]

Downstream toxics:
Proxy has no Downstream toxics enabled.
```

Now, go back to the Goldpinger UI in the browser and refresh. You will still see all four instances reporting healthy and happy (the 250 ms delay fits within the default time-out of 300 ms). But if you open the heatmap, this time it will tell a different story. The row with `goldpinger-chaos` pod will be marked in red (problem threshold), implying that all its peers detected slowness. See figure 10.17 for a screenshot.

Our hypothesis was correct: Goldpinger correctly detects and reports the slowness, and at 250 ms, below the default time-out of 300 ms, the Goldpinger graph UI reports all as healthy. And you did all of that without modifying the existing pods.

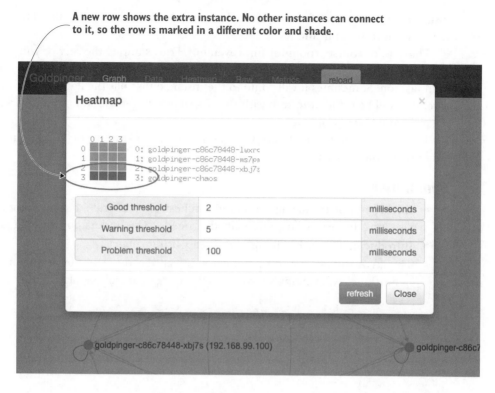

A new row shows the extra instance. No other instances can connect to it, so the row is marked in a different color and shade.

Figure 10.17 Goldpinger heatmap, showing slowness accessing pod `goldpinger-chaos`

This wraps up the experiment, but before we go, let's clean up the extra pod. To do that, run the following command to delete everything you created using the gold-pinger-chaos.yml file:

```
kubectl delete -f goldpinger-chaos.yml
```

Let's discuss our findings.

EXPERIMENT 2 DISCUSSION

How well did you do? You took some time to learn new tools, but the entire implementation of the experiment boiled down to a single YAML file and a handful of commands with Toxiproxy. You also had a tangible benefit of working on a copy of the software that you wanted to test, leaving the existing running processes unmodified. You effectively rolled out extra capacity and then had 25% of running software affected, limiting the blast radius.

Does that mean you could do that in production? As with any sufficiently complex question, the answer is, "It depends." In this example, if you wanted to verify the robustness of some alerting that relies on metrics from Goldpinger to trigger, this could be a good way to do it. But the extra software could also affect the existing instances in a more profound way, making it riskier. At the end of the day, it really depends on your application.

There is, of course, room for improvement. For example, the service you're using to access the Goldpinger UI is routing traffic to any instance matched in a pseudorandom fashion. Sometimes it will route to the instance that has the 250 ms delay. In our case, that will be difficult to spot with the naked eye, but if you wanted to test a larger delay, it could be a problem.

Time to wrap up this first part. Coming in part 2: making your chaos engineer life easier with PowerfulSeal.

Summary

- Kubernetes helps manage container orchestration at scale, but in doing that, it also introduces its own complexity that needs to be understood and managed.
- Introducing failure by killing pods is easy using `kubectl`.
- Thanks to Kubernetes, it's practical to inject network issues by adding an extra network proxy; by doing so, you can also better control the blast radius.

Automating Kubernetes experiments

11

This chapter covers

- Automating chaos experiments for Kubernetes with PowerfulSeal
- Recognizing the difference between one-off experiments and ongoing SLO verification
- Designing chaos experiments on the VM level using cloud provider APIs

In this second helping of Kubernetes goodness, you'll see how to use higher-level tools to implement chaos experiments. In the previous chapter, you set up experiments manually to build an understanding of how to implement the experiment. But now I want to show you how much more quickly you can go when using the right tools. Enter PowerfulSeal.

11.1 Automating chaos with PowerfulSeal

It's often said that software engineering is one of the very few jobs where being lazy is a good thing. And I tend to agree with that; a lot of automation or reducing toil can be seen as a manifestation of being too lazy to do manual labor. Automation also reduces operator errors and improves speed and accuracy.

The tools for automation of chaos experiments are steadily becoming more advanced and mature. For a good, up-to-date list of available tools, it's worth checking out the Awesome Chaos Engineering list (https://github.com/dastergon/awesome-chaos-engineering). For Kubernetes, I recommend PowerfulSeal (https://github.com/powerfulseal/powerfulseal), created by yours truly, and which we're going to use here. Other good options include Chaos Toolkit (https://github.com/chaostoolkit/chaostoolkit) and Litmus (https://litmuschaos.io/).

In this section, we're going to build on the two experiments you implemented manually in chapter 10 to make you more efficient the next time. In fact, we're going to reimplement a slight variation of these experiments, each in 5 minutes flat. So, what's PowerfulSeal again?

11.1.1 What's PowerfulSeal?

PowerfulSeal is a chaos engineering tool for Kubernetes. It has quite a few features:

- Interactive mode, helping you to understand how software on your cluster works and to manually break it
- Integrating with your cloud provider to take VMs up and down
- Automatically killing pods marked with special labels
- Autonomous mode supporting sophisticated scenarios

The latter point in this list is the functionality we'll focus on here.

The *autonomous mode* allows you to implement chaos experiments by writing a simple YAML file. Inside that file, you can write any number of *scenarios*, each listing the steps necessary to implement, validate, and clean up after your experiment. There are plenty of options you can use (documented at https://powerfulseal.github.io/powerfulseal/policies), but at its heart, autonomous mode has a very simple format. The YAML file containing scenarios is referred to as a *policy file*.

To give you an example, take a look at listing 11.1. It contains a simple policy file, with a single scenario, with a single step. That single step is an HTTP probe. It will try to make an HTTP request to the designated endpoint of the specified service, and fail the scenario if that doesn't work.

Listing 11.1 Minimal policy (powerfulseal-policy-minimal.yml)

```
scenarios:
- name: Just check that my service responds
  steps:
  - probeHTTP:            ◁──┤ Instructs PowerfulSeal to
      target:                 │ conduct an HTTP probe
        service:              ┤ Targets service my-service
          name: my-service ◁──┤ in namespace myapp
          namespace: myapp
      endpoint: /healthz   ◁──┤ Calls the /healthz endpoint
                              │ on that service
```

Once you have your policy file ready, you can run PowerfulSeal in many ways. Typically, it tends to be used either from your local machine—the same one you use to interact with the Kubernetes cluster (useful for development)—or as a deployment running directly on the cluster (useful for ongoing, continuous experiments).

To run, PowerfulSeal needs permission to interact with the Kubernetes cluster, either through a ServiceAccount, as you did with Goldpinger in chapter 10, or through specifying a `kubectl` config file. If you want to manipulate VMs in your cluster, you also need to configure access to the cloud provider. With that, you can start PowerfulSeal in autonomous mode and let it execute your scenario.

PowerfulSeal will go through the policy and execute scenarios step by step, killing pods and taking down VMs as appropriate. Take a look at figure 11.1, which shows what this setup looks like.

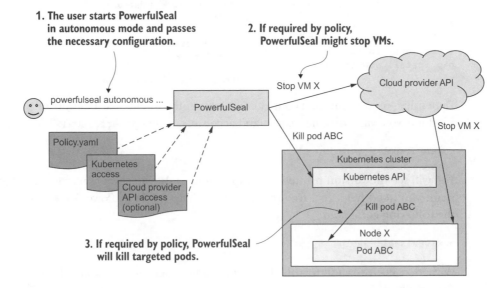

Figure 11.1 Setting up PowerfulSeal

And that's it. Point PowerfulSeal at a cluster, tell it what your experiment is like, and watch it do the work for you! We're almost ready to get our hands dirty, but before we do, you need to install PowerfulSeal.

Pop quiz: What does PowerfulSeal do?

Pick one:

1 Illustrates—in equal measures—the importance and futility of trying to pick up good names in software
2 Guesses what kind of chaos you might need by looking at your Kubernetes clusters
3 Allows you to write a YAML file to describe how to run and validate chaos experiments

See appendix B for answers.

11.1.2 *PowerfulSeal installation*

PowerfulSeal is written in Python, and it's distributed in two forms:

- A pip package called `powerfulseal`
- A Docker image called `powerfulseal/powerfulseal` on Docker Hub

For our two examples, running PowerfulSeal locally will be much easier, so let's install it through pip. It requires Python3.7+ and pip available.

To install it using a `virtualenv` (recommended), run the following commands in a terminal window to create a subfolder called env and install everything in it:

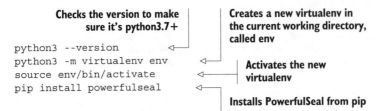

```
python3 --version
python3 -m virtualenv env
source env/bin/activate
pip install powerfulseal
```

Checks the version to make sure it's python3.7+

Creates a new virtualenv in the current working directory, called env

Activates the new virtualenv

Installs PowerfulSeal from pip

Depending on your internet connection, the last step might take a minute or two. When it's done, you will have a new command accessible, called `powerfulseal`. Try it out:

```
powerfulseal --version
```

You will see the version printed, corresponding to the latest version available. If at any point you need help, feel free to consult the help pages of PowerfulSeal by running the following command:

```
powerfulseal --help
```

With that, we're ready to roll. Let's see what experiment 1 would look like using PowerfulSeal.

11.1.3 *Experiment 1b: Killing 50% of pods*

As a reminder, this was our plan for experiment 1:

1. Observability: use the Goldpinger UI to see if any pods are marked as inaccessible; use `kubectl` to see new pods come and go.
2. Steady state: all nodes are healthy.
3. Hypothesis: if you delete one pod, you should see it marked as failed in the Goldpinger UI, and then be replaced by a new, healthy pod.
4. Run the experiment!

We have already covered the observability, but if you closed the browser window with the Goldpinger UI, here's a refresher. Open the Goldpinger UI by running the following command in a terminal window:

```
minikube service goldpinger
```

And just as before, you'd like to have a way to see which pods were created and deleted. To do that, you leverage the `--watch` flag of the `kubectl get pods` command. In another terminal window, start a `kubectl` command to print all changes:

```
kubectl get pods --watch
```

Now, to the actual experiment. Fortunately, it translates one-to-one to a built-in feature of PowerfulSeal. Actions on pods are done using `PodAction` (I'm good at naming like that). Every `PodAction` consists of three steps:

1 Match some pods; for example, based on labels.
2 Filter the pods (various filters are available; for example, take a 50% subset).
3 Apply an action on pods (for example, kill them).

This translates directly into experiment1b.yml that you can see in the following listing. Store it or clone it from the repo.

Listing 11.2 PowerfulSeal scenario implementing experiment 1b (experiment1b.yml)

```
config:
  runStrategy:          Runs the scenario only
    runs: 1             once and then exits
scenarios:
- name: Kill 50% of Goldpinger nodes
  steps:                          Selects all pods in
  - podAction:                    namespace default, with
      matches:                    labels app=goldpinger
        - labels:
            selector: app=goldpinger
            namespace: default
      filters:                    Filters out to take only 50%
        - randomSample:           of the matched pods
            ratio: 0.5
      actions:        Kills the pods
        - kill:
            force: true
```

You must be itching to run it, so let's not wait any longer. On Minikube, the `kubectl` config is stored in ~/.kube/config, and it will be automatically picked up when you run PowerfulSeal. So the only argument you need to specify is the policy file flag (`--policy-file`). Run the following command, pointing to the experiment1b.yml file:

```
powerfulseal autonomous --policy-file experiment1b.yml
```

You will see output similar to the following (abbreviated). Note the lines indicating it found three pods, filtered out two, and selected a pod to be killed (bold font):

```
(...)
2020-08-25 09:51:20 INFO __main__ STARTING AUTONOMOUS MODE
2020-08-25 09:51:20 INFO scenario.Kill 50% of Gol Starting scenario 'Kill 50%
    of Goldpinger nodes' (1 steps)
```

```
2020-08-25 09:51:20 INFO action_nodes_pods.Kill 50% of Gol Matching 'labels'
    {'labels': {'selector': 'app=goldpinger', 'namespace': 'default'}}
2020-08-25 09:51:20 INFO action_nodes_pods.Kill 50% of Gol Matched 3 pods for
    selector app=goldpinger in namespace default
2020-08-25 09:51:20 INFO action_nodes_pods.Kill 50% of Gol Initial set
    length: 3
2020-08-25 09:51:20 INFO action_nodes_pods.Kill 50% of Gol Filtered set
    length: 1
2020-08-25 09:51:20 INFO action_nodes_pods.Kill 50% of Gol Pod killed: [pod
    #0 name=goldpinger-c86c78448-8lfqd namespace=default containers=1
    ip=172.17.0.3 host_ip=192.168.99.100 state=Running
    labels:app=goldpinger,pod-template-hash=c86c78448 annotations:]
2020-08-25 09:51:20 INFO scenario.Kill 50% of Gol Scenario finished
(...)
```

If you're quick enough, you will see a pod becoming unavailable and then replaced by a new pod in the Goldpinger UI, just as you did the first time you ran this experiment. And in the terminal window running kubectl, you will see the familiar sight, confirming that a pod was killed (goldpinger-c86c78448-8lfqd) and then replaced with a new one (goldpinger-c86c78448-czbkx):

```
NAME                        READY   STATUS            RESTARTS   AGE
goldpinger-c86c78448-lwxrq  1/1     Running           1          45h
goldpinger-c86c78448-tl9xq  1/1     Running           0          40m
goldpinger-c86c78448-xqfvc  1/1     Running           0          8m33s
goldpinger-c86c78448-8lfqd  1/1     Terminating       0          41m
goldpinger-c86c78448-8lfqd  1/1     Terminating       0          41m
goldpinger-c86c78448-czbkx  0/1     Pending           0          0s
goldpinger-c86c78448-czbkx  0/1     Pending           0          0s
goldpinger-c86c78448-czbkx  0/1     ContainerCreating 0          0s
goldpinger-c86c78448-czbkx  1/1     Running           0          2s
```

That concludes the first experiment and shows you the ease of use of higher-level tools like PowerfulSeal. But we're just warming up. Let's take a look at experiment 2 once again, this time using the new toys.

11.1.4 *Experiment 2b: Introducing network slowness*

As a reminder, this was our plan for experiment 2:

1 Observability: use the Goldpinger UI's graph and heatmap to read delays.
2 Steady state: all existing Goldpinger instances report healthy.
3 Hypothesis: if you add a new instance that has a 250 ms delay, the connectivity graph will show all four instances as being healthy, and the 250 ms delay will be visible in the heatmap.
4 Run the experiment!

It's a perfectly good plan, so let's use it again. But this time, instead of manually setting up a new deployment and doing the gymnastics to point the right port to the right place, you'll leverage the clone feature of PowerfulSeal.

It works like this. You point PowerfulSeal at a source deployment that it will copy at runtime (the deployment must exist on the cluster). This is to make sure that you don't break the existing running software, and instead add an extra instance, just as you did before. Then you can specify a list of mutations that PowerfulSeal will apply to the deployment to achieve specific goals. Of particular interest is the Toxiproxy mutation. It does almost exactly the same thing that you did:

- Adds a Toxiproxy container to the deployment
- Configures Toxiproxy to create a proxy configuration for each port specified on the deployment
- Automatically redirects the traffic incoming to each port specified in the original deployment to its corresponding proxy port
- Configures any toxics requested

The only real difference between what you did before and what PowerfulSeal does is the automatic redirection of ports, which means that you don't need to change any port configuration in the deployment.

To implement this scenario using PowerfulSeal, you need to write another policy file. It's pretty straightforward. You need to use the clone feature and specify the source deployment to clone. To introduce the network slowness, you can add a mutation of type `toxiproxy`, with a toxic on port 8080, of type `latency`, with the latency attribute set to 250 ms. And just to show you how easy it is to use, let's set the number of replicas affected to 2. This means that two replicas out of the total of five (three from the original deployment plus these two), or 40% of the traffic, will be affected. Also note that at the end of a scenario, PowerfulSeal cleans up after itself by deleting the clone it created. To give you enough time to look around, let's add a wait of 120 seconds before that happens.

When translated into YAML, it looks like the file experiment2b.yml that you can see in the following listing. Take a look.

Listing 11.3 PowerfulSeal scenario implementing experiment 2b (experiment2b.yml)

```
config:
  runStrategy:
    runs: 1
scenarios:
- name: Toxiproxy latency          Uses the clone feature
  steps:                            of PowerfulSeal
    - clone:            ◁──┐
        source:            │        Clones the deployment
          deployment:      ◁─────── called "goldpinger" in
            name: goldpinger         the default namespace
            namespace: default
        replicas: 2        ◁──┐     Uses two replicas
        mutations:            │     of the clone
          - toxiproxy:
              toxics:
```

```
        - targetProxy: "8080"          ⟵    Targets port 8080 (the one
          toxicType: latency                that Goldpinger is running on)
          toxicAttributes:
            - name: latency            ⟵    Specifies latency
              value: 250                      of 250 ms
    - wait:
        seconds: 120       ⟵    Waits for 120 seconds
```

TIP If you got rid of the Goldpinger deployment from experiment 2, you can bring it back up by running the following command in a terminal window:

```
kubectl apply -f goldpinger-rbac.yml
kubectl apply -f goldpinger.yml
```

You'll see a confirmation of the created resources. After a few seconds, you will be able to see the Goldpinger UI in the browser by running the following command:

```
minikube service goldpinger
```

You will see the familiar graph with three Goldpinger nodes, just as in chapter 10. See figure 11.2 for a reminder of what it looks like.

Let's execute the experiment. Run the following command in a terminal window:

```
powerfulseal autonomous --policy-file experiment2b.yml
```

You will see PowerfulSeal creating the clone, and then eventually deleting it, similar to the following output:

```
(...)
2020-08-31 10:49:32 INFO __main__ STARTING AUTONOMOUS MODE
2020-08-31 10:49:33 INFO scenario.Toxiproxy laten Starting scenario
    'Toxiproxy latency' (2 steps)
2020-08-31 10:49:33 INFO action_clone.Toxiproxy laten Clone deployment
    created successfully
2020-08-31 10:49:33 INFO scenario.Toxiproxy laten Sleeping for 120 seconds
2020-08-31 10:51:33 INFO scenario.Toxiproxy laten Scenario finished
2020-08-31 10:51:33 INFO scenario.Toxiproxy laten Cleanup started (1 items)
2020-08-31 10:51:33 INFO action_clone Clone deployment deleted successfully:
    goldpinger-chaos in default
2020-08-31 10:51:33 INFO scenario.Toxiproxy laten Cleanup done
2020-08-31 10:51:33 INFO policy_runner All done here!
```

During the 2-minute wait you configured, check the Goldpinger UI. You will see a graph with five nodes. When all pods come up, the graph will show all as being healthy. But there is more to it. Click the heatmap, and you will see that the cloned pods (they will have chaos in their names) are slow to respond. But if you look closely, you will notice that the connections they are making to themselves are unaffected. That's because PowerfulSeal doesn't inject itself into communications on localhost.

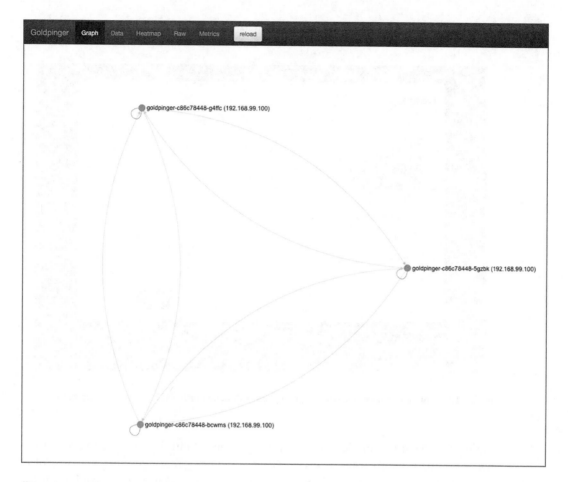

Figure 11.2   Goldpinger UI in action

Click the heatmap button. You will see a heatmap similar to figure 11.3. Note that the squares on the diagonal (pods calling themselves) remain unaffected by the added latency.

That concludes the experiment. Wait for PowerfulSeal to clean up after itself and then delete the cloned deployment. When it's finished (it will exit), let's move on to the next topic: ongoing testing.

11.2   Ongoing testing and service-level objectives

So far, all the experiments we've conducted were designed to verify a hypothesis and call it a day. Like everything in science, a single counterexample is enough to prove a hypothesis wrong, but absence of such a counterexample doesn't prove anything. And sometimes our hypotheses are about normal functioning of a system, where various events might occur and influence the outcome.

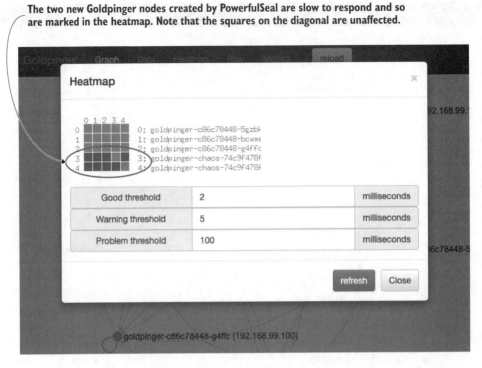

The two new Goldpinger nodes created by PowerfulSeal are slow to respond and so are marked in the heatmap. Note that the squares on the diagonal are unaffected.

Figure 11.3   Goldpinger heatmap showing two pods with added latency, injected by PowerfulSeal

To illustrate what I mean, let me give you an example. Think of a typical SLA that you might see for a platform as a service (PaaS). Let's say that your product is to offer managed services, similar to AWS Lambda (https://aws.amazon.com/lambda/): the client can make an API call specifying a location of some code, and your platform will build, deploy, and run that service for them. Your clients care deeply about the speed at which they can deploy new versions of their services, so they want an SLA for the time it takes from their request to their service being ready to serve traffic. To keep things simple, let's say that the time for building their code is excluded, and the time to deploy it on your platform is agreed to be 1 minute.

As the engineer responsible for that system, you need to work backward from that constraint to set up the system in a way that can satisfy these requirements. You design an experiment to verify that a typical request you expect to see in your clients fits in that timeline. You run it, it turns out it takes only about 30 seconds, the champagne cork is popping, and the party starts! Or does it?

When you run the experiment like this and it works, what you've actually proved is that the system behaved the expected way *during the experiment*. But does that guarantee it will work the same way in different conditions (peak traffic, different usage patterns, different data)? Typically, the larger and more complex the system, the harder it is to answer that question. And that's a problem, especially if the SLAs you signed have financial penalties for missing the goals.

Fortunately, chaos engineering really shines in this scenario. Instead of running an experiment once, you can run it continuously to detect any anomalies, experimenting every time on a system in a different state and during the kind of failure you expect to see. Simple yet effective.

Let's go back to our example. You have a 1-minute deadline to start a new service. Let's automate an ongoing experiment that starts a new service every few minutes, measures the time it took to become available, and alerts if it exceeds a certain threshold. That threshold will be your internal SLO, which is more aggressive than the legally binding version in the SLA that you signed, so that you can get alerted when you get close to trouble.

It's a common scenario, so let's take our time and make it real.

11.2.1 Experiment 3: Verifying pods are ready within (n) seconds of being created

Chances are that PaaS you're building is running on Kubernetes. When your client makes a request to your system, it translates into a request for Kubernetes to create a new deployment. You can acknowledge the request to your client, but this is where things start to get tricky. How do you know that the service is ready?

In one of the previous experiments, you used `kubectl get pods --watch` to print to the console all changes to the state of the pods you cared about. All of them are happening asynchronously, in the background, while Kubernetes is trying to converge to the desired state. In Kubernetes, pods can be in one of the following states:

- `pending`—The pod has been accepted by Kubernetes but hasn't been set up yet.
- `running`—The pod has been set up, and at least one container is still running.
- `succeeded`—All containers in the pod have terminated in success.
- `failed`—All containers in the pod have terminated, at least one of them in failure.
- `unknown`—The state of the pod is unknown (typically, the node running it stopped reporting its state to Kubernetes).

If everything goes well, the happy path is for a pod to start in `pending` and then move to `running`. But before that happens, a lot of things need to happen, many of which will take a different amount of time every time; for example:

- *Image download*—Unless already present on the host, the images for each container need to be downloaded, potentially from a remote location. Depending on the size of the image and on how busy the location from which it needs to be downloaded is at the time, it might take a different amount of time every time. Additionally, like everything on the network, the download is prone to failure and might need to be retried.

- *Preparing dependencies*—Before a pod is run, Kubernetes might need to prepare dependencies it relies on, like (potentially large) volumes, configuration files, and so on.
- *Actually running the containers*—The time to start a container will vary depending on how busy the host machine is.

In a not-so-happy path, for example, if an image download gets interrupted, you might end up with a pod going from `pending` through `failed` to `running`. The point is that you can't easily predict how long it's going to take to actually have it running. So the next best thing you can do is to continuously test it and alert when it gets too close to the threshold you care about.

With PowerfulSeal, that's easy to do. You can write a policy that will deploy an example application to run on the cluster, wait the time you expect it to take, and then execute an HTTP request to verify that the application is running correctly. It can also automatically clean up the application when it's done, and provide a means to get alerted when the experiment fails.

Normally, you would add some type of failure, and test that the system withstands that. But right now, I just want to illustrate the idea of ongoing experiments, so let's keep it simple and stick to verifying our SLO on the system without any disturbance.

Leveraging that, you can design the following experiment:

1 Observability: read PowerfulSeal output (and/or metrics).
2 Steady state: N/A.
3 Hypothesis: when you schedule a new pod and a service, it becomes available for HTTP calls within 30 seconds.
4 Run the experiment!

That translates into a PowerfulSeal policy that runs the following steps indefinitely:

1 Create a pod and a service.
2 Wait 30 seconds.
3 Make a call to the service to verify it's available; fail if it's not.
4 Remove the pod and service.
5 Rinse and repeat.

Take a look at figure 11.4, which illustrates this process. To write the actual Powerful-Seal policy file, you're going to use three more features:

- A step of type `kubectl` behaves as you expect it to: it executes the attached YAML just as if you used `kubectl apply` or `kubectl delete`. You'll use that to create the pods in question. You'll also use the option for automatic cleanup at the end of the scenario, called `autoDelete`.
- You'll use the wait feature to wait for the 30 seconds you expect to be sufficient to deploy and start the pod.
- You'll use `probeHTTP` to make an HTTP request and detect whether it works. `probeHTTP` is fairly flexible; it supports calling services or arbitrary URLs, using proxies and more.

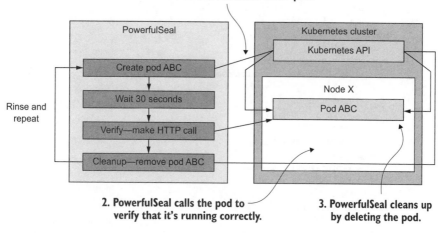

Figure 11.4 Example of an ongoing chaos experiment

You also need an actual test app to deploy and call. Ideally, you'd choose something that represents a reasonable approximation of the type of software that the platform is supposed to handle. To keep things simple, you can deploy a simple version of Gold-pinger again. It has an endpoint /healthz that you can reach to confirm that it started correctly.

Listing 11.4 shows experiment3.yml, which is what the preceding list looks like when translated into a YAML file. Unlike in the previous experiments, where you configured the policy to run only once, here you configure it to run continuously (the default) with a 5- to 10-second wait between runs. Take a look; you'll run that file in just a second.

Listing 11.4 PowerfulSeal scenario implementing experiment 3 (experiment3.yml)

```
config:
  runStrategy:
    minSecondsBetweenRuns: 5          ◁── Configures the seal to run
    maxSecondsBetweenRuns: 10              continuously with 5- to 10-
scenarios:                                second wait between runs
- name: Verify pod start SLO
  steps:
  - kubectl:                          ◁── The kubectl command
      autoDelete: true                    is equivalent to kubectl
      # equivalent to `kubectl apply -f -`  apply -f.
      action: apply
      payload: |                      Cleans up whatever was
        ---                           created here at the end
        apiVersion: v1                of the scenario
        kind: Pod
        metadata:
```

```
        name: slo-test
        labels:
          app: slo-test
      spec:
        containers:
        - name: goldpinger
          image: docker.io/bloomberg/goldpinger:v3.0.0
          env:
          - name: HOST
            value: "0.0.0.0"
          - name: PORT
            value: "8080"
          ports:
          - containerPort: 8080
            name: goldpinger
      ---
      apiVersion: v1
      kind: Service
      metadata:
        name: slo-test
      spec:
        type: LoadBalancer
        ports:
          - port: 8080
            name: goldpinger
        selector:
          app: slo-test
# wait the minimal time for the SLO
- wait:
    seconds: 30
# make sure the service responds
- probeHTTP:
    target:
      service:
        name: slo-test
        namespace: default
        port: 8080
    endpoint: /healthz
```

Waits for the arbitrarily chosen 30 seconds

Makes an HTTP call to the specified service (the one created above in the kubectl section)

Calls the /healthz endpoint just to verify the server is up and running

We're almost ready to run this experiment, but I have just one caveat to get out of the way. If you're running this on Minikube, the service IPs that PowerfulSeal uses to make the call in probeHTTP need to be accessible from your local machine. Fortunately, that can be handled by the Minikube binary. To make them accessible, run the following command in a terminal window (it will ask for a sudo password):

```
minikube tunnel
```

After a few seconds, you will see it start to periodically print a confirmation message similar to the following. This is to show you that it detected a service, and that it made local routing changes to your machine to make the IP route correctly. When you stop the process, the changes will be undone:

```
Status:
        machine: minikube
        pid: 10091
        route: 10.96.0.0/12 -> 192.168.99.100
        minikube: Running
        services: [goldpinger]
    errors:
                minikube: no errors
                router: no errors
                loadbalancer emulator: no errors
```

With that, you are ready to run the experiment. Once again, to have a good view of what's happening to the cluster, let's start a terminal window and run the kubectl command to watch for changes:

```
kubectl get pods --watch
```

In another window, run the actual experiment:

```
powerfulseal autonomous --policy-file experiment3.yml
```

PowerfulSeal will start running, and you'll need to stop it at some point with Ctrl-C. A full cycle of running the experiment will look similar to the following output. Note the lines creating the pod, making the call, and getting a response and doing the cleanup (all in bold font):

```
(...)
2020-08-26 09:52:23 INFO scenario.Verify pod star Starting scenario 'Verify
    pod start SLO' (3 steps)
2020-08-26 09:52:23 INFO action_kubectl.Verify pod star pod/slo-test created
    service/slo-test created
2020-08-26 09:52:23 INFO action_kubectl.Verify pod star Return code: 0
2020-08-26 09:52:23 INFO scenario.Verify pod star Sleeping for 30 seconds
2020-08-26 09:52:53 INFO action_probe_http.Verify pod star Making a call:
    http://10.101.237.29:8080/healthz, get, {}, 1000, 200, , , True
2020-08-26 09:52:53 INFO action_probe_http.Verify pod star Response:
    {"OK":true,"duration-ns":260,"generated-at":"2020-08-26T08:52:53.572Z"}
2020-08-26 09:52:53 INFO scenario.Verify pod star Scenario finished
2020-08-26 09:52:53 INFO scenario.Verify pod star Cleanup started (1 items)
2020-08-26 09:53:06 INFO action_kubectl.Verify pod star pod "slo-test"
    deleted
service "slo-test" deleted
2020-08-26 09:53:06 INFO action_kubectl.Verify pod star Return code: 0
2020-08-26 09:53:06 INFO scenario.Verify pod star Cleanup done
2020-08-26 09:53:06 INFO policy_runner Sleeping for 8 seconds
```

PowerfulSeal says that the SLO was being respected, which is great. But we only just met, so let's double-check that it actually deployed (and cleaned up) the right stuff on the cluster. To do that, go back to the terminal window running kubectl. You should see the new pod appear, run, and disappear, similar to the following output:

```
slo-test                    0/1        Pending            0        0s
slo-test                    0/1        Pending            0        0s
slo-test                    0/1        ContainerCreating  0        0s
slo-test                    1/1        Running            0        1s
slo-test                    1/1        Terminating        0        30s
slo-test                    0/1        Terminating        0        31s
```

So there you have it. With about 50 lines of verbose YAML, you can describe an ongoing experiment and detect when starting a pod takes longer than 30 seconds. The Goldpinger image is pretty small, so in the real world, you'd pick something that more closely resembles the type of thing that will run on the platform. You could also run multiple scenarios for multiple types of images you expect to deal with. And if you wanted to make sure that the image is downloaded every time so that you deal with the worst-case scenario, that can easily be achieved by specifying `imagePullPolicy`: `Always` in your pod's template (http://mng.bz/A0lE).

This should give you an idea of what an ongoing, continuously verified experiment can do for you. You can build on that to test other things, including but not limited to the following:

- *SLOs around pod healing*—If you kill a pod, how long does it take to be rescheduled and ready again?
- *SLOs around scaling*—If you scale your deployment, how long does it take for the new pods to become available?

As I write this, the weather outside is changing; it's getting a little bit . . . cloudy. Let's take a look at that now.

Pop quiz: When does it make sense to run chaos experiments continuously?

Pick one:

1 When you want to detect when an SLO is not satisfied
2 When an absence of problems doesn't prove that the system works well
3 When you want to introduce an element of randomness
4 When you want to make sure that there are no regressions in the new version of the system
5 All of the above

See appendix B for answers.

11.3 Cloud layer

So far, we've focused on introducing failure to particular pods running on a Kubernetes cluster—a bit like a reverse surgical procedure, inserting a problem with high precision. And the ease with which Kubernetes allows us to do that is still making me feel warm and fuzzy inside to this day.

But there is more. If you're running your cluster in a cloud, private or public, it's easy to simulate failure on the VM level by simply taking machines up or down. In Kubernetes, a lot of the time you can stop thinking about the machines and data centers that your clusters are built on. But that doesn't mean that they stop existing. They are very much still there, and you still need to obey the rules of physics governing their behavior. And with a bigger scale come bigger problems. Let me show you some napkin math to explain what I mean.

One of the metrics to express the reliability of a piece of hardware is the *mean time to failure* (*MTTF*). It's the average time that the hardware runs without failure. It's typically established empirically by looking at historical data. For example, let's say that the servers in your datacenter are of good quality, and their MTTF is five years. On average, each server will run about five years between times it fails. Roughly speaking, on any given day, the chance of failing for each of your servers is 1 in 1826 (5 × 365 + leap year). That's a 0.05% chance. This is, of course, a simplification, and other factors would need to be taken into account for a serious probability calculation, but this is a good enough estimate for our needs.

Now, depending on your scale, you're going to be more or less exposed to that. If the failures were truly independent in a mathematical sense, with just 20 servers you'd have a daily chance of failure of 1%, or 10% with 200 servers. And if that failed server is running multiple VMs that you use as Kubernetes nodes, you're going to end up with a chunk of your cluster down. If your scale is in the thousands of servers, the failure is a daily occurrence.

From the perspective of a chaos-engineering-practicing SRE, that means one thing— you should test your system for the kind of failure coming from hardware failure:

- Single machines going down and back up
- Groups of machines going down and back up
- Entire regions/datacenters/zones going down and back up
- Network partitions that make it look like other machines are unavailable

Let's take a look at how to prepare for this kind of issue.

11.3.1 *Cloud provider APIs, availability zones*

Every cloud provider offers an API you can use to create and modify VMs, including taking them up and down. This includes self-hosted, open source solutions like OpenStack. They also provide GUIs, CLIs, libraries, and more to best integrate with your existing workflow.

To allow for effective planning against outages, cloud providers also structure their hardware by partitioning it into regions (or an equivalent) and then using availability zones (or an equivalent) inside the regions. Why is that?

Typically, regions represent different physical locations, often far away from each other, plugged into separate utility providers (internet, electricity, water, cooling, and so on). This is to ensure that if something dramatic happens in one region (storm, earthquake, flood), other regions remain unaffected. This approach limits the blast radius to a single region.

Availability zones are there to further limit that blast radius within a single region. The actual implementations vary, but the idea is to leverage things that are redundant (power supply, internet provider, networking hardware) to put the machines that rely on them in separate groups. For example, if your datacenter has two racks of servers, each plugged into a separate power supply and separate internet supply, you could mark each rack as an availability zone, because failure within the components in one zone won't affect the other.

Figure 11.5 shows an example of both regions and availability zones. The West Coast region has two availability zones (W1 and W2), each running two machines. Similarly, the East Coast region has two availability zones (E1 and E2), each running two machines. A failure of a region wipes out four machines. A failure of an availability zone wipes out two.

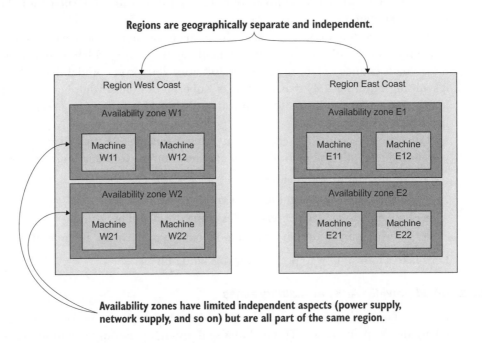

Figure 11.5   Regions and availability zones

With this partitioning, software engineers can design their applications to be resilient to the different problems we mentioned earlier:

- Spreading your application across multiple regions can make it immune to an entire region going down.
- Within a region, spreading your application across multiple availability zones can help make it immune to an availability zone going down.

To automatically achieve this kind of spreading, we often talk about *affinity* and *anti-affinity*. Marking two machines with the same affinity group simply means that they should (soft affinity) or must (hard affinity) be running within the same partition (availability zone, region, others). Anti-affinity is the opposite: items within the same group shouldn't or mustn't be running in the same partition.

And to make planning easier, cloud providers often express their SLOs by using regions and availability zones—for example, promising to keep each region up 95% of the time, but at least one region up 99.99% of the time.

Let's see how you'd go about implementing an on-demand outage to verify your application.

11.3.2 Experiment 4: Taking VMs down

On Kubernetes, the application you deploy is going to be run on a physical machine somewhere. Most of the time, you don't care which one that is—until you want to ensure a reasonable partitioning with respect to outages. To make sure that multiple replicas of the same application aren't running on the same availability zones, most Kubernetes providers set labels for each node that can be used for anti-affinity. Kubernetes also allows you to set your own criteria of anti-affinity and will try to schedule pods in a way that respects them.

Let's assume that you have a reasonable spread and want to see that your application survives the loss of a certain set of machines. Take the example of Goldpinger from the previous section. In a real cluster, you would be running an instance per node. Earlier, you killed a pod, and you investigated how that was being detected by its peers. Another way of going about that would be to take down a VM and see how the system reacts. Will it be detected as quickly? Will the instance be rescheduled somewhere else? How long will it take for it to recover, after the VM is brought back up? These are all questions you could investigate using this technique.

From the implementation perspective, these experiments can be very simple. In its most crude form, you can log in to a GUI, select the machines in question from a list, and click Shutdown or write a simple bash script that uses the CLI for a particular cloud. Those steps would absolutely do it.

The only problem with these two approaches is that they are cloud-provider specific, and you might end up reinventing the wheel each time. If only an open source solution supporting all major clouds would let you do that. Oh, wait, PowerfulSeal can do that! Let me show you how to use it.

PowerfulSeal supports OpenStack, AWS, Microsoft Azure, and Google Cloud Platform (GCP), and adding a new driver involves implementing a single class with a handful of methods. To make PowerfulSeal take VMs down and bring them back up, you need to do these two things:

1 Configure the relevant cloud driver (see `powerfulseal autonomous --help`).
2 Write a policy file that performs the VM operations.

The cloud drivers are configured in the same way as their respective CLIs. Unfortunately, your Minikube setup only has a single VM, so it won't be any good for this section. Let me give you two examples of two different ways of taking VMs down.

First, similar to `podAction`, which you used in the previous experiments, you can use `nodeAction`. It works the same way: it matches, filters, and takes action on a set of nodes. You can match on names, IP addresses, availability zones, groups, and state.

Take a look at listing 11.5, which represents an example policy for taking down a single node from any availability zone starting with `WEST`, and then making an example HTTP request to verify that things continue working, and finally cleaning up after itself by restarting the node.

Listing 11.5   PowerfulSeal scenario implementing experiment 4a (experiment4a.yml)

```
config:
  runStrategy:
    runs: 1
scenarios:
- name: Test load-balancing on master nodes
  steps:
  - nodeAction:
      matches:
        - property:              ◁── Selects one VM from
            name: "az"               any availability zone
            value: "WEST.*"          starting with WEST
      filters:                   ◁── Selects one VM randomly
        - randomSample:              from within the matched set
            size: 1              ◁──
      actions:                       Stops the VM, but auto-restarts
        - stop:                  ◁── it at the end of the scenario
            autoRestart: true
  - probeHTTP:                   ◁── Makes an HTTP request to some kind of URL
      target:                        to confirm that the system keeps working
        url: "http://load-balancer.example.com"
```

Second, you can also stop VMs running a particular pod. You use `podAction` to select the pod, and then use the `stopHost` action to stop the node that the pod is running on. Listing 11.6 shows an example. The scenario selects a random pod from the mynamespace namespace and stops the VM that runs it. PowerfulSeal automatically restarts the machines it took down.

Listing 11.6   PowerfulSeal scenario implementing experiment 4b (experiment4b.yml)

```
scenarios:
- name: Stop that host!
  steps:
  - podAction:
      matches:                          Selects all pods in namespace
        - namespace: mynamespace   ◁──  "mynamespace"
      filters:
        - randomSample:            ◁──  Selects one pod randomly from
            size: 1                     within the matched set
```

```
actions:
  - stopHost:                          Stops the VM, but auto-restarts
      autoRestart: true                it at the end of the scenario
```

Both of these policy files work with any of the supported cloud providers. And if you'd like to add another cloud provider, feel free to send pull requests on GitHub to https://github.com/powerfulseal/powerfulseal!

It's time to wrap up this section. Hopefully, this gives you enough tools and ideas to go forth and improve your cloud-based applications' reliability. In chapter 12, you'll take a step deeper into the rabbit hole by looking at how Kubernetes works under the hood.

Pop quiz: What can PowerfulSeal not do for you?

Pick one:

1. Kill pods to simulate processes crashing
2. Take VMs up and down to simulate hypervisor failure
3. Clone a deployment and inject simulated network latency into the copy
4. Verify that services respond correctly by generating HTTP requests
5. Fill in the discomfort coming from the realization that if there are indeed infinite universes, there exists, theoretically, a version of you that's better in every conceivable way, no matter how hard you try

See appendix B for answers.

Summary

- High-level tools like PowerfulSeal make it easy to implement sophisticated chaos engineering scenarios, but before jumping into using them, it's important to understand how the underlying technology works.
- Some chaos experiments work best as an ongoing validation, such as verifying that an SLO isn't violated.
- You can easily simulate machine failure by using the cloud provider's API to take VMs down and bring them back up again, just like the original Chaos Monkey did.

12

Under the hood of Kubernetes

This chapter covers

- Understanding how Kubernetes components work together under the hood
- Debugging Kubernetes and understanding how the components break
- Designing chaos experiments to make your Kubernetes clusters more reliable

Finally, in this third and final chapter on Kubernetes, we dive deep under the hood and see how Kubernetes really works. If I do my job well, by the end of this chapter you'll have a solid understanding of the components that make up a Kubernetes cluster, how they work together, and what their fragile points might be. It's the most advanced of the triptych, but I promise it will also be the most satisfying. Take a deep breath, and let's get straight into the thick of it. Time for an anatomy lesson.

12.1 *Anatomy of a Kubernetes cluster and how to break it*

As I'm writing, Kubernetes is one of the hottest technologies out there. And it's for a good reason; it solves a lot of problems that come from running a large number of applications on large clusters. But like everything else in life, it comes with costs.

One of them is the complexity of the underlying workings of Kubernetes. And although this can be somewhat alleviated by using managed Kubernetes clusters so that most day-to-day management of Kubernetes is someone else's problem, you're never fully insulated from the consequences. And perhaps you're reading this on your way to a job managing Kubernetes clusters, which is yet another reason to understand how things work.

Regardless of whose problem this is, it's good to know how Kubernetes works under the hood and how to test that it works well. And as you're about to see, chaos engineering fits right in.

> **NOTE** In this section, I describe things as they stand for Kubernetes v1.18.3. Kubernetes is a fast-moving target, so even though special care was taken to keep the details in this section as future-proof as possible, the only constant is change in Kubernetes Land.

Let's start at the beginning—with the control plane.

12.1.1 *Control plane*

The Kubernetes control plane is the brain of the cluster. It consists of the following components:

- `etcd`—The database storing all the information about the cluster
- `kube-apiserver`—The server through which all interactions with the cluster are done, and that stores information in `etcd`
- `kube-controller-manager`—Implements an infinite loop reading the current state, and attempts to modify it to converge into the desired state
- `kube-scheduler`—Detects newly created pods and assigns them to nodes, taking into account various constraints (affinity, resource requirements, policies, and so forth)
- `kube-cloud-manager` (optional)—Controls cloud-specific resources (VMs, routing)

In the previous chapter, you created a deployment for Goldpinger. Let's see, on a high level, what happens under the hood in the control plane when you run a `kubectl apply` command.

First, your request reaches the `kube-apiserver` of your cluster. The server validates the request and stores the new or modified resources in `etcd`. In this case, it creates a new deployment resource. Once that's done, `kube-controller-manager` gets notified of the new deployment. It reads the current state to see what needs to be done, and eventually creates new pods through another call to `kube-apiserver`. Once `kube-apiserver` stores it in `etcd`, `kube-scheduler` gets notified about the new pods, picks the best node to run them, assigns the node to them, and updates them back in `kube-apiserver`.

As you can see, `kube-apiserver` is at the center of it all, and all the logic is implemented in asynchronous, eventually consistent loops in loosely connected components. See figure 12.1 for a graphic representation.

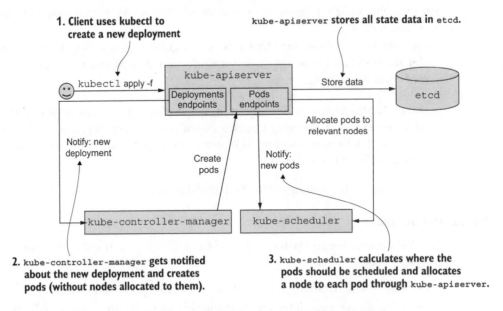

1. Client uses kubectl to create a new deployment

`kube-apiserver` **stores all state data in** `etcd`.

2. `kube-controller-manager` **gets notified about the new deployment and creates pods (without nodes allocated to them).**

3. `kube-scheduler` **calculates where the pods should be scheduled and allocates a node to each pod through** `kube-apiserver`.

Figure 12.1   Kubernetes control plane interactions when creating a deployment

Let's take a closer look at each of these components and see their strengths and weaknesses, starting with `etcd`.

ETCD

Legend has it that `etcd` (https://etcd.io/) was first written by an intern at a company called CoreOS that was bought by Red Hat that was acquired by IBM. Talk about bigger fish eating smaller fish. If the legend is to be believed, it was an exercise in implementing a distributed consensus algorithm called Raft (https://raft.github.io/). What does consensus have to do with `etcd`?

Four words: availability and fault tolerance. In chapter 11, I spoke about MTTF and how with just 20 servers, you were playing Russian roulette with a 0.05% probability of losing your data every day. If you have only a single copy of the data, when it's gone, it's gone. You want a system that's immune to that. That's *fault tolerance.*

Similarly, if you have a single server and it's down, your system is down. You want a system that's immune to that. That's *availability.*

To achieve fault tolerance and availability, you really can't do much other than run multiple copies. And that's where you run into trouble: the multiple copies have to somehow agree on a version of reality. In other words, they need to reach a *consensus.*

Consensus is agreeing on a movie to watch on Netflix. If you're by yourself, there is no one to argue with. When you're with your partner, consensus becomes almost impossible, because neither of you can gather a majority for a particular choice. That's when power moves and barter comes into play. But if you add a third person, then whoever convinces them gains a majority and wins the argument.

That's pretty much exactly how Raft (and by extension, etcd) works. Instead of running a single etcd instance, you run a cluster with an odd number of nodes (typically three or five), and then the instances use the consensus algorithm to decide on the leader, who basically makes all decisions while in power. If the leader stops responding (Raft uses a system of heartbeats, or regular calls between all instances, to detect that), a new election begins where everyone announces their candidacy, votes for themselves, and waits for other votes to come in. Whoever gets a majority of votes assumes power. The best thing about Raft is that it's relatively easy to understand. The second best thing about Raft is that it works.

If you'd like to see the algorithm in action, the Raft official website has a nice animation with heartbeats represented as little balls flying between bigger balls representing nodes (https://raft.github.io/). I took a screenshot showing a five-node-cluster (S1 to S5) in figure 12.2. It's also interactive, so you can take nodes down and see how the rest of the system copes.

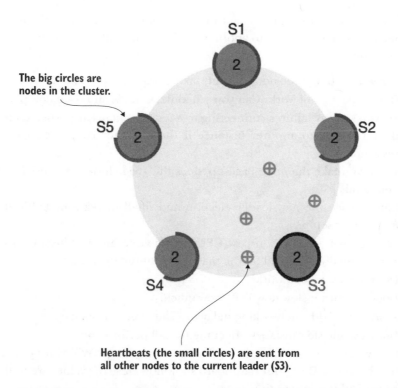

Figure 12.2　Animation showing Raft consensus algorithm in action (https://raft.github.io/)

I could talk (and I have talked) about etcd and Raft all day, but let's focus on what's important from the chaos engineering perspective. etcd holds pretty much all of the data about a Kubernetes cluster. It's strongly consistent, meaning that the data you write to etcd is replicated to all nodes, and regardless of which node you connect to, you get the up-to-date data.

The price you pay for that is in performance. Typically, you'll be running in clusters of three or five nodes, because that tends to give enough fault tolerance, and any extra nodes just slow the cluster with little benefit. And odd numbers of members are better, because they actually decrease fault tolerance.

Take a three-node cluster, for example. To achieve a quorum, you need a majority of two nodes (n / 2 + 1 = 3 / 2 + 1 = 2). Or looking at it from the availability perspective, you can lose a single node, and your cluster keeps working. Now, if you add an extra node for a total of four, you need a majority of three to function. You still can survive only a single node failure at a time, but you now have more nodes in the cluster that can fail, so overall you are worse off in terms of fault tolerance.

Running etcd reliably is not easy. It requires an understanding of your hardware profiles, tweaking various parameters accordingly, continuous monitoring, and keeping up-to-date with bug fixes and improvements in etcd itself. It also requires building an understanding of what actually happens when failure occurs and whether the cluster heals correctly.

And that's where chaos engineering can really shine. The way that etcd is run varies from one Kubernetes offering to another, so the details will vary too, but here are a few high-level ideas:

- *Experiment 1*—In a three-node cluster, take down a single etcd instance.
  - Does kubectl still work? Can you schedule, modify, and scale new pods?
  - Do you see any failures connecting to etcd? Its clients are expected to retry their requests to another instance if the one they connected to doesn't respond.
  - When you take the node back up, does the etcd cluster recover? How long does it take?
  - Can you see the new leader election and small increase in traffic in your monitoring setup?
- *Experiment 2*—Restrict resources (CPU) available to an etcd instance to simulate an unusually high load on the machine running the instance.
  - Does the cluster still work?
  - Does the cluster slow down? By how much?
- *Experiment 3*—Add a networking delay to a single etcd instance.
  - Does a single slow instance affect the overall performance?
  - Can you see the slowness in your monitoring setup? Will you be alerted if that happens? Does your dashboard show how close the values are to the limits (the values causing time-outs)?

- *Experiment 4*—Take down enough nodes for the `etcd` cluster to lose the quorum.
  - Does `kubectl` still work?
  - Do the pods already on the cluster keep running?
  - Does healing work?
    - If you kill a pod, is it restarted?
    - If you delete a pod managed by a deployment, will a new pod be created?

This book gives you all the tools you need to implement all of these experiments and more. `etcd` is the memory of your cluster, so it's crucial to test it well. And if you're using a managed Kubernetes offering, you're trusting that the people responsible for running your clusters know the answers to all these questions (and that they can prove it with experimental data). Ask them. If they're taking your money, they should be able to give you reasonable answers!

Hopefully, that's enough for a primer on `etcd`. Let's pull the thread a little bit more and look at the only thing actually speaking to `etcd` in your cluster: `kube-apiserver`.

KUBE-APISERVER

`kube-apiserver`, true to its name, provides a set of APIs to read and modify the state of your cluster. Every component interacting with the cluster does so through `kube-apiserver`. For availability reasons, `kube-apiserver` also needs to be run in multiple copies. But because all the state is stored in `etcd`, and `etcd` takes care of its consistency, `kube-apiserver` can be stateless.

This means that running it is much simpler, and as long as enough instances are running to handle the load of requests, we're good. There is no need to worry about majorities or anything like that. It also means that they can be load-balanced, although some internal components are often configured to skip the load balancer. Figure 12.3 shows what this typically looks like.

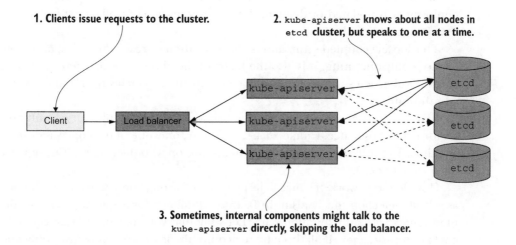

Figure 12.3 `etcd` and `kube-apiserver`

From a chaos engineering perspective, you might be interested in knowing how slowness on kube-apiserver affects the overall performance of the cluster. Here are a few ideas:

- *Experiment 1*—Create traffic to kube-apiserver.
  - Since everything (including the internal components responsible for creating, updating, and scheduling resources) talks to kube-apiserver, creating enough traffic to keep it busy could affect how the cluster behaves.
- *Experiment 2*—Add network slowness.
  - Similarly, adding a networking delay in front of the proxy could lead to a buildup of queuing of new requests and adversely affect the cluster.

Overall, you will find kube-apiserver start up quickly and perform pretty well. Despite the amount of work it does, running it is pretty lightweight. Next in the line: kube-controller-manager.

KUBE-CONTROLLER-MANAGER

kube-controller-manager implements the infinite control loop, continuously detecting changes in the cluster state and reacting to them to move it toward the desired state. You can think of it as a collection of loops, each handling a particular type of resource.

Do you remember when you created a deployment with kubectl in the previous chapter? What actually happened is that kubectl connected to an instance of kube-apiserver and requested creation of a new resource of type deployment. That was picked up by kube-controller-manager, which in turn created a ReplicaSet. The purpose of the latter is to manage a set of pods, ensuring that the desired number runs on the cluster. How is it done? You guessed it: a replica set controller (part of kube-controller-manager) picks it up and creates pods. Both the notification mechanism (called watch in Kubernetes) and the updates are served by kube-apiserver.

See figure 12.4 for a graphical representation. A similar cascade happens when a deployment is updated or deleted; the corresponding controllers get notified about the change and do their bit.

This loosely coupled setup allows for separation of responsibilities; each controller does only one thing. It is also the heart of the ability of Kubernetes to heal from failure. Kubernetes will attempt to correct any discrepancies from the desired state ad infinitum.

Like kube-apiserver, kube-controller-manager is typically run in multiple copies for failure resilience. Unlike kube-apiserver, only one of the copies is doing work at a time. The instances agree among themselves on who the leader is through acquiring a lease in etcd.

How does that work? Thanks to its property of strong consistency, etcd can be used as a leader-election mechanism. In fact, its API allows for acquiring a *lock*—a distributed mutex with an expiration date. Let's say that you run three instances of kube-controller-manager. If all three try to acquire the lease simultaneously, only one will succeed. The lease then needs to be renewed before it expires. If the leader stops

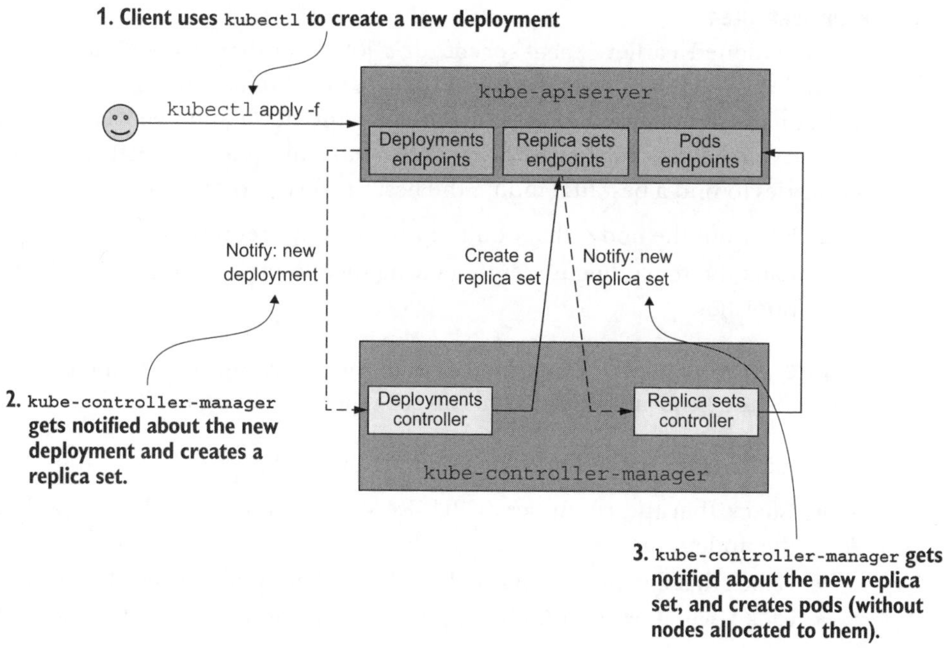

1. Client uses `kubectl` to create a new deployment

Figure 12.4 Kubernetes control plane interactions when creating a deployment—more details

working or disappears, the lease will expire and another copy will acquire it. Once again, `etcd` comes in handy and allows for offloading a difficult problem (leader election) and keeping the component relatively simple.

From the chaos engineering perspective, here are some ideas for experiments:

- *Experiment 1*—How does `kube-apiserver`'s amount of traffic affect the speed at which your cluster converges toward the desired state?
  - `kube-controller-manager` gets all its information about the cluster from `kube-apiserver`. It's worth understanding how any extra traffic on `kube-apiserver` affects the speed at which your cluster is converging toward the desired state. At what point does `kube-controller-manager` start timing out, rendering the cluster broken?
- *Experiment 2*—How does your lease expiry affect how quickly the cluster recovers from losing the leader instance of `kube-controller-manager`?
  - If you run your own Kubernetes cluster, you can choose various time-outs for this component. That includes the expiry time of the leadership lease. A shorter value will increase the speed at which the cluster restarts converging toward the desired state after losing the leader `kube-controller-manager`, but it comes at the price of increased load on `kube-apiserver` and `etcd`.

When `kube-controller-manager` is done reacting to the new deployment, the pods are created, but they aren't scheduled anywhere. That's where `kube-scheduler` comes in.

KUBE-SCHEDULER

As I mentioned earlier, kube-scheduler's job is to detect pods that haven't been scheduled on any nodes and to find them a new home. They might be brand-new pods, or a node that used to run the pod might go down and need a replacement.

Every time kube-scheduler assigns a pod to run on a particular node in the cluster, it tries to find a best fit. Finding the best fit consists of two steps:

1 Filter out the nodes that don't satisfy the pod's requirements.
2 Rank the remaining nodes by a giving them scores based on a predefined list of priorities.

NOTE   If you'd like to know the details of the algorithm used by the latest version of the kube-scheduler, you can see it at http://mng.bz/ZPoj.

For a quick overview, the filters include the following:

- Check that the resources (CPU, RAM, disk) requested by the pod can fit in the node.
- Check that any ports requested on the host are available on the node.
- Check whether the pod is supposed to run on a node with a particular hostname.
- Check that the affinity (or anti-affinity) requested by the pod matches (or doesn't match) the node.
- Check that the node is not under memory or disk pressure.

The priorities taken into account when ranking nodes include the following:

- *The highest amount of free resources after scheduling*—The higher the better; this has the effect of enforcing spreading.
- *Balance between the CPU and memory utilization*—The more balanced, the better.
- *Anti-affinity*—Nodes matching the anti-affinity setting are least preferred.
- *Image locality*—Nodes already having the image are preferred; this has the effect of minimizing the number of image downloads.

Just like kube-controller-manager, a cluster typically runs multiple copies of kube-scheduler, but only the leader does the scheduling at any given time. From the chaos engineering perspective, this component is prone to basically the same issues as kube-controller-manager.

From the moment you ran the kubectl apply command, the components you just saw worked together to figure out how to move your cluster toward the new state you requested (the state with a new deployment). At the end of that process, the new pods were scheduled and assigned a node to run. But so far, we haven't seen the actual component that starts the newly scheduled process. Time to take a look at Kubelet.

Pop quiz: Where is the cluster data stored?

Pick one:

1. Spread across the various components on the cluster
2. In /var/kubernetes/state.json
3. In `etcd`
4. In the cloud, uploaded using the latest AI and machine learning algorithms and leveraging the revolutionary power of blockchain technology

See appendix B for answers.

Pop quiz: What's the control plane in Kubernetes jargon?

Pick one:

1. The set of components implementing the logic of Kubernetes converging toward the desired state
2. A remote-control aircraft, used in Kubernetes commercials
3. A name for Kubelet and Docker

See appendix B for answers.

12.1.2 Kubelet and pause container

Kubelet is the agent starting and stopping containers on a host to implement the pods you requested. Running a Kubelet daemon on a computer turns it into a part of a Kubernetes cluster. Don't be fooled by the affectionate name; Kubelet is a real workhorse, doing the dirty work ordered by the control plane.

Like everything else on a cluster, Kubelet reads the state and takes its orders from `kube-apiserver`. It also reports the data about the factual state of what's running on the node, whether it's running or crashing, how much CPU and RAM is actually used, and more. That data is later leveraged by the control plane to make decisions and make it available to the user.

To illustrate how Kubelet works, let's do a thought experiment. Let's say that the deployment you created earlier always crashes within seconds after it starts. The pod is scheduled to be running on a particular node. The Kubelet daemon is notified about the new pod. First, it downloads the requested image. Then, it creates a new container with that image and the specified configuration. In fact, it creates two containers: the one you requested, and another special one called pause. What is the purpose of the pause container?

It's a pretty neat hack. In Kubernetes, the unit of software is a pod, not a single container. Containers inside a pod need to share certain resources and not others. For example, processes in two containers inside a single pod share the same IP address and can communicate via localhost. Do you remember namespaces from chapter 5 on Docker? The IP address sharing is implemented by sharing the network namespace.

But other things (for example, the CPU limit) are applicable to each container separately. The reason for pause to exist is simply to hold these resources while the other containers might be crashing and coming back up. The pause container doesn't do much. It starts and immediately goes to sleep. The name is pretty fitting.

Once the container is up, Kubelet will monitor it. If the container crashes, Kubelet will bring it back up. See figure 12.5 for a graphical representation of the whole process.

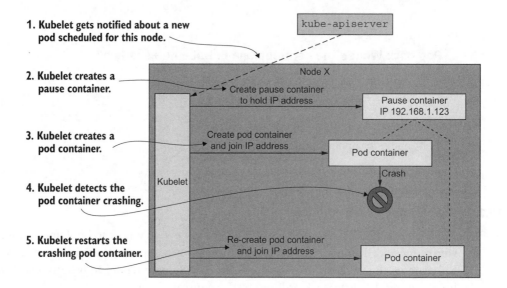

Figure 12.5   Kubelet starting a new pod

When you delete the pod, or perhaps it gets rescheduled somewhere else, Kubelet takes care of removing the relevant containers. Without Kubelet, all the resources created and scheduled by the control plane would remain abstract concepts.

This also makes Kubelet a single point of failure. If it crashes, for whatever reason, no changes will be made to the containers running on that node, even though Kubernetes will happily accept your changes. They just won't ever get implemented on that node.

From the perspective of chaos engineering, it's important to understand what actually happens to the cluster if Kubelet stops working. Here are a few ideas:

- *Experiment 1*—After Kubelet dies, how long does it take for pods to get rescheduled somewhere else?
  - When Kubelet stops reporting its readiness to the control plane, after a certain time-out it's marked as unavailable (NotReady). That time-out is configurable

and defaults to 5 minutes at the time of writing. Pods are not immediately removed from that node. The control plane will wait another configurable time-out before it starts assigning the pods to another node.

- If a node disappears (for example, if the hypervisor running the VM crashes), you're going to need to wait a certain minimal amount of time for the pods to start running somewhere else.
- If the pod is still running, but for some reason Kubelet can't connect to the control plane (network partition) or dies, then you're going to end up with a node running whatever it was running before the event, and it won't get any updates. One of the possible side effects is to run extra copies of your software with potentially stale configuration.
- The previous chapter covered the tools to take VMs up and down, as well as killing processes. PowerfulSeal also supports executing commands over SSH;, for example, to kill or switch off Kubelet.
- *Experiment 2*—Does Kubelet restart correctly after crashing?
  - Kubelet typically runs directly on the host to minimize the number of dependencies. If it crashes, it should be restarted.
  - As you saw in chapter 2, sometimes setting things up to get restarted is harder than it initially looks, so it's worth checking that different patterns of crashing (consecutive crashes, time-spaced crashes, and so on) are all covered. This takes little time and can avoid pretty bad outages.

So the question now remains: How exactly does Kubelet run these containers? Let's take a look at that now.

Pop quiz: Which component starts and stops processes on the host?
Pick one:

1. `kube-apiserver`
2. `etcd`
3. `kubelet`
4. `docker`

See appendix B for answers.

12.1.3 *Kubernetes, Docker, and container runtimes*

Kubelet leverages lower-level software to start and stop containers to implement the pods that you ask it to create. This lower-level software is often called *container runtimes*. Chapter 5 covered Linux containers and Docker (their most popular representative), and that's for a good reason. Initially, Kubernetes was written to use Docker directly, and you can still see some naming that matches one-to-one to Docker; even the `kubectl` CLI feels similar to the Docker CLI.

Today, Docker is still one of the most popular container runtimes to use with Kubernetes, but it's by no means the only option. Initially, the support for new runtimes was baked directly into Kubernetes internals. To make it easier to add new supported container runtimes, a new API was introduced to standardize the interface between Kubernetes and container runtimes. It is called the *Container Runtime Interface* (*CRI*), and you can read more about its introduction in Kubernetes 1.5 in 2016 at http://mng.bz/RXln.

Thanks to that new interface, interesting things happened. For example, since version 1.14, Kubernetes has had Windows support. Kubernetes uses Windows containers (http://mng.bz/2eaN) to start and stop containers on machines running Windows. And on Linux, other options have emerged; for example, the following runtimes leverage basically the same set of underlying technologies as Docker:

- *containerd* (https://containerd.io/)—The emerging industry standard that seems poised to eventually replace Docker. To make matters more confusing, Docker versions 1.11.0 and higher use containerd under the hood to run containers.
- *CRI-O* (https://cri-o.io/)—Aims to provide a simple, lightweight container runtime optimized for use with Kubernetes.
- *rkt* (https://coreos.com/rkt)—Initially developed by CoreOS, the project now appears to be no longer maintained. It was pronounced *rocket*.

To further the confusion, the ecosystem has more surprises for you. First, both containerd (and therefore Docker, which relies on it) and CRIO-O share some code by leveraging another open source project called runc (https://github.com/opencontainers/runc), which manages the lower-level aspects of running a Linux container. Visually, when you stack the blocks on top of one another, it looks like figure 12.6. The

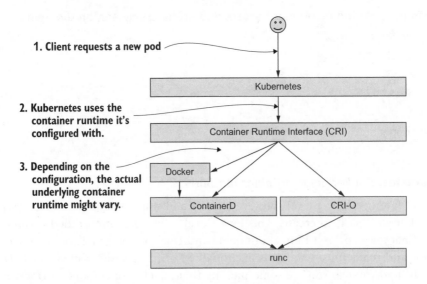

Figure 12.6   Container Runtime Interface, Docker, containerd, CRI-O, and runc

user requests a pod, and Kubernetes reaches out to the container runtime it was configured with. It might go to Docker, containerd, or CRI-O, but at the end of the day, it all ends up using runc.

The second surprise is that in order to avoid having different standards pushed by different entities, a bunch of companies led by Docker came together to form the Open Container Initiative (or OCI for short; https://opencontainers.org/). It provides two specifications:

- *Runtime Specification*—Describes how to run a *filesystem bundle* (a new term to describe what used to be called a Docker image downloaded and unpacked)
- *Image Specification*—Describes what an *OCI image* (a new term for a Docker image) looks like, and how to build, upload, and download one

As you might imagine, most people didn't just stop using names like *Docker images* and start prepending everything with *OCI*, so things can get a little bit confusing at times. But that's all right. At least there is a standard now!

One more plot twist. In recent years, we've seen a few interesting projects pop up that implement the CRI, but instead of running Docker-style Linux containers, get creative:

- *Kata Containers* (https://katacontainers.io/)—Runs "lightweight VMs" instead of containers that are optimized for speed, to offer a "container-like" experience, but with stronger isolation offered by different hypervisors.
- *Firecracker* (https://github.com/firecracker-microvm/firecracker)—Runs "micro-VMs," also a lightweight type of VM, implemented using Linux Kernel Virtual Machine, or KVM (http://mng.bz/aozm). The idea is the same as Kata Containers, with a different implementation.
- *gVisor* (https://github.com/google/gvisor)—Implements container isolation in a different way than Docker-style projects do. It runs a user-space kernel that implements a subset of syscalls that it makes available to the processes running inside the sandbox. It then sets up the program to capture the syscalls made by the process and execute them in the user-space kernel. Unfortunately, that capture and redirection of syscalls introduces a performance penalty. You can use multiple mechanisms for the capture, but the default leverages `ptrace` (briefly mentioned in chapter 6), so it takes a serious performance hit.

Now, if we plug these into the previous figure, we end up with something along the lines of figure 12.7. Once again, the user requests a pod, and Kubernetes makes a call through the CRI. But this time, depending on which container runtime you are using, the end process might be running in a container or a VM.

If you're running Docker as your container runtime, everything you learned in chapter 5 will be directly applicable to your Kubernetes cluster. If you're using containerd or CRI-O, the experience will be mostly the same, because they all use the same underlying technologies. gVisor will differ in many aspects because of its different approach to implementing isolation. If your cluster uses Kata Containers or

1. Client requests a new pod

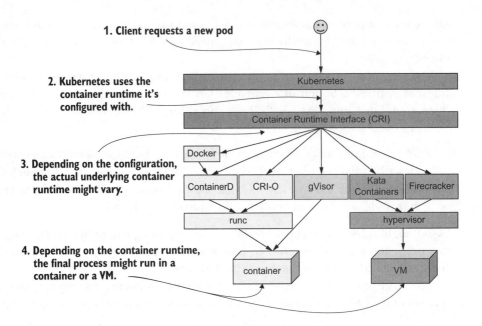

2. Kubernetes uses the container runtime it's configured with.

3. Depending on the configuration, the actual underlying container runtime might vary.

4. Depending on the container runtime, the final process might run in a container or a VM.

Figure 12.7 Runc-based container runtimes, alongside Kata Containers, Firecracker and gVisor

Firecracker, you're going to be running VMs rather than containers. This is a fast-changing landscape, so it's worth following the new developments in this zone. Unfortunately, as much as I love these technologies, we need to wrap up. I strongly encourage you to at least play around with them.

Let's take a look at the last piece of the puzzle: the Kubernetes networking model.

> **Pop quiz: Can you use a different container runtime than Docker?**
> Pick one:
>
> 1 If you're in the United States, it depends on the state. Some states allow it.
> 2 No, Docker is required for running Kubernetes.
> 3 Yes, you can use a number of alternative container runtimes, like CRI-O, containerd, and others.
>
> See appendix B for answers.

12.1.4 *Kubernetes networking*

There are three parts of Kubernetes networking that you need to understand to be effective as a chaos engineering practitioner:

- Pod-to-pod networking
- Service networking
- Ingress networking

I'll walk you through them one by one. Let's start with pod-to-pod networking.

POD-TO-POD NETWORKING

To communicate between pods, or have any traffic routed to them, pods need to be able to resolve each other's IP addresses. When discussing Kubelet, I mentioned that the pause container was holding the IP address that was common for the whole pod. But where does this IP address come from, and how does it work?

The answer is simple: It's a made-up IP address that's assigned to the pod by Kubelet when it starts. When configuring a Kubernetes cluster, a certain range of IP addresses is configured, and then subranges are given to every node in the cluster. Kubelet is then aware of that subrange, and when it creates a pod through the CRI, it gives it an IP address from its range. From the perspective of processes running in that pod, they will see that IP address as the address of their networking interface. So far, so good.

Unfortunately, by itself, this doesn't implement any pod-to-pod networking. It merely attributes a fake IP address to every pod and then stores it in kube-apiserver.

Kubernetes then expects you to configure the networking independently. In fact, it gives you only two conditions that you need to satisfy, and doesn't really care how you achieve that (http://mng.bz/1rMZ):

- All pods can communicate to all other pods on the cluster directly.
- Processes running on the node can communicate with all pods on that node.

This is typically done with an overlay network (https://en.wikipedia.org/wiki/Overlay_network); the nodes in the cluster are configured to route the fake IP addresses among themselves, and deliver them to the right containers.

Once again, the interface for dealing with the networking has been standardized. It's called the Container Networking Interface (CNI). At the time of writing, the official documentation lists 29 options for implementing the networking layer (http://mng.bz/PPx2). To keep things simple, I'll show you an example of how one of the most basic works: Flannel (https://github.com/coreos/flannel).

Flannel runs a daemon (flanneld) on each Kubernetes node and agrees on subranges of IP addresses that should be available to each node. It stores that information in etcd. Every instance of the daemon then ensures that the networking is configured to forward packets from different ranges to their respective nodes. On the other end, the receiving flanneld daemon delivers received packets to the right container. The forwarding is done using one of the supported existing backends; for example, Virtual Extensible LAN, or VXLAN (https://en.wikipedia.org/wiki/Virtual_Extensible_LAN).

To make it easier to understand, let's walk through a concrete example. Let's say that your cluster has two nodes, and the overall pod IP address range is 192.168.0.0/16. To keep things simple, let's say that node A was assigned range 192.168.1.0/24, and node B was assigned range 192.168.2.0/24. Node A has a pod A1, with an address 192.168.1.1, and it wants to send a packet to pod B2, with an address 192.168.2.2 running on node B.

When pod A1 tries to connect to pod B2, the forwarding set up by Flannel will match the node IP address range for node B and encapsulate and forward the packets there. On the receiving end, the instance of Flannel running on node B will receive the packets, undo the encapsulation, and deliver them to pod B. From the perspective of a pod, our fake IP addresses are as real as anything else. Take a look at figure 12.8, which shows this in a graphical way.

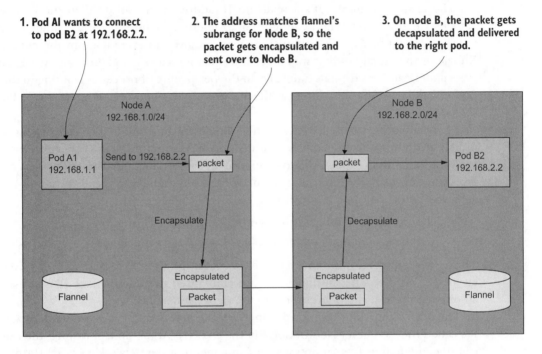

1. Pod A1 wants to connect to pod B2 at 192.168.2.2.

2. The address matches flannel's subrange for Node B, so the packet gets encapsulated and sent over to Node B.

3. On node B, the packet gets decapsulated and delivered to the right pod.

Figure 12.8   High-level overview of pod networking with Flannel

Flannel is pretty bare-bones. There are much more advanced solutions, doing things like allowing for dynamic policies that dictate which pods can talk to what other pods in what circumstances, and much more. But the high-level idea is the same: the pod IP addresses get routed, and a daemon is running on each node that makes sure that happens. And that daemon will always be a fragile part of the setup. If it stops working, the networking settings will be stale and potentially wrong.

That's the pod networking in a nutshell. There is another set of fake IP addresses in Kubernetes: service IP addresses. Let's take a look at that now.

SERVICE NETWORKING

As a reminder, services in Kubernetes give a shared IP address to a set of pods that you can mix and match based on the labels. In the previous example, you had some pods with the label `app=goldpinger`; the service used that same label to match the pods and give them a single IP address.

Just like the pod IP addresses, the service IP addresses are completely made up. They are implemented by a component called `kube-proxy`, which also runs on each node on your Kubernetes cluster. `kube-proxy` watches for changes to the pods matching the particular label, and reconfigures the host to route these fake IP addresses to their respective destinations. They also offer some load-balancing. The single service IP address will resolve to many pod IP addresses, and depending on how `kube-proxy` is configured, you can load-balance them in different fashions.

`kube-proxy` can use multiple backends to implement the networking changes. One of them is to use iptables (https://en.wikipedia.org/wiki/Iptables). We don't have time to dive into how iptables works, but at a high level, it allows you to write a set of rules that modify the flow of the packets on the machine.

In this mode, `kube-proxy` will create rules that forward the packets to particular pod IP addresses. If there is more than one pod, each will have rules, with corresponding probabilities. The first rule to match wins. Let's say you have a service that resolves to three pods. On a high level, they would look something like this:

1 If IP == SERVICE_IP, forward to pod A with probability 33%
2 If IP == SERVICE_IP, forward to pod B with probability 50%
3 If IP == SERVICE_IP, forward to pod C with probability 100%

This way, on average, the traffic should be routed roughly equally to the three pods.

The weakness of this setup is that iptables evaluates all the rules one by one, until it hits a rule that matches. As you can imagine, the more pod services and pods you're running on your cluster, the more rules there will be, and therefore the bigger overhead this will create.

To alleviate that problem, `kube-proxy` can also use IP Virtual Server, or IPVS (https://en.wikipedia.org/wiki/IP_Virtual_Server), which scales much better for large deployments.

From a chaos engineering perspective, that's one of the things you need to be aware of. Here are a few ideas for chaos experiments:

- *Experiment 1*—Does the number of services affect the speed of networking?
  - If you're using iptables, you will find that just creating a few thousand services (even if they're empty) will suddenly and significantly slow the networking on all nodes. Do you think your cluster shouldn't be affected? You're one experiment away from checking that.
- *Experiment 2*—How good is the load balancing?
  - With probability-based load balancing, you might sometimes find interesting results in terms of traffic split. It might be a good idea to verify your assumptions about that.
- *Experiment 3*—What happens when `kube-proxy` is down?
  - If the networking is not updated, it is quite possible to end up with not only stale routing that doesn't work, but also routing to the wrong service. Can

your setup detect when that happens? Would you be alerted if requests start flowing to the wrong destinations?

Once you have a service configured, one last thing that you want to do with it is to make it accessible outside the cluster. That's what ingresses are designed for. Let's take a look at that now.

INGRESS NETWORKING

Having the routing work inside the cluster is great, but the cluster won't be of much use if you can't access the software running on it from the outside. That's where ingresses come in.

In Kubernetes, an *ingress* is a natively supported resource that effectively describes a set of hosts and the destination service that these hosts should be routed to. For example, an ingress could say that requests for *example.com* should go to a service called `example`, in the namespace called `mynamespace`, and route to port 8080. It's a first-class citizen, natively supported by the Kubernetes API.

But once again, creating this kind of resource doesn't do anything by itself. You need to have an ingress controller installed that will listen on changes to the resources of this kind and implement them. And yes, you guessed it, there are multiple options. As I'm looking at it now, the official docs list 15 options at http://mng.bz/JDlp.

Let me use the NGINX ingress controller (https://github.com/kubernetes/ingress-nginx) as an example. You saw NGINX in the previous chapters. It's often used as a reverse proxy, receiving traffic and sending it to some kind of server upstream. That's precisely how it's used in the ingress controller.

When you deploy it, it runs a pod on each host. Inside that pod, it runs an instance of NGINX, and an extra process that listens to changes on resources of type `ingress`. Every time a change is detected, it regenerates a config for NGINX, and asks NGINX to reload it. NGINX then knows which hosts to listen on, and where to proxy the incoming traffic. It's that simple.

It goes without saying that the ingress controller is typically the single point of entry to the cluster, and so everything that prevents it from working well will deeply affect the cluster. And like any proxy, it's easy to mess up its parameters. From the chaos engineering perspective, here are some ideas to get you started:

1 What happens when a new ingress is created or modified and a config is reloaded? Are the existing connections dropped? What about corner cases like WebSockets?

2 Does your proxy have the same time-out as the service it proxies to? If you time out quicker, not only can you have outstanding requests being processed long after the proxy dropped the connection, but the consequent retries might accumulate and take down the target service.

We could chat about that for a whole day, but this should be enough to get you started with your testing. Unfortunately, all good things come to an end. Let's finish with a summary of the key components covered in this chapter.

> ## Pop quiz: Which component did I just make up?
> Pick one:
>
> 1 `kube-apiserver`
> 2 `kube-controller-manager`
> 3 `kube-scheduler`
> 4 `kube-converge-loop`
> 5 `kubelet`
> 6 `etcd`
> 7 `kube-proxy`
>
> See appendix B for answers.

12.2   Summary of key components

We covered quite a few components in this chapter, so before I let you go, I have a little parting gift for you: a handy reference of the key functions of these components. Take a look at table 12.1. If you're new to all of this, don't worry; it will soon start feeling like home.

Table 12.1   Summary of the key Kubernetes components

Component	Key function
`kube-apiserver`	Provides APIs for interacting with the Kubernetes cluster
`etcd`	The database used by Kubernetes to store all its data
`kube-controller-manager`	Implements the infinite loop converging the current state toward the desired one
`kube-scheduler`	Schedules pods onto nodes, trying to find the best fit
`kube-proxy`	Implements the networking for Kubernetes services
Container Networking Interface (CNI)	Implements pod-to-pod networking in Kubernetes—for example, Flannel, Calico
Kubelet	Starts and stops containers on hosts, using a container runtime
Container runtime	Actually runs the processes (containers, VMs) on a host—for example, Docker, containerd, CRI-O, Kata, gVisor

And with that, it's time to wrap up!

Summary

- Kubernetes is implemented as a set of loosely coupled components, using `etcd` as the storage for all data.
- The capacity of Kubernetes to continuously converge to the desired state is implemented through various components reacting to well-defined situations and updating the part of the state they are responsible for.
- Kubernetes can be configured in various ways, so implementation details might vary, but the Kubernetes APIs will work roughly the same wherever you go.
- By designing chaos experiments to expose various Kubernetes components to expected kinds of failure, you can find fragile points in your clusters and make your cluster more reliable.

Chaos engineering (for) people

This chapter covers

- Understanding mindset shifts required for effective chaos engineering
- Getting buy-in from the team and management for doing chaos engineering
- Applying chaos engineering to teams to make them more reliable

Let's focus on the other type of resource that's necessary for any project to succeed: people. In many ways, human beings and the networks we form are more complex, dynamic, and harder to diagnose and debug than the software we write. Talking about chaos engineering without including all that human complexity would therefore be incomplete.

In this chapter, I would like to bring to your attention three facets of chaos engineering meeting human brains:

- First, we'll discuss the kind of mindset that is required to be an effective chaos engineer, and why sometimes that shift is hard to make.
- Second is the hurdle to get buy-in from the people around you. You will see how to communicate clearly the benefits of this approach.

- Finally, we'll talk about human teams as distributed systems and how to apply the same chaos engineering approach we did with machines to make teams more resilient.

If that sounds like your idea of fun, we can be friends. First stop: the chaos engineering mindset.

13.1   Chaos engineering mindset

Find a comfortable position, lean back, and relax. Take control of your breath and try taking in deep, slow breaths through your nose, and release the air with your mouth. Now, close your eyes and try to not think about anything. I bet you found that hard; thoughts just keep coming. Don't worry, I'm not going to pitch my latest yoga and mindfulness classes (they're all sold out for the year)!

I just want to bring to your attention that a lot of what you consider "you" is happening without your explicit knowledge. From the chemicals produced inside your body to help process the food you ate and make you feel sleepy at the right time of the night, to split-second, subconscious decisions on other people's friendliness and attractiveness based on visual cues, we're all a mix of rational decisions and rationalizing the automatic ones.

To put it differently, parts of what makes up your identity are coming from the general-purpose, conscious parts of the brain, while others are coming from the subconscious. The conscious brain is much like implementing things in software—easy to adapt to any type of problem, but costlier and slower. That's opposed to the quicker, cheaper, and more-difficult-to-change logic implemented in the hardware.

One of the interesting aspects of this duality is our perception of risk and rewards. We are capable of making the conscious effort to think about and estimate risks, but a lot of this estimation is done automatically, without even reaching the level of consciousness. And the problem is that some of these automatic responses might still be optimized for surviving in the harsh environments the early human was exposed to—and not doing computer science.

The *chaos engineering mindset* is all about estimating risks and rewards with partial information, instead of relying on automatic responses and gut feelings. This mindset requires doing things that feel counterintuitive at first—like introducing failure into computer systems—after careful consideration of the risk-reward ratio. It necessitates a scientific, evidence-based approach, coupled with a keen eye for potential problems. In the rest of this chapter, I illustrate why.

Calculating risks: The trolley problem

If you think that you're good at risk mathematics, think again. You might be familiar with the trolley problem (https://en.wikipedia.org/wiki/Trolley_problem). In the experiment, participants are asked to make a choice that will affect other people—by either keeping them alive, or not.

A trolley is barreling down the tracks. Ahead, five people are tied to the tracks. If the trolley hits them, they die. You can't stop the trolley, and there is not enough time to detach even a single person. However, you notice a lever. Pulling the lever will redirect the trolley to another set of tracks, which has only one person attached to it. What do you do?

You might think most people would calculate that one person dying is better than five people dying, and pull the lever. But the reality is that most people wouldn't do it. There is something about it that makes the basic arithmetic go out the window.

Let's take a look at the mindset of an effective chaos engineering practitioner, starting with failure.

13.1.1 *Failure is not a maybe: It will happen*

Let's assume that we're using good-quality servers. One way of expressing the quality of being *good quality* in a scientific manner is the mean time between failure (MTBF). For example, if the servers had a very long MTBF of 10 years, that means that on average, each of them would fail every 10 years. Or put differently, the probability of the machine failing today is 1 / (10 years × 365.25 days in a year) ~= 0.0003, or 0.03%. If we're talking about the laptop I'm writing these words on, I am only 0.03% worried it will die on me today.

The problem is that small samples like this give us a false impression of how reliable things really are. Imagine a datacenter with 10,000 servers. How many servers can be expected to fail on any given day? It's 0.0003 × 10,000 ~= 3. Even with a third of that, at 3333 servers, the number would be 0.0003 × 3333 ~= 1. The scale of modern systems we're building makes small error rates like this more pronounced, but as you can see, you don't need to be Google or Facebook to experience them.

Once you get the hang of it, multiplying percentages is fun. Here's another example. Let's say that you have a mythical, all-star team shipping bug-free code 98% of the time. That means, on average, with a weekly release cycle, the team will ship bugs more than once a year. And if your company has 25 teams like that, all 98% bug free, you're going to have a problem every other week—again, on average.

In the practice of chaos engineering, it's important to look at things from this perspective —a calculated risk—and to plan accordingly. Now, with these well-defined values and elementary school-level multiplication, we can estimate a lot of things and make informed decisions. But what happens if the data is not readily available, and it's harder to put a number to it?

13.1.2 *Failing early vs. failing late*

One common mindset blocker when starting with chaos engineering is that we might cause an outage that we would otherwise most likely get away with. We discussed how to minimize this risk in chapter 4, so now I'd like to focus on the mental part of the equation. The reasoning tends to be like this: "It's currently working, its lifespan is X years, so chances are that even if it has bugs that would be uncovered by chaos engineering, we might not run into them within this lifespan."

There are many reasons a person might think this. The company culture could be punitive for mistakes. They might have had software running in production for years, and bugs were found only when it was being decommissioned. Or they might simply have low confidence in their (or someone else's) code. And there may be plenty of other reasons.

A universal reason, though, is that we have a hard time comparing two probabilities we don't know how to estimate. Because an outage is an unpleasant experience, we're wired to overestimate how likely it is to happen. It's the same mechanism that makes people scared of dying of a shark attack. In 2019, two people died of shark attacks in the entire world (http://mng.bz/goDv). Given the estimated population of 7.5 billion people in June 2019 (www.census.gov/popclock/world), the likelihood of any given person dying from a shark attack that year was 1 in 3,250,000,000. But because people watched the movie *Jaws*, if interviewed on the street, they will estimate that likelihood very high.

Unfortunately, this just seems to be how we are. So instead of trying to convince people to swim more in shark waters, let's change the conversation. Let's talk about the cost of failing early versus the cost of failing late. In the best-case scenario (from the perspective of possible outages, not learning), chaos engineering doesn't find any issues, and all is good. In the worst-case scenario, the software is faulty. If we experiment on it now, we might cause the system to fail and affect users within our blast radius. We call this *failing early*. If we don't experiment on it, it's still likely to fail, but possibly much later (*failing late*).

Failing early has several advantages:

- Engineers are actively looking for bugs, with tools at the ready to diagnose the issue and help fix it as soon as possible. Failing late might happen at a much less convenient time.
- The same applies to the development team. The further in the future from the code being written, the bigger the context switch the person fixing the bug will have to execute.
- As a product (or company) matures, usually the users expect to see increased stability and decreased number of issues over time.
- Over time, the number of dependent systems tends to increase.

But because you're reading this book, chances are you're already aware of the advantages of doing chaos engineering and failing early. The next hurdle is to get the people around you to see the light too. Let's take a look at how to achieve that in the most effective manner.

13.2 Getting buy-in

To get your team from zero to chaos engineering hero, you need team members to understand the benefits it brings. And for them to understand those benefits, you need to be able to communicate them clearly. Typically, you're going to be pitching to two groups of people: your peers/team members and your management. Let's start by looking at how to talk to the latter.

13.2.1 Management

Put yourself in your manager's shoes. The more projects you're responsible for, the more likely you are to be risk-averse. After all, what you want is to minimize the number of fires to extinguish, while achieving your long-term goals. And chaos engineering can help with that.

So to play some music to your manager's ears, perhaps don't start with breaking things on purpose in production. Here are some elements that managers are much more likely to react well to:

- *Good return on investment (ROI)*—Chaos engineering can be a relatively cheap investment (even a single engineer can experiment on a complex system in a single-digit number of days if the system is well documented) with a big potential payoff. The result is a win-win situation:
  - If the experiments don't uncover anything, the output is twofold: first, increased confidence in the system; second, a set of automated tests that can be rerun to detect any regressions later.
  - If the experiments uncover a problem, it can be fixed.
- *Controlled blast radius*—It's good to remind them again that you're not going to be randomly breaking things, but conducting a well-controlled experiment with a defined blast radius. Obviously, things can still go sideways, but the idea is not to set the world on fire and see what happens. Rather, it's to take a calculated risk for a large potential payoff.
- *Failing early*—The cost of resolving an issue found earlier is generally lower than if the same issue is found later. You can then have faster response time to an issue found on purpose, rather than at an inconvenient time.
- *Better-quality software*—Your engineers, knowing that the software will undergo experiments, are more likely to think about the failure scenarios early in the process and write more resilient software.
- *Team building*—The increased awareness of the importance of interaction and knowledge sharing has the potential to make teams stronger (more on this later in this chapter).
- *Increased hiring potential*—You'll have a real-life proof of building solid software. All companies talk about the quality of their product. Only a subset puts their

money where their mouth is when it comes to funding engineering efforts in testing.

- Solid software means fewer calls outside working hours, which means happier engineers.
- Remember the shininess factor: using the latest techniques helps attract engineers who want to learn them and have them on their CVs.

If delivered correctly, the tailored message should be an easy sell. It has the potential to make your manager's life easier, make the team stronger, the software better quality, and hiring easier. Why would you not do chaos engineering?!

How about your team members?

13.2.2 *Team members*

When speaking to your team members, many of the arguments we just covered apply in equal measure. Failing early is less painful than failing later; thinking about corner cases and designing all software with failure in mind is often interesting and rewarding. Oh, and office games (we'll get to them in just a minute) are fun.

But often what really resonates with the team is simply the potential of getting called less. If you're on an on-call rotation, everything that minimizes the number of times you're called in the middle of the night is helpful. So framing the conversation around this angle can really help with getting the team onboard. Here are some ideas of how to approach that conversation:

- *Failing early and during work hours*—If there is an issue, it's better to trigger it before you're about to go pick up your kids from school or go to sleep in the comfort of your own home.
- *Destigmatizing failure*—Even for a rock-star team, failure is inevitable. Thinking about it and actively seeking problems can remove or minimize the social pressure of not failing. Learning from failure always trumps avoiding and hiding failure. Conversely, for a poorly performing team, failure is likely a common occurrence. Chaos engineering can be used in preproduction stages as an extra layer of testing, allowing the unexpected failures to be rarer.
- *Chaos engineering is a new skill, and one that's not that hard to pick up*—Personal improvement will be a reward in itself for some. And it's a new item on a CV.

With that, you should be well equipped to evangelize chaos engineering within your teams and to your bosses. You can now go and spread the good word! But before you go, let me give you one more tool. Let's talk about game days.

13.2.3 *Game days*

You might have heard of teams running *game days*. Game days are a good tool for getting buy-in from the team. They are a little bit like those events at your local car dealership. Big, colorful balloons, free cookies, plenty of test drives and miniature cars for your kid, and boom—all of a sudden you need a new car. It's like a gateway drug, really.

Game days can take any form. The form is not important. The goal is to get the entire team to interact, brainstorm ideas of where the weaknesses of the system might lie, and have fun with chaos engineering. It's both the balloons and the test drives that make you want to use a new chaos engineering tool.

You can set up recurring game days. You can start your team off with a single event to introduce them to the idea. You can buy some fancy cards for writing down chaos experiment ideas, or you can use sticky notes. Whatever you think will get your team to appreciate the benefits, without feeling like it's forced upon them, will do. Make them feel they're not wasting their time. Don't waste their time.

That's all I have for the buy-in—time to dive a level deeper. Let's see what happens if you apply chaos engineering to a team itself.

13.3 Teams as distributed systems

What's a *distributed system*? Wikipedia defines it as "a system whose components are located on different networked computers, which communicate and coordinate their actions by passing messages to one another" (https://en.wikipedia.org/wiki/Distributed_computing). If you think about it, a team of people behaves like a distributed system, but instead of computers, we have individual humans doing things and passing messages to one another.

Let's imagine a team responsible for running customer-facing ticket-purchasing software for an airline. The team will need varied skills to succeed, and because it's a part of a larger organization, some of the technical decisions will be made for them. Let's take a look at a concrete example of the core competences required for this team:

- *Microsoft SQL database cluster management*—That's where all the purchase data lands, and that's why it is crucial to the operation of the ticket sales. This also includes installing and configuring Windows OS on VMs.
- *Full-stack Python development*—For the backend receiving the queries about available tickets as well as the purchase orders, this also includes packaging the software and deploying it on Linux VMs. Basic Linux administration skills are therefore required.
- *Frontend, JavaScript-based development*—The code responsible for rendering and displaying the user-facing UI.
- *Design*—Providing artwork to be integrated into the software by the frontend developers.
- *Integration with third-party software*—Often, the airline can sell a flight operated by another airline, so the team needs to maintain integration with other airlines' systems. What it entails varies from case to case.

Now, the team is made of individuals, all of whom have accumulated a mix of various skills over time as a function of their personal choices. Let's say that some of our Windows DB admins are also responsible for integrating with third parties (the

Windows-based systems, for example). Similarly, some of the full-stack developers also handle integrations with Linux-based third parties. Finally, some of the frontend developers can also do some design work. Take a look at figure 13.1, which shows a Venn diagram of these skill overlaps.

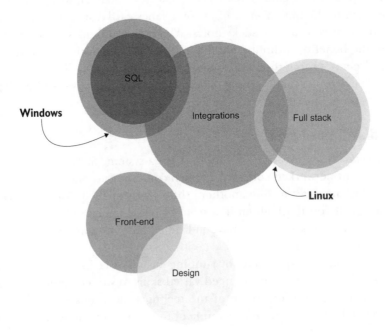

Figure 13.1   Venn diagram of skill overlaps in our example team

The team is also lean. In fact, it has only six people. Alice and Bob are both Windows and Microsoft SQL experts. Alice also supports some integrations. Caroline and David are both full stack developers, and both work on integrations. Esther is a frontend developer who can also do some design work. Franklin is the designer. Figure 13.2 places these individuals onto the Venn diagram of the skill overlaps.

Can you see where I'm going with this? Just as with any other distributed system, we can identify the weak links by looking at the architecture diagram. Do you see any weak links? For example, if Esther has a large backlog, no one else on the team can pick it up, because no one else has the skills. She's a single point of failure. By contrast, if Caroline or David is distracted with something else, the other one can cover: they have redundancy between them. People need holidays, they get sick, and they change teams and companies, so in order for the team to be successful long term, identifying and fixing single points of failure is very important. It's pretty convenient that we had a Venn diagram ready!

One problem with real life is that it's messy. Another is that teams rarely come nicely packaged with a Venn diagram attached to the box. Hundreds of different skills

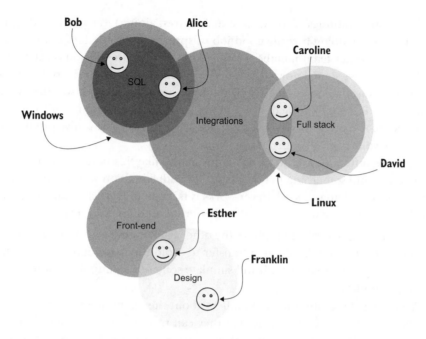

Figure 13.2   Individuals on the Venn diagram of skill overlaps

(hard and soft), constantly shifting technological landscapes, evolving requirements, personnel turnaround, and the sheer scale of some organizations are all factors in how hard it can be to ensure no single points of failure. If only there was a methodology to uncover systemic problems in a distributed system . . . oh, wait!

To discover systemic problems within a team, let's do some chaos experiments. The following experiments are heavily inspired by Dave Rensin, who described them in his talk, "Chaos Engineering for People Systems" (https://youtu.be/sn6wokyCZSA). I strongly recommend watching that talk. They are also best sold to the team as "games" rather than experiments. Not everyone wants to be a guinea pig, but a game sounds like a lot of fun and can be a team-building exercise if done right. You could even have prizes!

Let's start with identifying single points of failure within a team.

13.3.1   Finding knowledge single points of failure: Staycation

To see what happens to a team in the absence of a person, the chaos engineering approach is to simulate the event and observe how the team members cope. The most lightweight variant is to just nominate a person and ask them to not answer any queries related to their responsibilities and work on something different than they had scheduled for the day. Hence, the name *Staycation*. Of course, it's a game, and should an actual emergency arise, it's called off and all hands are on deck.

If the team continues working fine at full (remaining) capacity, that's great. It means the team is doing a really good job of spreading knowledge. But chances are that sometimes other team members will need to wait for the person on staycation to come back, because some knowledge wasn't replicated sufficiently. It could be work in progress that wasn't documented well enough, an area of expertise that suddenly became relevant, tribal knowledge the newer people on the team don't have yet, or any number of other reasons. If that's the case, congratulations: you've just discovered how to make your team stronger as a system!

People are different, and some will enjoy games like this much more than others. You'll need to find something that works for the individuals on your team. There is no single best way of doing this; whatever works is fair game. Here are some other knobs to tweak in order to create an experience better tailored for your team:

- Unlike a regular vacation, where the other team members can predict problems and execute some knowledge transfer to avoid them, it might be interesting to run this game by surprise. It will simulate someone falling sick, rather than taking a holiday.
- You can tell the other team members about the experiment . . . or not. Telling them will have the advantage that they can proactively think about things they won't be able to resolve without the person on staycation. Telling them only after the fact is closer to a real-life situation, but might be seen as distraction. You know your team; suggest what you think will work best.
- Choose your timing wisely. If team members are working hard to meet a deadline, they might not enjoy playing games that eat up their time. Or, if they are very competitive, they might like that, and having more things going on might create more potential for knowledge-sharing issues to arise.

Whichever way works for your team, this can be a really inexpensive investment with a large potential payout. Make sure you take the time to discuss the findings with the team, lest they might find the game unhelpful. Everyone involved is an adult and should recognize when a real emergency arises. But even if the game goes too far, failing early is most likely better than failing late, just as with the chaos experiments we run in computer systems.

Let's take a look at another variant, this time focusing not on absence, but on false information.

13.3.2 *Misinformation and trust within the team: Liar, Liar*

In a team, information flows from one team member to another. A certain amount of trust must exist among members for effective cooperation and communication—but also a certain amount of distrust, so that we double-check and verify things, instead of just taking them at face value. After all, to err is human.

We're also complex human beings, and we can trust the same person more on one topic than a different one. That's very helpful. You reading this book shows some trust in my chaos engineering expertise, but that doesn't mean you should trust my carrot cake (the last one didn't look like a cake, let alone a carrot!) And that's perfectly fine; these checks should be in place so that wrong information can be eventually weeded out. We want that property of the team, and we want it to be strong.

Liar, Liar is a game designed to test how well your team is dealing with false information circulating. The basic rules are simple: nominate a person who's going to spend the day telling very plausible lies when asked about work-related stuff. Some safety measures: write down the lies, and if they weren't discovered by others, straighten them out at the end of the day, and in general be reasonable with them. Don't create a massive outage by telling another person to click Delete on the whole system.

This game has the potential to uncover situations in which other team members skip the mental effort of validating their inputs and just take what they heard at face value. Everyone makes a mistake, and it's everyone's job to reality-check what you heard before you implement it. Here are some ideas of how to customize this game:

- Choose the liar wisely. The more the team relies on their expertise, the bigger the blast radius, but also the bigger the learning potential.
- The liar's acting skills are pretty useful here. Being able to keep up the ruse for the whole day, without spilling the beans, should have a pretty strong wow effect on other team members.
- You might want to have another person on the team know about the liar, to observe and potentially step in if they think the situation might have some consequences they didn't think of. At a minimum, the team leader should always know about this!

Take your time to discuss the findings within the team. If people see the value in doing this, it can be good fun. Speaking of fun, do you recall what happened when we injected latency in the communications with the database in chapter 4? Let's see what happens when you inject latency into a team.

13.3.3 Bottlenecks in the team: Life in the Slow Lane

The next game, Life in the Slow Lane, is about finding who's a bottleneck within the team, in different contexts. In a team, people share their respective expertise to propel the team forward. But everyone has a maximum throughput of what they can process. Bottlenecks form as some team members need to wait for others before they can continue with their work. In the complex network of social interactions, it's often difficult to predict and observe these bottlenecks, until they become obvious.

The idea behind this game is to add latency to a designated team member by asking them to take at least X minutes to respond to queries from other team members. By artificially increasing the response time, you will be able to discover bottlenecks more easily: they will be more pronounced, and people might complain about them directly! Here are some tips to ponder:

- If possible, working from home might be useful when implementing the extra latency. It limits the amount of social interaction and might make it a bit less weird.

- Going silent when others are asking for help is suspicious, might make you uncomfortable, and can even be seen as rude. Responding to queries with something along the lines of, "I'll get back to you on this; sorry, I'm really busy with something else right now," might help greatly.
- Sometimes resolving found bottlenecks might be the tricky bit. Policies might be in place, cultural norms or other constraints may need to be taken into account, but even just knowing about the potential bottlenecks can help planning ahead.
- Sometimes the manager of the team will be a bottleneck. Reacting to that might require a little bit more self-reflection and maturity, but it can provide invaluable insights.

So this one is pretty easy, and you don't need to remember the syntax of tc to implement it! And since we're on a roll, let's cover one more. Let's see how to use chaos engineering to test out your remediation procedures.

13.3.4 *Testing your processes: Inside Job*

Your team, unless it was started earlier today, has a set of rules to deal with problems. These rules might be well structured and written down, might be tribal knowledge in the collective mind of the team, or as is the case for most teams, somewhere between the two. Whatever they are, these "procedures" of dealing with different types of incidents should be reliable. After all, that's what you rely on in stressful times. Given that you're reading a book on chaos engineering, how do you think we could test them out?

With a gamified chaos experiment, of course! I'm about to encourage you to execute an occasional act of controlled sabotage by secretly breaking a subsystem you reasonably expect the team to be able to fix using the existing procedures, and then sit and watch them fix it.

Now, this is a big gun, so here are a few caveats:

- Be reasonable about what you break. Don't break anything that would get you in trouble.
- Pick the inside group wisely. You might want to let the stronger people on the team in on the secret, and let them "help out" by letting the other team members follow the procedures to fix the issue.
- It might also be a good idea to send some people to training or a side project, to make sure that the issue can be solved even with some people out.
- Double-check that the existing procedures are up-to-date before you break the system.
- Take notes while you're observing the team react to the situation. See what takes up their time, what part of the procedure is prone to mistakes, and who might be a single point of failure during the incident.
- It doesn't have to be a serious outage. It might be a moderate-severity issue, which needs to be remediated before it becomes serious.

If done right, this can be a very useful piece of information. It increases the confidence in the team's ability to fix an issue of a certain type. And again, it's much nicer to be dealing with an issue just after lunch, rather than at 2 a.m.

Would you do an inside job in production? The answer will depend on many factors we covered earlier in chapter 4 and on the risk/reward calculation. In the worst-case scenario, you create an issue that the team fails to fix in time, and the game needs to be called off and the issue fixed. You learn that your procedures are inadequate and can take action on improving them. In many situations, this might be perfectly good odds.

You can come up with an infinite number of other games by applying the chaos engineering principles to the human teams and interaction within them. My goal here is to introduce you to some of them to illustrate that human systems have a lot of the same characteristics as computer systems. I hope that I piqued your interest. Now, go forth and experiment with and on your teams!

Summary

- Chaos engineering requires a mindset shift from risk averse to risk calculating.
- Good communication and tailoring your message can facilitate getting buy-in from the team and management.
- Teams are distributed systems, and can also be made more reliable through the practice of experiments and office games.

13.4 *Where to go from here?*

This is the last section of the last chapter of this book, and I'd be lying if I said it didn't feel weird. It really does. For the last year or so, writing this book has been a sort of daily ritual for me. Forcing myself out of bed hours too early to keep pushing was hard, but it made this book possible. And now my Stockholm syndrome is kicking in and I'm finding myself wondering what I'm going to do with all this free time!

With a topic as broad as chaos engineering, choosing what should go into the book and what to leave out was objectively tricky. My hope is that the 13 chapters give you just enough information, tools, and motivation to help you continue your journey on making better software. At the same time, it's been my goal to remove all fluff and leave only a thin layer of padding in the form of a few jokes and "rickrolls" (if you don't know what that means, I know you haven't run the code samples!). If you'd like to see some things that didn't make it into the main part of the book, see appendix C. And if you're still hungry for more after that, head straight to appendix D!

If you're looking for a resource that's updated more often than a book, check out https://github.com/dastergon/awesome-chaos-engineering. It's a good list of chaos engineering resources in various shapes and forms.

If you'd like to hear more from me, ping me on LinkedIn (I love hearing people's chaos engineering stories) and subscribe to my newsletter at http://chaosengineering .news.

As I mentioned before, the line between chaos engineering and other disciplines is a fine one. In my experience, coloring outside these lines from time to time tends to make for better craftsmanship. That's why I encourage you to take a look at some of these:

- SRE
  - The three books from Google (https://landing.google.com/sre/books/):
    - *Site Reliability Engineering* (O'Reilly, 2016) edited by Betsy Beyer, Chris Jones, Jennifer Petoff, and Niall Richard Murphy
    - *The Site Reliability Workbook* (O'Reilly, 2018) edited by Betsy Beyer, Niall Richard Murphy, David K. Rensin, Kent Kawahara, and Stephen Thorne
    - *Building Secure & Reliable Systems* (O'Reilly, 2020) by Heather Adkins, Betsy Beyer, Paul Blankinship, Piotr Lewandowski, Ana Oprea, and Adam Stubblefield
- System performance
  - *Systems Performance: Enterprise and the Cloud* (Addison-Wesley, 2020) by Brendan Gregg
  - *BPF Performance Tools* (Addison-Wesley, 2020) by Brendan Gregg
- Linux kernel
  - *Linux Kernel Development* (Addison-Wesley, 2010) by Robert Love
  - *The Linux Programming Interface: A Linux and UNIX System Programming Handbook* (No Starch Press, 2010) by Michael Kerrisk
  - *Linux System Programming: Talking Directly to the Kernel and C Library* (O'Reilly, 2013) by Robert Love
- Testing
  - The Art of Software Testing (Wiley, 2011) by Glenford J. Myers, Corey Sandler, and Tom Badgett
- Other topics to observe
  - Kubernetes
  - Prometheus, Grafana

Two chaos engineering conferences are worth checking out:

- Conf42: Chaos Engineering (www.conf42.com); I'm involved in organizing it.
- Chaos Conf (www.chaosconf.io).

Finally *Chaos Engineering: System Resiliency in Practice* (O'Reilly, 2020) by Casey Rosenthal and Nora Jones is a good complement to this read. Unlike this book, which is pretty technical, it covers more high-level stuff and offers firsthand experience from people working at companies in various industries. Give it a read.

And with that, time to release you into the wild world of chaos engineering. Good luck and have fun!

appendix A
Installing chaos
engineering tools

This appendix will help you install the tools you need in order to implement chaos engineering experiments in this book. All of the tools we discuss here (with the exception of Kubernetes) are also preinstalled in the VM that ships with this book, so the easiest way to benefit from the book is to just start the VM.

If you'd like to use the tools directly on any host, let's see how to do that now.

A.1   Prerequisites

You're going to need a Linux machine. All of the tools and examples in this book have been tested on kernel version 5.4.0. The book uses Ubuntu (https://ubuntu .com/), a popular Linux distribution, version 20.04 LTS, but none of the tools used in the book are Ubuntu-specific.

The book assumes the x86 architecture, and none of the examples have been tested on other architectures.

There aren't specific machine specification requirements per se, although I recommend using a machine with at least 8 GB of RAM and multiple cores. The most power-hungry chapters (chapters 10, 11, and 12) use a small virtual machine to run Kubernetes, and I recommend 4 GB of RAM for that machine.

You're also going to need an internet connection to download all the tools we cover here. With these caveats out of the way, let's go for it.

A.2   *Installing the Linux tools*

Throughout the book, you will need tools available through the Ubuntu package management system. To install them, you can run the following command in a terminal window (replace PACKAGE and VERSION with the correct values):

```
sudo apt-get install PACKAGE=VERSION
```

For example, to install Git in version 1:2.25.1-1ubuntu3, run the following command:

```
sudo apt-get install git=1:2.25.1-1ubuntu3
```

Table A.1 summarizes the package names, the versions I used in testing, and a short description of where the package is used.

> **NOTE** I've added this table for completeness, but in the fast-moving Wild West of open source packaging, the versions used here will probably be outdated by the time these words are printed. Some of these versions might no longer be available (this is one of the reasons I prebuilt the VM image for you). When in doubt, try to go for the latest packages.

Table A.1   Packages used in the book

Package name	Package version	Notes
git	1:2.25.1-1ubuntu3	Used to download the code accompanying this book.
vim	2:8.1.2269-1ubuntu5	A popular text editor. Yes, you can use Emacs.
curl	7.68.0-1ubuntu2.2	Used in various chapters to make HTTP calls from the terminal window.
nginx	1.18.0-0ubuntu1	An HTTP server used in chapters 2 and 4.
apache2-utils	2.4.41-4ubuntu3.1	A suite of tools including Apache Bench (ab), used in multiple chapters to generate load on an HTTP server.
docker.io	19.03.8-0ubuntu1.20.04	Docker is a container runtime for Linux. Chapter 5 covers it.
sysstat	12.2.0-2	A collection of tools for measuring performance of a system. Includes commands like iostat, mpstat, and sar. Covered in chapter 3, we use them across the book.
python3-pip	20.0.2-5ubuntu1	Pip is a package manager for Python. We use it to install packages in chapter 11.
stress	1.0.4-6	Stress is a tool to . . . stress test a Linux system, by generating load (CPU, RAM, I/O). Covered in chapter 3 and used in many chapters.

Table A.1 Packages used in the book *(continued)*

Package name	Package version	Notes
bpfcc-tools	0.12.0-2	The package for BCC tools (https://github.com/iovisor/bcc) that provide various insights into Linux kernel using eBPF. Covered in chapter 3.
cgroup-lite	1.15	Cgroup utilities. Covered in chapter 5.
cgroup-tools	0.41-10	Cgroup utilities. Covered in chapter 5.
cgroupfs-mount	1.4	Cgroup utilities. Covered in chapter 5.
apache2	2.4.41-4ubuntu3.1	An HTTP server. Used in chapter 4.
php	2:7.4+75	PHP language installer. Used in chapter 4.
wordpress	5.3.2+dfsg1-1ubuntu1	A blogging engine. Used in chapter 4.
manpages	5.05-1	Manual pages for various commands. Used throughout the book.
manpages-dev	5.05-1	Manual pages for sections 2 (Linux system calls) and 3 (library calls). Used in chapter 6.
manpages-posix	2013a-2	POSIX flavor of the manual pages. Used in chapter 6.
manpages-posix-dev	2013a-2	POSIX flavor of the manual pages for sections 2 (Linux system calls) and 3 (library calls). Used in chapter 6.
libseccomp-dev	2.4.3-1ubuntu3.20.04.3	Libraries necessary to compile code using seccomp. See chapter 6.
openjdk-8-jdk	8u265-b01-0ubuntu2~20.04	Java Development Kit (OpenJDK flavor). Used to run Java code in chapter 7.
postgresql	12+214ubuntu0.1	PostgreSQL is a very popular, open source SQL database. Used in chapter 9.

On top of that, the book uses a few other tools that aren't packaged, and need to be installed by downloading them. Let's take a look at doing that now.

A.2.1 Pumba

To install Pumba, you need to download it from the internet, make it executable, and place it somewhere in your PATH. For example, you can run the following command:

```
curl -Lo ./pumba \
"https://github.com/alexei-led/pumba/releases/download/0.6.8/
    pumba_linux_amd64"
chmod +x ./pumba
sudo mv ./pumba /usr/bin/pumba
```

A.2.2 *Python 3.7 with DTrace option*

In chapter 3, you'll use a Python binary that's compiled in a special way. It's so you we can get extra insight into its inner workings, thanks to DTrace. To download and compile Python 3.7 from sources, run the following command (note that it might take a while, depending on your processing power):

```
# install the dependencies
sudo apt-get install -y build-essential
sudo apt-get install -y checkinstall
sudo apt-get install -y libreadline-gplv2-dev¶
sudo apt-get install -y libncursesw5-dev
sudo apt-get install -y libssl-dev
sudo apt-get install -y libsqlite3-dev
sudo apt-get install -y tk-dev
sudo apt-get install -y libgdbm-dev
sudo apt-get install -y libc6-dev
sudo apt-get install -y libbz2-dev
sudo apt-get install -y zlib1g-dev
sudo apt-get install -y openssl
sudo apt-get install -y libffi-dev
sudo apt-get install -y python3-dev
sudo apt-get install -y python3-setuptools
sudo apt-get install -y curl
sudo apt-get install -y wget
sudo apt-get install -y systemtap-sdt-dev
# download
cd ~
curl -o Python-3.7.0.tgz \
    https://www.python.org/ftp/python/3.7.0/Python-3.7.0.tgz
tar -xzf Python-3.7.0.tgz
cd Python-3.7.0
./configure --with-dtrace
make
make test
sudo make install
make clean
./python -version
cd ..
rm Python-3.7.0.tgz
```

A.2.3 *Pgweb*

The easiest way to install pgweb is to download it from GitHub. At the command-line prompt, use the following command to get the latest version available:

```
sudo apt-get install -y unzip
curl -s https://api.github.com/repos/sosedoff/pgweb/releases/latest \
| grep linux_amd64.zip \
| grep download \
| cut -d '"' -f 4 \
| wget -qi - \
&& unzip pgweb_linux_amd64.zip \
&& rm pgweb_linux_amd64.zip \
&& sudo mv pgweb_linux_amd64 /usr/local/bin/pgweb
```

A.2.4 Pip dependencies

To install the `freegames` package used in chapter 3, run the following command:

```
pip3 install freegames
```

A.2.5 Example data to look at for pgweb

In chapter 9, you'll look at PostgreSQL, which you just installed in section A.2. An empty database is not particularly exciting, so to make it more interesting, let's fill it in with some data. You can use the examples that come with pgweb. To clone them and apply them to your database, run the following command:

```
git clone https://github.com/sosedoff/pgweb.git /tmp/pgweb
cd /tmp/pgweb
git checkout v0.11.6
sudo -u postgres psql -f ./data/booktown.sql
```

A.3 Configuring WordPress

In chapter 4, you'll look at a WordPress blog and how to apply chaos engineering to it. In section A.2, you installed the right packages, but you still need to configure Apache and MySQL to work with WordPress. To do that, a few more steps are required.

First, create an Apache configuration file for WordPress by creating a new file /etc/apache2/sites-available/wordpress.conf with the following content:

```
Alias /blog /usr/share/wordpress
<Directory /usr/share/wordpress>
    Options FollowSymLinks
    AllowOverride Limit Options FileInfo
    DirectoryIndex index.php
    Order allow,deny
    Allow from all
</Directory>
<Directory /usr/share/wordpress/wp-content>
    Options FollowSymLinks
    Order allow,deny
    Allow from all
</Directory>
```

Second, you need to activate the WordPress configuration in Apache, so the new file is taken into account. Run the following commands:

```
a2ensite wordpress
service apache2 reload || true
```

Third, you need to configure WordPress to use MySQL. Create a new file at /etc/wordpress/config-localhost.php with the following content:

```
<?php
define('DB_NAME', 'wordpress');¶define('DB_USER', 'wordpress');
define('DB_PASSWORD', 'wordpress');
define('DB_HOST', '127.0.0.1');
```

```
define('WP_CONTENT_DIR', '/usr/share/wordpress/wp-content');
define('WP_DEBUG', true);
Finally, you need to create a new database in MySQL for WordPress to use:
cat <<EOF | sudo mysql -u root
CREATE DATABASE wordpress;
CREATE USER 'wordpress'@'localhost' IDENTIFIED BY 'wordpress';
GRANT SELECT,INSERT,UPDATE,DELETE,CREATE,DROP,ALTER
ON wordpress.* TO wordpress@localhost;
FLUSH PRIVILEGES;
quit
EOF
```

After that, you will be able to browse to localhost/blog and see the WordPress blog configuration page.

A.4 Checking out the source code for this book

Throughout this book, I refer to the various examples that are available in your VM and on GitHub. To clone them on your machine, use `git`. Run the following command to copy all the code coming with this book to a folder called src in your home directory:

```
git clone https://github.com/seeker89/chaos-engineering-book.git ~/src
```

A.5 Installing Minikube (Kubernetes)

For chapters 10, 11, and 12, you need a Kubernetes cluster. Unlike all the previous chapters, I recommend against doing that from the VM shipped with this book. This is for two reasons:

- Minikube (https://github.com/kubernetes/minikube) is officially supported by the Kubernetes team, and runs on Windows, Linux, and macOS, so there is no need to reinvent the wheel.
- Minikube works by starting a VM with all the Kubernetes components preconfigured, and we want to avoid running a VM inside of a VM.

Besides, if you haven't used Minikube before and you're new to Kubernetes, knowing how to use it is a valuable skill in its own way. Let's go ahead and install it.

Minikube runs on Linux, macOS, and Windows, and the installation is pretty straightforward. Go through the necessary steps for your operating system that are detailed next. For troubleshooting instructions, feel free to consult https://minikube.sigs.k8s.io/docs/.

A.5.1 Linux

First, check that virtualization is supported on your system. To do that, run the following command in a terminal window:

```
grep -E --color 'vmx|svm' /proc/cpuinfo
```

You should see a non-empty output. If it's empty, your system won't be able to run any VMs, so you won't be able to use Minikube, unless you're happy to run the processes directly on the host (there are some caveats, so read https://minikube.sigs.k8s.io/docs/drivers/none/ to learn more, if you'd like to take that route).

The next step is to download and install `kubectl`:

```
curl -LO https://storage.googleapis.com/kubernetes-release/release/$(curl -s
    https://storage.googleapis.com/kubernetes-release/release/stable.txt)/
    bin/linux/amd64/kubectl
chmod +x ./kubectl
sudo mkdir -p /usr/local/bin/
sudo mv ./kubectl /usr/local/bin/kubectl
kubectl version --client
```

You will see the `kubectl` version printed to the console. Finally, you can install the actual Minikube CLI:

```
curl -Lo minikube https://storage.googleapis.com/minikube/releases/latest/
    minikube-linux-amd64
chmod +x minikube
sudo install minikube /usr/local/bin/
minikube version
```

If you see the Minikube version printed, then voilà, you're all done here. Otherwise, for troubleshooting, see the docs at https://github.com/kubernetes/minikube.

A.5.2   macOS

Just as on Linux, check that virtualization is supported on your system. Run the following command in a terminal window:

```
sysctl -a | grep -E --color 'machdep.cpu.features|VMX'
```

On any modern Mac, you should see VMX in the output to tell you that your system supports running VMs. The next step is to download and install `kubectl`. It looks similar to Linux. Run the following commands:

```
curl -LO https://storage.googleapis.com/kubernetes-release/release/$(curl -s
    https://storage.googleapis.com/kubernetes-release/release/stable.txt)/
    bin/darwin/amd64/kubectl
chmod +x ./kubectl
sudo mv ./kubectl /usr/local/bin/kubectl
kubectl version --client
```

You will see the `kubectl` version printed to the console. Finally, you can install the actual Minikube CLI:

```
curl -Lo minikube https://storage.googleapis.com/minikube/releases/latest/
    minikube-darwin-amd64
chmod +x minikube
sudo install minikube /usr/local/bin/
minikube version
```

You will see the version printed out, and you're good to go. Finally, let's cover Windows.

A.5.3   *Windows*

Once again, first you need to check that your system supports virtualization. On Windows, this can be done by running the following command in a Windows terminal:

```
systeminfo
```

Find the section Hyper-V Requirements. It will mention whether the virtualization is supported. If it isn't, you won't be able to run Minikube.

    Second, you need to install kubectl. This is done by downloading the file from the official link (http://mng.bz/w9P7) and adding the binary to your PATH. To confirm that it's working, run the following command:

```
kubectl version --client
```

You will see the kubectl version printed to the console. Let's now install the actual Minikube. Similar to kubectl, it can be had by downloading it from Google servers (http://mng.bz/q9dK) and adding it to your PATH. Confirm that it works by running the following command in a terminal:

```
minikube version
```

You will see the version printed out, and you're ready to rock. Let's rock.

appendix B
Answers to the pop quizzes

This appendix provides answers to the exercises spread throughout the book. Correct answers are marked in bold.

Chapter 2

Pick the false statement:

1. Linux processes provide a number that indicates the reason for exiting.
2. Number 0 means successful exit.
3. Number 143 corresponds to SIGTERM.
4. **There are 32 possible exit codes.**

What's OOM?:

1. A mechanism regulating the amount of RAM any given process is given
2. **A mechanism that kills processes when the system runs low on resources**
3. A yoga mantra
4. The sound that Linux admins make when they see processes dying

Which step is not a part of the chaos experiment template?

1. Observability
2. Steady state
3. Hypothesis
4. **Crying in the corner when an experiment fails**

What's a blast radius?

1. The amount of stuff that can be affected by our actions
2. **The amount of stuff that we want to damage during a chaos experiment**

3 The radius, measured in meters, that's a minimal safe distance from coffee being spilled when the person sitting next to you realizes their chaos experiment went wrong and suddenly stands up and flips the table

Chapter 3

What's USE?

1 A typo in USA

2 A method of debugging a performance issue, based around measuring utilization, severity, and exiting

3 A command showing you the usage of resources on a Linux machine

4 **A method of debugging a performance issue, based around measuring utilization, saturation and errors**

Where can you find kernel logs?

1 /var/log/kernel

2 **dmesg**

3 kernel --logs

Which command does not help you see statistics about disks?

1 df

2 du

3 iostat

4 biotop

5 **top**

Which command does not help you see statistics about networking?

1 sar

2 tcptop

3 **free**

Which command does not help you see statistics about CPU?

1 top

2 **free**

3 mpstat

Chapter 4

What can Traffic Control (tc) not do for you?

1 Introduce all kinds of slowness on network devices

2 Introduce all kinds of failure on network devices

3 **Give you permission for landing the aircraft**

When should you test in production?

1 When you are short on time
2 When you want to get a promotion
3 **When you've done your homework, tested in other stages, applied common sense, and see the benefits overweighing the potential problems**
4 When it's failing in the test stages only intermittently, so it might just pass in production

Pick the true statement:

1 Chaos engineering renders other testing methods useless.
2 Chaos engineering only makes sense only in production.
3 Chaos engineering is about randomly breaking things.
4 **Chaos engineering is a methodology to improve your software beyond the existing testing methodologies.**

Chapter 5

What's an example of OS-level virtualization?

1 **Docker container**
2 VMware virtual machine

Which statement is true?

1 Containers are more secure than VMs.
2 **VMs typically offer better security than containers.**
3 Containers are equally secure as VMs.

Which statement is true?

1 Docker invented containers for Linux.
2 **Docker built on top of existing Linux technologies to provide an accessible way of using containers, rendering them much more popular.**
3 Docker is the chosen one in *The Matrix* trilogy.

What does chroot do?

1 Change the root user of the machine
2 Change permissions to access the root filesystem on a machine
3 **Change the root of the filesystem from the perspective of a process**

What do namespaces do?

1 **Limit what a process can see and access for a particular type of resource**
2 Limit the resources that a process can consume (CPU, memory, and so forth)
3 Enforce naming conventions to avoid name clashes

What do cgroups do?

1 Give extra control powers to groups of users
2 Limit what a process can see and access for a particular type of resource
3 **Limit the resources that a process can consume (CPU, memory, and so forth)**

What is Pumba?

1 A really likable character from a movie
2 A handy wrapper around namespaces that facilitates working with Docker containers
3 A handy wrapper around cgroups that facilitates working with Docker containers
4 **A handy wrapper around tc that facilitates working with Docker containers, and that also lets you kill containers**

Chapter 6

What are syscalls?

1 A way for a process to request actions on physical devices, such as writing to disk or sending data on a network
2 A way for a process to communicate with the kernel of the operating system it runs on
3 A universal angle of attack for chaos experiments, because virtually every piece of software relies on syscalls
4 **All of the above**

What can strace do for you?

1 **Show you what syscalls a process is making in real time**
2 Show you what syscalls a process is making in real time, without incurring a performance penalty
3 List all places in the source code of the application, where a certain action, like reading from disk, is performed

What's BPF?

1 Berkeley Performance Filters: an arcane technology designed to limit the amount of resources a process can use, to avoid one client using all available resources
2 A part of the Linux kernel that allows you to filter network traffic
3 A part of the Linux kernel that allows you execute special code directly inside the kernel to gain visibility into various kernel events
4 **Options 2, 3, and much more!**

Is it worth investing some time into understanding BPF, if you're interested in system performance?

1 **Yes**
2 **Definitely**

   3 **Absolutely**

   4 **Positively**

Chapter 7

What's `javaagent`?

   1 A secret service agent from Indonesia from a famous movie series

   2 **A flag used to specify a JAR that contains code to inspect and modify the code loaded into THE JVM on the fly**

   3 Archnemesis of the main protagonist in a knockoff version of the movie *The Matrix*

Which of the following is not built into the JVM?

   1 A mechanism for inspecting classes as they are loaded

   2 A mechanism for modifying classes as they are loaded

   3 A mechanism for seeing performance metrics

   4 **A mechanism for generating enterprise-ready names from regular, boring names. For example: "butter knife" -> "professional, stainless-steel-enforced, dishwasher-safe, ethically sourced, low-maintenance butter-spreading device"**

Chapter 8

When is it a good idea to build chaos engineering into the application?

   1 When you can't get it right on the lower levels, such as infrastructure or syscalls

   2 **When it's more convenient, easier, safer, or you have access to only the application level**

   3 When you haven't been certified as a chaos engineer yet

   4 When you downloaded only this chapter instead of getting the full book!

What is not that important when building chaos experiments into the application itself?

   1 Making sure the code implementing the experiment is executed only when switched on

   2 Following the best practices of software deployment to roll out your changes

   3 **Rubbing the ingenuity of your design into everyone else's faces**

   4 Making sure you can reliably measure the effects of your changes

Chapter 9

What is `XMLHttpRequest`?

   1 A JavaScript class that generates XML code that can be sent in HTTP requests

   2 An acronym standing for *Xeno-Morph! Little Help to them please Request*, which is horribly inconsistent with the timeline in the original movie *Alien*

   3 **One of the two main ways for JavaScript code to make requests, along with the Fetch API**

To simulate a frontend application loading slowly, which one of the following is the best option?

1 Expensive, patented software from a large vendor
2 An extensive, two-week-long training session
3 **A modern browser, like Firefox or Chrome**

Pick the true statement:

1 JavaScript is a widely respected programming language, famous for its consistency, and intuitive design that allows even beginner programmers to avoid pitfalls.
2 Chaos engineering applies to only the backend code.
3 **JavaScript's ubiquitous nature combined with its lack of safeguards makes it very easy to inject code to implement chaos experiments on the fly into existing applications.**

Chapter 10

What's Kubernetes?

1 A solution to all of your problems
2 Software that automatically renders the system running on it immune to failure
3 **A container orchestrator that can manage thousands of VMs and will continuously try to converge the current state into the desired state**
4 A thing for sailors

What's a Kubernetes deployment?

1 A description of how to reach software running on your cluster
2 **A description of how to deploy some software on your cluster**
3 A description of how to build a container

What happens when a pod dies on a Kubernetes cluster?

1 Kubernetes detects it and sends you an alert.
2 **Kubernetes detects it, and will restart it as necessary to make sure the expected number of replicas are running.**
3 Nothing.

What's Toxiproxy?

1 **A configurable TCP proxy that can simulate various problems, such as dropped packets or network slowness**
2 A K-pop band singing about the environmental consequences of dumping large amounts of toxic waste sent to developing countries through the use of proxy and shell companies

Chapter 11

What does PowerfulSeal do?

1 Illustrates—in equal measures—the importance and futility of trying to pick up good names in software

2 Guesses what kind of chaos you might need by looking at your Kubernetes clusters

3 **Allows you to write a YAML file to describe how to run and validate chaos experiments**

When does it make sense to run chaos experiments continuously?

1 When you want to detect when an SLO is not satisfied

2 When an absence of problems doesn't prove that the system works well

3 When you want to introduce an element of randomness

4 When you want to make sure that there are no regressions in the new version of the system

5 **All of the above**

What can PowerfulSeal not do for you?

1 Kill pods to simulate processes crashing

2 Take VMs up and down to simulate hypervisor failure

3 Clone a deployment and inject simulated network latency into the copy

4 Verify that services respond correctly by generating HTTP requests

5 **Fill in the discomfort coming from the realization that if there are indeed infinite universes, there exists, theoretically, a version of you that's better in every conceivable way, no matter how hard you try**

Chapter 12

Where is the cluster data stored?

1 Spread across the various components on the cluster

2 In /var/kubernetes/state.json

3 **In etcd**

4 In the cloud, uploaded using the latest AI and machine learning algorithms and leveraging the revolutionary power of blockchain technology

What's the control plane in Kubernetes jargon?

1 **The set of components implementing the logic of Kubernetes converging toward the desired state**

2 A remote-control aircraft, used in Kubernetes commercials

3 A name for Kubelet and Docker

Which component actually starts and stops processes on the host?

1 `kube-apiserver`

2 `etcd`

3 **kubelet**

4 `docker`

Can you use a different container runtime than Docker?

1 If you're in the United States, it depends on the state. Some states allow it.

2 No, Docker is required for running Kubernetes.

3 **Yes, you can use a number of alternative container runtimes, like CRI-O, containerd, and others.**

Which component did I just make up?

1 `kube-apiserver`

2 `kube-controller-manager`

3 `kube-scheduler`

4 **kube-converge-loop**

5 `kubelet`

6 `etcd`

7 `kube-proxyNo index entries found.`

appendix C
Director's cut
(aka the bloopers)

True story: during my final review, one of the reviewers asked what would go into the book if I did a director's cut. And boom, next thing I know, I have to uncheck the Finished checkbox, call off the party, and go back to writing. The people at my door were disappointed to hear the news, but they must understand—the idea was just too good to let go!

In this appendix, you will find a collection of scenes that didn't make it into the movie for various reasons. Apparently, this being an appendix means that the publisher cut me a bit more slack, so this is in the form of a friendly chat, rather than serious teaching. Either the rules are different, or the PR team didn't read this far. Let's go before they change their minds!

C.1   Cloud

The winner of the Yearly Award for the Most Abused Word for Years 2006 to 2020—*cloud*—has been haunting me throughout the process of writing this book. Some people expressed their surprise to not see a chapter called "Cloud" in the table of contents.

I chose not to have a dedicated chapter for various reasons, including but not limited to the following. (When I was 6.5 years old, I had a short period of time when I stopped wanting to be an astronaut-archaeologist and wanted to be a lawyer. It lasted about two weeks, from what I'm told, but maybe my penchant for reasoned arguments remains.)

- I already covered a multi-cloud solution for taking VMs up and down in chapter 11 with PowerfulSeal.

- Different cloud providers have their own tools and API, and I wanted to focus on things that are as portable as possible.
- While it's true that cloud-based applications are getting more and more popular, at the end of the day, it's just someone else's computer. This book focuses on technologies that I expect to be relevant for the foreseeable future.

C.2   Chaos engineering tools comparison

I was tempted to create a large table with all the chaos engineering tools I know of. But when I started to create it, I realized the following:

- Different open source projects get different levels of support; some flourish, some slowly degrade; so creating a detailed table like this would produce value mainly for the archaeologists who might dig it out a few thousand years later.
- It's better for you to form your own opinions anyway.

I still covered a few tools (Pumba, PowerfulSeal, Chaos Toolkit) that I'm fairly confident will stay relevant for a while. For an up-to-date list, I recommend this site: http://mng.bz/7V1x.

C.3   Windows

One of the (valid) criticisms of this book is that it's entirely Linux-based. And although you can apply a large portion of it to other *nix operating systems, there is a gaping hole in the shape of Windows.

I don't cover Windows mainly because I would be out of my depth. I spent the vast majority of my professional life with Linux, and I don't know the Windows ecosystem well enough to write about it.

The mindset and the methodology are universal, and will work regardless of which operating system you use. The tooling, on the other hand, will differ.

Besides, with Windows Subsystem for Linux (https://docs.microsoft.com/en-us/windows/wsl/about), Microsoft publicly acknowledged defeat, so perhaps you're covered anyway.

If you're reading this (whether you work in Redmond or not), and would like to add a Windows section to the second edition, give me a shout!

C.4   Runtimes

We looked briefly at DTrace with Python, but various languages, runtimes, and frameworks often offer metrics out of the box that can be useful from the perspective of observability. This subject could be a book in itself, so I didn't even try to include it in these pages.

C.5 Node.js

For some reason beyond my cognitive abilities, a sizable crowd of people kept suggesting that I add a chapter similar to chapter 8 (application-level chaos engineering), but in Node.js. This goes back to the previous point, but it was a surprisingly persistent question.

So far, I've managed to successfully parry that using a combination of these two arguments:

- If you understand my points from chapter 8 in Python, you can replicate that in JavaScript.
- I already cover JavaScript, albeit of the browser variety, in chapter 9.

I'm hoping that works for you too.

C.6 Architecture problems

Various people I spoke to while writing the book mentioned architecture problems as an exciting topic to include in the book. Although I see the value in looking at case studies like that, this book attacks chaos testing from a slightly different angle.

If I tried to include all the relevant practices on how to design reliable systems, I would probably die of old age before I finished. Instead, this book attempts to give you the mindset, with all the tools and techniques you need to verify that systems behave the way you expect them to and detect when they don't. It leaves the actual fixing part to the users. There are shelves and shelves of books on designing good software. This one is about checking how well you've done.

C.7 The four steps to a chaos experiment

One of the thoughtful reviewers asked a question that's been on the back of my mind every time I wrote the word *four* in this book: "Why isn't there a fifth step called *analysis*?"

It's a good question. An experiment is useless if you don't analyze your findings at the end. Ultimately, I decided against adding the fifth step, primarily for the promotional reasons: fewer steps sound easier and are admittedly catchier. The analysis part is implied.

In a way, I feel like I sacrificed some of the "correctness" on the altar of "easier sells." But then again, if this book doesn't sell well, no one will care anyway. Now I have to live with that decision.

C.8 You should have included <tool X>!

We all have our favorites, and in this book I had to make decisions on which tools to cover, decisions that are by definition going to surprise some people. In particular, some folks expected to see commercial offerings on these pages.

The main motivation for the selections I made aligns with point C.2: this entire chaos engineering ecosystem is young, and I expect it to move a lot in the coming years. The basics will likely stay the same, but the specifics might look very different in just a short while. I would like this book to stay relevant for a few years.

C.9   Real-world failure examples!

Another thing that didn't make the cut was my attempt to gather some real-life failures detected using chaos engineering. Although people are pretty excited to talk about their experiences with chaos engineering, it's a completely different story when it's about going on record and telling others why your system was badly designed before you fixed it.

A fair amount of stigma surrounds this topic, and I expect this is unlikely to go away anytime soon. The reason is simple: we all know that software is hard, but we all want to appear to be good at writing it.

The unfortunate side effect is that I failed to gather stories for a chapter on specific failures that went unnoticed and eventually were uncovered by chaos engineering. Well, I guess that's what the live events are for!

C.10   "Chaos engineering" is a terrible name!

There, I said it. The *chaos* part makes it interesting but goes a long way toward generating initial friction for adoption. It's a little too late to say, "OK everyone, we're renaming it; just cross out the chaos part!" But with a bit of luck, people will eventually stop worrying about the name and focus on what it does.

You probably heard that there are only three hard things in computer science: naming things and off-by-one errors. I named one project PowerfulSeal and another Goldpinger, so don't look at me for better ideas!

C.11   Wrap!

It was nice to let some steam off, but now I'm feeling a little bit peckish (that's British for "as I can't be sure whether I'm actually famished or just bored, I shall err on the side of caution and devour something imminently"). Check out appendix D if you're just a little bit peckish yourself!

appendix D
Chaos-engineering recipes

Writing books makes you hungry. Well, at the very least, it makes me hungry. If my manuscript was in a paper form, it would smell of all of the following things.

Legal disclaimer 1

I'm not a doctor, dietician or even a cook. What you find below is a result of letting a software engineer loose in the kitchen. Oh, and THE RECIPES ARE PROVIDED "AS IS," WITHOUT WARRANTY OF ANY KIND, EXPRESS OR IMPLIED, INCLUDING BUT NOT LIMITED TO THE WARRANTIES OF MERCHANTABILITY, FITNESS FOR A PARTICULAR PURPOSE, AND NONINFRINGEMENT. IN NO EVENT SHALL THE AUTHORS OR COPYRIGHT HOLDERS BE LIABLE FOR ANY CLAIM, DAMAGES, OR OTHER LIABILITY, WHETHER IN AN ACTION OF CONTRACT, TORT OR OTHERWISE, ARISING FROM, OUT OF OR IN CONNECTION WITH THE SOFTWARE OR THE USE OR OTHER DEALINGS IN THE SOFTWARE.

Legal disclaimer 2

Previous returns are no guarantee of future performance. In other words, the fact that I lived through eating these things doesn't guarantee that you will. Use at your own risk, preferably under adult supervision. As a rule of thumb, don't do anything your mum would disapprove of.

D.1 SRE ('ShRoomEee) burger

I like the taste of burgers, but I don't like what the meat industry is doing to the planet and to the meat. Also, making common mushrooms edible appears to be easier than cooking meat (Figure D.1). And it's cheaper. For these three reasons,

Figure D.1   The real reason I didn't become a food photographer

I've been experimenting with multiple veggie burger recipes, and debugging burger recipes turns out to be generally easier than debugging software.

D.1.1   Ingredients

Patties:

- Makes three to four medium-sized patties, depending on how hungry you are.
- 8 ounces (250 g) of mushrooms (any edible variety, preferably sliced already)
- One large onion
- Two large cloves of garlic
- Your favorite seasoning
- Smoked tofu—2 to 4 ounces (50 to 100 g), as a function of how much you like it
- Wheat flour
- Some oil for frying (coconut is good, because it has a higher burning temperature)

Miscellaneous:

- Bread to put the patties in-between—you can make your own or buy ready-made
- One large avocado—adds creaminess
- Sauce—BBQ, ketchup, mayo, whatever you like
- Any customary additives your culture expects you to throw in, like lettuce, an extra slice of onion, cheese—whatever floats your boat

D.1.2 *Hidden dependencies*

- Frying equipment—a stove and a pan
- A spatula to turn things over in the pan

Listen in. If you try hard, you can hear all the seasoned (pun intended!) software engineers sighing in concert at how vague this list of ingredients is. The very senior ones will be positively surprised that there is at least one quantifiable amount (8 ounces) in the list, but don't worry: they too will be disappointed when they see that during cooking, mushrooms give away a variable amount of water, depending on the type of mushroom used. Yep, it's freestyle!

D.1.3 *Making the patty*

1. Clean, cut (unless already sliced), and fry the mushrooms until they're edible.
    - Most varieties will release water, which you can discard; you want the mushrooms to be reasonably dry.
    - (Parallelism) While the mushrooms are frying, slice the garlic and the onion, and chop the tofu to your liking.
2. Once the mushrooms are deemed edible, take them out of the frying pan and repeat the process with the onion and garlic.
3. Once the onion looks nothing like it did when you cut it, and is nice and soft, add the mushrooms back in with all of your favorite seasonings (no one will judge you).
4. Take the mixture out of the pan and put it in a bowl.
5. Throw in tofu, chopped into small pieces. The smokiness of it should trigger the parts of your brain that recognize burger meat.
6. Mix it as much as you like. You can make the texture pretty uniform, or leave out larger chunks. Both have their merits.
7. Finally, glue the ingredients together. This is done by leveraging gluten in the flour. Repeat the following steps:
    - Add 2 to 3 teaspoons (10 g) of flour and mix it in well, so that the moisture from the mixture reaches the flour. The more flour you add, the less moist the patty will be.
    - Try to form a small ball. If it sticks together, break the loop. If it's too runny and/or sticky, keep going.
8. Form the mixture into three or four balls.
9. Warm up the frying pan with a little oil.
10. Squash the balls in the frying pan to form patties. Fry until piping hot inside. The thicker they are, the longer they will take to cook.
    - Alternatively, you can fry them a little to give them shape and then bake them in the oven for the rest of the process.
    - Once the flour mixed with water from the mixture was heated to a high temperature, the gluten in it should have bound and the patty should hold its shape.

11 Switch off any appliances with the potential of burning down your house.

12 Take a photo and post it on LinkedIn or Twitter. Make sure to tag me!

D.1.4 Assembling the finished product

Once the patties are done, wrap them in two slices of bread and add whatever toppings you like. After you've done it once, you will feel the urge to experiment further. Give into that urge. Try adding chickpeas, pickled onions, or dying the patty with a small amount of beetroot, to make it look meatier. I recommend A/B testing, and scoring the different attempts for observability reasons.

D.2 Chaos pizza

I used to think that making pizza was difficult, until I discovered the real secret: it all relies on baking the pizza directly on a hot surface. The heat transfer through direct contact is what leads to this crispy base that I associate with a successful attempt (figure D.2). You can buy a dedicated pizza stone, but preheating a thick metal tray can also do the trick.

Pizza is happiness. With about half an hour of your time, you can turn a rainy day into a holiday. And it can be as healthy or unhealthy as you want it to be.

Figure D.2 Another reason I really should have gotten a professional photographer to take pictures of these foods

D.2.1 Ingredients

Pizza base:

- Active dry yeast (about 1 ½ teaspoons, or 7 g per pizza)
- 2 cups (250 g) flour (for two medium-sized, thin-crust bases)
- 1 tablespoon of olive oil
- Salt, oregano, any other flavoring you like
- Water
- ¼ teaspoon of sugar

Toppings that go into the oven:

- Sauce—tomato, BBQ, pesto, ajvar, your grandma's famous sauce, whatever you like
- Melt-friendly cheese, like mozzarella or a mozzarella-style vegan alternative
- Absolutely anything else you want:
  - Onions
  - Mushrooms (best precooked)
  - Olives
  - Tofu
  - Meat or fish (precooked)
  - Leftovers from the fridge that magically turn into a tasty experience

Toppings that don't go into the oven (you add them after baking):

- Leafy vegetables, like arugula or spinach
- Dried meats, like prosciutto—if you're into that kind of stuff

D.2.2 Preparation

1. Prepare the yeast.
   - Take a half glass of warm (not boiling) water.
   - Add sugar.
   - Add dry yeast.
   - Mix it until it becomes muddy.
2. Make the dough.
   - Put the flour in a bowl.
   - Slowly pour in the yeast mixture while mixing with a spoon.
   - Add salt, oregano, olive oil.
   - Get the consistency right:
     - You need to be able to knead the dough with your hands.
     - If it's too runny or sticky, add extra flour.
     - If it's too hard, or there are visible bits of flour in it, add more water.
   - Once the mixture is kneadable, knead the dough for a couple of minutes until you feel like ordering a DNA test to track down your Italian ancestry.

- Leave the dough in a bowl to rise for about 20 minutes. (The rising process happens because you've just fed the dehydrated yeast some sugar and water, and let it rest; the poor thing will start growing, creating bubbles of air in your dough; and then you're going to bake and eat it. It really is a cruel world.)

3 Preheat the oven to about 400°F (200°C, or 180°C fan), including a pizza stone, or a thick tray equivalent.

4 Take out a sheet of parchment or wax paper, and spread a small amount of flour on it to prevent sticking (alternatively, you can use more olive oil).

5 Take half of the dough from the bowl and spread it on the paper.
- You can use your hands or a rolling pin.
- Or attempt the rotate-the-dough-in-the-air-until-it's-flat thing. (You have a redundant copy in the pipe; no one will know.)
- Spread the sauce.
- Add all the bake-able toppings.

6 Bake for about 10 to 12 minutes.
- It's ready when the dough is baked (but not carbonized) and the cheese is melted.

7 Take it out; decorate with non-bake-able toppings.

8 Take a photo and post it on LinkedIn or Twitter. Make sure to tag me!

That's it. Now you know how to vote for the best food recipe in a tech book. If there ever was a tasteful ending to a programming book, hopefully this is one.

index